ASPHODEL PLANTATION 113

CLINTON COURTHOUSE 30

RICHARD KOCH—DISTRICT OFFICER. DRAWN BY — ALVYK BOYD CRUISE.

MAP
OF THE
STATE OF
LOUISIANA

SHOWING
BAYOUS, RIVERS,
EARLY TRAILS
AND
IMPORTANT PLANTATIONS

WORKS PROGRESS ADMINISTRATION
SPONSORED FEDERAL PROJECT N°2
HISTORIC AMERICAN BUILDINGS SURVEY

83	HOMELAND — LULING	135	WAVERLY — BAINS
43	EVERGREEN — WALLACE	182	GREENWOOD (PERRY) BARROW
42	WHITNEY — WALLACE	17	LIVE OAK — WEYANOKE
94	CHRIST CHURCH — NAPOLEONVILLE	16	GREENWOOD (VENTRESS) BAINS
20	WOODLAWN — NAPOLEONVILLE	105	ELLERSLIE — BAINS
139	ST. JOHN'S — THIBODEAUX	137	STONE HOUSE — CLINTON
110	SIMEON SMITH HOUSE — FRANKLIN	63	CHASE HOUSE — CLINTON
163	OAK LAWN — FRANKLIN	31	LAWYERS' ROW — CLINTON
119	DARBY HOUSE — BALDWIN	108	CONRAD — CONRAD POINT
69	MELROSE — NATCHITOCHES	32	HERMITAGE — GEISMAR
171	PINK HOUSE — BAYOU LIBERTY	26	HOUMAS AT BURNSIDE
35	FANNIE RICHÉ — NEW ROADS	51	WELHAM — WELHAM P.O.
77	RAMSEY — MIX	14	ANGELINA — MOUNT AIRY
62	BELMONT — MARINGOIN	12	GARCONNIERE AT ST. ROSE
35	WAKEFIELD — BAINS	184	CARRIERE - DU BOURG — BAYOU LIBERTY
84	MATTHEW BELL — FRANKLIN	179	DRAKE OUTBUILDING — ST. JOSEPH

SCALE OF 0 5 10 15 20 25 30 35 40 MILES

BRAEME HOUSE 40

LABATUT PLANTATION 117

VICKSBURG

PORT GIBSON

SIDNEY

WASHINGTON

MISSISSIPPI

LIBERTY

FELICIANAS
WILSON
CLINTON
FLUKER

FLORIDA PARISHES

N
S

MADEWOOD PLANTATION 68

BATON ROUGE

GERMAN COAST
WHITE CASTLE

LAKE MAUREPAS

MADISONVILLE

LAKE PONTCHARTRAIN

NEW ORLEANS

LAKE BORGNE

LAKE DES ALLEMANDS

NAPOLEONVILLE

BILOXI

BRETON SOUND

HICKORY HILL 114

ROSEDOWN

HEBRARD HOUSE 63

HETERICK MEMORIAL LIBRARY
OHIO NORTHERN UNIVERSITY
ADA, OHIO 45810

Y0-BRY-658

Louisiana Buildings, 1720–1940

LOUISIANA BUILDINGS 1720–1940

The Historic American Buildings Survey

EDITED BY

JESSIE POESCH AND
BARBARA SoRELLE BACOT

LOUISIANA STATE UNIVERSITY PRESS

BATON ROUGE AND LONDON

Copyright © 1997 by Louisiana State University Press
All rights reserved
Manufactured in the United States of America
First printing
05 04 03 02 01 00 99 98 97 96   5 4 3 2 1

Designer: Melanie O'Quinn Samaha
Typeface: AGaramond
Typesetter: Impressions Book and Journal Services, Inc.
Printer and binder:

LIBRARY OF CONGRESS CATALOGING-IN-PUBLICATION DATA

Louisiana buildings, 1720–1940 : the historic American buildings
    survey / edited by Jessie Poesch and Barbara SoRelle Bacot.
        p.   cm.
    Includes bibliographical references and index.
      ISBN 0-8071-2054-5 (cloth : alk. paper)
        1. Architecture—Louisiana.   2. Decoration and ornament,
Architectural—Louisiana.   3. Historic buildings—Louisiana.
I. Poesch, Jessie J. II. Bacot, Barbara SoRelle.
NA730.L8L68   1996
720'.9763—dc20   96-16959
                                                      CIP

This volume is a joint project of the Louisiana Department of Culture, Recreation and Tourism, Office of Cultural Development, Division of Historic Preservation, and Tulane University. The publication of the volume has been financed in part with Federal funds from the National Park Service, U.S. Department of the Interior. However, the contents and opinions do not necessarily reflect the views or policies of the Department of the Interior. This program receives Federal financial assistance for identification and protection of historic properties. Under Title VI of the Civil Rights Act of 1964, Section 504 of the Rehabilitation Act of 1973, and the Age Discrimination Act of 1975, as amended, the U.S. Department of the Interior prohibits discrimination on the basis of race, color, national origin, or disability or age in its federally assisted programs. If you believe you have been discriminated against in any program, activity, or facility as described above, or if you desire further information, please write to Office for Equal Opportunity, National Park Service, P.O. Box 37127, Washington, D.C. 20013–7127.

The endpapers of this book are reproduced by courtesy of the Historic New Orleans Collection (accession nos. 1961.15.1, 1961.15.2). The frontispiece, *View of Baton Rouge* (1855), a hand-colored steel engraving by Frederick Piercy, is reproduced by courtesy of the Louisiana State University Museum of Art, Baton Rouge.

The paper in this book meets the guidelines for permanence and durability of the Committee on Production Guidelines for Book Longevity of the Council on Library Resources. ♾

720.9763
L 888

CONTENTS

Plates

Acknowledgments

In large measure, this volume owes its existence to the Louisiana Department of Culture, Recreation and Tourism, where the Division of Historic Preservation and the Division of the Arts, both within the Office of Cultural Development, provided grants and staff support. Among the staff there, the editors would especially like to thank Donna Fricker for invaluable assistance in the editing of several chapters and in the selection and handling of some of the photographs. We are also grateful for the significant contributions of other staff members, including Christy Ball, Betty Chauvin, Lori Durio, and Ann Russo.

For a thoughtful and thorough reading of the manuscript, and the addition and correction of crucial information, we must thank John C. Ferguson. Others to whom we are indebted for their comments and advice are Julian W. Adams, H. Parrott Bacot, Charles Hammond, and Mary "Mimi" Warren Miller. We are conscious, as well, of our debt to Jim Zietz, a truly gifted photographer.

All Louisiana's preservationists are deeply beholden to the lifetime pioneering efforts of Richard Koch (1889–1971), who served as director of the Louisiana Historic American Buildings Survey from 1933 to 1941, of Fred B. Kniffen (1900–1993), a seminal scholar in the study of vernacular architecture and folk housing in the United States, and of Samuel Wilson, Jr. (1911–1993), a renowned architect and scholar of Louisiana architectural history.

We also wish to express our gratitude for assistance from Jim Blanchard, Ann Butler, Robert Brantley, William R. Cullison III, Thomas H. Eubanks, George T. Fore, Robert Gamble, Anne Glynn, Ethel S. Goodstein, Sid Gray, Jack Holden, Pat Chapoton Holden, William DeMarigny Hyland, Davis L. Jahncke, Trent L. James, Dr. and Mrs. Robert C. Judice, Patricia "Pat" Lee Kahle, Bernard Lemann, Mr. and Mrs. Arthur A. Lemann, Jr., Frank Masson,

William Obier, Christian L. Olivier, Jr., Carol Layton Parsons, Robert S. Reich, Lloyd Sensat, Jr., Robert E. Smith, Mr. and Mrs. George Thompson, William K. Turner, Bill Wiener, Jr., and Mr. and Mrs. Frank W. Wurzlow, as well as the late John Lawrence.

We have received generous help in compiling and preparing this work from numerous institutions and their staff: the Avery Architectural and Fine Arts Library, at Columbia University, and Angela Giral there; the Gallier House Museum, and Ann M. Masson; the Hermann-Grima House, and Jan Bradford; the Historic New Orleans Collection, and Pamela D. Arceneaux, Jan White Brantley, Mary Louise Christovich, Elizabeth Kellner, Jon Kukla, John T. Magill, and Sally Spier Stassi; Koch and Wilson Architects, and Robert J. Cangelosi; the Library of Congress, and Marilyn Ibach; the Louisiana State Museum, and Patricia Eischen, Claudia K. Kheel, Milita Rios-Samaniego, Jeff Rubin, and James Sefcik; the Fred B. Kniffen Cultural Resources Laboratory, of the Department of Geography and Anthropology at Louisiana State University, and Jay D. Edwards; the School of Architecture at LSU, and William Brockway, David Connick, Barrett Kennedy, and Michael Pitts; the LSU Libraries, and V. Faye Phillips; the LSU Museum of Art, and H. Parrott Bacot; the Louisiana State University at Shreveport Archives, and Laurie Street; Louisiana Tech University, and F. Lestar Martin; the Maryland Historical Society, and Jeff D. Goldman; the New Orleans Historic District Landmarks Commission, and Lary P. Hesdorffer; the New Orleans Museum of Art, and Tara J. Alt and E. John Bullard; the New Orleans Notarial Archives, and Sally Kittredge Reeves; the River Road Historical Society, and Irene Tastet; the Southeastern Architectural Archive, at Tulane University, and Gary A. Van Zante and Kevin Williams; the University of Southwestern Louisiana, and Dan Branch; and the Vieux Carre Commission, and Marc Cooper, Jim Cripps, and Hilary Irvin. We are grateful to our editor at LSU Press, Barry L. Blose, and to the Press's managing editor, John Easterly.

LOUISIANA BUILDINGS, 1720–1940

INTRODUCTION

Jessie Poesch

THE AIM OF THIS VOLUME IS TO PRESENT A BROAD VIEW OF THE HISTORY OF building in Louisiana, taking the superb records of the Historic American Buildings Survey as a point of departure. Perhaps more than most of us realize, those who created the HABS records—as this remarkable archive is called—have from 1934 to the present quietly alerted us to the historical and artistic significance of buildings in our midst. In so doing they have delighted the eye and stimulated the mind. The chapters that follow provide a frame of reference for interpreting the data about Louisiana assembled by HABS and also call attention to many other structures that are part of the history of building in the state.

In 1983, when HABS was observing its fiftieth anniversary, Charles E. Peterson (1906–), whose brainchild the project was, wrote, "The Historic American Buildings Survey did not begin in a bureaucratic routine. It was founded a half century ago by a handful of public servants in a burst of idealism and energy." Born as a federal program during the Great Depression, conceived largely by architects, the project set out to record with measured drawings "important antique buildings," thereby giving work to unemployed architects. Simple, inexpensive materials were to be used: T squares, drawing boards, paper, pencils, and erasers. Relevant historical information, and on occasion photographs, might supplement the drawings.[1]

The initial proposal, penned on a Sunday afternoon in November, 1933, declared that "from the cultural standpoint an enormous contribution to the history and aesthetics of American life could be made" by a general canvass

1. Charles E. Peterson, "The Historic American Buildings Survey: Its Beginnings," in *Historic America: Buildings, Structures, and Sites,* ed. C. Ford Peatross (Washington, D.C., 1983), 7; Charles E. Peterson, "The Historic American Buildings Survey Continued," *Journal of the Society of Architectural Historians,* XVI (1957), 29–31.

of structures erected "between the earliest times and (say) 1860," covering buildings in styles roughly classifiable as Jacobean, Georgian, Early Republic, and Greek Revival, with special attention to early work in New Orleans and Santa Fe. One part of the genius of the initial proposal was to suggest in fine, straightforward language, trusting the judgment of the participants, that "the list of building types should be almost a complete resume of the builder's art. It should include public buildings, churches, residences, bridges, forts, barns, mills, shops, rural outbuildings, and any other kind of structure of which good specimens are extant."[2]

In the first group recruited to carry out the project was Richard Koch, of New Orleans, who had pursued an interest in early Louisiana architecture since the 1920s and had already made precise measured drawings of some structures for his own ends. Some early publicity about the project in the Washington *Star* on April 5, 1934, showed a photograph Koch had taken of a building in the French Quarter of New Orleans. In the Introduction to the Louisiana HABS Catalog, at the back of this book (see below, pp. 349–53), there is mention of the list of 150 buildings Koch presented for consideration. True to the early criteria, a country store, a small cottage, and a church, along with grander plantation complexes, including outbuildings, are represented; all the structures were in poor condition, facing destruction by man or nature.

HABS has continued to the present day, with a hiatus during World War II; it is an open-ended archive and now includes structures built well after 1860. If its early participants were an idealistic lot, so too are those who have followed. Nowadays the survey teams are mainly students in schools of architecture and in related university departments. In recent years, students and faculty at the Tulane University School of Architecture, the Louisiana State University School of Architecture, the Department of Geography and Anthropology at Louisiana State University, the Department of Architecture at the University of Southwestern Louisiana, and the Department of Architecture at Louisiana Tech University have all participated in compiling records of buildings for HABS. Recently recorded buildings include a livestock pavilion, a parish courthouse, a railroad depot, some houses, and the structures in a lumbermill town and on several plantations.

Louisiana is boot shaped, with the sole of the boot rippled by the waterways communicating with the Gulf of Mexico (Front endpaper). In the east the nation's biggest river empties into the Gulf by way of a delta (Figure 1), and farther west lie swamps that constitute one of the largest wetlands of the continent. Before Europeans began to explore the land and waters of the area, Native Americans belonging to three broad linguistic groups—Tunican, Caddoan, and Muskhogean—made their home there. Many lived in

2. Peterson, "The Historic American Buildings Survey Continued," 29–31.

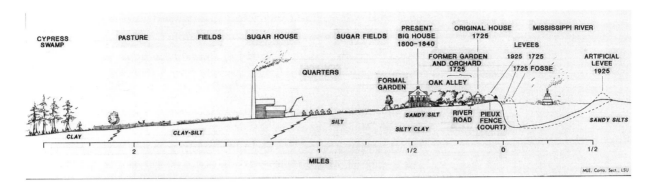

FIGURE 1 Cross section of the Mississippi. The highest and, therefore best, arable land was closest to the river, sloping from the natural levee to the back swamp. The natural levee and the slope away from it result from flooding. When rivers overflow, carrying loads of silt, the heaviest deposits occur closest to the bank. Man-made levees were built at the crest of the natural levees.

Courtesy of Jay D. Edwards, Fred B. Kniffen Cultural Resources Laboratory, Department of Geography and Anthropology, LSU.

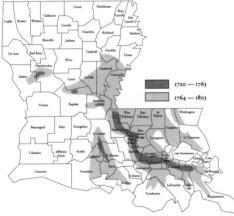

FIGURE 2 Settlement in the colonial era, 1699–1803. Under the French (1699–1763), settlement was concentrated along the lower Mississippi and its bayous and to the northwest along the Red River. In the era of Spanish administration (1763–1803), settlement spread farther up the Mississippi, along the western bayous and into the Florida parishes.

Thomas H. Eubanks, Louisiana Division of Archaeology.

villages near rivers or streams, growing Indian corn, beans, pumpkins, and melons, and relying also on fish and game for sustenance. As early as 1519 a Spaniard had found the mouth of the Mississippi; in 1542–1553, survivors of de Soto's expedition probably came down the lower Mississippi. But it was some 140 years later, on April 9, 1682, that the explorer Robert Cavelier de La Salle boldly claimed for France all the lands drained by the great river. He called the region Louisiane, for Louis XIV. Less than two decades later, in 1699, a group of French Canadians under Pierre Lemoyne d'Iberville established a temporary camp on Biloxi Bay as a way to thwart the Spanish. In 1714, the French constructed a military outpost at Natchitoches, on the Cane River, a branch of the Red River, to keep the Spaniards of Texas and Mexico from advancing into French territory. Three years after that, John Law, a Scot, received an exclusive charter from the French crown to develop Louisiana, and the flurry of speculation his Mississippi Scheme excited brought German settlers in 1718 and slaves in 1719. In 1718, Jean Baptiste Lemoyne de Bienville, a younger brother of Iberville who had taken charge after Iberville's death, selected the land New Orleans today occupies as the site for a commercial and military base.[3]

In 1721, French military engineers began laying out the city along a great bend, or crescent, of the river, ninety or so miles from the river's mouth. It was high ground in a swampy area thick with canebrakes, though some of the area behind it was still below sea level, and an Indian portage route between the river and the nearby lake, now called Lake Pontchartrain, traversed it. By 1724 a number of the streets had been named. Although the foothold of the French was not the firmest in the first few decades of settlement, they sustained their claim to the lower Mississippi and the coastal region along the Gulf of Mexico (Figure 2), holding what is now Louisiana until about 1763.

The Spanish, under the terms of two treaties with France and Britain, obtained control in 1762 and 1763, but the officials and residents of Louisiana did not learn of the transfer until 1764, and Spanish rule was ten-

3. *Louisiana Almanac, 1995–96,* ed. Milburn Calhoun (Gretna, La., 1995), is a useful volume.

4

FIGURE 3   Louisiana parishes

Thomas H. Eubanks, Louisiana Division of Archaeology.

uous until 1769. Political and religious ties with Havana thereafter became close. The population of the colony grew during the years of Spanish governance, especially with the addition of around four thousand French-speaking Acadian (Cajun) refugees whom the British expelled from Nova Scotia. Most of the exiles settled in the bayou country west of New Orleans and near the wetlands bordering the Gulf. Canary Islanders (Isleños) were among the Spanish subjects who came to the area. In 1791, the colony welcomed French-speaking refugees, white and black, from Saint Domingue (French Hispaniola) after the slave revolution there. By then Americans from the newly formed United States who were settling in the Ohio River valley were pressing the Spanish for commercial access to New Orleans and the mouth of the Mississippi. The Spanish, however, were unyielding, despite their support of the American Revolution.

In negotiations that obtained concessions regarding Italy from Napoleon, Spain retroceded the area to France in 1801, and in 1803 President Thomas Jefferson's agents negotiated with the French and made the famous Louisiana Purchase. The area south of 33 degrees, the present northern border of the state, was marked off as the Territory of Orleans, and in 1812 it became the state of Louisiana. The extension of the Florida panhandle—now called the Florida parishes—east of the Mississippi and north of Lake Pontchartrain, was annexed to the state in 1819, setting the present boundaries. In a place that had once been under French and Spanish rule, with most of the people's roots in lands bordering the Mediterranean and the Caribbean, the Americans were the newcomers but an increasingly evident element of the population.

In 1805, the territorial legislative council established counties as local units of government, and then in 1807, without abolishing the counties, it created parish jurisdictions. In 1812, when the area became a state, the term *parish* was adopted instead of *county.* The early parishes were roughly similar in contour to the Roman Catholic church divisions, the *paroisse* of the French and the *parroquia* of the Spanish. In the chapters that follow, buildings in rural settings are identified by the parishes in which they are located.

The names of the parishes often reflect the parishes' history (Figure 3). Among the earliest were those of the southern tier of the state, for example, the parishes of St. Charles, St. James, St. John the Baptist, and Ascension along the Mississippi, and Assumption, St. Martin, and St. Mary in the adjacent bayous. These names are redolent of the French and Spanish Catholic traditions. Elsewhere there are names based on the Indians who once inhabited the lands, like Natchitoches, in the central part of the state along the Cane and Red rivers, and Ouachita, in the northern tier. Natchitoches Parish is the site of the oldest settlement in the Louisiana Purchase, and Ouachita of the Indian mounds first explored by de Soto. Calcasieu Parish, in the southwest, is probably named for an Atakapa chief. Parishes formed after statehood sometimes took the names of figures in American history. Washington Parish, on the border with the state of Mississippi, was established in 1819. Jefferson Parish, close to Orleans Parish, was created in 1825. In 1845, Jackson Parish, originally part of the Natchitoches territory, was named for President Andrew Jackson. Grant Parish, an area of forest in the central part of the state, received its name in 1869 from the post–Civil War legislature. The final two parishes to be named were each cut out of Calcasieu Parish in 1912 as the population grew. Allen and Jefferson Davis are both named after Confederate leaders, the first a governor of Louisiana and the other the president of the Confederacy. The year, 1912, saw also what might be called an antebellum revival in architecture, with columnar mansions coming into vogue again—a southern variation on the Colonial Revival movement taking place in other parts of the nation.

Building names, place names, and architectural terms primarily from the French, but occasionally from the Spanish have crept into the English now almost exclusively in use in the state. In New Orleans, the two major public buildings flanking the Cathedral of Saint Louis, King of France, on Jackson Square, are the Cabildo (named using the Spanish word for a governing body) and the Presbytère (named using the French word for a priest's residence or a parsonage), yet the difference in the origins of the names occurs to few natives of the city. The diversity in the names probably arose because the Cabildo was built under the Spanish regime, in 1795–1799, whereas the construction of the Presbytère, though inaugurated in 1795, continued to a partial completion in 1813 and to completion of the rear portions only in 1840, during which time the language of the neighborhood probably affected what the building was called. The name of the old quarter of the city, the Vieux Carre—probably not widely used until the last quarter of the nineteenth century—is now usually printed without the acute accent over the final *e.*

The English word *gallery* is employed in Louisiana to identify both narrow balconies and covered porches along the front or side of buildings and derives from the French *galerie. Bousillage* and *briquette entre poteaux* refer to the filling between timbers or posts, a mixture of mud and moss or bricks. The character of the mud or daub mix, or the bricks, used in Louisiana may have differed in small ways from what was customary in other areas in the same period, but the use of exotic terms may make it seem as if there were more pronounced differences than there were from the timber-frame construction of Europe and England. Other architectural terminology of French inheritance—including *cabinet, garçonnière, pigeonnier,* and *poteaux en terre*—will be defined in context later in the volume.

The following chapters are in roughly chronological sequence and have focuses or themes connected with the special circumstances or patterns of development in Louisiana. The first three chapters deal with buildings by early generations of settlers: structures of Mediterranean or Creole heritage in the south of the state, urban construction in New Orleans, and folk fabrications in the Anglo and Scotch-Irish settlements in the north or central areas mainly postdating Louisiana's entrance into the Union.

Chapter 4 looks at plantation buildings, and Chapter 5 at public and private buildings in urban settings between 1815 and 1880. The chapter on plantations encompasses rural structures built from approximately 1815 into the early twentieth century, because Louisiana was largely rural until about 1950, with sugar, cotton, and rice the most important crops. In 1840, the population of Louisiana had been 69.1 percent rural and 29.95 percent urban. A hundred years later, in 1940, 59 percent of the population remained rural, with 41 percent urban. It was not until 1950 that the urban population exceeded the rural, and then it amounted to only 50.8 percent.[4] Because of the growth and prosperity of the southern agricultural economy before the Civil War, and the consequent number of buildings erected in the countryside, it is the plantation complex, particularly the "big house"—which was not always especially large—that has come to symbolize the region, in what is often an all too romantic image.

Chapter 5, on urban growth in the Romantic era, looks above all at New Orleans, which from its founding to the present time, has been the largest city in the state. It grew by leaps and bounds in the booming pre–Civil War era; a more modest but steady growth continued in subsequent years. Until relatively recent times, when interstate highways and air service made quicker travel to other places possible, New Orleans was *the* city not only for Louisianians but for people in neighboring states like Mississippi and Alabama. Other leading urban centers in the state include Baton Rouge, the state capital; Alexandria-Pineville, in the central part of the state; Shreveport–Bossier City, in the northwest, on the Red River; Monroe, in the north-central area; and Lake Charles, in the southwest. A large number of buildings survive from the years between 1815 and 1880.

In both Chapter 4 and Chapter 5, the survival of architectural features from the early Creole period is noted. Among these are galleries, narrow roofed balconies or porches, in both city and country buildings. On plantation houses the piers and posts of the early years gave way to Greek Revival columns, but the galleries were retained. In cities the galleries gave a uniform texture to street vistas even as styles of architecture changed. In New Orleans, the transition from the Greek Revival style to the Italianate and even to the preferences of later-nineteenth-century taste, such as the Stick style and the Colonial Revival style, is more subtle than elsewhere. There is a ubiquitous presence of galleries and sheltering porches supported by columns, more columns, and a variety of turned posts. Also surviving from the Creole

4. *Hammond's World Atlas and Gazetteer* (New York, 1952), 52.

period are the economical floor plans favored in both country and city, which most likely come out of the Mediterranean, Latin, and African traditions. Little space is given over to halls and foyers, and movement is from room to room, on either rectangular or linear plans, that is, in *en suite* or *enfilade* arrangements.

Given Louisiana history, these are now conveniently identified as Creole architectural traditions. Still, it is doubtful that any builder or architect living in the eighteenth or nineteenth century spoke of the buildings he erected as Creole. The word *Creole* has a long history, and there are endless discussions of its etymology and meaning. In colonial Portuguese, Spanish, and French, the word and its cognates referred to people born (created) in the colonies. In Louisiana it has meant people descended from the early French or Spanish settlers or from those associated with them; it has also meant those who spoke French or a Creole patois, including whites and blacks and people of mixed race. The word only gradually gained application apart from persons. The current, and now more frequent, use of it to label Louisiana's ambience and circumstances, and hence as an adjective conveying that something—such as food—has diverse origins, probably became current only around 1880, when George Washington Cable and Lafcadio Hearn wrote, respectively, *Old Creole Days,* published in 1879, and *La Cuisine Creole,* published in 1885.

An obvious basis for both rural and urban prosperity before the Civil War was the steamboat, which immensely facilitated shipping of agricultural products and other goods. But the steamboat is but one of the mechanical and technological innovations that helped shape the built environment of Louisiana. Chapter 6 is devoted to the buildings that are part of this story, over its long time span. Warehouses, railroad stations and hotels, lumber mills and lumber towns, and even the motels of the automobile era enter into the account.

Chapters 7 and 8 also carry the history of Louisiana building into the twentieth century. In the recovery after the Civil War, Louisiana shared in the many changes that took place in the late nineteenth and early twentieth centuries. Some structural types uncommon elsewhere became popular. The shotgun cottages in New Orleans, built as middle- and working-class housing in many sections of the city, often on speculation, are as distinctive a component of the architecture of New Orleans as the galleried buildings of the French Quarter. And remarkably fine examples of early Modernism sprang up in Shreveport in the 1930s.

The National Historic Preservation Act of 1966 ruled that buildings fifty years old or older may be considered historic. Not all buildings of that age should be viewed as historic or recorded as part of the Historic American Buildings Survey. Nonetheless, there is a need to be alert to the special qualities of buildings from the decades up to the 1940s and, as time passes, into and beyond the present. Selections are still made according to the original criteria and include major monuments as well as typical buildings.

Peterson recalled that HABS had its beginnings in a burst of idealism and energy. From the first efforts to compile a historic record by making drawings, many of the participants soon moved on to preservation—to working for the repair of old buildings so that these might endure for the next generations to see and enjoy. In the effort is not only idealism but also realism, since it is apparent that many surviving buildings have economic as well as educational value. Sometime around 1940, Samuel Wilson, Jr. (1911–1993), told listeners in New Orleans that the architecture of the French Quarter was beginning to attract visitors and predicted that the buildings would be an asset to the city: "Each year brings visitors in great numbers. When the possibilities of the Quarter have been developed to their utmost limits, the amount of money that the Quarter will bring into New Orleans will easily make it the major business of the city."[5]

The vibrant ambience of the French Quarter has given enjoyment, a sense of place, and a sense of history to Louisianians and to many visitors. Tourism has become an important business of the city. There are, however, now moments when those who love the old buildings fear there are too many visitors.[6] The danger exists that the balance between residential and commercial, between insiders and outsiders, will be lost, making for an artificial setting rather than the lively urban neighborhood and community that is.

Those now carrying out HABS's work, and the many people who appreciate their efforts, continue to take the long view. They have faith in the educational and spiritual values gained by preserving the architectural heritage of Louisiana, and the nation, and are resolute in the conviction that if we are aware and care for our built environment, we are caring for future generations.

5. Samuel Wilson, Jr., "The Old French Quarter as a Community Asset" (Typescript in Samuel Wilson, Jr., Papers, HABS Folder, Southeastern Architectural Archive, Tulane University).
6. Marc Cooper, "The Vieux Carre—New Orleans' Heart and Soul," *Cultural Vistas,* XVI (1995), 64; Walter W. Gallas, "French Quarter Group Pushes Preservation of Buildings and Neighborhoods Since 1920s," *Preservation in Print,* XXII (1995), 24.

I

BEGINNINGS: CREOLE ARCHITECTURE FOR THE LOUISIANA SETTING

Eugene Darwin Cizek

IN 1682, WHEN ROBERT CAVELIER DE LA SALLE TRAVELED THE GREAT LAKES from French Canada and descended the Mississippi to the Gulf of Mexico, he claimed all the lands drained by this great water system in the name of Louis XIV, king of France. He called the new colonial territory Louisiane in honor of the king (Figure 1). In 1685, he returned to the Gulf of Mexico to establish a permanent settlement on the Mississippi, but he was unable to locate the river's mouth and landed instead in Texas.

In 1699, Pierre Lemoyne d'Iberville found the mouth and reclaimed the territory for France. In that same year, a brother of his, Jean Baptiste Lemoyne de Bienville, persuaded an exploration party sent out by England to turn back at what is now called English Turn, the first oxbow downriver from New Orleans. Early in the sixteenth century, the Spanish had explored the Louisiana Territory and its large river, and the English later became interested and curious, but it was the French who persevered and finally laid claim. Their language and culture were to be fundamental for Creole Louisiana.

The vast territory adjacent to the Mississippi provided France with uninterrupted passage from Canada to the Gulf of Mexico and the Caribbean through the heartland of North America. The immense ecological system at the river's mouth would henceforth be intertwined with the culture, technology, and commerce of the New World and Europe. Water transportation was the key to power and control in the intense competition between colonizing nations.

To the New World the Europeans brought their centuries of traditions in military engineering, public and private architecture, and official policy. They brought, besides, the knowledge they had acquired in two hundred years of adaptation to their colonial empires. Creolization is a concept to

FIGURE 1   Henri Joutel, *The Gulf of Mexico,* in the journal Joutel kept during La Salle's last voyage (Paris, 1713; London, 1714). New Orleans, at the end of the great Mississippi system, became a key location for the eventual settlement and control of the North American continent. Soon New Orleans was a regular port of call for the ships that connected other colonies—Cartagena, Santo Domingo, Campeche, Veracruz, and Havana—with Europe. During the initial French period, the majority of the slaves brought into Louisiana were from Senegal and Gambia, a region of Africa where people were known for their abilities in building, woodcrafting, and farming in a hot, humid climate. Their cuisine was based on seafood, vegetables, and rice. The Louisiana colony's free people of color were primarily from the French colonial islands of the Caribbean: St. Maarten, Martinique, Guadeloupe, and Haiti. They too were skilled in the building crafts and agriculture. The Germans came from the Rhineland and also knew how to build and farm.

Library of Congress

FIGURE 2 Marie Adrien Persac, *Plantations of the Mississippi River from Natchez to New Orleans* (Norman's Chart), 1857, detail of East Baton Rouge and West Baton Rouge parishes. The manner of subdividing the land gave each landholder a narrow frontage on the water and resulted in elongated parcels of land. That bestowed an appearance of linear suburbia along the roads that paralleled the levees on the river and the related bayous. Most movement of goods and people was by water. At the intersection of levee roads, such as where a bayou met its river artery, or of highland roads that interconnected inland locations, urban development might occur.

LSU Libraries

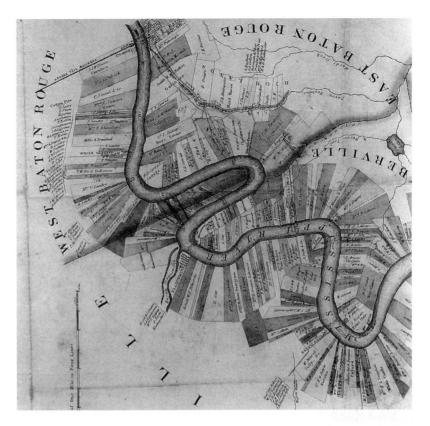

which cling the many mutations of the idea of what it is to be a Creole. But whatever the derivation of the concept, it has come to comprise the adaptation of a mother country's ideals to, and their integration with, those of Native Americans and of the Africans who came either as slaves or as free people of color from the islands, as well as with those of the other Europeans inhabiting the region under the mother country's governance. In Louisiana, it was the melding of the French mother country's values not only with those of the Spaniards who preceded and followed the French settlement but also with those of the American Indians and blacks that constituted creolization.

The hot, humid subtropical climate in the lower portions of the territory, with its sudden swings between bountiful rain and blistering sun, between gentle breeze and violent hurricane or tornado, compelled the attention of builders. The complex topography, predominantly flat throughout the vast floodplains, prairies, and coastal marshes, imposed the need for careful siting. Higher ground existed only along the natural levees of the bayous and rivers, on the hills and terraces adjacent to most floodplains, and on the blufflands to the north.

In the interest of maximizing the number of properties that could be carved out along the bayous and rivers, long-lot subdivision prevailed (Figure 2); the result was land parcels with narrow widths at the water's edge and lengths many times the width extending inland. Access to water and water

FIGURE 3 François Mugnier, *Cypresses, ca.* 1895. This Creole photographer from New Orleans has given posterity some of its rarest images of late-nineteenth-century Louisiana. The huge cypress trees provided building materials for Louisiana.

Collection of the Louisiana State Museum

FIGURE 4 Alexandre de Batz, *Temple des Sauvages* and *Cabane du Chef,* 1732. The early-eighteenth-century drawings dispel any doubt about the sophistication and beauty of indigenous American architecture. Today only experiences in Central and South America can provide a firsthand understanding of what such early civilizations were like. Modern archaeology has also established the extent and complexity of ancient cultures.

Peabody Museum of Archaeology and Ethnology, Harvard University. Photograph by Hillel Burger.

FIGURE 5 François Mugnier, *Palmetto House, ca.* 1890. The picture was taken in Bayou Lacombe, St. Tammany Parish. Some early colonists adopted this indigenous sort of palmetto-covered wood-frame house for their first dwellings. The Isleños, Spanish people who came to St. Bernard Parish from the Canary Islands in the late eighteenth century, found that palmetto houses suited their needs, and many continued to build them into the early twentieth century.

Collection of the Louisiana State Museum

transportation was paramount for both urban and rural development throughout the colonial period.

The Native Americans, to whom the New World was far from new, had developed a culture in great harmony with nature. Those living near the floodplains of the river system around the lower Mississippi drew great advantage from the relatively flat topography. They designed their villages to catch the cooling breezes so as to contrive a degree of comfort. The flora and fauna of south Louisiana were abundant and diverse. Fishing and hunting afforded a great variety in the diet, but care always had to be taken against

FIGURE 6 Jean Baptiste Michel Le Bouteux, *Veuë du Camp de la Concession de Monseigneur Law, au Nouveau Biloxy, Coste de la Louisianne,* December 10, 1720. At New Biloxi, the French drew upon forms from their homeland at the same time that they appropriated shapes, forms, and materials from Native American construction.

Courtesy of Edward E. Ayer Collection, The Newberry Library, Chicago.

the menace of snakes, alligators, bears, and wildcats, and the annoyance of insects, which sometimes—as with mosquitoes—could all too easily turn into a menace. Giant cypress trees touched the edges of the water system and grew from the low slopes of the natural levees to the higher elevations where live oaks and pines thrived (Figure 3). The wooded lands lasted as a source of superior building materials for both Native Americans and colonists until the early twentieth century. Photographs from the nineteenth century show the lush and glorious landscape that was soon to be logged to build a growing nation.

In 1732, Alexandre de Batz made a drawing of the well-crafted and skillfully adorned temple and chief's cabin of the Colapissa Indians (Figure 4). He recorded that all the Indian structures were round and of similar construction, with roofs of palmetto thatch. The indigenous fill of mud, moss, and animal hair was later adopted by the French, who called it *bousillage.* In Louisiana, this fill was used between heavy timbers well into the nineteenth century.

In an alluvial valley without rock and stone, the Louisiana Indians' most imposing construction was their huge earthen mounds in a stepped design. A temple, having a thatched roof supported by posts in the ground as the only foundation, stood on the uppermost earthen platform. The image achieved was powerful and may have related to the social hierarchy. In larger settlements there could be several mounds serving as ceremonial centers. The arrangement of the mounds is at times of such a scale that it is possible to make out the pattern only from a viewpoint high above the earth.

The French soon realized the wisdom of raising structures above the wet

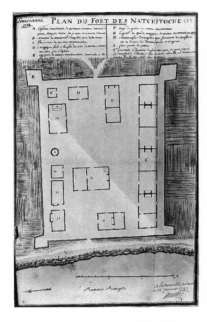

FIGURE 7   Ignace François Broutin, *Plan du Fort des Natchitoche*, 1733. In the twentieth century, the architectural firm of Koch and Wilson relied on this plan to reconstruct the fortification, duplicating the materials and techniques of the period, near the original site in Natchitoches.

Archives Nationales, Centre des Archives d'Outre-Mer. All rights of reproduction reserved. Photograph in Samuel Wilson, Jr., Collection. Courtesy of Koch and Wilson Architects.

ground, perhaps having been instructed by the example of the Native Americans, who continued to build in that manner into the early twentieth century. A late-nineteenth-century photograph shows a traditional Louisiana palmetto house in Bayou Lacombe (Figure 5). A drawing by Jean Baptiste Michel Le Bouteux of the camp at New Biloxi, in Mississippi, in 1720 displays a French-style structure with posts in the ground and tents of both European cloth and palmetto fronds (Figure 6).

In 1714, Louis Juchereau de St. Denis established Fort St. Jean Baptiste as the first permanent French settlement in what is now Louisiana (Figure 7). Engineering drawings and field notes survive showing the fort that became Natchitoches. The drawings depict a rectangular stockade of posts in the ground, along with individual buildings that have walls of similar construction and hip and gable roofs of hand-split cypress shingles. The joining of French form and style with native building materials was to persist in Creole architecture.

Spain had begun settlements in the New World by 1500 and was forever working to enlarge Spanish territories. In 1717, Spain established the Mission of San Miguel de los Adais fourteen miles southwest of Natchitoches to restrict the westward expansion of the French into the territories of New Spain. In 1721, a *presidio* was set up at the mission, and this served as the capital of the province of Texas until 1773. Archival drawings confirm that during this period the Spanish and the French were constructing buildings that looked much alike.

In 1718, Bienville founded New Orleans on the natural levee of a great curve of the Mississippi, near the portage of Bayou St. John, long used by Native Americans to transfer goods between Lake Pontchartrain and the river. In 1708 there had been French land grants relating to what became the city's site. Bienville named the new city in honor of the regent of France, Philippe, duc d'Orleans. An early plan displaying all the structures built from September 3, 1722, up to the end of December, 1722, presents the city with its ancient colonial form of a tight grid of squares three hundred feet to a side (Figure 8). Each square was divided into lots 60 feet wide and 120 feet deep—in French feet, which were 12 3/4 English and American inches—leaving one lot of 60 by 150 feet facing each side street. The Place d'Armes, a public square that the church and other public buildings faced, was at the center of the plan. To each side of the public square the city was to extend across five urban squares. The entire city was to be eleven squares wide and only six squares deep from the river. Eighteen buildings that served the public and social needs of a colonial town appeared in the plan, including the church, the hospital, and the carpenters' barracks. The utility of barracks for workmen of different nationalities and trades lay in the multinational profile of Louisiana's settlers from its inception. Large numbers of Germans and Acadians came in the early years, after the first wave of immigration. The Acadians had been forced to flee Nova Scotia

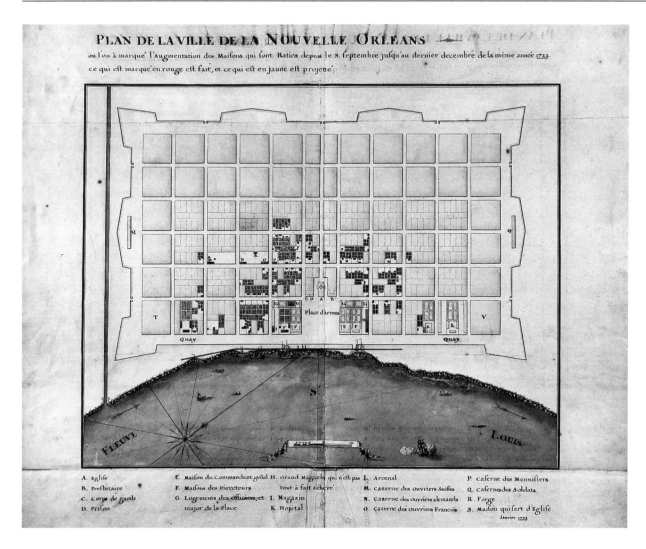

PLAN DE LA VILLE DE LA NOUVELLE ORLEANS

A. Eglife
B. Presbitaire
C. Corps de garde
D. Prison
E. Maifon du Commandant genal
F. Maifons des Directeurs
G. Logements des officiers, et major de la Place
H. Grand Magazin qui n'est pas tout à fait acheve'
I. Magazin
K. Hopital
L. Arcenal
M. Cazerne des Ouvriers Suiffes
N. Cazerne des Ouvriers alemands
O. Cazerne des Ouvriers Francois
P. caferne des Menuifiers
Q. caferne des Soldats
R. Forge
S. Maifon qui fert d'Eglife

FIGURE 8 *Plan de la Ville de la Nouvelle Orleans, ca.* 1723. Shown in this plan are the houses built in New Orleans between September 3 and December 31, 1722. Although unsigned, the document is undoubtedly a copy of the plan sent to the Company of the Indies by Pierre Leblond de La Tour with his letter of January 15, 1723. Key: A, church; B, presbytère; C, guardhouse; D, prison; E, commander's house; F, directors' houses; G, lodgings of adjutant and officers; H, large warehouse that is incomplete; I, warehouse; K, hospital; L, arsenal; M, Swiss workmen's barracks; N, German workmen's barracks; O, French workmen's barracks; P, carpenters' barracks; Q, soldiers' barracks; R, forge; S, house serving as a church; T, V, open frontage along the river.

Courtesy of Edward E. Ayer Collection, The Newberry Library, Chicago

when the English began to expand their holdings in the New World and to expel the French who rebelled against their government. Later in the eighteenth century and throughout the nineteenth century the Spanish-speaking presence grew as emigrants from Spain and Spain's subjects from other territories arrived. The Spanish also welcomed French-speaking refugees, coreligionists both white and black, from Saint Domingue. Anglo-Americans streamed in in great numbers after 1803, the year of the Louisiana Purchase.

FIGURE 9   Jean Pierre Lassus, *Veüe et Perspective de la Nouvelle Orleans*, 1726. The small clearing in the vast forest foretells how the city's development will dominate the landscape. The swamps and forests would disappear with increasing settlement.

Archives Nationales, Centre des Archives d'Outre-Mer. All rights of reproduction reserved. Photograph in Samuel Wilson, Jr., Collection. Courtesy of Koch and Wilson Architects.

FIGURE 10   Pierre Leblond de La Tour, *La Direction*, January 3, 1723. The narrow one-and-a-half-room floor plan, the long french windows, and the raised construction allowed the movement of air for the sake of comfort in the hot, humid climate of Louisiana. The heavy timber construction, often referred to as a Norman truss system since it reflected a way of building in Normandy, gave the huge roof strength to weather the intense rains and winds of Louisiana. Deep overhangs, galleries, and shutters would be added to later examples of this traditional French architecture.

Archives Nationales, Centre des Archives d'Outre-Mer. All rights of reproduction reserved. Photograph in Samuel Wilson, Jr., Collection. Courtesy of Koch and Wilson Architects.

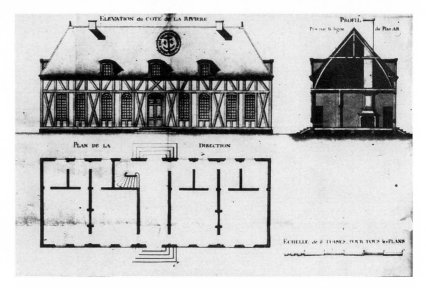

New Orleans was a picturesque city from the beginning. In a drawing Jean Pierre Lassus prepared in 1726 (Figure 9), the settlement's public buildings are readily identifiable and the urban development met the edge of the uncleared cypress forest. The vast wilderness appeared to go on forever. The first public structures were designed by engineers trained by the royal institutes in current theory and policy. Many think La Direction, which was headquarters for the directors of the Company of the Indies (Figure 10), the most beautiful building in the city, and it served as a model for distinguished private dwellings. The people of the city were particularly fond of the geometric patterns the exposed timbers created on the surface of the walls, though the exposed timbers later proved to be a problem in the relentless rain and humidity. The design document was signed January 3, 1723, by the chief engineer of Louisiana, Leblond de La Tour.

Upon the death of La Tour in October, 1724, Adrien de Pauger became chief engineer. The preceding May he had signed the documents for the construction of the parish church of St. Louis (Figure 11), a replacement building for the first congregation to be organized in New Orleans. The new

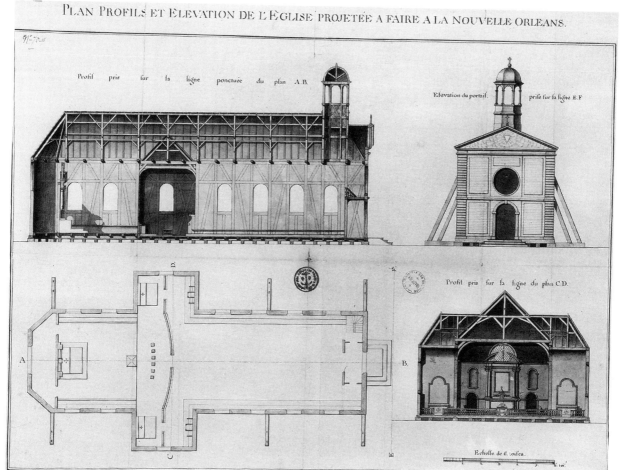

PLAN PROFILS ET ELEVATION DE L'EGLISE PROJETÉE A FAIRE A LA NOUVELLE ORLEANS.

FIGURE 11   Adrien de Pauger, *Plan, Profils et Elevation de l'Eglise Projetée à Faire à la Nouvelle Orleans,* May 29, 1724. Reflected here are French traditions in both religious and military architecture. The simple buttresses are an acknowledgment that extra support may be needed to withstand local hurricanes.

Archives Nationales, Centre des Archives d'Outre-Mer. All rights of reproduction reserved. Photograph in Samuel Wilson, Jr., Collection. Courtesy of Koch and Wilson Architects.

church was of heavy timber with a fill of brick and a stuccoed exterior. The Company of the Indies opened the city's first brickyard in 1725, on Bayou Road, and its harder bricks may have been what allowed de Pauger to omit the side buttresses the church's design called for. Because the hurricane of September, 1722, had destroyed the previous church and many other structures, de Pauger was wary of the extreme wind loads experienced in Louisiana. His church survived until the fire of 1788.

In 1730, Dumont de Montigny produced sketches of the early architecture and landscape in the new colony (Figure 12). One included his own house in New Orleans, in addition to what stood near it: a kitchen and house for blacks, a pavilion, a willow tree in use as a hen house, a trellis for vines, two gardens, two ponds, a ladder for roosting, and an oven. A palisade fence enclosed the principal house, along with the rear gardens, which were of a geometric configuration in the formal French fashion. The second sketch, of Concession plantation, downriver from New Orleans, included structures and gardens remarkably similar to those appearing in the urban drawing, but there were a greater number of buildings, gardens, and yards related to agri-

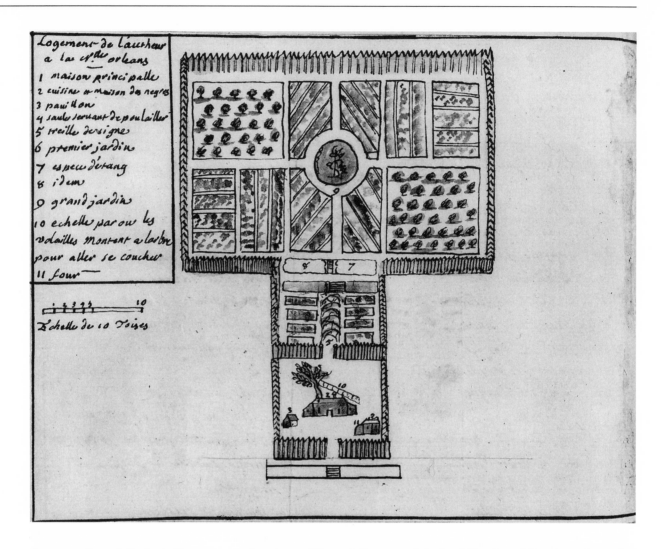

Logement de l'autheur
a la v.lle orleans
1 maison principalle
2 cuisine o maison des neg.res
3 pauillon
4 saule seruant de poulailler
5 treille de signe
6 premier jardin
7 espece d'etang
8 idem
9 grand jardin
10 echelle par ou les
volailles montent a l'arbre
pour aller se coucher
11 four —

Echelle de 10 Toises

FIGURE 12 François Benjamin Dumont de Montigny, *Logement de l'Autheur à la Nlle. Orleans, ca.* 1730. The drawing exhibits the complex arrangement of structures that settlers devised for living in the New World. The structures here do not have the deep roof overhangs and galleries that were eventually incorporated by the more environmentally responsive Creole design.

Courtesy of Edward E. Ayer Collection, The Newberry Library, Chicago.

cultural uses (Plate A). Layouts of the land like those Montigny pictured—especially of the gardens—retained a popular appeal into the early nineteenth century. But none of the structures he represented in his two sketches had the galleries that are common in later Creole architecture.

Military engineers designed many of the buildings in the new colony, though the extent of their architectural contribution was not known until the architect-historian Samuel Wilson, Jr., stimulated by his work on the HABS drawings in 1934, did research in France. Through his discovery in the French archives of drawings by the military engineers, we have learned most of what we know about the earliest structures. The HABS drawings of the few buildings surviving from the late eighteenth and early nineteenth century round out that knowledge.

The design for a barracks that Bernard Forest de Belidor presented in *La Science des ingénieurs,* published in 1729 (Figure 13), may have inspired the plans Ignace François Broutin produced in 1732 for a barracks adjacent to the

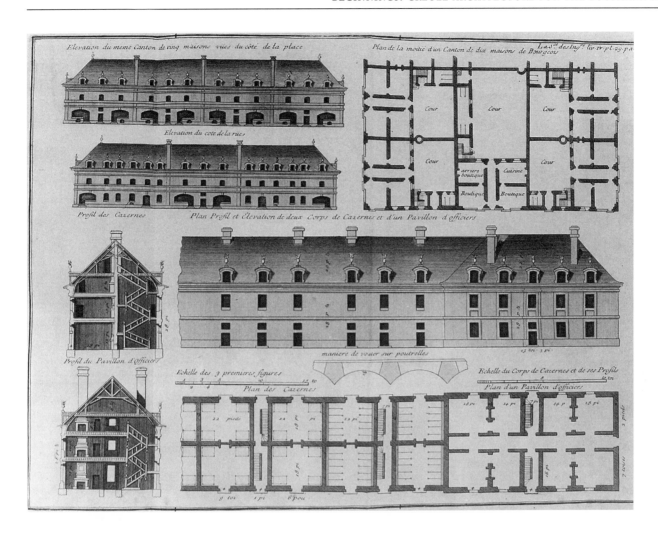

FIGURE 13 Bernard Forest de Belidor, *Design for a Barracks,* in *La Science des ingénieurs,* 1729. This was a prototype for Broutin's plans for the barracks and the second Ursuline Convent, in New Orleans. By way of engineer's designs published in Paris, construction in the Americas had continuity with European ideas.

Archives Nationales, Centre des Archives d'Outre-Mer. All rights of reproduction reserved. Photograph in Samuel Wilson, Jr., Collection. Courtesy of Koch and Wilson Architects.

public square. The drawings of both men show two-and-a-half-story buildings made of brick and heavy timber with high hip roofs, a flare at the eaves, and prominent dormers. A plan in 1731 for a fort at the Balise, at the Southeast Pass, near the mouth of the Mississippi, involves the employment of wood pilings as a foundation—here to support masonry fortifications. The commandant's lodge has a gallery. Drawings for a guardhouse and prison at the Balise, signed by Bernard Deverges in 1734 (Figure 14), are among the first showing a gallery under the main roof. The climatic conditions of Louisiana were primarily responsible for perpetuating that innovation in later designs.

The Gonichon Plan for New Orleans, drawn in 1731 (Figure 15), exhibits a city of high hip roofs. Some of the houses had galleries, many set at or near the sidewalk, or banquette, and bordered on three sides by gardens. There had been no serious problems with the local Indians, and major fortifications had not been constructed. The larger houses were usually timber-frame with

FIGURE 14   Bernard Deverges, *Elevation, Section, and Plan of a Guardhouse and Prison for the Balise near the Mouth of the Mississippi,* February 28, 1734. The addition of a gallery is a clear mark of Creolization. The overhang and gallery adjust the air and light admitted to the interior.

Archives Nationales, Centre des Archives d'Outre-Mer. All rights of reproduction reserved. Photograph in Samuel Wilson, Jr., Collection. Courtesy of Koch and Wilson Architects.

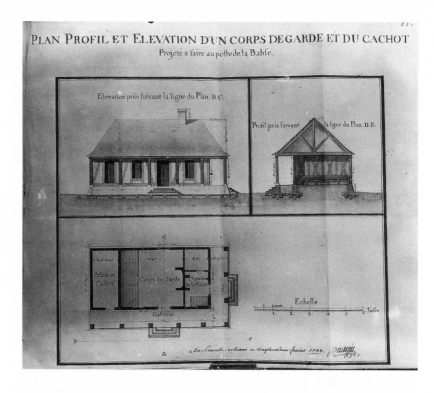

FIGURE 15   Gonichon, *Plan de la Nouvelle Orleans,* 1731. This plan illustrates how the houses of French New Orleans were situated in gardens and often set back from the sidewalk and street. New Orleans was a city of urban pavilions in garden settings.

Archives Nationales, Centre des Archives d'Outre-Mer. All rights of reproduction reserved. Photograph in Samuel Wilson, Jr., Collection. Courtesy of Koch and Wilson Architects.

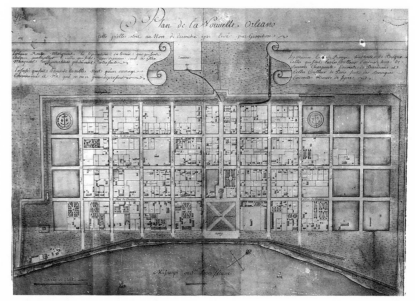

brick between the posts. These and the better wooden houses had roofs of cypress shingle. Huts had roofs of bark.

The first Ursuline Convent was begun in 1727 and completed in 1734. The elevations Broutin signed in 1733 depict a heavy timber structure of three stories with a hip roof capped by a lantern (Figures 16, 17). The fram-

FIGURE 16 Ignace François Broutin, *Elevation de la Façade du Quay du Bâtiment des R. Urselines,* March 19, 1733. This design for the first Ursuline Convent's facade facing the river is similar to an earlier design by de Batz and to the later design of the second, existing convent. The archival research of Samuel Wilson, Jr., established the sequence of the buildings of the Ursuline Convent.

Archives Nationales, Centre des Archives d'Outre-Mer. All rights of reproduction reserved. Photograph in Samuel Wilson, Jr., Collection. Courtesy of Koch and Wilson Architects.

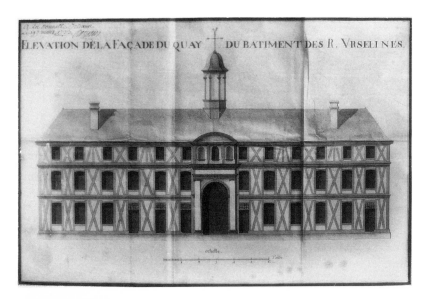

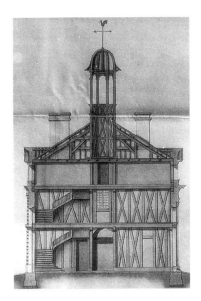

FIGURE 17 Ignace François Broutin, *Des Plans du Bâtiment des R. Ursulines,* March 19, 1733. The techniques of construction for the first Ursuline Convent were similar to those for the second. Displayed here is the basic structural section the engineers prescribed. It was employed afterward in both public and residential architecture in French Louisiana. The original stairway was installed in the second convent.

Archives Nationales, Centre des Archives d'Outre-Mer. All rights of reproduction reserved. Photograph in Samuel Wilson, Jr., Collection. Courtesy of Koch and Wilson Architects.

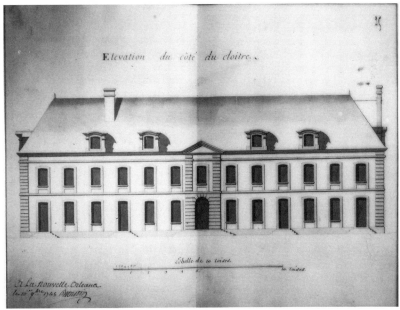

FIGURE 18 Ignace François Broutin, *Elevation du Côte de Cloitres,* November 10, 1745. This drawing of the second Ursuline Convent presents the original design before it was decided to widen the central bay. The expanded later plan was executed between 1749 and 1753 by the builder Claude Joseph Villan Dubreuil.

Archives Nationales, Centre des Archives d'Outre-Mer. All rights of reproduction reserved. Photograph in Samuel Wilson, Jr., Collection. Courtesy of Koch and Wilson Architects.

ing was exposed, and the unprotected wood and an inadequate foundation contributed to the building's short life-span. A design for the second Ursuline Convent that Broutin signed in 1745 shows a solid masonry structure of elegant proportions (Figure 18). Like the barracks for which Broutin may

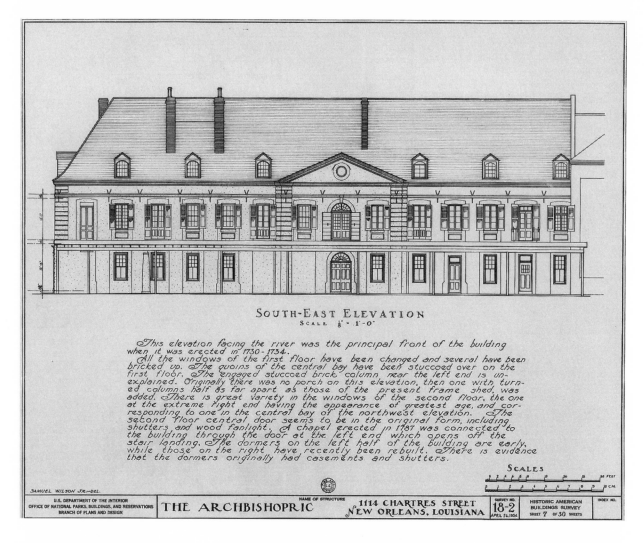

SOUTH-EAST ELEVATION

SCALE ⅛" = 1'-0"

This elevation facing the river was the principal front of the building when it was erected in 1730-1734. All the windows of the first floor have been changed and several have been bricked up. The quoins of the central bay have been stuccoed over on the first floor. The engaged stuccoed brick column near the left end is unexplained. Originally there was no porch on this elevation, then one with turned columns half as far apart as those of the present frame shed, was added. There is great variety in the windows of the second floor, the one at the extreme right end having the appearance of greatest age, and corresponding to one in the central bay of the northwest elevation. The second floor central door seems to be in the original form, including shutters and wood fanlight. A chapel erected in 1787 was connected to the building through the door at the left end and which opens off the stair landing. The dormers on the left half of the building are early, while those on the right have recently been rebuilt. There is evidence that the dormers originally had casements and shutters.

SCALES

SAMUEL WILSON JR.—DEL.

| U.S. DEPARTMENT OF THE INTERIOR OFFICE OF NATIONAL PARKS, BUILDINGS, AND RESERVATIONS BRANCH OF PLANS AND DESIGN | THE ARCHBISHOPRIC | NAME OF STRUCTURE | 1114 CHARTRES STREET NEW ORLEANS, LOUISIANA | SURVEY NO. 18-2 APRIL 26,1934 | HISTORIC AMERICAN BUILDINGS SURVEY SHEET 7 OF 30 SHEETS | INDEX NO. |

FIGURE 19   Ursuline Convent (Archbishopric), New Orleans, designed 1745, completed 1749–1753. The river, or southwest, elevation of the second convent includes the changes made during construction. Later changes, primarily on the first floor, occurred when the entrance was shifted from the river facade to the cloister facade, on Chartres Street. The convent saw use as the archbishopric from 1824 to 1899.

HABS, 1934, Library of Congress

have found inspiration in *La Science des ingénieurs,* it has two and a half stories and a high hip roof with a flare at the eaves and prominent dormers; the original principal entrance was a single bay with a small pediment. Broutin's design was altered during construction to widen the central bay and include two additional windows. The entire building was thus lengthened and two extra dormers installed. The facade, which faced the river, was even more elegant than in the original proposal. This second Ursuline Convent is the only surviving documented example of early French Colonial architecture in Louisiana (Figure 19).

Details now seen to define French Colonial architecture are evident in the drawings: the segmental arched windows with multipaned transoms, the pairs of shuttered ten-light casement windows, the brick stuccoed to create moldings and quoins. Inspection of the end elevation and the cross section at center line discloses the correlation between external and internal linea-

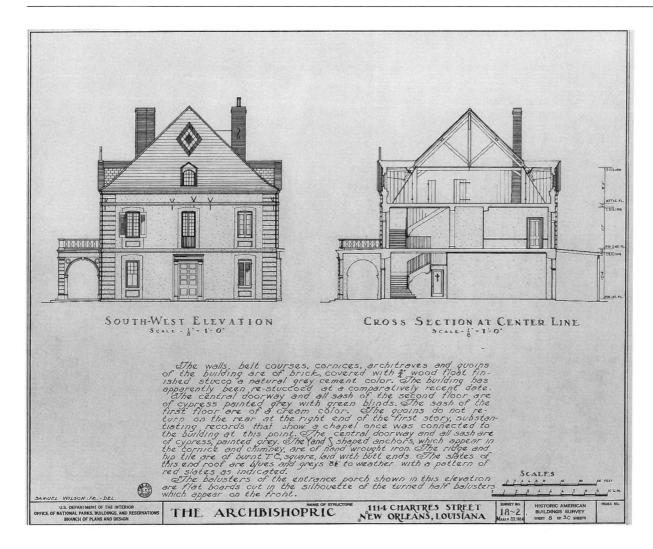

SOUTH-WEST ELEVATION
SCALE - ⅛" - 1'-0"

CROSS SECTION AT CENTER LINE
SCALE - ⅛" - 1'-0"

The walls, belt courses, cornices, architraves and quoins of the building are of brick, covered with ¾" wood float finished stucco a natural grey cement color. The building has apparently been re-stuccoed at a comparatively recent date.
The central doorway and all sash of the second floor are of cypress painted grey with green blinds. The sash of the first floor are of a cream color. The quoins do not return on the rear at the right end of the first story, substantiating records that show a chapel once was connected to the building at this point. The central doorway and all sash are of cypress, painted grey. The I and S shaped anchors, which appear in the cornice and chimney, are of hand wrought iron. The ridge and hip tile are of burnt T.C. square, laid with butt ends. The slates of this end roof are blues and greys th to weather with a pattern of red slates as indicated.
The balusters of the entrance porch shown in this elevation are flat boards cut in the silhouette of the turned half balusters which appear on the front.

SAMUEL WILSON JR.-DEL.

SCALES

| U.S. DEPARTMENT OF THE INTERIOR OFFICE OF NATIONAL PARKS, BUILDINGS, AND RESERVATIONS BRANCH OF PLANS AND DESIGN | NAME OF STRUCTURE **THE ARCHBISHOPRIC** | 1114 CHARTRES STREET NEW ORLEANS, LOUISIANA | SURVEY NO. 18~2 MARCH 20, 1934 | HISTORIC AMERICAN BUILDINGS SURVEY SHEET 8 OF 30 SHEETS | INDEX NO. |

FIGURE 20 Ursuline Convent. The end elevation and cross section show the high-pitched roof with the slight double pitch at the edge, which is a characteristic of later Creole buildings, such as the main house at Homeplace plantation, in St. Charles Parish. This slight double pitch provided better dispersal of rainwater and protected intersections of roof with plaster wall.

HABS, 1934, Library of Congress

ments (Figure 20). The stairway appearing in the cross section was saved from the first convent and installed in the second (Figures 21, 22). The Norman roof truss of mortise-and-tenon construction, which was the norm for all well-built structures, continued to be used into the nineteenth century. The Ursuline Convent's details typify every aspect of early Creole design (Figures 23, 24). From dormer construction to hardware, to the slight jutting of the roof overhang, each, whether subtle or bold in impression, continues into subsequent Creole architecture.

Of French Colonial religious structures in Louisiana, only the Ursuline Convent remains virtually intact. Disguised by a late-nineteenth-century remodeling, St. Gabriel Church, in Iberville Parish, has a late-eighteenth-century timber frame and arched windows that survive (Figure 25). De Pauger's plan of 1724 for the Church of St. Louis, in New Orleans, is reflected in both St. Gabriel Church and the second St. Francis Church, in Pointe Coupee

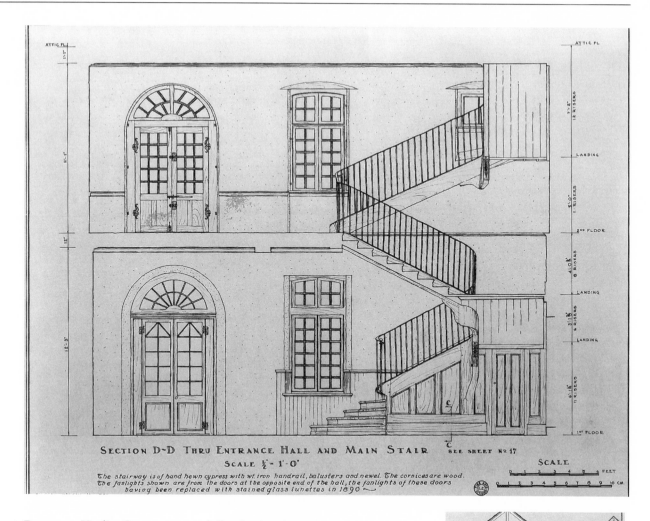

FIGURE 21   Ursuline Convent, entrance hall and main stairway
HABS, 1934, Library of Congress

FIGURE 22   Ursuline Convent, stairway moved from the first convent to the present building.
HABS, 1934, Library of Congress

FIGURE 23   Ursuline Convent. The details show the Norman truss roof structure and dormer design that were features of Louisiana Creole architecture through much of the eighteenth and nineteenth centuries.
HABS, 1934, Library of Congress

FIGURE 24   Ursuline Convent, hardware.

HABS, 1934, Library of Congress

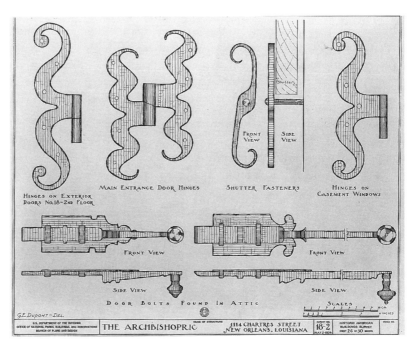

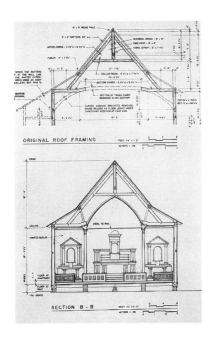

FIGURE 25   St. Gabriel Catholic Church, St. Gabriel, Iberville Parish, 1774–1776. The church originally had the traditional double-pitched Creole roof common in both Louisiana and the West Indies. The original framing is now hidden by a late-nineteenth-century remodeling.

HABS, 1993, Louisiana State Archives

Parish (Figure 26). A photograph from the 1880s of the demolished church bespeaks simplicity and elegance, with a highly pitched roof and cupola bell tower that are Creole in character.

In 1749, Broutin signed plans for the Intendance (Plate B), the earliest known drawing for Louisiana of a two-story galleried structure with a double-pitched roof. Broutin's design illustrates features that regularly recurred in plantation houses in Louisiana well into the early 1800s. Travelers of the period often commented on the frequency of the West Indies style, with a double-pitched hip roof nestled like a pavilion in a tropical garden.

The only structure still standing with the profile of the Intendance is the principal house of Destrehan plantation, on the east bank in St. Charles Parish (Chapter 4, Figures 18, 19). In January, 1787, during Louisiana's Spanish period, Robert Antoine Robin de Logny entered into a contract with Charles, a free mulatto carpenter, to construct the house for his family. Completed in 1790, the house is a masterpiece of Creole architecture built for a Frenchman during the Spanish period by a free man of color. It is truly the quintessence of creolization in its evolved sense (see above, pp. 1–2). As built, Destrehan had peripteral galleries on both floors. The ground floor is brick, and originally had brick columns. The upper, principal floor is *bousillage,* and originally had wood posts. The huge pavilion roof is supported by a Norman truss and has a second pitch to cover the galleries. The depth of the gallery ensures that the sun never touches the exterior walls of the living spaces during the hot months. The massive brick chimneys hold winter heat. *Bousillage* was as effective an insulation as any available at the time.

FIGURE 26 St. Francis Catholic Church, near New Roads, Pointe Coupee Parish, 1880s. This rare antique photograph shows the traditional Creole roof as it was used in church architecture from the mid-1700s. The church was erected around 1760. It was destroyed by a change in the course of the Mississippi in 1895.

Southeastern Architectural Archive, Tulane University Library.

FIGURE 27 Homeplace, St. Charles Parish, *ca.* 1800. The great umbrella roof and wide galleries shelter the house, giving some relief from the sweltering heat. The ground-floor walls are masonry, and the upper, timber frame filled with *bousillage.* The ground level includes a dining room with black-and-white marble floor, two rooms for storing wine, a pantry, and two other service rooms. The ground-floor location made the dining room more convenient to the separate kitchen at the rear.

HABS, 1934, Library of Congress

It is believed that the master builder Charles also constructed Homeplace, across the river on the west bank (Figure 27). It has a straight hip roof with a kick at the eaves and retains original exterior stairs at one corner of the gallery in the Creole manner (Figures 28, 29). The truss system and colonnettes are much less weighty than those of Destrehan, and the house is smaller despite having four rooms across (Figure 30). Whitney, on the west bank in St. John the Baptist Parish, is a house of the same type. Its upper rear loggia has a wall of louvers (Figures 31, 32), a device for ventilation once com-

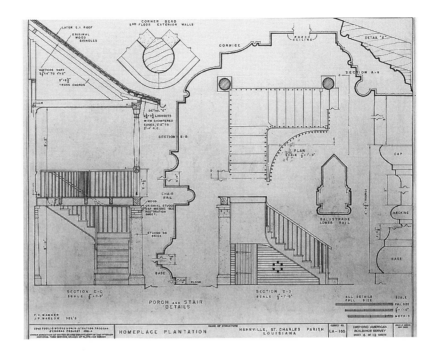

FIGURE 28 Homeplace, rear stairs. Stuccoed brick piers support the gallery, and slender wooden colonnettes support the roof. The high hip roof has a kick, a slight outward cant at the eaves.

HABS, 1934, Library of Congress

FIGURE 29 The rear stairs at Homeplace. Galleries are the corridors, and sheltered stairs at the left rear corner—and formerly at the right front—joined upper and lower corridors.

Richard Koch Collection, Southeastern Architectural Archive, Tulane University. Photograph by Richard Koch for HABS.

mon in Louisiana and still prevalent in the former French and Spanish colonies of the Caribbean.

Two surviving dwellings in Natchitoches Parish are excellent examples of the Creole marriage of imported forms and French style with local building materials. Both were built at the Isle de Brevelle as principal houses of small farms on the Cane River, which connected the hinterland and the village of Natchitoches to the larger Red River and eventually the Mississippi. The craftsmen who built the houses were Creoles of color descended from French colonists and Africans. Some may also have had Native American ancestry. They continued the early traditions and achieved beautifully proportioned structures. The Roque House, of the late eighteenth century, has a steeply pitched hip roof supported on gallery columns of hand-hewn cypress (Figure 33). All interior and exterior walls are of cypress posts joined by mortise and tenon to horizontal members, with the sill lying directly on a slightly raised foundation. The Badin-Roque House, of the nineteenth century, equally drew on techniques from much earlier times (Figure 34). It is *bousillage,* and its major walls are supported directly with posts in the ground. Cypress shingles cover the gables.

In the nineteenth century the Acadians, especially those who had settled on the bayous, developed an architecture that combined their own French and Canadian traditions with local Creole elements (Figure 35). The Acadian cottage generally had two rooms across the front and a full gallery under a gable-end roof. It was truly small and was raised only a few feet off the ground. It may have had an interior or exterior chimney. It was often two

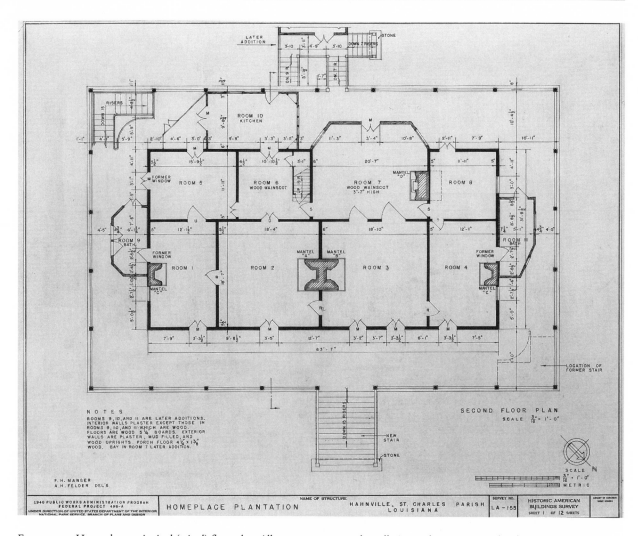

FIGURE 30 Homeplace, principal (raised) floor plan. All rooms open onto the galleries, and most onto each other. Cross-ventilation brought relief in the warm months. In the twentieth century, the kitchen was moved so as to be adjacent to the rear gallery and a rear room was widened for use as the dining room. Bathrooms were added on the side galleries.

HABS, 1940, Library of Congress

FIGURE 31 Whitney, St. John the Baptist Parish, *ca.* 1800–1815, rear elevation. The louvers completely screen the loggia on the second floor, affording shade and ventilation. Louvered shutters in the wall of fixed louvers allowed further control of air flow. Canvas awnings that could be rolled or pulled up were more common.

Courtesy of William Brockway, LSU School of Architecture.

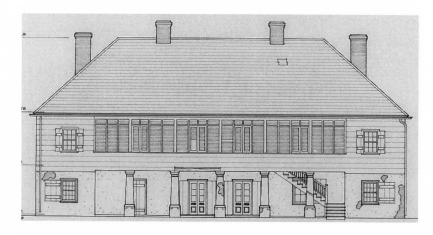

FIGURE 32   Whitney, principal floor plan.

Courtesy of William Brockway, LSU School of Architecture.

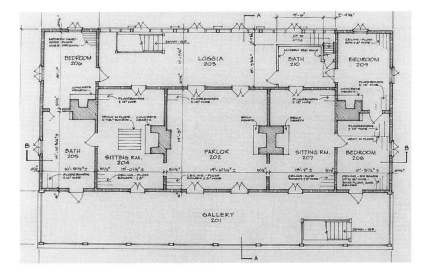

FIGURE 33   Roque House, Natchitoches Parish, *ca.* 1780. Built along the Cane River, the hip-roof Creole structure was relocated to another site on the Cane River, in Natchitoches. The walls of the house are of *bousillage* between posts, and covered on the exterior with clapboards. The posts of the gallery are driven directly into the earth.

Photograph by Eugene Darwin Cizek

FIGURE 34   Badin-Roque House, Natchitoches Parish, *ca.* 1850. The last surviving example of a complete post-in-ground structure in Louisiana is on the Cane River. Creoles of color built it. The original roof and attic gable walls were covered with long hand-split cypress shingles. Post-in-ground construction requires digging a deep trench, setting the sharpened points of vertical timbers in it, and fitting the upper, tenoned ends of those timbers into mortises cut into a horizontal timber plate. The space between timbers is filled with *bousillage* on lath.

Photograph by Eugene Darwin Cizek

FIGURE 35 An Acadian cottage. This simple gable-end building exemplifies the directness and beauty of vernacular architecture in Louisiana. Acadian architecture is a variation of Creole design that evolved from building practices in the French colony in Nova Scotia.

Courtesy of Fred B. Kniffen Cultural Resources Laboratory, Department of Geography and Anthropology, LSU.

rooms deep, with a porch or a *cabinet,* a small room to the rear. The distinctive feature was a set of stairs on the front gallery, leading to the attic, which was used as a sleeping loft. Only in Acadian houses was the attic used for living. Hip-roof and gable-end Creole houses often had dormers and sometimes access stairs, but in these houses the attic was for ventilation and insulation.

In Louisiana's extensive floodplains and marshes very special adaptations were needed. Houses high above the water on stilts were a picturesque Creole expedient (Figure 36). A community of runaway slaves made its home on the tiny island of San Malo, in Lake Borgne, in St. Bernard Parish. When many of them returned to the city after participating in the Battle of New Orleans, other inhabitants moved in. Even the vegetable gardens and animal pens were on platforms. Hurricanes in the twentieth century destroyed the settlement, which was not rebuilt.

On November 3, 1762, in an attempt to increase the security of France's older and more profitable territories in the New World, Louis XV made a gift of all of Louisiana lying west of the Mississippi and of the Ile d'Orleans, the land lying on the east bank of the Mississippi downriver from Bayou Manchac, to his cousin, Charles III of Spain. In 1763, the Treaty of Paris, terminating the Seven Years' War, confirmed the transfer of Louisiana to Spain. The Florida parishes—those north of Lake Pontchartrain, from the Mississippi, at the west, to the Pearl River, at the east—were ceded to England, with Baton Rouge becoming New Richmond. These parishes were not to join the state and the nation until 1819, seven years after Louisiana gained statehood and four years after the American victory at the Battle of New Orleans. When the French colonists of Louisiana learned of the transfer Louis XV had made to Spain, they petitioned him to rescind the gift, but to no

Battaille's House.

Farewell to St. Malo.

El Maestro's House.

Bayou St. Malo

Oldest House in St. Malo

THE LACUSTRINE VILLAGE OF SAINT MALO, LOUISIANA.—Drawn by Charles Graham from Sketches by J. O. Davidson.—[See Page 198.]

FIGURE 36   Charles Graham, *The Lacustrine Village of Saint Malo, Louisiana.* There was a Creole village entirely on stilts in Lake Borgne, in St. Bernard Parish. One small knoll supported a large live oak tree. The giant hip roofs shed the rain and withstood ravaging hurricanes. Continuous galleries afforded protection from the sun and tempered the breezes. Vegetable and baking ovens were on platforms above the water. Indigenous, French, Spanish, and African heritages were all evident. The collection of structures began as a refuge for runaway slaves, then housed a Filipino community. It was finally destroyed by neglect and the forces of nature.

The Historic New Orleans Collection, 1974.25.4.133.

avail. France had often neglected its Louisiana colony, and Spain waited until 1766 to send a commissioner, Antonio de Ulloa. He was coldly received. The colonists, already isolated, had strong nationalistic feelings, and in 1768 New Orleans became one of the first colonial capitals to revolt against its European ruler, beginning the end of the Old World order. Insurgents took over the city, and Ulloa departed for Cuba. Alejandro O'Reilly, Irish-born but reared in Spain, arrived in 1769 with twenty-four ships and two thousand soldiers. Spain took control of its new possession and established a government, the Cabildo. But Spain's influence was primarily administrative, and the French Creole culture remained dominant. The transfer neither halted French and German immigration nor brought a great influx of Spanish colonists. The Isleños, from the Canary Islands, were the most numerous Spanish settlers outside New Orleans, in St. Bernard Parish. What the transfer did bring was a determination to put the new lands under cultivation. Under Spain's regime, the number of inhabitants increased more than sixfold, from about 7,500 in 1762 to approximately 50,000 in 1803, at the time of the Louisiana Purchase. Spain not only offered sanctuary to its coreligionists but also opened its coffers to relocate thousands of Acadians from Nova

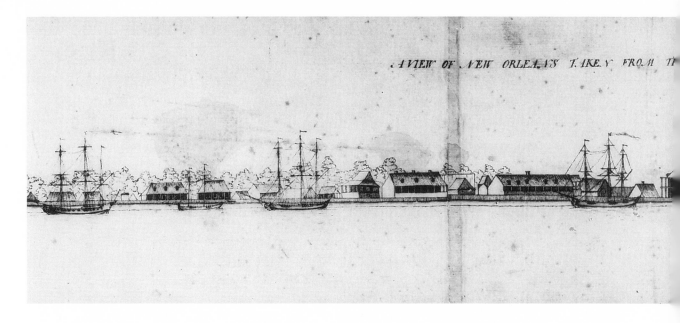

A VIEW OF NEW ORLEANS TAKEN FROM TH

FIGURE 37   *View of New Orleans from the Opposite Side of the River,* 1765. Probably by Captain Philip Pittman, the drawing shows the waterfront of the growing Creole city. The pavilions and gardens gave New Orleans much the same look as French colonial outposts in Martinique, Guadeloupe, and St. Maarten. Creolization lent a similar appearance to such Spanish colonial urban settlements as Santiago, Cuba, and the small coastal towns of Costa Rica, Guatemala, and Santo Domingo.

Collection of the Louisiana State Museum

Scotia. The earliest immigrants settled upriver from New Orleans, and later arrivals, whose descendants are known as Cajuns, moved westward into the bayous. The new arrivals reinforced the French influence. As governor, Don Alejandro set official immigration policy, which granted tracts fronting a river or bayou of six to eight arpents (an arpent being 192 English feet) in width and forty arpents in depth to settlers who agreed to occupy the land, clear river frontage, and maintain roads and levees. From the 1760s through the 1780s, Spain helped transport, feed, and equip the new colonists—an undertaking "very costly to the exchequer," according to the governor.

New Orleans had long been a major port on the trade routes of the Gulf of Mexico and the Caribbean islands, with European ships sailing between the Caribbean and the mainland for over two centuries. The drawing *View of New Orleans Taken from the Opposite Side of the Mississippi River,* from 1765 and possibly by Captain Philip Pittman, shows the distinctive character of the city (Figure 37). Almost every building has a gallery of some kind. One-story structures have a gallery across the front; two-story structures often have galleries at both levels. Each building stands separately to benefit from the prevailing winds. The steep roofs and pronounced overhangs provide shelter from the heavy rain and the intense sun.

Little of New Orleans survived the fire of 1788, but the city apparently rebuilt much as it had been. The Spanish, celebrated for sound building regulations, did not impose their own standards. Madame John's Legacy was reconstructed close to its original form and partly of its original materials. Of surviving buildings, it best illustrates the larger and finer Creole urban houses (Figures 38, 39). A contract dated April 1, 1788, between Manuel Lanzos and the American builder Robert Jones stipulated the construction of the

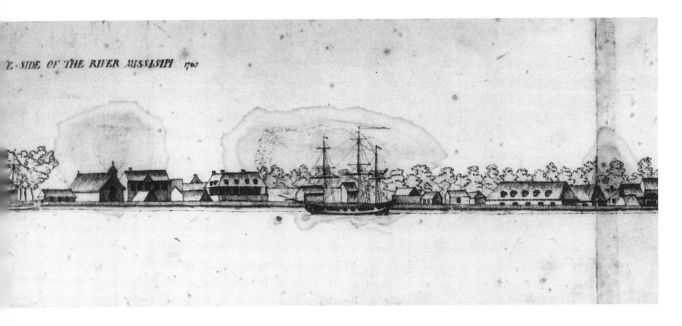

FIGURE 38 Madame John's Legacy, New Orleans, 1788.

Photograph by Barbara SoRelle Bacot

new dwelling using some materials "salvaged from his burned house." Earlier documents record the subdividing, and thus reduction, of the land attached to the earlier building. Madame John's Legacy is very like several houses in the 1765 view, with a raised basement, a gallery across the front with colonnettes, and a double-pitched roof with dormers. The front wall is flush with the sidewalk, and there are heavy batten doors that lead to service rooms and storage. A loggia is at the rear, framed at each end with *cabinets.* This is a city house with strong resemblances to the style already in general use by the 1750s for plantation houses outside New Orleans. The main floor is comparable to that of the larger plantation houses. The steep roof has a double pitch, with dormer windows. During this period, dormers were the best way

FIGURE 39 Madame John's Legacy, facade and rear elevation. The house built for Manuel Lanzos by Robert Jones in 1788, after the city's first great fire, is a town house of the traditional Creole pavilion style.

HABS, 1994, Louisiana State Archives

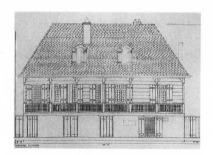

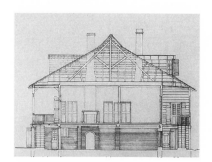

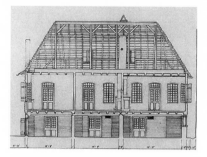

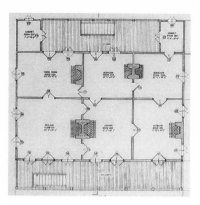

FIGURE 40 Madame John's Legacy, cross section. Apparent here are some of the primary characteristics of Creole architecture. The overall shape of the house is typical of the French Creole period, but the courtyard spaces formed between the main house and the service buildings reflect the closeness and density that prevailed during the Spanish Creole period.

HABS, 1994, Louisiana State Archives

FIGURE 41 Madame John's Legacy, cross section along roof ridge. The spatial feeling inside the Creole house is in abundant evidence. French doors and windows allow cross-ventilation. The dressed and beaded beams and ceilings and relatively simple millwork became an elegant accompaniment to fine furniture and the deft touches of the decorative arts.

HABS, 1994, Louisiana State Archives

FIGURE 42 Madame John's Legacy, plan of principal floor. The Creole spatial arrangement includes no hallway. All the rooms open onto protected exterior spaces. The tightness of the courtyard is favorable to cool shade and shadow. The service building, one room deep, housed a kitchen on the ground floor.

HABS, 1994, Louisiana State Archives

to ventilate a hip roof, and in the winter the closed attic constituted an insulating air space (Figures 40, 41).

Floor plans did not have to be symmetrical, and single *cabinets* might be found on smaller buildings. The facade was often not symmetrical, and little significance was given to the alignment of gallery posts with openings (Figure 42). On the interior, however, the openings of the parlor onto the gallery were carefully symmetrical (Figure 43). The timber-frame and *briquette entre poteaux* construction of the principal level of Madame John's Legacy was originally stuccoed on the front and on the rear loggia. Only the exterior walls not sheltered by galleries were protected by clapboards. Eventually, with the realization that the rain blew, the owners replaced deteriorated stucco with flush boarding. Recent research has discovered that the original colors were subdued: the entire exterior, front and rear, was white, and all windows, doors, frames, and shutters, as well as the exposed-beam porch ceiling, were

FIGURE 43   Parlor of Madame John's Legacy. The mantel with overmantel, as well as the size of the room, confirm that this room is the parlor. All windows and doors open in, for all openings have batten-and-panel blinds that open out. Shorter interior doors without an overlight allow passage from room to room with no need to exit to the galleries. Hand-wrought-iron ramshorn hinges, head and foot bolts, throw bolts, gravity latches, and shutter hooks complement the elegant strength of the building.

Photograph by Eugene Darwin Cizek

painted a dull khaki or moss green. A feature not yet known to have been re-peated in other buildings is the oxblood or dark barn red paint on the gable ends and the baseboards.

The house of 1788 matches the description of the earlier house on the property: a "pavilion raised on a brick wall." The use of the ground level as a warehouse or as storage chambers was typical of urban housing of the time and continued well into the nineteenth century. The same arrangement served for government and public buildings. The Spanish government build-ing of 1765, seen on the Tanesse map of 1817, had a similar exterior (Chapter 5, Figure 1). Madame John's Legacy is truly a Creole building, constructed by an American for a Spaniard, and it is the only building of its type to have sur-vived within the Vieux Carre.

In 1794, New Orleans was struck by a second devastating fire, and this time the Spanish decreed stringent new building regulations. The French

Creole city was again rebuilt, but now under stronger Spanish influence, apparent mainly in the enclosed courtyards, the low-pitched roofs, and the wrought-iron balconies. Fireproof construction, usually solid masonry, became the norm. The pavilion houses in garden settings were no longer the ideal. Outside New Orleans, though, the French Creole building tradition was largely untouched by Spanish influence.

For information about native American building traditions, the works under References (pp. 391–94) by Fred B. Kniffen and J. Ashley Sibley, Jr., have been useful. Material in the Smithsonian Miscellaneous Collections relating to drawings that A. DeBatz produced between 1732 and 1735 has also been consulted. For colonial Louisiana architecture, publications issued by the Bureau of Governmental Research of the City of New Orleans, along with "The Origins of Creole Architecture," by Jay D. Edwards, and *The Architecture of Colonial Louisiana: Collected Essays of Samuel Wilson, Jr., F.A.I.A.,* edited by Jean M. Farnsworth and Ann M. Masson, both of these titles listed under References, have been pertinent. On paints and finishes, two unpublished studies by George Fore, "Destrehan Manor House: Interior and Exterior Paint Analysis" (1982) and "Madame John's Legacy: Finishes Analysis" (1981), on file at the houses under discussion and at the Louisiana Division of Historic Preservation, were informative. Indexes of building contracts for Orleans, Jefferson, and St. Bernard parishes are available in New Orleans at the Notarial Archives in City Hall, the New Orleans Public Library, the Louisiana State Museum, and the Southeastern Architectural Archive of Tulane University. This chapter is also based on personal experience in preparing HABS drawings of a number of early buildings.

2

NEW ORLEANS AFTER THE FIRES
Barbara SoRelle Bacot

On Good Friday of 1788 a great conflagration "reduced to ashes eight hundred and fifty buildings, among which [were] all the business houses and the residences of the most aristocratic families" of New Orleans. The records of the Cabildo added that four-fifths of the populated section of the city burned, including the Church of St. Louis, the timber-frame Cabildo, the Corps de Garde, and the jail.[1] Only the blocks near the river and downstream from the Place d'Armes, which included the Ursuline Convent, escaped the flames.

The new Cabildo, church, and Presbytère visibly defined New Orleans as the seat of Spanish colonial administration (Figure 1). The new designs preserved the symmetry that Adrien de Pauger had envisioned for the Place d'Armes, with the church as its focal point. Like Pauger, the architect of the replacement buildings was a military engineer, Don Gilberto Guillemard. Although born in France, he had been in Spanish military service since 1770, and his designs reflect those of other Spanish colonies.[2] The Cabildo and Presbytère, flanking the church, were the two most important buildings of the Spanish regime. The first of the two was named for the colony's governing body, which it housed, and the second was planned to quarter the priest and his assistants.

Guillemard's designs of 1791 bore strong likenesses to such buildings as the Spanish government offices constructed at Antequera, Mexico, in 1781, and at Havana in the 1780s.[3] The Cabildo and Presbytère reflect the neoclassicism current in both France and Spain in the second half of the eighteenth century. Commissioned to design the new church and rectory, Guillemard

1. Samuel Wilson, Jr., *The Architecture of Colonial Louisiana* (Lafayette, La., 1987), 342–43.
2. *Ibid.,* 285, 302–305.
3. Jessie Poesch, *The Art of the Old South* (New York, 1983), 134.

FIGURE I Jackson Square, New Orleans, *ca.* 1920. The view across the former Place d'Armes, renamed in honor of the victorious commander of the Battle of New Orleans, shows the brick Upper Pontalba Building, the Cabildo with the mansard roof and cupola from 1847, de Pouilly's St. Louis Cathedral, of 1849, and the Presbytère, from which the cupola has been removed.

The Historic New Orleans Collection, 1974.25.14.29.

obviously designed all three buildings as a complex. The site of the new Cabildo incorporated that of the single-story Corps de Garde on the corner, constructed in 1751, as well as the land on which the timber-frame Cabildo and the brick jail had stood. The massive brick walls of the Corps de Garde had survived the fire, and they, with four square piers, a wide gallery, and five arched windows on the side street, form the first three bays of the ground floor of the new building. The Presbytère appears so exact a counterpart to the Cabildo that the governing council quibbled about paying for the plans, which appeared to duplicate those for its own building. In fact, the Presbytère is a few feet wider than the building it complements, with wider arches. Skillful and thrifty, Guillemard managed to salvage what he could of earlier buildings on the site, but he was also so sensitive an architect that the church appears to be centered on the block and the flanking buildings to balance exactly.

The construction of the new Cabildo was delayed for several years by

FIGURE 2   The Cabildo, 1795–1799,
1847, facade.

HABS, 1934, Library of Congress

disagreements over funding. Neither the crown nor the local government wanted to pay for it. The generosity of Don Andrés Almonester y Roxas made it possible to begin construction. Shortly after the fire, the Spanish-born entrepreneur and merchant had undertaken to rebuild the church and the lodging for the priests at his own expense. Prompted by piety and hopes for a title, Don Andrés commissioned Don Gilberto for the designs and was paying for work on the church and the Cabildo before he began to help pay for the Presbytère. His death in 1798 delayed the completion of the Presbytère. It stood as a single-story building until 1813, when its upper story was added. It was never used for its intended purpose of housing all the clerics serving at the Church of Saint Louis. At least Don Andrés got to see the church completed, and it was there that he was buried.

Both the Cabildo, erected between 1795 and 1799 (Figure 2) and the Presbytère, erected between 1791 and 1813 (Figure 3), have open arcades of

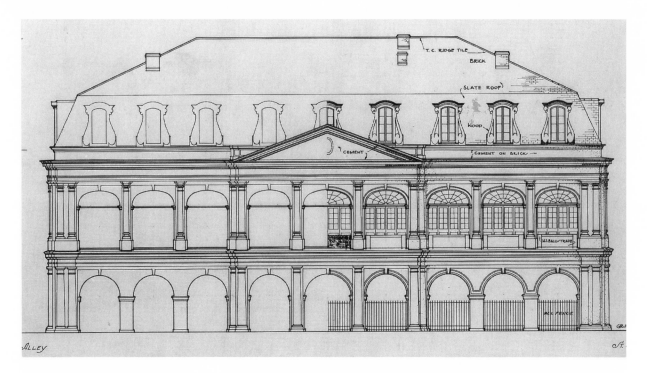

FIGURE 3   The Presbytère, 1791–1813, 1847, facade. The additions begun in 1847 included both the mansard roof and the cupola matching the Cabildo's.

HABS, 1934, Library of Congress

nine bays, with molded piers and pilasters supporting round arches and groin vaults. The segmental arches of the upper arcades are glazed and have elegant wrought-iron railings set in the window embrasures (Figure 4). The three central bays project slightly, with Tuscan columns supporting the first-floor entablature and Ionic columns supporting the second-floor entablature and pediment. The pilasters of the second and principal floor are also Ionic. The plaster bas-relief in the Cabildo's pediment features an eagle with military trophies, a truly American replacement in 1821 of the original Spanish coat of arms in an oval cartouche with garlands. Balustrades hid the low pitched roofs until the remodeling of 1847 added mansard roofs with cupolas and elaborately voluted dormer windows.[4]

The notable surviving feature of the Cabildo's interior is the monumental stairs rising to the principal floor (Figure 5). The black walnut balustrade has an interesting pattern of crosses and is similar to the exterior balustrades of a number of country houses. The primary room is the Salle Capitulaire. It was there that the signing of the Louisiana Purchase in 1803 transferred to the United States as a territory the French colony, which had been retroceded to the French by the Spanish in 1800.[5]

The complex, with the church flanked by a pair of monumental matching government buildings, made the public square it faced the most impres-

4.   *Ibid.,* 132–35; Rowles photograph 1979.120.173, in Louisiana State Museum.
5.   The interior of the Cabildo has been greatly modified over time. In the 1960s, Samuel Wilson, Jr., effected a careful conjectural reconstruction of the Salle Capitulaire on the basis of period interiors. The hall and upper floor were restored after the fire of 1988.

B.Proctor Del.

U.S. DEPARTMENT OF THE INTERIOR
OFFICE OF NATIONAL PARKS, BUILDINGS, AND RESERVATIONS
BRANCH OF PLANS AND DESIGN

THE CABILDO

NAME OF STRUCTURE
JACKSON SQUARE
NEW ORLEANS LOUISIANA

SURVEY NO.
18-4
OCT-22-1934

HISTORIC AMERICAN
BUILDINGS SURVEY
SHEET 18 OF 22 SHEETS

INDEX NO.

FIGURE 4   The Cabildo, wrought-iron
balustrade made by Marcelino
Hernandez.

HABS, 1934, Library of Congress

sive in the United States at its completion. Even as poorly depicted as the
buildings are in the 1817 map of New Orleans (Chapter 5, Figure 1), its formal grandeur is evident. Looking with a trained eye, the architect Benjamin
Henry Latrobe was critical of the details, but he admired the "symmetry, and
the good proportions and strong relief of the facades of the Two." He added
that the "solid mass" of the cathedral produced an "admirable effect when
seen from the river or the levee."[6] The effect was even more admirable after
the addition in 1820 of the central tower Latrobe designed.

   The church, begun in 1789, was consecrated as the Cathedral of St.
Louis, King of France, for the new diocese of Louisiana on Christmas Day,
1794. It, too, was of Spanish Colonial design, with its nave defined by a two-
story slightly projecting portico that had two pairs of columns on the first

6.   Poesch, *The Art of the Old South,* 134–35.

FIGURE 5   The stairway of the Cabildo
Photograph by Susan Gandolfo

floor supporting two pairs of columns with a pediment on the second story. A pair of three-story octagonal towers projected forward and were capped with high polygonal roofs. Even with Latrobe's tower, the cathedral was scarcely universally admired. In 1835–1836, a writer visiting New Orleans found it dilapidated and weather-beaten and declared that "its utter insignificance as a work of art would deprive it of all claim to notice, were it not that in the earlier and best points of New Orleans it occupies a position as prominent as to induce one to suppose the Orleanois had put their best feet forward, and were willing to make the most of a doubtful ornament."[7] Both "Orleanois" and the diocese came to agree with the criticisms, and the church was completely rebuilt between 1849 and 1851 to the designs of J. N. B. de Pouilly. Although not resulting in the handsomest of American churches, Guillemard's design, with a projecting central bay and clearly defined first and second stories, made the cathedral the perfect focal point between the two flanking buildings and complemented their pedimented porticos and strong horizontal massing. All three buildings were built of brick stuccoed and scored in a pattern of stone blocks. The facade of the church was painted to resemble white marble.

The church begun in 1789 was not completed when another fire swept through the city, in December, 1794. The edifice was spared, but most of the new buildings upriver from the Cabildo were reduced to ashes. The minutes of the governing body of the colony record the legislation that implemented a building code for the city:

> In order to prevent fires in the future, similar to those experienced in this City in the year 1788 and during last year . . . the two story houses of two apartments . . . to be built, should all be constructed of brick or lumber and filled with brick between the upright posts, the posts to be covered with cement of at least one inch thick, covered with a flat roof of tile or brick. That the wooden houses covered with the same material must not be of more than 30 feet deep including the galleries. That all houses which are to be built of brick or lumber must precisely have their front facing the street, and nobody is allowed to build them with the rear or sides to the street except those persons whose lots have not a frontage of 30 feet.

John Pintard's description of the city in 1801 shows the impact of the legislation:

> The city of course is much improved and will be regenerated as a much handsomer form & with safer materials. The Houses facing the levee as before remarked are neat—of two Stories with a gallery in front—As no cellar can be dug in this flat country. The first story is appropriated as a warehouse—carriage houses offices & etc after the Spanish fashion—the Family resides on the [upper] floor with back buildings for the Kitchen &

7.   Edward Durrell [H. Didimus], *New Orleans As I Found It* (New York, 1845), 18.

Negroes—The rooms are neatly disposed and furnished within—Glass windows or doors opening in the middle down to the first floor for the benefit of air in the warm climate.[8]

The second rebuilding gave New Orleans a different appearance from what it had before. Although laid out in long narrow lots by 1794, the city retained the sense of pavilions set in gardens. None survive of these early timber-frame houses on high basements, with galleries and vast roofs, all surrounded by yards and gardens. Only one house, Madame John's Legacy (Chapter 1, Figures 38–42), which was rebuilt after the fire of 1788, compares with the many seen in earlier views of the French colonial capital, since the legislation of 1795 prohibited building additional houses of this type. George Washington Cable, a popular writer of the late nineteenth century, gave the house this name. It can be said of him, as he said of one of his characters, that he knew "the history of every old house in the French Quarter; or if he happens not to know one, he can make one up as he goes along."[9]

After the fires, the texture of the New Orleans streetscape became more dense. Houses set in yards and spacious gardens gave way to buildings fronting the sidewalk, with common side walls or only a narrow passage between neighbors. At the time of the census of 1785, only five thousand people, half of them slaves and twelve hundred of them free people of color, lived in the city. By 1803, the total population had increased to twelve thousand. The Spanish colonial administration encouraged immigration, especially of Catholic Acadians, but even Protestant Americans were welcome. The great influx of French Creoles, including free people of color, who were fleeing the slave rebellion of 1796 in Saint Domingue (now Haiti) reinforced French culture in the colony.

The kind of house most evocative of early New Orleans is the four-room cottage. One example of this, at 941 Bourbon Street, is romantically known as Lafitte's Blacksmith Shop, but it has nothing to do with Lafitte or any blacksmith and once again a name arises from the popularity of a story by Cable (Figures 6, 7). Built before 1808, and possibly around 1788, the house has the simplest of almost-square plans: it is divided into four rooms with double chimneys between the two front and the two back rooms. There is no interior corridor. In this and similar *en suite* plans, movement is from room to room, or through one room to the next. Such use of space is typical of both four-room cottages and larger houses in Louisiana. The hip roof has a kick at the eaves, and the construction is of heavy timber frame with brick between the posts. In accordance with the law enacted in 1795, the brick and posts were originally protected by stucco. Added in the HABS drawing is the

8. Records of the Cabildo, in New Orleans Public Library, 10.9.1795; John Pintard, "New Orleans, 1801," ed. David Lee Sterling, *Louisiana Historical Quarterly,* XXXV (1951), 224.

9. George Washington Cable, "Café des Exiles," in *Old Creole Days* (New York, 1879).

FIGURE 6   941 Bourbon Street (Lafitte's Blacksmith Shop), New Orleans, *ca.* 1788, facade. The present windows are sash, but casement windows may have preceded them, and many houses began with only shutters. The shutters were essential, whereas glazing could be added a generation or generations later.

HABS, 1934, Library of Congress. Drawn by Samuel Wilson, Jr.

FIGURE 7   941 Bourbon Street
Photograph by Barbara SoRelle Bacot

wide overhanging roof that projected over the sidewalk and protected both passersby and the walls of the house from rain.[10]

The cottage at 1218–1220 Burgundy Street, La Rionda, was built around 1810 and is a slightly later dwelling of the same type (Figure 8). The four-room plan remains the same, but a rear loggia and *cabinets* added to the com-

10.   Wilson, *The Architecture of Colonial Louisiana*, 346.

FIGURE 8   1218–1220 Burgundy Street
(La Rionda Cottage), New Orleans, *ca.*
1800, elevations and section.

HABS, 1939, Library of Congress

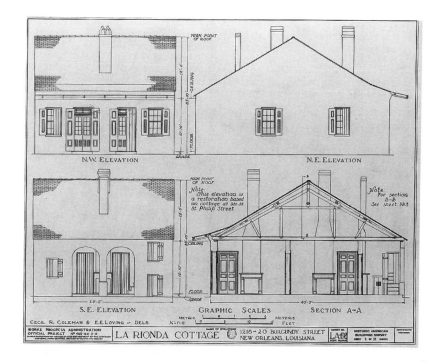

fort and, although more costly, became part of the preferred plan in the nineteenth century (Figure 9). Like the cottage at 941 Burgundy, this one has the
typical pattern of openings in the facade: window, french door, french door,
window (Figure 10). But many other cottages from the period have the alternative pattern, with doors separated by two windows (Figure 11). Over
time newer cottages came to be built with somewhat higher ceilings and
Classical details, and much of the woodwork inside 1218–1220 Burgundy
Street was changed some years after construction to conform to the Greek
Revival taste. Later cottages had only french doors on the facade, and gable
roofs came to be preferred to hip (Figure 12). Tile was the most common
roofing, but slate was increasingly available. The original roof of the cottage
was tile; the slate is a replacement. Otherwise the building's exterior retains
its early-nineteenth-century appearance.

Latrobe greatly admired the Creole plan of architecture for its maximum
use of interior space. He noted that Americans "derive from the English the
habit of desiring that every one of our rooms should be separately accessible,
and we consider rooms that are thoroughfares as useless. The French and
Continental Europeans generally live, I believe, as much to their own satisfaction in their houses as we do in ours, and employ the room they have to
more advantage because they do not require so much space for passages."[11]

11.   Edward C. Carter II, ed., *The Papers of Benjamin Henry Latrobe: The Journals of Benjamin
Henry Latrobe, 1799–1820, From Philadelphia to New Orleans* (New Haven, 1980), 194 (February 19,
1819); Samuel Wilson, Jr., ed., *Impressions Respecting New Orleans by Benjamin Henry Boneval Latrobe*
(New York, 1951), 42.

FIGURE 9   1218–1220 Burgundy Street, plan.

HABS, 1939, Library of Congress

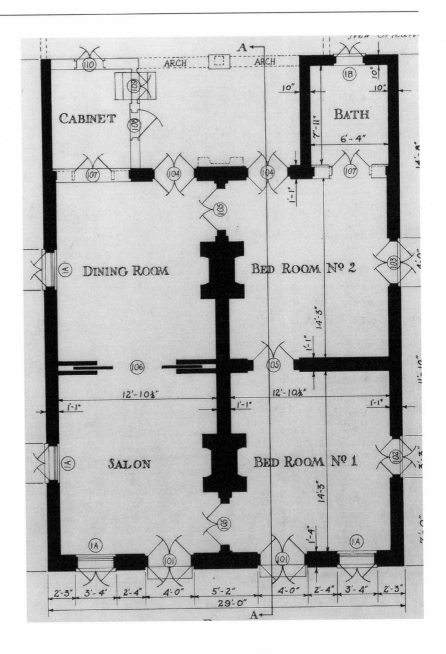

His son, John H. B. Latrobe, visited the city fifteen years later and was himself impressed with Creole cottages. In 1834, he

found entire squares without a single two story building but composed of rows of one storied dwellings with sheds projecting from the eaves over the pavements. Windows were of the French fashion, opening like doors, and were very frequently placed on the inside of the wall so as to put the window seat in the street. Walls were generally painted yellow with white pilasters on the corners, and white facings to all the openings. The sheds just mentioned besides giving a singular and highly picturesque appearance to the street, answer many useful purposes. They shade the house from the

FIGURE 10   1218–1220 Burgundy Street

Richard Koch Collection, Southeastern Architectural Archive, Tulane University. Photograph by Richard Koch for HABS.

FIGURE 11   1028–1030 Ursuline Street, New Orleans, *ca.* 1800, photographed in the early 1930s. Long destroyed, the brick-between-posts four-room cottage had casement windows.

Richard Koch Collection, Southeastern Architectural Archive, Tulane University. Photograph by Richard Koch for HABS.

sun and shield it from the rain, and perform the same office to the foot passenger, whom they further benefit in the unpaved street by keeping in some measure the ground dry under his feet.[12]

Such four-room cottages are aptly named Creole, in one of the most venerable senses of the word, for they are truly children born in the New

12.   John H. B. Latrobe, *Southern Travels,* ed. Samuel Wilson, Jr. (New Orleans, 1986), 48.

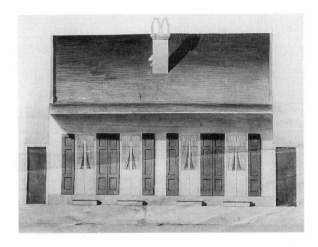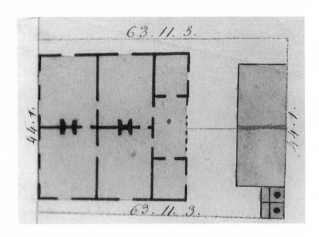

FIGURE 12   613–615 Dumaine Street,
New Orleans, *ca.* 1820. The plan is the
same as for 1218–1220 Burgundy Street,
and both dwellings had two-story service
buildings, which customarily stood
across the yard from one-story houses.

*New Orleans Notarial Archives, Book 40,
folio 31, dated 1847.*

World of European parentage. Their ancestors are the houses of the western
Mediterranean, as is clear from two manuscripts of the same title, "On Domestic Architecture," written in the sixteenth century by the architect Sebastiano Serlio, who was born in Italy around 1497 and worked in France from
1541 until his death in 1554. His personal manuscript was written in the years
between roughly 1537 and 1549, and the presentation manuscript he dedicated to Henri II of France was written early in the king's reign. A third manuscript appears to have been the source for printer's proofs for a never published French edition around 1700. Serlio's prominence as architect to
François I of France from 1541 to 1547, as well as the high regard in which his
published works were held, suggests that his treatise, the first on housing for
the common man, received a wide reading.[13]

Serlio drew four small houses whose facades bear a close likeness to the
New Orleans cottages (Figure 13). I suggest that Serlio was not so much creating new designs here as using forms familiar in both France and Italy for
affirming his conviction that even the humblest dwellings were worthy of intellectual attention. Labeled houses for poor artisans, the four share the basic
elements of the Creole cottage: one story, four bays, a width of two rooms,
placement only slightly above grade, a steep roof, and central chimneys. The
meanest of the plans is for a structure of four rooms with two center chimneys (Figure 13D). Each room houses a family, with an inset enclosure providing a more private space. This adumbrates both the four-room cottage
with its almost square rooms and the small *cabinets* of New Orleans. There
the cottage could house one family—or two, one on each side—with or

13.   Sebastiano Serlio, *On Domestic Architecture: Different Dwellings from the Meanest Level to
the Most Ornate Palace . . .—the Sixteenth-Century Manuscript of Book VI in the Avery Library of Columbia University,* ed. Myra Nan Rosenfeld, intro. James S. Ackerman (New York, 1978), Plate
XLVIII, 19, 27–34, 61–62, 68–70, 82. In an unpublished paper, "The Bolduc House, St. Genevieve,"
presented at the meeting of the Society of Architectural Historians in January, 1968, Ernest Allen
Connally pointed out the similarities between the Bolduc House, in Missouri on the upper Mississippi, and Serlio's designs for French farmhouses. In *The Art of the Old South,* Jessie Poesch noted the
relationship between Creole cottages and Serlio's houses for artisans (see pp. 53, 133).

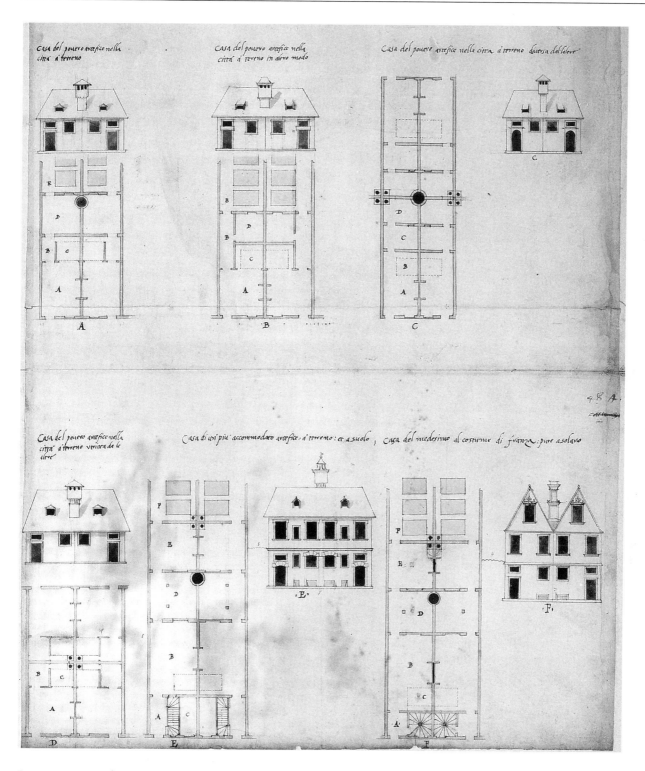

FIGURE 13   Houses for poor urban artisans, in Sebastiano Serlio's "On Domestic Architecture," *ca.* 1537–1549, Plate XLVIII. A, B, and C show pairs of cottages with each dwelling one room wide and three rooms deep and having at least one smaller room. D shows a cottage with four rooms of equal size, each a separate dwelling.

Avery Architectural and Fine Arts Library, Columbia University in the City of New York

without rear *cabinets* (Plate C). Artisans in dwellings like those in Serlio's other three plans occupied one side, three rooms deep—a linear succession of rooms forming a miniature *enfilade*.

A comparison of these mid-sixteenth-century drawings with New Orleans' late-eighteenth- and early-nineteenth-century cottages discloses resemblances not only of facade and plan but also of detail. Even the fanciful chimneys of 1218–1220 Burgundy Street and 613–615 Dumaine Street echo the almost Venetian chimney pots in Serlio's drawings. They are even more like the chimneys of Guyenne, a region of southwest France the rivers of which meet the Atlantic near Bordeaux, which was one of the chief ports of embarkation for France's American colonies. Serlio drew his houses for artisans with party walls, to be built in rows. In New Orleans, only the narrowest of passages separates a cottage from its neighbors, and short rows of identical cottages were built in the city. Downriver in the lower French Quarter and in the adjoining neighborhoods of Treme and Marigny, numerous artisans and tradesmen, many of them free people of color, dwelt in Creole cottages designed for their degree of wealth.[14]

Creoles built European urban houses in urban New Orleans, and people of some substance considered a house such as 613–615 Dumaine Street a "valuable property" into the middle of the nineteenth century. Brick-between-posts or solid masonry construction set cottages like it apart in cost and desirability from less expensive frame cottages. Frame cottages often occurred in rows. Literary travelers found the houses, whether stucco or frame, cheerfully painted ocher or gray or even orangish red. The watercolors A. Boyd Cruise painted in the 1930s and 1940s show that cottages continued in those colors into the twentieth century.[15] What the New World contributed to the design of the houses are the standardization of the four-room plan, with the addition of an open rear loggia flanked by *cabinets* and the provision of a separate building for the kitchen and servants.

The loggia with *cabinets* appears in a variety of residences in Louisiana, both urban and rural. A uniquely urban variation existed both in New Orleans and in Natchitoches, the northernmost French colonial settlement in the state. The timber-frame Lemee House, in Natchitoches, opening directly onto the sidewalk, has a three-room plan with rear loggia (Figure 14). The now demolished Troxler Cottage, on St. Philip Street, in New Orleans, likewise timber-frame, had the same plan, but the narrow side faced the street and the loggia led to a side yard (Figure 15). The plan of the Troxler Cottage recurs later in the nineteenth century in the variation of the single shotgun

14. Elsie Burch Donald, *The French Farmhouse* (New York, 1995), 75; Mary Louise Christovich and Roulhac Toledano, eds., *Faubourg Treme and the Bayou Road* (Gretna, La., 1980), 17–24, Vol. VI of *New Orleans Architecture,* 7 vols. Donald also remarks, on p. 153, that galleries are a prominent feature of the farmhouses of Guyenne.

15. 613–615 Dumaine Street, Proceedings, G. Giroux, notary, Book 40, folio 31, January 24, 1849, in New Orleans Notarial Archives. A. Boyd Cruise's watercolors are held by HABS, the Historic New Orleans Collection, and the Louisiana State Museum.

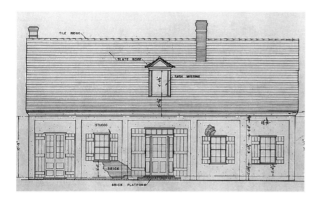

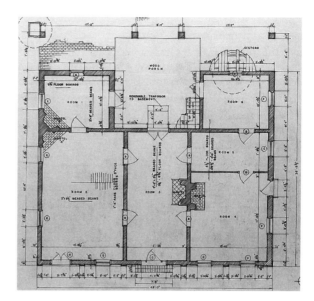

FIGURE 14   Lemee House, Front Street, Natchitoches, 1830s, facade and plan. Despite the symmetry, the center room is not a passage hall. It shares a chimney with the room to the right; the room on the left originally had no fireplace. The flat pilasters are a feature of two- and three-story buildings in New Orleans.

HABS, 1940, Library of Congress

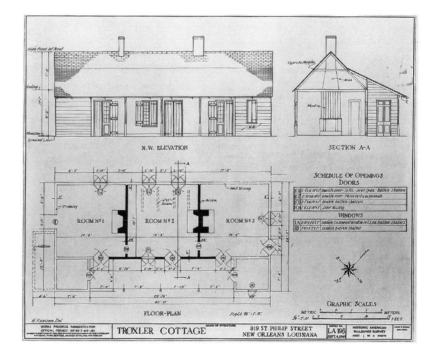

FIGURE 15   Troxler Cottage, formerly at 919 St. Phillip Street, New Orleans, *ca.* 1810, plan, elevation, and section; HABS, 1940.

HABS, 1940, Library of Congress

house—one room wide and three to four rooms deep—for which entrance is through a *cabinet* that screens the open side gallery from the street (Chapter 7, Figure 21). The obscure origins of the shotgun house may include this Creole cottage, with its ubiquitous loggia and its *cabinets* reoriented.[16]

16.   John Michael Vlach, "The Shotgun House: An African Architectural Legacy," in *Common Places: Readings in American Vernacular Architecture,* ed. Dell Upton and John Michael Vlach (Athens, Ga., 1986). In *The African-American Tradition* (Cleveland, 1978), Vlach also proposes African origins for the shotgun house. Jay D. Edwards has in lectures presented persuasive evidence for the African origin of elements of Creole houses, particularly relative to their galleries and piers.

FIGURE 16   723 Toulouse Street (Casa Flinard), New Orleans, *ca.* 1825, facade and rear elevation; HABS, 1937. The shed-roof service wing at right angles to the rear of the house is frequent with houses of more than one story. The wing is always one room deep with lower ceilings.

HABS, 1937, Library of Congress

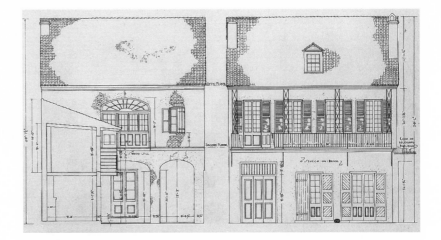

The more prosperous of New Orleans tended to live in two- or three-story town houses without interior halls and stairs. The house at 723 Toulouse Street, Casa Flinard, has its living quarters on the principal, second, floor and a shop at ground level (Figure 16). A side passage leads to the courtyard and the stairs. The arched loggias, originally open on both floors, serve as the stair halls. The residence is in essence a two-story variation of the four-room cottage with a rear loggia. Box chimneys extend into the rooms, a common positioning in multistory residences in the limited space of party-wall construction. The box or wraparound mantel makes a strong statement, even in large rooms, and architects and carpenters lavished their skills on it. The box mantel was the pièce de résistance of Creole interiors, functioning almost as a fine piece of furniture. The parlor mantel of 723 Toulouse Street has carving and gougework that follow neoclassical patterns of Federal decoration (Figures 17, 18).

The house at 536–542 Chartres Street adapts the same sort of plan to three-story row houses (Figure 19). Because there is no side passage, entrance to the upstairs residential quarters is from the side street to the rear stairs or through the ground-floor commercial space. Like the house itself the separate three-story service wing is brick, and the colonnettes and plain balustrade reproduce on this lesser building the type of gallery common on French Creole pavilions. The early nineteenth century saw the introduction of the double parlor, here with folding panel doors, giving a more spacious venue for entertaining. In the three-story plan, bedrooms occupied the third floor and sometimes the upper level of the service wing.

In 1795, Bartolome Bosque, a Spanish-born shipowner and merchant, built a town house at 617 Chartres Street (Figures 20, 21). A spacious carriage way, a rare convenience, leads to the stairs and service yard, with its kitchen and quarters.[17] The first floor facing the street is a commercial space, and the

17.   Jay D. Edwards, "Cultural Identifications in Architecture: The Case of the New Orleans Townhouse," *Traditional Dwellings and Settlements Review,* I (1993), 17–32.

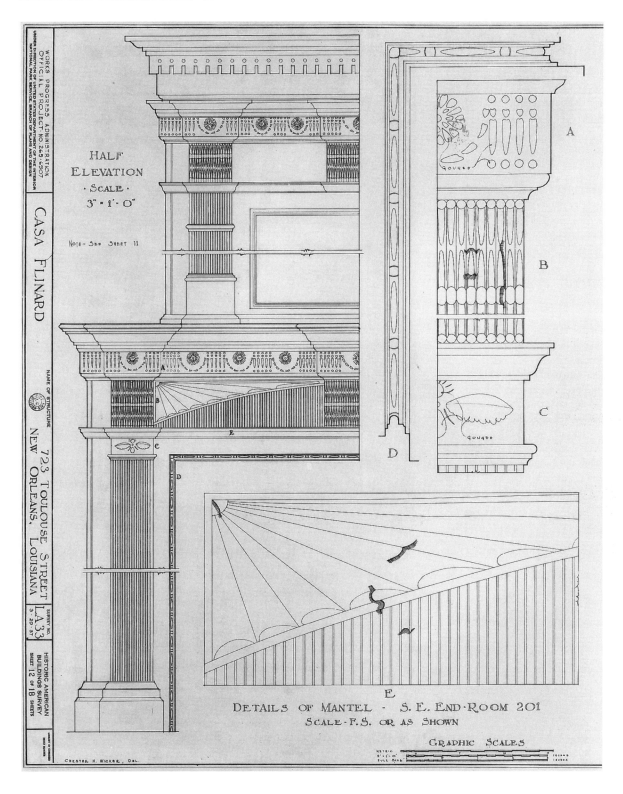

FIGURE 17   723 Toulouse Street, parlor mantel
HABS, 1937, Library of Congress

FIGURE 18   723 Toulouse Street, gougework detail from another room.

Richard Koch Collection, Southeastern Architectural Archive, Tulane University. Photograph by Richard Koch for HABS.

FIGURE 19   536–542 Chartres Street (Gally House), New Orleans, *ca.* 1830. The ground-floor openings of this building have batten shutters and arched transoms made secure with iron rods. Paneled shutters secure the doors and windows on the upper floors. Stylish Federal transoms over the french doors on the second floor provide additional light, and superb cables and swags decorate the cornice.

Richard Koch Collection, Southeastern Architectural Archive, Tulane University. Photograph by Richard Koch for HABS.

stair hall in the rear loggia leads up to the principal residential rooms, an unusual three deep. In the front parlor, the overmantel has pilasters supporting a pediment in the Classical taste (Figure 22). Four pairs of french doors open onto a projecting balcony, which originally continued along the side.

Marcellino Hernandez, a local blacksmith who produced the decorative ironwork of the Cabildo, most likely forged the Bosque House balustrade as well. The ornamental wrought iron was something new in New Orleans, and one of the architectural influences that the Spanish regime brought to the city. A balcony extending over the sidewalk was such a novel idea that in 1791 a hopeful householder, desiring "to give more beauty and comfort to a house" that he planned, petitioned for permission to construct it "with a porch on the edge of the sidewalk, and far be it from obstructing the traffic of pedestrians, said porch will afford protection in time of rain and strong sun."[18]

18.   Wilson, *The Architecture of Colonial Louisiana,* 344, 339.

FIGURE 20 619 Chartres Street (Bartolome Bosque House), New Orleans, 1795, facade
HABS, 1938, Library of Congress

FIGURE 21   619 Chartres Street, view from the carriage way across the paved yard to the rear service wing. Originally strictly utilitarian, the yards have been adapted in the twentieth century to serve as patios in the Spanish manner.

HABS, 1938, Library of Congress

An act of sale dated 1810 describes Bosque's dwelling as a "beautiful house situated in this city on Chartres Street, fully plastered and of brick with a terrace roof, the major part of which has an upper story." The sectional drawing depicts the line of a very low pitched roof such as was favored during the Spanish period (Figure 23). Latrobe's watercolor of a gentleman lounging in an armchair on the roof readily explains the popularity of combining roof and terrace (Figure 24). Cottages were also built with terrace roofs, but 707–709 Dumaine Street, with its stacked tile balustrade, may be the only one left unaltered (Figure 25). As Eugene Darwin Cizek has observed, in many Latin American countries with rain and humidity similar to Louisiana's, flat tiled terraces are a dominant form of roof. The difference is in the building materials that were available. In Latin America, sand of volcanic origin was the prime ingredient in waterproof construction. In New Orleans, waterproofing—tile or stucco on planks—invariably failed, and

FIGURE 22   619 Chartres Street, parlor
mantel, now located in the
Rosamunde E. and Emile Kuntz Rooms,
New Orleans Museum of Art.

Courtesy of New Orleans Museum of Art.
Photograph by Owen F. Murphy, Jr.

later generations ended up replacing the terrace roofs with roofs of much
steeper pitch. Most of the new roofs were tile, too, a more expensive but
more fireproof material, and tiled roofs were considered Spanish even after
the Louisiana Purchase (Figure 26).[19]

19.   *Ibid.,* 343; Eugene Darwin Cizek, personal communication.

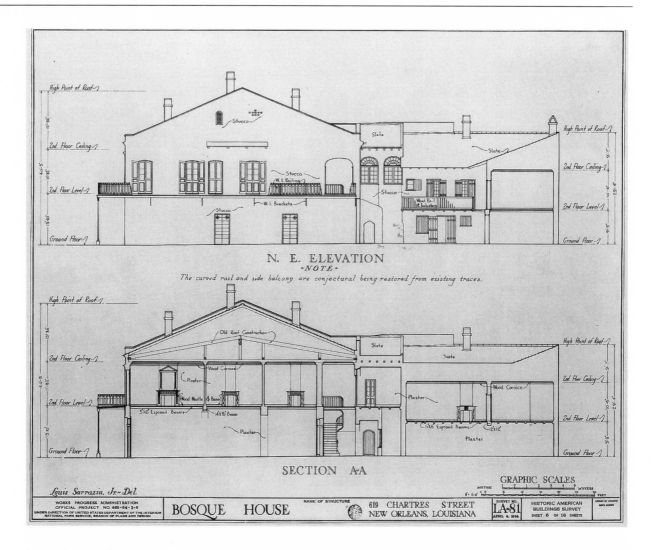

N. E. ELEVATION
-NOTE-
The curved rail and side balcony are conjectural being restored from existing traces.

SECTION A-A

FIGURE 23   619 Chartres Street, section and side elevation. The original but superseded roof was a terrace. That the rooms were accorded increasing importance as they were farther from the stairway and closer to the front of the house is evident in the progressively larger size of the rooms toward the front and even more clearly in the progressively greater grandeur and embellishment of their mantels. The investigations of Samuel Wilson, Jr., disclose that the carriage way was one story tall and that the second-story side rooms opened onto the terrace supported by the carriage way's roof.

HABS, 1938, Library of Congress

The most impressive Creole town house surviving in New Orleans is the one completed in 1815 at 500 Chartres Street for Nicholas Girod, mayor of the city (Figure 27). Of stuccoed brick, the three-story house has its original flat tiles on a high hip roof. The dormers are arched, and there is a low octagonal cupola under an ogee-arched roof. The plan was complex, since it incorporated an existing house that faced the side street and that the mayor's brother had owned (Figure 28). In floor space and height the new structure was one of the largest residences of its era. Tall french doors of twelve lights each open onto scrolled wrought-iron balconies supported on brackets in the center bays of the second floor. Tall double casement windows with paneled lower rails frame each balcony (Figure 29). Low iron railings at the windows provide safety, as do those in all the french doors on the third floor. Through full-height openings the maximum possible ventilation and light are ensured for the upper floors. In the early nineteenth century, french doors did not presuppose a balcony or gallery, but the use of french doors in place of win-

FIGURE 24 Benjamin Henry Latrobe, Sketch from Hotel Window, New Orleans, 1819.

Maryland Historical Society, Baltimore

FIGURE 25 Dumaine Street, New Orleans, *ca.* 1890. The building at 617–619 Dumaine Street (foreground) still stands.

Collection of the Louisiana State Museum. Photograph by François Mugnier (Old Houses, Ursuline Street, erroneously titled).

9081. OLD HOUSES, URSULINE STREET.

FIGURE 26   House with tile roof on St. Peter Street, New Orleans, *ca.* 1800, drawn in 1844. Barrel tiles cover the roof. Although the house has gable ends, it also has decorative chimney pots and a projecting canopy supported by iron rods.

Collection of the Louisiana State Museum. Photograph by François Mugnier, ca. *1890.*

FIGURE 27   500 Chartres Street, (Nicholas Girod House, now Old Napoleon House), New Orleans, 1814–1815.

HABS, 1934, Library of Congress

FIGURE 28   500 Chartres Street, Toulouse Street facade
HABS, 1934, Library of Congress

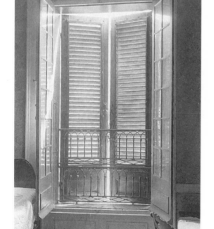

FIGURE 29   500 Chartres Street, pair of
interior second-story casement windows
with louvered shutters and wrought iron
grill, which was doubled later for safety.

*Richard Koch Collection, Southeastern
Architectural Archive, Tulane University.
Photograph by Richard Koch for HABS, ca.
1936.*

dows made the later addition of the elaborate cast iron galleries to other similar houses an easy modification.

The wrought iron of the balustrades and brackets was the master smith's
work, but the hardware on every opening needed skill at the forge. The hardware on all of these houses differed from that found on the North American
continent outside the regions of French influence. The tradition of casement
windows and french doors imposed special requirements in hardware (Figures
30, 31). Shutters are supported on strap hinges that fit onto pintles driven into
the frames of doors and windows and on into the frame of the building. Dou-
ble-leaf french doors have bolts on both the upper and lower stiles to attach
them to the top and bottom of the frame. Gravity latches are frequently used
in place of handles or doorknobs, and a privacy latch on the upper stiles holds
paired doors tightly shut. The hardware on houses of the late eighteenth and
early nineteenth centuries differs little from that on the Ursuline Convent of
1742 (Chapter 1, Figure 24). The way the hardware operated was largely inde-
pendent of the size of the building. Flat-mounted butt hinges came into use
only as Americans moved into Louisiana with their own notions.

The building contract for Girod's house must have been similar to that
for the house erected across the street the next year for Bernard de Marigny:

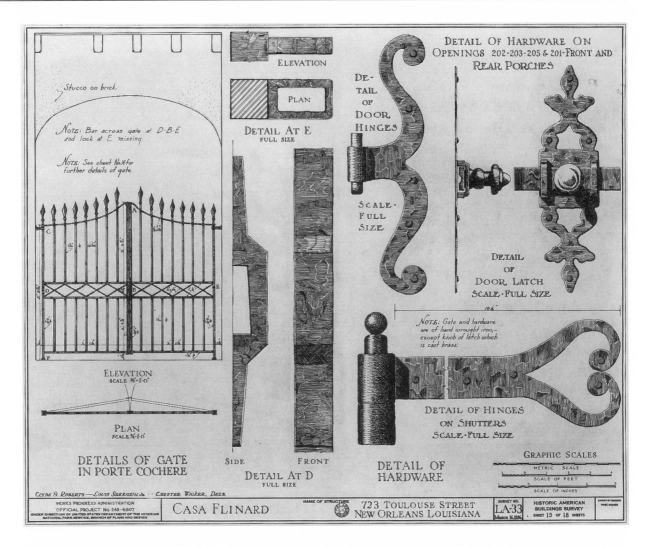

WORKS PROGRESS ADMINISTRATION
OFFICIAL PROJECT No. 265-6807
UNDER DIRECTION OF UNITED STATES DEPARTMENT OF THE INTERIOR
NATIONAL PARK SERVICE, BRANCH OF PLANS AND DESIGN

FIGURE 30   723 Toulouse Street, details of hardware. Ramshorn hinges, as they are known in Louisiana, may be installed on both the window or door and the frame, or the frame may have only a pintle; in either case, shutters and doors can be lifted off the hardware attached to the frame.

HABS, 1936, Library of Congress

All the walls of this house shall be made with bricks of the country of good quality, and coated [with stucco]—the doors of the store shall be one inch and a half in thickness, and shall open and fold in the manner of those of the exchange [bifold]—all the apartments of the upper story shall have ceilings and shall have cornices—there shall be outside Venetian blinds [louvered shutters] on the openings of the front—the chimneys shall be properly panelled, and those of the salon [parlor] in an elegant manner—all the woodwork as well as the hardware shall be in the French fashion—there shall be made use . . . only of cypress wood—The whole shall be painted with two coats in white, except the outside [louvered shutters], which shall be in green and the doors of the store which shall be of a dark color—the court shall be properly paved in bricks.[20]

The lozenge design and tapered pilasters in favor in the eighteenth century decorate the mantel and overmantel in the secondary chamber (Figure 32).

20.   Wilson, *The Architecture of Colonial Louisiana*, 360 (bracketed insertions mine).

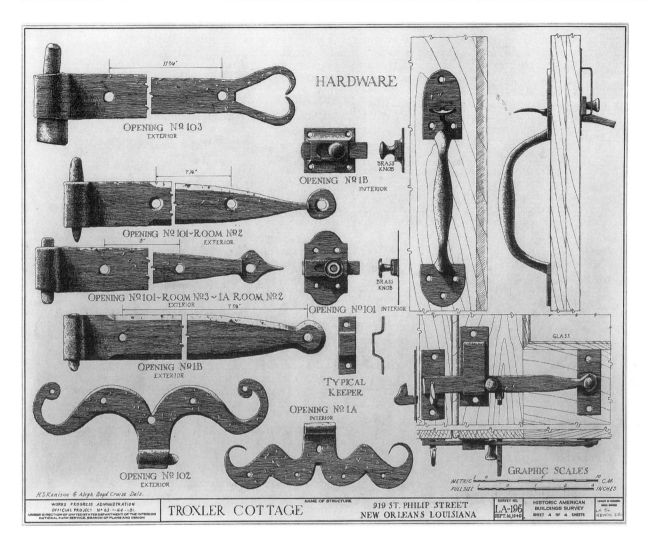

HARDWARE

OPENING Nº 103
EXTERIOR

OPENING Nº 101~ROOM Nº2
EXTERIOR

OPENING Nº 101~ROOM Nº3~1A ROOM Nº2
EXTERIOR

OPENING Nº1B
EXTERIOR

OPENING Nº 102
EXTERIOR

OPENING Nº 1B
INTERIOR

BRASS
KNOB

OPENING Nº 101 INTERIOR

BRASS
KNOB

TYPICAL
KEEPER

OPENING Nº 1A
INTERIOR

GLASS

GRAPHIC SCALES
METRIC C.M.
FULLSIZE INCHES

H.S.Kenison & Alvyk Boyd Cruise Dels.

WORKS PROGRESS ADMINISTRATION
OFFICIAL PROJECT Nº 65-1-64-181.
UNDER DIRECTION OF UNITED STATES DEPARTMENT OF THE INTERIOR
NATIONAL PARK SERVICE, BRANCH OF PLANS AND DESIGN

NAME OF STRUCTURE
TROXLER COTTAGE

919 ST. PHILIP STREET
NEW ORLEANS LOUISIANA

SURVEY NO.
LA-196
SEPT. 16,1940

HISTORIC AMERICAN
BUILDINGS SURVEY
SHEET 4 OF 4 SHEETS

FIGURE 31   Troxler Cottage, details of hardware. The hardware on a small house could be as elaborate and well made as on more costly buildings.

HABS, 1940, Library of Congress

As Samuel Wilson, Jr., has commented, the far more elaborate parlor mantel and arched overmantel, with winged victories bearing laurel wreaths and blowing trumpets, recall a Roman triumphal arch (Figure 33). These embellishments certainly were in keeping with the taste of the Napoleonic Empire, but it is equally possible that the stars and triumphant angels were commissioned to commemorate the American victory over the English at the Battle of New Orleans, on January 8, 1815.[21]

The same writer who found the Cathedral of St. Louis a building of "utter insignificance as a work of art" visited a bachelor's house that in 1835–1836 was the "only pure specimen of a peculiar style of Spanish architecture, called the 'entre suelo' now remaining in the city. The first, or ground floor, he appropriated exclusively to his horses; the second, or 'entre suelo,' to the stowage of grain and hay, and for servants' room; while the

21.   *Ibid.,* 361.

FIGURE 32   500 Chartres Street, secondary mantel
Richard Koch Collection, Southeastern Architectural Archive, Tulane University. Photograph by Richard Koch for HABS, ca. 1940.

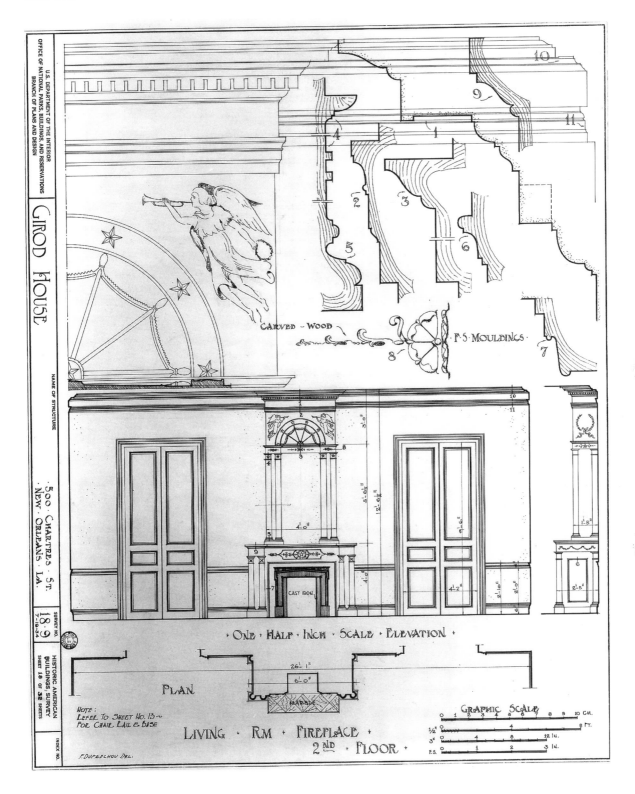

FIGURE 33   500 Chartres Street, principal parlor and mantel
HABS, 1934, Library of Congress

FIGURE 34   517 Decatur Street, New Orleans, 1785
New Orleans Notarial Archives, Book 44, folio 23, dated 1852

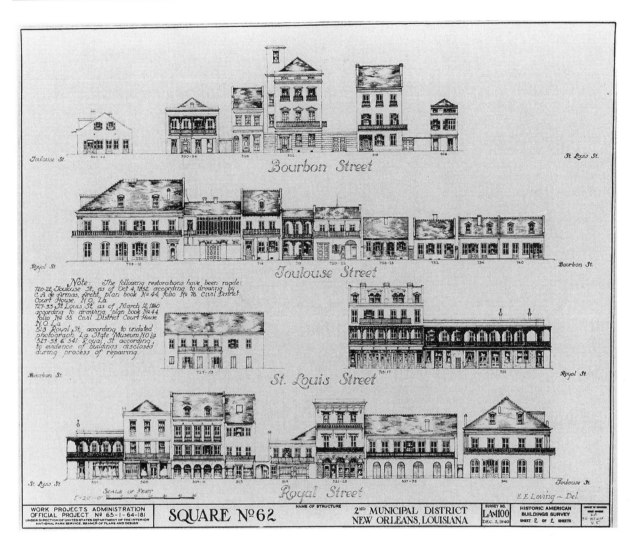

Bourbon Street

Toulouse Street

St. Louis Street

Royal Street

WORK PROJECTS ADMINISTRATION OFFICIAL PROJECT Nº 65-1-64-181
UNDER DIRECTION OF UNITED STATES DEPARTMENT OF THE INTERIOR NATIONAL PARK SERVICE, BRANCH OF PLANS AND DESIGN

SQUARE Nº 62

NAME OF STRUCTURE

2ND MUNICIPAL DISTRICT
NEW ORLEANS, LOUISIANA

SURVEY NO. LA-1100 DEC. 3, 1940

HISTORIC AMERICAN BUILDINGS SURVEY SHEET 2 OF 2 SHEETS

FIGURE 35   Square No. 62, the block bounded by Royal, St. Louis, Bourbon, and Toulouse Streets, New Orleans.

HABS, 1940, Library of Congress

third or upper story, contains his own private apartments; thus retaining in the disposition of the different parts of his house to the several uses, the original design of its architect."[22] Although the writer does not name an address, he was quite likely the guest of the owner of 517 Decatur Street, which is among the few *entresol* buildings remaining in the city. Originally, when the house stood on what was then Levee Street, adjacent to the docks and shipping, the ground floor was for commerce. A drawing in the New Orleans Notarial Archives shows it with the original tile roof and a wooden shed canopy over the sidewalk (Figure 34).[23]

Not only *entresol* houses were recognizably Spanish. Both they and two- and three-story houses built after 1795 may owe much to Havana, the principal Spanish port with which New Orleans traded. Travelers to New Orleans in the early nineteenth century observed that the city was Spanish in its

22.   Durrell, *New Orleans As I Found It*, 53.
23.   New Orleans Notarial Archives, Book 44, Folio 23, May 5, 1852.

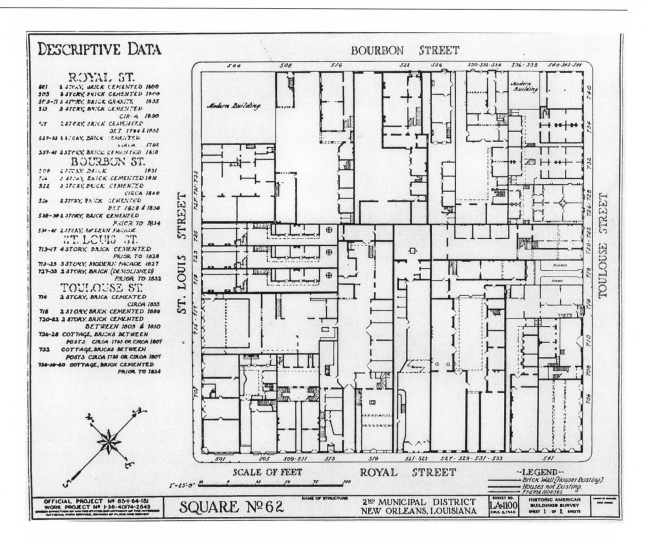

Figure 36   Square No. 62, plan
HABS, 1940, Library of Congress

features. Mrs. Basil Hall, an aristocratic Englishwoman traveling on both American continents in 1827 and 1828, judged New Orleans particularly pleasing. She admired the "appearance of the houses with their queerly shaped, high roofs and iron balconies [and the] delightful dark *portes cocheres* and Spanish *patios* look[ing] deliciously cool for summer use" (Plate D).[24] Since the outspoken Mrs. Hall found much not to her liking, this was high praise indeed. The courtyards were more utilitarian than she supposed, but twentieth-century plumbing has freed them for a new use. Throughout the French Quarter, the humble service areas have now become patios in the Spanish manner. Some blocks in the French Quarter still look much as they did to Mrs. Hall. The character of Creole New Orleans, with its dense plan and variety of housing, is seen in Municipal District 3, Square No. 62 (Figures 35, 36).

24.   Mrs. Basil Hall, *The Aristocratic Journey, 1827–1828*, ed. Una Pope-Hennessy (New York, 1931), 253. Both Mrs. Hall and her husband wrote of their travels.

The Battle of New Orleans marked the true onset of the Americaniza-
tion of the city. That victory proved that the young United States would survive as a nation. Spurred by the opportunities that the commercial success of
sugarcane and cotton offered, people poured in from the eastern seaboard
and Europe. In a generation, New Orleans was to become one of the great
ports of America. With the new residents came a preference for new styles
and architects trained in the new tastes (Plate E).

3

THE FOLK ARCHITECTURE OF THE APPALACHIAN UPLANDERS

Jonathan Fricker

APPALACHIAN UPLANDERS WERE THE LARGEST GROUP OF PIONEERS IN THE areas of the state beyond steady French influence—mainly in north Louisiana and the Florida parishes. They were of hardy stock, typically Scotch-Irish, that enabled them to come to a hostile environment and, with little in the way of resources, make it their own. From what they found, they created a distinctive built environment quite unlike the Creole plantations of south Louisiana and Natchitoches Parish. They were a ruggedly individualistic population that came a long way, over several centuries, to leave an extraordinarily interesting architectural legacy.

The Scotch-Irish were descendants of Lowland Scottish Presbyterians who emigrated to northern Ireland in the early decades of the seventeenth century to work the large manorial farms owned by English and Scottish planters. Between 1725 and 1775 these Ulster Scots, as they were known in Ireland, emigrated again, this time to the British colonies of North America, many of them settling in the frontier areas of Pennsylvania. There they encountered Pennsylvania Germans, known as the Pennsylvania Dutch, who had come to the colony in the 1680s. (*Dutch* was a corruption of *Deutsch,* the German word for *German.*) The Scotch-Irish and the Germans shared the region for about a generation, trading words, customs, and most important, methods of construction.[1]

Cultural geographers believe that this cross-fertilization created a hardy pioneer culture that could quickly claim the heavily wooded Appalachian hinterland. Log construction enabled the Scotch-Irish to exploit the region's vast resources of virgin timber. Indeed, it is evidence of their adaptability

---

1. Robert McCrum, William Cran, and Robert MacNeil, *The Story of English* (New York, 1987), 152.

that they mastered the technique in just a generation. For though the log cabin was not part of the native heritage of the Scotch-Irish, they made it an American frontier commonplace and symbol. Constructing buildings by placing logs horizontally one upon another, and connecting the corners with interlocking notches in Lincoln Log fashion, dates back to the Middle Stone Age. At one time log construction was common in much of Europe, but by the early Middle Ages it was restricted to the heavily wooded areas of central Europe and Scandinavia. The Pennsylvania Germans used the kind of log construction they had known in their native land, and examples of it can still be found in Bohemia, Moravia, and Silesia.[2]

Log construction in early America may have had antecedents besides this. The cultural geographer Terry Jordan relates that log buildings were erected in the small Delaware Valley colony of New Sweden, which lasted from 1638 to 1655. Certain features of the structures there, which reflect the colony's Swedish and Finnish heritage, resembled log buildings that were later built in many parts of the South.[3]

Theodore Roosevelt described the Scotch-Irish as the "kernel of the distinctively and intensely American stock who were the pioneers of our people in their march westward." Flourishing on the Appalachian frontier, filling the Shenandoah Valley and the Carolina Piedmont, they spread so quickly that on the eve of the American Revolution they had covered most of the southern Appalachian region.[4] In the succeeding years they spread farther westward, penetrating Louisiana about 1790.

By roughly the 1830s, the Appalachian Scotch-Irish had taken possession of north Louisiana and the Florida parishes, bringing their Jacksonian politics and a distinctive way of life. They created what the late Milton Newton called an "uncouth" landscape, punctuated by rambling ridge roads, scattered hamlets, and irregular fields. Farms and dwellings were widely dispersed, and the settlers left much forest and meadowland undeveloped for grazing.[5] Their pattern of land use was much in contrast to the neat and tightly packed villages and towns of the East Coast tidewater.

The inhabitants of isolated Uplander piney-woods hamlets earned a reputation for a remarkable self-sufficiency. Writing in 1869, Samuel Lockett described the families in a remote community on Bundick's Creek, near present-day Fort Polk, in Vernon Parish: "The good people of this settlement had

2. Milton Newton, "Cultural Preadaptation and the Upland South," *Geoscience and Man,* V (1974), 146–47; Fred B. Kniffen and Henry Glassie, "Building in Wood in the Eastern United States," *Geographical Review,* LVI (1966), 58–59.

3. Terry Jordan, "Cultural Preadaptations and the American Frontier: The Role of New Sweden," in *Re-Reading Cultural Geography,* ed. Kenneth E. Foote *et al.* (Austin, Tex., 1994), 215–36.

4. McCrum, Cran, and MacNeil, *The Story of English,* 156; Newton, "Cultural Preadaptation," 150.

5. Milton Newton, "The Historical Settlement of Louisiana" (Typescript of report prepared for Louisiana Division of Historic Preservation, 1980), 49–53.

a church, a school house, and a Masonic lodge. Each family had its herd of cattle, flock of sheep, and drove of hogs. They all made their own cotton, corn, potatoes, rice, sugar and tobacco; spun and wove their own clothes for summer and winter wear, made their own leather, and in fact supplied nearly all of their necessities by home products."[6]

Pioneer communities were quick to build churches. A prospectus compiled in 1886 to attract settlers to north Louisiana stressed the abundance of churches. Asserting that "it is always safe to settle among a church-going population," the pamphlet boasted that "there is no settlement without its church and some have two or three."[7] But although a community's life may have revolved around worship, the church was seldom at the geographical center of town, as it would have been in other cultures. Often the Scotch-Irish built their churches in relatively remote settings, as illustrated by the line from an old popular song, "Come to the church in the wildwood."

Walnut Creek Baptist Church, in Lincoln Parish (Figure 1), is a case in point. It is set on a semiwooded hilltop with no other building visible from the cemetery or grounds. Although a late example (*ca.* 1870), it is the kind of stark gable-fronted church that many pioneer communities erected in the nineteenth century. It is a very much watered-down version of the Greek Revival temple-style churches of the 1830s and 1840s. Stripped of almost all details, it presents a stark yet well-proportioned appearance, with a plain plank interior and hard pews. In seeming almost deliberately unadorned, Walnut Creek Church is typical of Uplander churches throughout north Louisiana. The historian James G. Leyburn offers a possible explanation for the severity of both Uplander buildings and the culture as a whole. He remarks that "nothing in the background of the Scotch-Irish, whether in Scotland or Ulster, had drawn their attention to painting, sculpture, or architecture, and music," and nothing in their American experience "provided an incentive to develop [any] interest in the finer arts."[8] Embellishment was not one of the preoccupations of the Uplander building tradition.

In a poetic sense, the hard, stark, and plain appearance of the Walnut Creek Church befits the kind of evangelical fundamentalism prevailing in Appalachian Uplands culture. In general, Uplanders belonged to the Baptist, Methodist, Presbyterian, and Church of Christ denominations. In churches such as Walnut Creek, long and blustery sermons smote the listeners with a message of fire and brimstone. Church services were also an opportunity for socializing, which was not always possible on the isolated farmstead.

6. Susan Roach-Langford, "The Regional Folklife of North Louisiana," in *Louisiana Folklife: A Guide to the State,* ed. Nicholas R. Spitzer (Baton Rouge, 1985), 94.

7. *Ibid.,* 91.

8. Walnut Creek Baptist Church (Lincoln Parish) National Register File, Louisiana Division of Historic Preservation; James G. Leyburn, *The Scotch-Irish: A Social History* (Chapel Hill, N.C., 1962), 324.

FIGURE I Walnut Creek Baptist
Church, near Simsboro, Lincoln Parish,
ca. 1870.

Photograph by Jim Zietz

Worship was not the only occasion for community gatherings. Accustomed to hardship, the Scotch-Irish had a long tradition of cooperative work, extending from clearing fields to shucking corn and constructing houses and other buildings. The so-called raising bee was a frontier institution. The piney woods were settled fairly quickly, and the need for farm buildings was urgent. For several days or weeks prior to a raising, the landowner and his family, sometimes with the help of friends who could spare a day or two from their labors, cut trees and squared off logs, leaving them on the ground near the building site. If the building to be raised was a house, it could vary from a sixteen-by-sixteen-foot one-room "single pen" to a two-room "double pen" to a dogtrot house—two complete rooms separated by a covered passageway open to the air. Shed lean-tos could be added front and rear, and thus the house could have as many as six rooms. Early in the morning on the appointed day, neighbors converged on the site. The first operation was to place the bottom logs, or sills, securely on heavy wood blocks or

FIGURE 2 Saddle notching, house at Mile Branch Settlement, Franklinton, Washington Parish.

Photograph by Jim Zietz

FIGURE 3 Square notching, Autrey House, near Dubach, Lincoln Parish, 1849.

Photograph by Jim Zietz

piles of stones. In Louisiana, the stone was a poor grade of yellowish iron-stone. Once the foundation was down, the floor was laid anywhere from one to three feet above the ground.[9]

As the log walls went up, four skilled axmen served as "cornermen," chopping and chiseling the ends of the logs so that they interlocked in neat corners. Notching, as this was known, was an art, sometimes involving fairly complex geometry. The simplest form was the saddle notch (Figure 2), which linked round logs by rounded cuts. More refined, and much employed in Louisiana, was the square notch, which enabled logs to interlock neatly at the corners (Figure 3). Even more complex were the half and full dovetail notches, with interlocking wedge shapes that allowed rainwater to drain away. Occasionally one or two of the cornermen did the notching differently from the others.[10] In general, the builders exercised greater care in fashioning the corners of a residence than of a barn, shed, or corncrib. In all but the poorest construction, logs did not protrude beyond the corners of the building. Actual practice was in sharp contrast to the popular image of log cabins—the kind of tourist cabins erected in our national parks during the 1920s and 1930s. In those deliberately rustic, Smokey the Bear style buildings, rough round logs extend as much as two feet beyond the corners.

During a raising there was a constant banter of jokes and "lively talk" to lighten the work. At midday the women served a huge meal on a makeshift table. The food might be boiled ham, pork, or pork or chicken stew, and it could include as well a pot of turnip greens, sweet potatoes, cornmeal dumplings, and—almost invariably—black coffee brewed so strong that Uplanders liked to say it could float a wedge of iron. After eating, the men returned to the job, normally completing the shell in a single day.[11] Once the log walls were up, the gaps between the logs were covered with long boards made of split timber, which resulted in more finished interior walls of horizontal paneling. In much of the South, mud or lime plaster filled the gaps between the logs. But chinking, as such primitive insulation was called, seems to have been relatively infrequent in Louisiana, possibly because of the state's mild climate. Often the final stage of a raising bee was hoisting the roof rafters, usually skinned poles, and setting them in place.

In folk building, or vernacular architecture, only a limited number of choices were available to the builders. Because far-flung neighbors cooperated on a project, the design and techniques had to be familiar to all. In consequence, the natural tendency was to perpetuate the old way of doing things and to resist innovations. In any case, folk builders were as a rule outside the reach of contemporary fashion. Isolated on the frontier, they simply never

9. Frank Lawrence Owsley, *Plain Folk of the Old South* (Baton Rouge, 1949), 104–106.

10. *Ibid.,* 107; Hiram F. Gregory, Department of Anthropology, Northwestern State University, Natchitoches, La., to author, May 7, 1992.

11. Owsley, *Plain Folk of the Old South,* 109–10.

FIGURE 4   Knight Cabin, Mile Branch
Settlement, Franklinton, 1857.

Photograph by Jim Zietz

considered that there might be a different way to build. For the Appalachian
Uplanders, following accepted practice meant log construction. As America
developed, the Uplanders were the only major pioneer group to view log
houses as the norm for permanent dwelling. The log house of the Uplanders
became a cultural symbol when, in the presidential election of 1840, William
Henry Harrison embraced homespun Jacksonian virtues, declaring that he
would be proud to live in a log cabin. In the "log cabin and hard cider campaign" that followed, the log house came to stand for domestic American
virtues such as ruggedness, honesty, simplicity, and courage.[12] Harrison won
the election, and in the succeeding generation the log cabin became the ideal
place for an aspiring politician to have been born.

A simple frontier log cabin of this type was the one George and Martha
Knight built in Washington Parish (Figure 4). This single pen, probably con-

12.   Kniffen and Glassie, "Building in Wood," 65; Hugh Morrison, *Early American Architecture:
From the First Colonial Settlements to the National Period* (New York, 1952), 13.

structed in 1857, may be regarded as typical for a pioneer family in Louisiana. Its logs are not fully squared but are half round, with the rounded side facing outward. Having square notched corners, the cabin is at the mean between the roughest of Louisiana log construction and the most refined. The single chimney, now reconstructed, is of stickwork encased in mud. Mud-and-stick chimneys were in general use despite their unfortunate readiness to catch fire. A family had to be prepared to rush out at any hour of the day or night to pull the burning chimney away from the house. In the hill parishes of Louisiana, the local ironstone was a more desirable material for chimneys, since it was fireproof, but it was not always obtainable in sufficient quantities. The Knight Cabin is a single room, with a partial sleeping loft reached by a ladder. Apart from the area beneath the sleeping loft, the cabin is completely open to the rafters. Many pioneer dwellings went without ceilings, as they did also glazing, often making do merely with shutters that closed over the window openings. The absence of glazing in some of the early dwellings is often overlooked today, inasmuch as the surviving cabins have almost always been fitted with sashes and glass panes.

It strains the late-twentieth-century imagination to think that a family of eight occupied the Knight Cabin's single room. Although such crowding suggests poverty, Knight and others like him were far from penniless. Census records from 1860 and 1870 disclose that Knight owned about 175 acres and had an annual farm income of over seven hundred dollars. By 1880, he owned 250 acres, with 25 under cultivation. His livestock included 2 horses, 2 oxen, 36 cows, 16 calves, 75 swine, and 30 fowl. This was a level of affluence undreamed of by sharecroppers of the period, and suggests that the crowding in the house would not in his time have been felt an exceptional hardship.[13]

The overall darkness of the interior of a cabin in the 1840s would be striking to anyone accustomed to the light in modern houses. Windows were small, and the wooden walls absorbed such light as came in unless the owner could procure whitewash. The furnishings were generally crude homemade beds, tables, benches, and perhaps a chair or two. Pegs for hanging things usually abounded, and over the door might be a long-barrel rifle.[14]

A cabin larger than the Knights', a two-room "double pen," was built by Nathaniel Washington Pigott in Washington Parish between 1865 and 1868 (Figure 5). Of square-notched logs, the Pigott House has a partition wall one plank thick between the two rooms, insufficient for any kind of acoustical privacy. Planks similar to those in the wall are mounted as a flat ceiling in both rooms. Also distinguishing the Pigott House as a "fine home" are its glass sash windows, which appear to be original, and its chamfered porch

13. Knight Cabin (Washington Parish) National Register File, Louisiana Division of Historic Preservation.
14. Owsley, *Plain Folk of the Old South*, 35.

FIGURE 5   Piggot House, Mile Branch
Settlement, Franklinton, 1865–1868.

Photograph by Jim Zietz

FIGURE 6   Countess' House,
Germantown, near Minden, Webster
Parish, *ca.* 1840.

Photograph by Jim Zietz

columns. Nathaniel Pigott and his wife, Permelia, reared nine children in the
house. The family continued to occupy the cabin until 1923 or 1924.[15]

The Countess' House (Figure 6), at Germantown, a communal religious
settlement founded near Minden, in Webster Parish, in 1836, is another well-

15.   Pigott House (Washington Parish) National Register File, Louisiana Division of Historic
Preservation.

preserved double pen. The "countess" was Elisa Leon, widow of the self-styled Count Leon, who led his forty-odd followers from Germany to Pennsylvania, and then to Natchitoches Parish, where he died and floods destroyed the settlement. The countess decided that the colony should start over again in nearby Webster Parish, where it acquired the name of Germantown. The community made extensive use of log construction, which they most likely learned from their American neighbors. Today only two original log buildings remain: the Countess' House and the communal kitchen and dining hall. Both employ dovetail notching.[16]

The standard dogtrot cabin consisted of two rooms flanking a central passageway completely open at both ends. There were also larger houses of the type, with four rooms, two on each side of the dogtrot corridor. Possessing one of the most interesting designs of southern houses, the dogtrot cabin was symmetrical, with a continuous roof line over both the open passageway and the rooms. To be a true dogtrot, the floor of the passageway must be at the same level as the floors inside the house.

One theory holds that the dogtrot house came into being as a way of dealing with the hot, humid summers of the middle and lower South. The idea is that the dogtrot provides a primitive form of air conditioning, for the flow of air accelerates through the passageway, rather in the way the flow of water does through a narrow stream bed. Although this theory is attractive, particularly to environmentalists, it has not won wide acceptance among cultural geographers. Anyway, the dogtrot also brought howling winds in the winter, for at best a trade-off in comfort. Another theory holds that the dogtrot house developed as the frontiersman's attempt to build a formal, symmetrical central-hall house.[17]

Whatever the impulses behind the design, the dogtrot cabin is the most spacious Uplander house commonly built in Louisiana. Although it was more often constructed than the smaller, double-pen house, relatively few examples survive from before the Civil War. Fewer still survive with their dogtrots open, since in the late nineteenth century owners began to convert the passageways into additional living space.

Absalom Autrey House, near Dubach, in Lincoln Parish (Figure 7), is a dogtrot cabin that retains not only its original open passageway but also its ironstone chimney. Absalom Autrey and his family, which included fourteen children, came to what is now Lincoln Parish in 1848, when the area was a howling wilderness. In the Autreys' first year there, they subsisted on little besides the abundant game, from which they took 544 deer as well as numerous squirrels and wild turkeys. In 1849, they built the present four-room square-notched log house, which was to see use not only as a residence for

16. Germantown (Webster Parish) National Register File, Louisiana Division of Historic Preservation.

17. Newton, "The Historical Settlement of Louisiana," 80.

FIGURE 7   Absalom Autrey House, near Dubach, 1849.

Photograph by Jim Zietz

the large family but also as a boardinghouse for teachers at the nearby Autrey School. The school also functioned as the meeting place for the local Primitive Baptist church. According to family accounts, people would gather at the Autrey House after services for meals and overnight lodging.[18] Restored in 1991 and 1992 by the Lincoln Parish Historical Society, the Autrey House is one of a very small number of well-maintained log buildings on their original sites.

Probably the finest dogtrot log cabin remaining in Louisiana, as well as one of the oldest, is the King House, in Washington Parish (Figures 8–10), constructed of large half-round logs with square notching. According to the family stories handed down by the Kings, Thomas Iverson King, a native of Georgia, built the house in 1831, when he married Lucy Bickham, of Washington Parish. Although it is impossible to verify that information, the architectural evidence supports a date of construction in the 1830s. Much about the house is of larger than ordinary scale. The dogtrot corridor is unusually wide, being twelve feet, as against the more customary eight. Huge timbers frame up the structure. The sills on which the house rests are each a single piece of wood forty-seven feet long. But what sets the King House apart is its elaborate and fine woodwork and details. Unlike other log houses with their skinned pole rafters and maybe a rough ceiling, the King House has ceilings of planed lumber, and ceiling beams and boards cut with a decorative bead. The glory of the King House is its pair of intricately

18. Autrey House (Lincoln Parish) National Register File, Louisiana Division of Historic Preservation.

FIGURE 8   King House, Mile Branch
Settlement, Franklinton, 1830s.
Photograph by Jim Zietz

FIGURE 9   Dogtrot detail of King
House.
Photograph by Jim Zietz

FIGURE 10   Mantel of King House
Photograph by Jim Zietz

worked mantels in a provincial Federal style, one of which bears the initials of the builder, T.I.K.[19]

Some owners of dogtrot cabins adapted their houses to their increasing wealth by applying clapboards to the walls, enclosing the passageways, and generally remodeling their dwellings in the Greek Revival style. But the emergence of high fashion on the frontier did not always blot out the earlier folk building tradition. In a few curious hybrid houses, fashion and the old tradition merged. The Allen House, built about 1848 in rural De Soto Parish (Figure 11), is a full-blown Greek Revival galleried house of wood-frame construction with an open dogtrot. The Scott House, also in De Soto Parish, is a two-story Greek Revival house that has a two-story pedimented portico. On the ground floor is an enclosed central hall, but upstairs the hall is an open dogtrot.

19.   King House (Washington Parish) National Register File, Louisiana Division of Historic Preservation.

FIGURE II Allen House, near Keatchie, De Soto Parish, *ca.* 1848.

Photograph by Jim Zietz

FIGURE 12 Robert D. Magee House, near State Line, Washington Parish, *ca.* 1845.

Photograph by Jim Zietz

Not all dogtrot houses started out as such. Some grew out of smaller houses. The Robert D. Magee House, near the rural community of State Line, in Washington Parish (Figure 12), is a case in point. Magee was a postmaster and community leader in Washington Parish during the final decades of the nineteenth century, but the house that currently bears his name dates to the antebellum period. There is architectural evidence placing construction of the original portion—a one-room square-notched log structure with a sleeping loft, and with the rare feature of vertical pegs inserted into drilled holes to hold the logs together—in the 1840s. Probably the builder was Alfred Richardson, a native of Mississippi who came to Washington Parish with his wife, Selena, in 1845. Figures from the 1860 census show that the Richardsons had nine children living in a house that probably still consisted of just one room. Some time after that, Richardson enlarged the house, with a second large room of frame construction and a dogtrot corridor. He also attached two small rooms to the rear and appended two brick chimneys, which were sounder than the original single chimney, undoubtedly of mud. He covered the old log house with boards and fitted the windows with the frontier luxury of movable glass sashes. In 1879, Magee bought the house and turned it into a still more prosperous-looking home. Clotilde Magee Carter, a daughter of Robert Magee who was born in the house in 1886, remembered that a dining room and a kitchen with a dirt floor and a mud chimney stood behind the house. Those two rooms were connected to the house by a breezeway. For a time the wing was occupied by a woman named Eller, who did housework for the Magees and helped rear their children. The wing no longer stands. The Magees vacated the house in the 1920s, and by the 1960s it had fallen into disrepair. In recent years it has been rescued, moved, and painstakingly restored as a country retreat.[20]

Of course, the pioneer farmscape included buildings besides dwellings. There were barns, cribs, smokehouses, well houses, and other buildings scattered over the land. People today think of a farmstead as a collection of rural buildings reached by a driveway from the main road. But the Uplander terrain was not nearly so consciously organized. Wagon roads developed in response to local needs, often crossing established farmsteads. The road frequently widened to form a "stomp" with a house, barns, gardens, and pens around it.[21]

The core unit of Uplander outbuildings was the crib, usually a four-sided enclosure made of logs, under a pitched roof. The typical barn combined a pair of cribs under a common roof with an open passageway between, rather like a dogtrot house. Many crib-style outbuildings had attached lean-to sheds, which could be used for anything from stabling mules to storing pumpkins. Early cribs were often built with considerable attention to detail, but as time passed, the construction of log barns, and of barns in general, became more and more perfunctory. By the early twentieth century, log barns were made from unpeeled logs joined with simple saddle notches.

A single-crib barn remains at Oakland plantation, in Natchitoches

20. Robert D. Magee House (Washington Parish) National Register File, Louisiana Division of Historic Preservation.
21. Newton, "Cultural Preadaptation," 151.

FIGURE 13   Oakland Barn, Natchitoches Parish, *ca.* 1840.

Photograph by Jim Zietz

Parish (Figure 13). Thought to be antebellum, the Oakland barn confirms that log-crib outbuildings enjoyed an acceptance extending beyond the rural farmstead of the Appalachian Uplander to plantations. At the center of the Oakland barn is a log crib very nearly two stories high, which is capped by a prominent gable roof and completely encased in lean-tos. One of the lean-tos contains a hayrack for feeding livestock.[22]

The largest log barn known to have survived in Louisiana is the King Barn, in Washington Parish (Figures 14, 15). An outbuilding to the King House, the barn, which measures sixty-four feet by thirty, consists of three log cribs separated by dogtrot passageways. An enormous pitched roof juts over a front porch with a dirt floor. The two eastern cribs have low doors, suggesting the likelihood that they were for oxen. The floors are dirt. Each of these cribs has a hayrack and a feeding trough made from a hollowed-out log. The western crib, with its raised plank floor, was a storehouse for corn. The walls of the cribs are of small, casually chopped-off logs with rough saddle notching. Across the rear of the barn are animal pens assembled from boards and slats. The pen at the eastern end was for milking cows. Although local preservationists believe that the barn was constructed at the same time as the King House, in the 1830s, all that the structural evidence establishes is that it was built before approximately 1880.[23]

In 1992, the Washington Parish Fair Association acquired the King Barn,

22.   Oakland Plantation (Natchitoches Parish) National Register File, Louisiana Division of Historic Preservation.

23.   King Barn (Washington Parish) National Register File, Louisiana Division of Historic Preservation.

FIGURE 14   King Barn, Mile Branch
Settlement, Franklinton, prior to *ca.*
1880.

Photograph by Jim Zietz

FIGURE 15   Crib of King Barn

Photograph by Jim Zietz

took it apart, and put it back together at Mile Branch Settlement, a museum
village of log buildings gathered from elsewhere in the parish. King House,
Pigott House, and Knight House are also now at Mile Branch. Unfortu-
nately, log houses and outbuildings tend not to survive outside a museum
setting. People who live in log houses often tack on one thing after another
until they become unrecognizable. Those that are unaltered are also usually
abandoned. Deteriorating, they face an uncertain future. The prospects for
log outbuildings are even grimmer. Such buildings are of absolutely no use

in modern agriculture and hence are either abandoned or sold for salvage lumber.

Appalachian Uplander farmsteads and hamlets were the dominant presence in the rural areas of Louisiana outside the French sphere through much of the nineteenth century, but after the 1870s things began to change. The prodigious construction of railroads after Reconstruction opened up much of the state, and new railroad towns such as Ruston and Arcadia became centers of commerce and industry. Railroads brought manufactured goods to the hinterland and ushered in the great Louisiana lumber boom, which destroyed much of the state's forest land within a single generation. The rural landscape was changing, as was the Uplander culture. But just how long the old traditions held out against technological civilization is arresting. By all accounts the Thomas Jackson House, in rural Calcasieu Parish, was built in 1903, well into the industrial era, yet the only difference between it and dogtrot cabins built a half century earlier is in the use of milled lumber in place of logs.[24] As milled lumber became available, log construction declined throughout the state, though it persisted in some areas into the twentieth century.

Sadly, what the distinctive building tradition of the Appalachian Uplanders produced is disappearing rapidly. With a few notable exceptions, this important architectural legacy is underappreciated, not only by owners but by the public at large. Preserving what remains will be a daunting challenge.

24.   Jackson House (Calcasieu Parish) National Register File, Louisiana Division of Historic Preservation.

4

THE PLANTATION

Barbara SoRelle Bacot

THE PLANTATION: AN AGRICULTURAL BUSINESS

For Americans the image of the plantation will always be Margaret Mitchell and David Selznick's celluloid Tara. But a plantation is more than a house. The word *plantation* refers to an extensive agricultural establishment for the production of a cash crop, however extensive the landholding and however humble the house.[1] Even the great number of houses for those who lived and worked on a plantation, including all the dependencies serving the dwellings and all the outbuildings supporting the agricultural operations, are not a plantation. A survey of plantation architecture manifests the complexity of plantation agriculture from the initial concessions by France's Company of the Indies to the mechanization of the twentieth century, and suggests the plantation's ties to the market, economy, and fashion of the world beyond Louisiana.

In Louisiana's colonial period—under France from 1699 to 1763, Spain from 1763 to 1800, and France again from 1800 to 1803—its principal crops were indigo, tobacco, rice, and wax myrtle. Indigo was a source of blue dye, and wax myrtle of candle wax. In the 1790s, two technological innovations made sugar and cotton highly profitable to cultivate, however, and these became the major crops of the nineteenth century. Eli Whitney's invention of the cotton gin, in 1793, enabled cotton growing to become commercially practical throughout the South. The gin, a mechanical device for removing seeds from the cotton boll, allowed the efficient production of cotton fiber for the mills of England and the East Coast. In semitropical Louisiana, planters had experimented with cultivating and granulating sugar, a lucrative tropical crop, around 1750. Only in 1795, though, did the planter and entre-

---

1. John Burkhardt Rehder, "Sugar Plantation Settlements of Southern Louisiana: A Cultural Geography" (Ph.D. dissertation, Louisiana State University, 1971), 5–10.

preneur Etienne de Boré and his master sugarmaker succeed in making granulated sugar in commercial quantities, thereby proving that it was a viable cash crop in the region. The loss of sugar-producing capacity in much of the Caribbean because of revolutions and political unrest in the late eighteenth century let Louisiana step into the market and become one of the principal producers in the world. Cotton and sugarcane were crops that created wealth and led to the accumulation of vast acreage. The fine family fortunes they generated built the grand houses that are central to the image of the South before the Civil War. King Cotton built the South, and King Sugar built south Louisiana.

The plantation system was well established in the New World by the beginning of the eighteenth century and was the basis for a form of American agriculture different from both yeoman family farms and Spanish ranches in Louisiana. The scale of the plantation system presupposes large tracts of fertile land, cheap and abundant labor, easy bulk-processing techniques, cheap transportation, and a marketing network. Louisiana and much of the South had conditions conducive to the system both before and after the Civil War. The plantation was both farm and factory and differed from the family farm, whether large or small. Farmers too grew sugarcane and cotton as cash crops. They ground cane with a mule press and boiled it for syrup. They sent cotton to the gin to be cleaned and baled. But it was the planter willing to make capital investments—in land, slaves, and processing that were sufficient to turn agriculture into a branch of manufacturing—who gave us the plantation.

The plantation had, besides, the dignity of a name. Some owners gave their plantations evocative names, like Shadows-on-the-Teche; other plantations were known by the name of the owner, like Uncle Sam, or by a family name, like Parlange. Some names recalled notable events, like Palo Alto, which commemorated the American victory over Mexico in 1846. Some paid homage to the houses of famous men like Hermitage, after Andrew Jackson's Hermitage, and some to nature, like Magnolia and Live Oak. The names might change with a change in ownership. Many, including the Shadows in the nineteenth century, were known as the "homeplace," and Homeplace then became a name, as at the Keller family's plantation in St. Charles Parish.

From its inception, the plantation was a planned community, complete with a levee and drainage system and a whole village of buildings. Although the big house was the most attractive building—and is often the only one remaining today—it was the least necessary. The crucial structures were those that made the plantation profitable: service and processing buildings such as sugar mills, cotton presses, and mule barns.

Not every plantation had a big house, particularly in Louisiana, where there was an unusually large incidence of absentee ownership. A family might own several plantations but live on only one, or for business or social reasons a planter might live in a nearby town rather than on the plantation. Natchez, Mississippi, developed as a town of homes for wealthy planters, many of whose holdings were across the Mississippi in Louisiana. Clinton, Franklin, Natchitoches, and other towns in Louisiana were also places where planters built houses.

One of the earliest plantations in the French colony, Concession des Chaouaches—its name was later shortened to Concession—operated under absentee ownership. Established in 1719 on a land grant on the Mississippi below New Orleans, it had a main house, but this was the residence of the manager. The plantation buildings were constructed around 1721, and a drawing prepared some sixteen years later shows the layout of the buildings and identifies the structures (Plate A). The plantations of the nineteenth century departed in some ways from the model Concession provided but made no changes in its fundamental concept. Except for the indigo sheds, which were replaced by sugarhouses and cotton presses, every one of the buildings in the early drawing existed on later plantations.

Traveling in Louisiana in 1834, the Yankee trader Joseph Holt Ingraham described a Mississippi River plantation:

> On my left, a few hundred yards from the house, and adjoining the pasture stood the stables and other plantation appurtenances, constituting a village in themselves—for planters always have a separate building for everything. To the right stood the humble yet picturesque village or "quarter" of the slaves, embowered in trees, beyond which, farther toward the interior of the plantation, arose the lofty walls and turreted chimneys of the sugarhouse, which, combined with the bell-tower, presented the appearance of a country village with its church-tower and the walls of some public edifice, lifting themselves above the trees.[2]

Ingraham was describing nothing new, and what was true of the plantation he visited upriver from New Orleans was true of plantations throughout the state. The same cluster of outbuildings occurred everywhere, beginning with the earliest plantation settlements, and slavery imparted to it the character Ingraham described. The South's "peculiar institution" necessitated the rows of houses that gave the appearance of village streets. Plantations continued to have the aspect of villages well after the Civil War.

PLANTATION LAYOUT

The first plantations were located along rivers and bayous, which were the main arteries of transportation and commerce before there was a network of railroads. In south Louisiana, the highest and the best land is directly beside the waterways on the natural levees, high ground built up over thousands of

2. Joseph Holt Ingraham, *Travels in the Southwest by a Yankee* (2 vols.; 1835; rpr. Ann Arbor, Mich., 1966), II, 242.

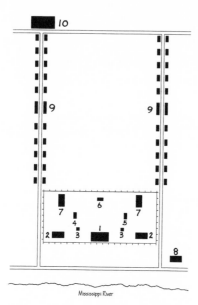

FIGURE 1   Evergreen plantation, St.
John the Baptist Parish, mid–nineteenth
century, plan. The double row of twenty-
two slave cabins upriver from the house
survives, as do the house, *garçonnières,*
kitchen, office, and privy. Key: 1, house;
2, *garçonnière;* 3, *pigeonnier;* 4, office; 5,
kitchen; 6, privy; 7, carriage house; 8,
overseer's house (moved); 9, quarters; 10,
sugarhouse; 11, boat landing. Not to
scale.

*LSU School of Architecture. Drawn by
David Connich.*

years of flooding and silt deposits. Away from the natural levees the land
slopes gently down to the back swamps (Introduction, Figure 2). The French
long-lot system of narrow and deep parcels of land accorded each property
access to transport and an equal proportion of the best-drained, and thus the
best-arable, land closest to the water. On the bayous, land could generally be
cultivated back to the twenty-arpent line (that is, 0.73 miles, an arpent being
192 feet), from which the property extended into the swamp. Along the vast
Mississippi, the initial land grants went back to the forty-arpent line. In the
nineteenth century, with improved techniques for drainage and haulage,
land was sold back to the eighty-arpent line. The plantation house was positioned at the front of the property, facing the water.

Three standard plantation layouts developed in Louisiana. One, called
the linear plan, had a deep and narrow configuration in which a single row
or double rows of slave houses ran at right angles to the river. It was especially
in use along the Mississippi, where the properties were deep. The second,
called the lateral plan, set other buildings parallel to the waterway, to the side
of the house, and was feasible where water frontage was relatively wide. The
third, called the block plan, permitted three or more rows of cabins, which
assumed the appearance of village streets. It was more common on the bayous of the southern parishes in which Americans had settled and was the
most likely plan where the whole housing and operational complex was located well back from the bayou.[3]

Evergreen, in St. John the Baptist Parish on the west bank (Figure 1),
survives as an excellent example of a linear plantation on the Mississippi.
New owners extensively remodeled the original house in 1832, as a building
contract documents.[4] The contract called for the construction of two *pigeonniers* (pigeon houses), a privy, and four "back buildings," which are now
considered a pair of *garçonnières* (residences for young men), a kitchen, and
a guest house. Just upriver, beside a double row of live oaks, stands what is
presumably the overseer's house, moved to the site and equal in size and
refinement to many main houses. The oak alley shades a double row of
twenty-two slave cabins set at right angles to the river frontage. On the east
bank upriver from Evergreen stood Uncle Sam plantation, the property
Samuel Fagot purchased in 1827. He bought neighboring properties on the
east bank in St. James Parish throughout his life and in the 1840s built his
magnificent residential complex (Figure 2). Fortunately, HABS drawings
and photographs were completed before its demolition, in 1940. The main
house faced the river, as did the kitchen and office, a pair of *garçonnières,* and
to the rear, a pair of *pigeonniers,* all of which lay within the house grounds.

3.   Rehder, "Sugar Plantation Settlements," 84–85, 94–96.
4.   Samuel Wilson, Jr., "The Building Contract for Evergreen Plantation, 1832," *Louisiana History,* XXXI (1990), 399–406; St. John the Baptist Courthouse, Conveyance Book H, folio 248, from
the research of Robert Cangelosi.

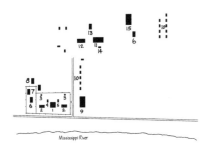

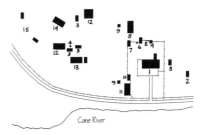

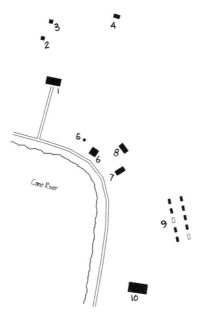

FIGURE 2 Uncle Sam plantation, St. James Parish, mid–nineteenth century (demolished 1940), plan. All the rows of slave housing line roads at right angles to the river, as in the typical linear plantation plan. Key: 1, house; 2, *garçonnière;* 3, *pigeonnier;* 4, kitchen; 5, office; 6, stable; 7, carriage house; 8, overseer's house; 9, hospital; 10, quarters; 11, sugarhouse; 12, sugar mill (here a separate structure); 13, scale house (for weighing sugarcane); 14, blacksmith shop; 15, barn. Not to scale.

LSU School of Architecture. Drawn by David Connich.

FIGURE 3 Magnolia plantation, Natchitoches Parish, mid–nineteenth century, plan. A double row of cabins, with both rows facing the Cane River, parallels the waterway in the lateral plan. Most of the buildings, including eight of the ten cabins, remain. Key: 1, house; 2, fattening pen; 3, privy; 4, corncrib; 5, *pigeonnier;* 6, small barn (blacksmith shop); 7, store; 8, hospital; 9, quarters; 10, cotton gin. Not to scale.

LSU School of Architecture. Drawn by David Connich.

FIGURE 4 Oakland plantation, Natchitoches Parish, mid–nineteenth century, plan. Only two cabins survive, and just one in its original location. Originally, rows of cabins paralleled the river in a lateral plan. Key to buildings still standing: 1, house; 2, cook's house (moved); 3, shed; 4, washhouse; 5, fattening pen; 6, chicken coop; 7, carpenter shop; 8, stable; 9, *pigeonnier;* 10, carriage house; 11, store; 12, barn; 13, doctor's house; 14, overseer's house; 15, quarters. Not to scale.

LSU School of Architecture. Drawn by David Connich.

Next upriver stood the stable and carriage house. Directly downriver was the slave hospital, with a row of cabins leading back from the river to the original sugarhouse and blacksmith's shop and to other ancillary buildings and cabins. Downriver from the sugarhouse and to its rear were another stable and barn and two more rows of cabins at right angles to the river. The distance between the rows of quarters on Uncle Sam owed to the later plantation's formation out of others. Although Uncle Sam started as a linear plantation, it eventually reached a sizable width, and the residential complex a breadth that was quite rare. Uncle Sam's symmetrical arrangement of highly styled buildings was unique to Louisiana. There were larger and more elaborate houses, and others flanked by paired dependencies, but never a grander prospect.

Two cotton plantations facing the Cane River in Natchitoches Parish and laid out according to the lateral plan have their dependencies largely intact. Both Magnolia and Oakland are from the early to mid-nineteenth century. Magnolia follows the curve of the river (Figure 3). The main house—recon-

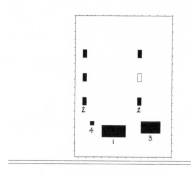

Mississippi River

FIGURE 5   Canebrake plantation, Concordia Parish, mid–nineteenth century, plan. Four of the six cabins stand in their original location; one was moved, and another destroyed. Two rows of cabins face each other behind the house. Key: 1, house; 2, quarters; 3, barn; 4, chicken coop. Not to scale.

LSU School of Architecture. Drawn by David Connich.

structed on the original site in 1899—faces the water and the road and has an axial approach with live oak trees. Behind it are a privy, a fattening pen, and a corncrib. Immediately downriver a *pigeonnier* and a small barn that served as a blacksmith shop are near the road. The hospital is set back facing a double row of eight—originally ten—midcentury brick slave cabins, which parallel the water between the hospital and the cotton gin. The store, built around 1890, is at the edge of the road, just below the hospital.

Oakland's layout too had the cabins facing the river (Figure 4). Oakland's original house and early garden remain, along with most of its nineteenth-century outbuildings. The privy and the kitchen, both subsequently moved, at first stood to the rear of the house. Along the rear-yard fence line are the carpenter's shed, the setting pen for the chickens, the chicken coop, a storage shed, the fattening pen for the pigs, and the washhouse. The stable lies slightly beyond the rear fence. The store, converted from an earlier structure to meet a new need after the Civil War, faces the road, and behind it is the carriage house. Two *pigeonniers,* one close to the carriage house, the other beyond the stable, are in the field beside the house. Also standing in the field are two barns, some sheds, and another coop. Of the state's plantations, none has its yard complex and garden more intact than Oakland.

A fourth plantation layout, uncommon in Louisiana along the Mississippi and the bayous but not in other parts of the South, is evident at Canebrake, on the Mississippi in Concordia Parish (Figure 5). Built around 1840, the main house survives with the dependencies constructed for it over the following twenty years: six slave dwellings, a barn, and a chicken house. Two rows of slave houses, one to the right and rear of the main house and the other to the left and rear of it, extend toward the back of the property. Like most of the agricultural land in the parish, Canebrake was owned by an absentee landlord from Natchez, across the river.[5] Like the owner, the layout was more closely tied to Mississippi than to Louisiana.

Since the outbuildings of few plantations survive, we must rely on documents and pictorial records for our knowledge of the most extensive villages of dependencies of the eighteenth and nineteenth centuries. Among the best-known pictorial records from either century is a series of landscapes that the architect and civil engineer Marie Adrien Persac painted between 1857 and 1861.[6] In Persac's paintings the main house was normally the focal point, but many of the outbuildings are also visible. Some buildings were clustered within the fences of the yard and were part of the running of the house; others, outside the residential complex, played a role in the production of cash crops. In the 1720s, only the barns, indigo sheds, cabins, and bell tower stood outside

5.   D. Clayton James, *Antebellum Natchez* (Baton Rouge, 1968), 148.

6.   There are public collections of Persac's landscapes at the Louisiana State University Museum of Art and at the Louisiana State Museum, in New Orleans. The Shadows-on-the-Teche holds two views of the Shadows. The major collections of Persac's urban images are in the Historic New Orleans Collection and the New Orleans Notarial Archives.

FIGURE 6   Marie Adrien Persac, *Palo Alto Plantation, ca.* 1857–1861. At Palo Alto plantation, in Ascension Parish, *ca.* 1850, the wood-frame sugarhouse stood in the fields behind the house, with two rows of slave cabins and the overseer's house to the side; another row of cabins stood much farther away from the main house. To the left of the house stood the kitchen, hidden by trees in the painting, and another small house with wood grilles on the front gallery. To the right were a *pigeonnier* and the schoolhouse, shown with curtains. A shed stood at the boat landing, and the sugarhouse is visible to the rear of the painting. Plantations all had bells; they were positioned, as here, by the overseer's house or to the rear of the big house.

Private collection

the palisade around the house, but by the mid–nineteenth century, the outlying structures serving agricultural operations might include not only the slave cabins, plantation bell, and barns but also the overseer's house, wagon sheds, corncribs, sawmills, sugarhouses, and cotton gins. The fences around, or at least in front of, the houses were decorative and set apart the house, kitchen, privies, cisterns, and washhouses. The yard often included *garçonnières, pigeonniers,* schoolhouses, and offices. Even a romantic cottage or a dollhouse for the children could gain a place in the yard, as could quarters for the house slaves, chicken houses, dairies, doghouses, and carriage houses.

A letter written in 1860 by a member of the Lemann family, of Palo Alto, on Bayou Lafourche in Ascension Parish, mentioned that, besides the house, built around 1850, and a sugarhouse, the property included a "sawmill, cotton gin, machinery, negro cabins, outhouses, etc. etc." The existence of a sawmill on the plantation indicates that there was logging in the back swamp, and the provision of both a sugarhouse and a cotton gin confirms that there was a planting of more than one crop. A letter written in 1867 added that "the place contains a fine dwelling house, stables, corn houses, corn mill, laborers houses etc."[7] The list of outbuildings for a plantation could go on indefinitely, since a planter really could have an outbuilding for everything, but the buildings that these letters refer to are the most likely ones. Persac's painting of Palo Alto shows the road, fences, storage house, kitchen, big house, *pigeonnier,* sugarhouse, school, bell, and overseer's house, as well as a double row of cabins (Figure 6). Leading away from the bayou,

7.   Bernard Lemann, *The Lemann Family* (New Orleans, 1965), 37–41. Jacob Lemann's letter of January 14, 1867, valued a cotton gin at a thousand dollars and a sawmill at two thousand. His letter of February 1, 1867, valued the house at three thousand dollars and the wooden sugarhouse with steam engine at six.

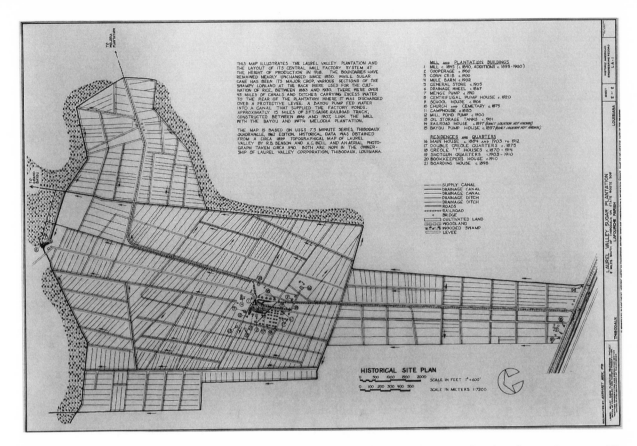

THIS MAP ILLUSTRATES THE LAUREL VALLEY PLANTATION AND THE LAYOUT OF ITS CENTRAL MILL FACTORY SYSTEM AT THE HEIGHT OF PRODUCTION IN 1918. THE BOUNDARIES HAVE REMAINED NEARLY UNCHANGED SINCE 1850. WHILE SUGAR CANE HAS BEEN ITS MAJOR CROP, VARIOUS SECTIONS OF THE SWAMPY LOWLAND AT THE BACK WERE USED FOR THE CULTIVATION OF RICE. BETWEEN 1883 AND 1930, THERE WERE OVER 43 MILES OF CANALS AND DITCHES CARRYING EXCESS WATER TO THE REAR OF THE PLANTATION WHERE IT WAS DISCHARGED OVER A PROTECTIVE LEVEE. A BAYOU PUMP FED WATER INTO A CANAL THAT SUPPLIED THE FACTORY PONDS. APPROXIMATELY 15 MILES OF 3 FT. GAUGE RAILROAD TRACK, CONSTRUCTED BETWEEN 1896 AND 1907 LINK THE MILL WITH THE BAYOU AND WITH MELODIA PLANTATION.

THE MAP IS BASED ON USGS 7.5 MINUTE SERIES, THIBODAUX QUADRANGLE, 1962 EDITION. HISTORICAL DATA WAS OBTAINED FROM A CIRCA 1899 TOPOGRAPHICAL MAP OF LAUREL VALLEY BY R.B. BENSON AND A.C. BELL AND AN AERIAL PHOTOGRAPH TAKEN CIRCA 1940. BOTH ARE NOW IN THE OWNERSHIP OF LAUREL VALLEY CORPORATION, THIBODAUX, LOUISIANA.

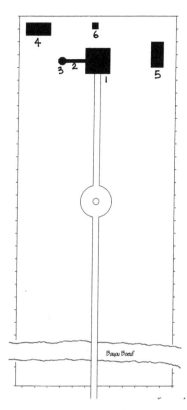

FIGURE 8   Oak Hall, Avoyelles Parish, 1923, plan. The plan is that of a country house with elaborate gardens. Key: 1, house; 2, pergola; 3, gazebo; 4, garage; 5, servants' house; 6, generator house. Not to scale.

LSU School of Architecture. Drawn by David Connich.

main. The brick sugarhouse and thirteen cabins date from the 1850s. Fire destroyed the original house from the 1850s, and it was not rebuilt until 1884. In the 1880s prosperity returned, and most of the tenant houses date from that decade. Laurel Valley plantation reached its largest size and greatest production in the first quarter of the twentieth century, profiting from the sugar booms from the 1890s to the mid-1920s. The great changes of the early twentieth century were the introduction of the narrow-gauge plantation railroad to haul cane to the mill and the expansion of the sugarhouse.

Laurel Valley ran as an industrial village amid fields of sugarcane. Even in the twentieth century, it was clearly an operation continuing from the nineteenth century. Oak Hall, in Avoyelles Parish, was a plantation for the new century. The house, surrounded by fields of sugarcane like its precursors, is a country house without a village of outbuildings (Figure 8). The owner sent his cane to the nearby Meeker Mill, built in 1911 and 1912 by midwestern investors, and the workers lived off the plantation (Chapter 6, Figure 16). In addition to the main house with its attached pergola and gazebo, this country seat includes a generator house, a garage, and a servants' cottage—trappings of the twentieth century—as well as an extensive ornamental garden. It followed the pattern of the suburban estate, not the plantation village of the past.

THE PLANTATION HOUSE

The plantation house was the big house, the residence of the owner. Whatever the house's size, it was always the largest one on the plantation. Some were little larger than the less cramped quarter cabins, and others were mansions that could rival any in America. They were humble or grandiose, plain or stylish, according to the wealth and inclinations of the owner. Some were log, for wealth and grandeur did not necessarily go hand in hand. Indivisible from their plantation, they were called by the same name. Plantations by their very nature required money to invest, and no one who owned land and slaves was poor. For most, the big house was the outward and visible sign of the planter's wealth, cultural taste, and social status. In 1818, one writer observed that "upon the banks of the Mississippi many of the sugar and cotton planters lived in edifices, where, within and without are exhibited all that artifice aided by wealth can produce."[8]

The observation would have been apt as early as the middle of the eighteenth century. The house built between 1750 and 1754 at Mon Plaisir, across the river from the Place d'Armes, in New Orleans, was truly My Pleasure for its proud owner, the Chevalier de Pradel, whose pride in it is apparent in his voluminous business and family correspondence with his brothers in France. The French planter furnished his residence in splendor. Although he em-

8. William Darby, *The Emigrant's Guide* (New York, 1818), 61.

ployed an architect for the plans, he followed precedent in plantation construction by getting the bricks, lumber, and shingles for the building from his own property. Despite that, he wrote in May, 1750, the costs were great, because the wages of the workers were high and the materials dear, especially the glass and hardware he imported from France. He complained that "he who builds lies, or building costs are deceptive: it always costs more in the end than one thought it would at first."[9]

Measured in the French foot of 12 3/4 inches, the house was 117 feet wide and 48 feet deep, including the galleries on all sides. An ell attached to the rear gallery extended back about 90 feet and included the dining room, the offices, the kitchen, and the laundry, as well as the room for making wax and candles from the wax myrtles on the plantation. In the center of the facade a "large and imposing flight of steps," in brick, led up to the front of the gallery. De Pradel assured his brothers that the "galleries are a great comfort to a country like this one . . . [and] although we are in a different world than France, we like our ease, and we look after our comforts as well as we can."[10]

In November, 1750, de Pradel wrote, "I agree that I did wrong in building it so large, and beautiful. . . . But the folly is made. . . . I have pleasurably occupied myself and I work every day with equal pleasure towards its embellishment." The main room was "very well proportioned," 24 by 26 feet, and 14 feet in height. It was wainscoted and had a ceiling of very fine painted wood. On each side there were two fine windows and what de Pradel described as a pair of doors but we would call french doors; the two-leaf door was 5 feet wide and 9 1/2 feet in height, "all panelled in glass" and painted. In May, 1754, after de Pradel had been living in the house for several months, he could conclude that it was "without doubt the most beautiful and comfortable here, and would pass for a small and very handsome château in our provinces." In letters dated the following year, he added that he covered the floor of the gallery with canvas that was painted to preserve it from rot and he exulted that the wooden columns supporting the gallery were "architecturally correct and . . . painted to look like white marble." Most likely these were Tuscan colonnettes, as in the Intendance design of 1749 (Plate B).[11]

West Indian was the appellation nineteenth-century travelers most often employed in their journals to describe the style of houses like Mon Plaisir.[12] The style was already the preferred one for Louisiana plantation houses in de Pradel's time, and it remained that for the rest of the eighteenth century and into the early nineteenth century. Many of the surviving houses in the style

9. Jean C. de Pradel, *Le Chevalier de Pradel: Vie d'un colon français en Louisiane au XVIII siècle,* ed. A. Baillardel and A. Prioult (Paris, 1928), 181; "Correspondence of the Chevalier de Pradel," trans. Henri Delville Sinclair (Works Progress Administration of Louisiana, 1937–38), 22.

10. De Pradel, *Le Chevalier,* 184; "Correspondence of the Chevalier de Pradel," 24.

11. De Pradel, *Le Chevalier,* 222–23, 236, 241, 245; "Correspondence of the Chevalier de Pradel," 46–47, 57, 60, 64.

12. Thomas Ashe, *Travels in America, Performed in 1806* (3 vols.; London, 1808), III, 11.

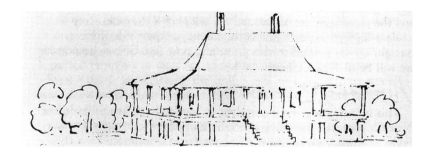

FIGURE 9 John H. B. Latrobe, *A Typical Louisiana Raised Cottage,* 1834. Latrobe commented that all the houses were built after the same model and that he could not better describe them than by this sketch.

Maryland Historical Society, Baltimore

date from after the Louisiana Purchase, in 1803, when the United States acquired the colony. In Louisiana, both the style and the traditional construction are now more commonly called Creole.

Creole plantation houses, like their owners, stemmed from an Old World lineage. The extensive gallery is the most prominent feature that the New World contributed. The uniting of galleries and the traditional steeply pitched French hip roof produced the distinctive double pitch of Creole roofs. The drawing Dumont de Montigny made in 1731 of the house on Concession plantation shows a simple dwelling, three rooms wide, with only steps leading to the front door—a house of France transposed to the Mississippi. The French had a long tradition of timber-frame construction, or *colombage.* The term *Norman truss* used for mortised, tenoned, and pegged roof framing recognizes its association with northern France. The colony's first permanent buildings, both official and residential, were timber-frame, at least one of the frames having been disassembled in the earlier French colony at Biloxi and reassembled in Louisiana (Chapter 1, Figure 6).

The title of West Indian had its basis primarily in the galleries that the French in Louisiana constructed, since these were already common in the Caribbean, where sugar first made planters wealthy. Two-story houses with two levels of galleries and a double-pitched roof had already appeared in the sugar-producing states of northeast Brazil by the seventeenth century. While traveling up the river below New Orleans in 1834, John H. B. Latrobe, the son of Benjamin Henry Latrobe, observed that "the farmhouses, or plantation houses rather, in this part of the world appear to have been built, all of them, after the same model. . . . The climate requires all the shade that can be procured, and to obtain it the body of the building is surrounded by galleries" (Figure 9). C. C. Robin, in his *Voyage to Louisiana,* recounting a visit in 1802, regarded galleries as the distinctive feature of local houses: "These wide Galleries have several advantages. First, they prevent the sun's rays from striking the walls of the house and thus to keep them cool. Also, they form a convenient and pleasant spot upon which to promenade during the day (one, of course, goes to the side away from the sun), one can eat or entertain there, and very often during the hot summer nights one sleeps there." There were no interior passage halls in Creole houses. Instead, galleries served as passageways and stair halls, besides being living and sleeping areas.[13] The wainscoting and highly decorative chair rails on some galleries and loggias continued to the exterior the aesthetics of the interior, for these were indispensable living rooms much of the year.

If Sebastiano Serlio's "On Domestic Architecture" suggests roots for Louisiana's cottage architecture in the dwellings of urban Mediterranean artisans (see above, pp. 48–49), it also points up the relationship between those less modest houses and Louisiana architecture. The plans and elevations for two urban Creole cottages, the Troxler Cottage, built around 1800 in New Orleans (Chapter 2, Figure 15) and the Lemee House, built around 1830 in Natchitoches (Chapter 2, Figure 14), closely resemble those Serlio presented for a middle-class farmhouse (Figure 10B2) and a merchant's house (Figure 11).[14] Serlio's drawings of buildings suitable for peasants, artisans, merchants, and farmers improved types that were traditional in his time. His models for high-style architecture, by contrast, adopted newer Renaissance forms inspired by Rome and conceived of as suitable for the nobility. But even in his simpler houses for France, he combined the local architectural vocabulary, such as steeply pitched roofs, with Roman forms, such as the loggia.

Serlio also provided the design of a farmhouse meant for a rich farmer (Figure 10C3). At first glance, the elevation looks like that of a two-story Creole house framed by a pair of *pigeonniers*. A closer examination, however, reveals that the house is flanked by wings and the ground-floor gallery is part of the colonnade. Still, the resemblance is close: posts with brackets, steep hip roof, and central chimney. The plan of a full gallery and three rooms across the front, with an end chamber divided into a pair of smaller rooms, is familiar in Louisiana, again confirmed by the region's reliance on a long Mediterranean tradition, both directly and by way of the Caribbean.[15]

13.   John H. B. Latrobe, *Southern Travels,* ed. Samuel Wilson, Jr. (New Orleans, 1986), 38; C. C. Robin, *Voyage to Louisiana,* ed. and trans. Stuart O. Landry, Jr. (New Orleans, 1966), 122; F. Fortescue Cuming, *Sketches of a Tour to the Western Country* (Pittsburgh, 1810), 311.

14.   Sebastiano Serlio, *On Domestic Architecture: Different Dwellings from the Meanest Level to the Most Ornate Palace . . .—the Sixteenth-Century Manuscript of Book VI in the Avery Library of Columbia University,* ed. Myra Nan Rosenfeld, intro. James S. Ackerman (New York, 1978), Plate I. Plates I, III, and V are of drawings on Italian paper, showing that Serlio (*ca.* 1497–1554) had begun his composition on domestic buildings before 1541, when he became architect to François I. Serlio designed only a few notable buildings, attaining fame primarily for his writings. He was one of a number of artists and architects, as famous as Leonardo da Vinci, who in the sixteenth century came to the French court, the principal source of the Renaissance. Serlio was the first to produce a treatise on housing for the lower classes, the builders of which included increasingly wealthy farmers, merchants, and professionals, who constructed both fine residences for themselves and rental housing for laborers. Domestic housing was a matter of interest throughout Europe at the time, and the architecture of the Italian Renaissance that the French crown introduced ultimately diffused into the countryside. James S. Ackerman, in *Distance Points: Studies in Theory and Renaissance Art and Architecture* (Cambridge, Mass., 1991), 303–24, presents a concise account of the continuity of the classical villa from its Roman origins through the Renaissance.

15.   Jay D. Edwards, "The Origins of Creole Architecture," *Winterthur Portfolio,* XXIX (1994), 155–89; Jay D. Edwards, *Louisiana's Remarkable French Vernacular Architecture, 1700–1900* (Baton Rouge, 1988); Jay D. Edwards, "Architectural Creolization: The Role of Africans in America's

FIGURE 10 Farmhouses, in Sebastiano Serlio's "On Domestic Architecture," *ca.* 1537–1549, Plate I. A1, for the poor, has two rooms of irregular size and a front gallery and hip roof similar to those of houses in Louisiana occupied by the early settlers and slaves. B2, for the middle class, has the *en suite* plan of central parlor, adjacent rooms, and loggia flanked by *cabinets* that is similar to Louisiana plantation and urban plans. C3, for the rich, shares many characteristics with Creole plantation houses raised on high basements. In Louisiana, pairs of *pigeonniers* sometimes give the appearance of a pair of wings, framing the approach to the house.

Avery Architectural and Fine Arts Library, Columbia University in the City of New York.

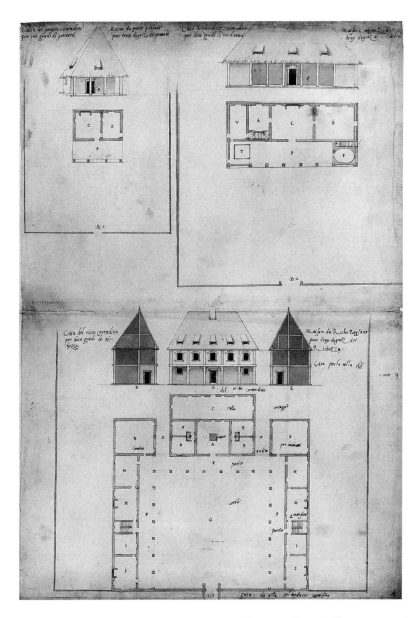

The prevailing feature is rooms *en suite,* that is, with no hall passage, and even more typically, *enfilade,* or in a line. In describing a notorious murder near Opelousas, Robin drew the plan of the three-room-wide house where it occurred and the path of the fatal bullet from one end—diagonally through two open doors—to the other. The house probably looked very like Latrobe's sketch (Figure 9), and the plan is the mirror image of Magnolia Mound, in Baton Rouge, as it was built in the 1790s. The houses in both Opelousas and

Vernacular Architecture" (Typescript). In these seminal studies, Edwards explores both the sources of Creole architecture and its diffusion. The Spanish most likely introduced the open loggia to Louisiana, since no clear instances of it predate the Spanish regime and it is found in Spanish colonies by the late sixteenth century.

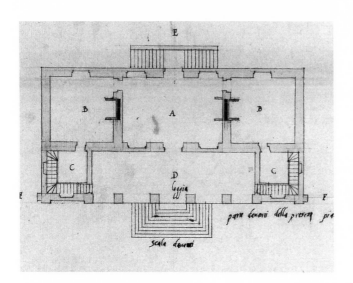
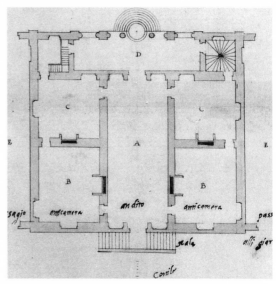

FIGURE 11 Merchants' houses, in Serlio's "On Domestic Architecture," Plates III, V. Both plans are similar to plans for the cores of symmetrical Louisiana houses with loggias. On the left, the steps from the loggia are in the same form as those at the front of Mon Plaisir and Concession.

Avery Architectural and Fine Arts Library, Columbia University in the City of New York.

FIGURE 12 Chrétien Point, St. Landry Parish, 1830, facade and principal floor plan. The HABS architects located the building contract during their research.

HABS, 1940, Library of Congress

Baton Rouge had peripteral galleries—galleries on all four sides—and one end of the building divided into two small rooms. The house at Destrehan, in St. Charles Parish, as completed in 1790, is three rooms wide, the house at Homeplace four (Chapter 1, Figure 30). Both are two rooms deep and two stories high with peripteral galleries at both levels. Not every plantation house in this style had all these galleries. The house at Chrétien Point, built in St. Landry Parish in 1830, has galleries only across the front. The rear open loggia seen in earlier plans has here become an enclosed stair hall (Figure 12). A small house using this plan could be only two rooms wide and one room deep, with an open loggia and *cabinets,* as at the Petit Pierre House (Kleinpeter House), in Baton Rouge (Figure 13), or three or four rooms wide, as at Maison Chenal, in Pointe Coupee Parish (Figure 14). These houses were modest in size, but it was possible to expand the same plan to a width of five

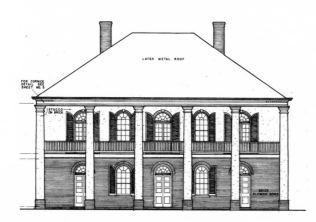
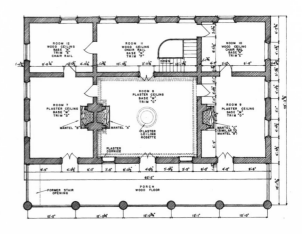

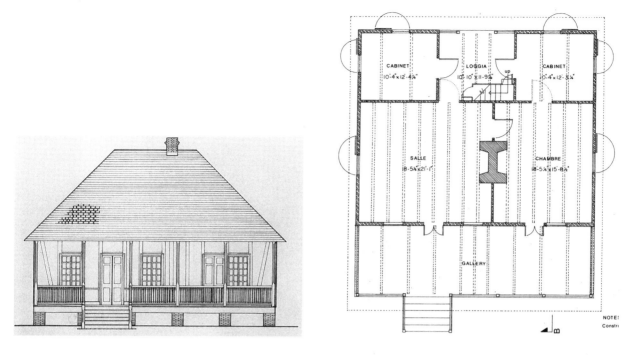

FIGURE 13 Petit Pierre House (Kleinpeter House), Baton Rouge, *ca.* 1815, facade and principal floor plan. Moved only a few miles from its site facing the road and the edge of the bluffs facing toward the Mississippi, the house now faces away from the bluff. The land along the bluffs was settled by German families and was known as the Dutch (Deutsch) Highlands.

Courtesy of Jay D. Edwards, Fred B. Kniffen Cultural Resources Laboratory, Department of Geography and Anthropology, LSU

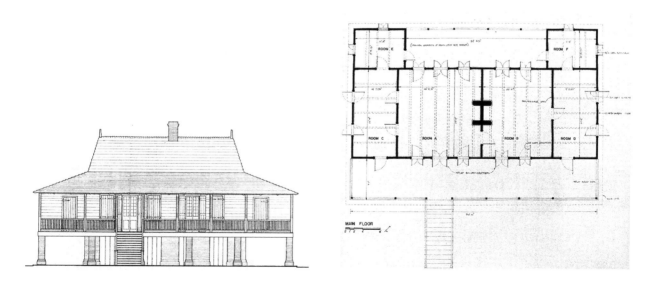

FIGURE 14 Maison Chenal, Pointe Coupee Parish, *ca.* 1790, facade and principal floor plan. The house has been moved from another site in the parish to the Chenal, the lower end of the cutoff of the Mississippi that resulted from a change of the river's course in 1722. In the new location, the house has been raised to include a high basement instead of the original lower piers.

Courtesy of Jay D. Edwards, Fred B. Kniffen Cultural Resources Laboratory, Department of Geography and Anthropology, LSU

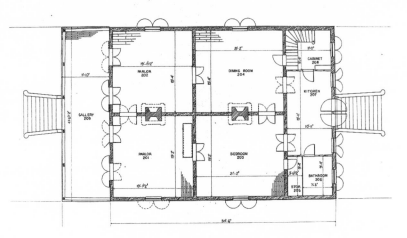

FIGURE 15   Lombard, Orleans Parish (now New Orleans), *ca.* 1810, facade and principal floor plan. The interior detailing is Federal.

HABS, 1983, Louisiana State Archives

large rooms, with sizable *cabinets,* as happened at the much grander house at Whitney plantation, in St. John the Baptist Parish (Chapter 1, Figure 32). Robin observed that another way of letting houses that started out three rooms wide gain two rooms in width was by filling in the side porches, and this is another possibility at Whitney.[16] But some houses began with smaller rooms the width of the porches around a core of larger principal rooms, though the plans for wider houses were not necessarily elaborations of smaller plans. It is equally likely that larger residences adapted the *enfilade* plans from villas and palaces, becoming diminutive versions of them.

The smaller one-story houses such as Magnolia Mound are called raised cottages. The four-room cottage plan so common in New Orleans also appears as a raised cottage. The plan of 1218–1220 Burgundy Street there (Chapter 2, Figure 10), with its four rooms, loggia, and pair of *cabinets,* is similar to that of the once-rural Lombard, in Orleans Parish, which is raised on a high basement with a gallery across the front (Figure 15). This plan could be adapted to include a central hall leading from the front porch to the rear loggia. By midcentury the central hall, introduced by the Americans, had become common. (In Louisiana, speakers of English were called American; the term *Anglo-American* became current later.) Two houses built around 1840 for two sisters at Crescent plantation, in St. James Parish, have central halls despite retaining their loggias and *cabinets,* central chimneys, and french doors.[17] Greek Revival cottages of the 1850s such as Palo Alto continue the combination of central hall and the Creole *cabinet.* The *en suite* plan of three rooms across, which was often symmetrical, likewise lent itself to the inclusion of a central hall. In such a case, the central parlor was reduced to a mere passage as at Labatut, in Pointe Coupee Parish (Figure 16). An asymmetrical

16.   Robin, *Voyage to Louisiana,* 122.
17.   Robicheaux House and Hymel House, St. James Parish, *ca.* 1840, in HABS, 1983.

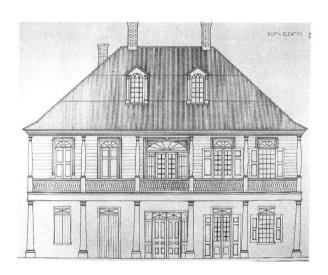
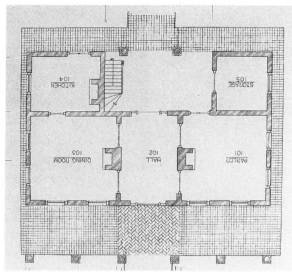

FIGURE 16   Labatut, Pointe Coupee Parish, *ca.* 1810, facade and ground floor plan. This is one of the finest Federal houses in the state. The usual central room was narrowed to a passage hall, but access to the upper floor remains by the stairs on the open loggias.

HABS, 1985, Louisiana State Archives

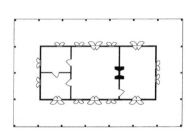
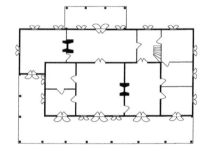
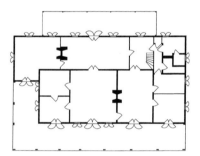

FIGURE 17   Magnolia Mound, floor plans, 1790s (left), *ca.* 1815 (middle), present (right). The house was remodeled after the marriage of Constance Joyce and Armand Duplantier in 1802 and before his death in 1827. An umbrella roof replaced the earlier double-pitched roof as part of the remodeling and enlargement. The original framing system was raised over the newly installed cove ceiling. Chamfered posts, most likely from the gallery dating from the 1790s, supported the new roof. The original double-pitched roof was unusual in attaching the porch to the frame within a few feet of the top of the frame rather than as in Latrobe's sketch (Figure 10).

Courtesy of Magnolia Mound Plantation, Baton Rouge. Drawn by George Fore.

plan could accommodate a passage hall, but not with grace.[18] A local modification of the full-length central hall was a short one leading directly to a rear central dining room. Wartelle, also known as Moundville, in St. Landry Parish, has the dining room at the end of such a hall, in an adaptation of Creole plans such as that employed at Magnolia Mound (Figure 17). Dining rooms continued in this location through the 1850s, and Armitage, in Terrebonne Parish, has this arrangement in an otherwise totally Greek Revival raised cottage.

The Creole plantation house has a heavy timber frame, mortised and

18.   Oakland, Natchitoches Parish, *ca.* 1820–21, in HABS, 1987. The Prudhommes decided to enlarge the house while it was under construction and added a hall from the front gallery to the rear loggia and another tier of rooms. The result is a three-room-wide building with an off-center full hall. An addition built at Butler-Greenwood, in West Feliciana Parish, around 1855 but now demolished had a similar layout.

tenoned together, and a steeply pitched heavy frame roof. The frame rests on brick piers, horizontal sections of cypress logs, or a brick high basement, often so high that the house becomes two stories, with the timber-frame principal living space on the second floor, a true *piano nobile.* Such a house has a dining room in the center of the brick lower story, but otherwise this area is generally given over to service and storage.

Another distinctive feature of this plantation house is the roofline. In the middle and late eighteenth century, the roof commonly had a double pitch. In the nineteenth century a single large hip roof, also called an umbrella roof, covered both rooms and galleries. A flare at the eaves was a refinement also frequently seen on French roofs. Structurally, this was possible through the installation of a false rafter, and the angled overhang gave further protection to the side walls. There are a number of examples of double-pitched roofs later modified to umbrella and still later to side-gable roofs. The umbrella roof sheds water more effectively than the double-pitched, but it is moot whether efficiency or taste prompted the change. The tumultuous winds of all-too-frequent hurricanes necessitated roof repairs, and damaged roofs may simply have been rebuilt in the current fashion, as was often the case in the early twentieth century.

Typically the main story of a Creole plantation house was timber frame, *colombage,* with fill between the timbers. Most common was *bousillage,* a mixture of mud, retted spanish moss, and animal hair shaped into loaves and laid, from the bottom up, on laths or slats between the posts. In some cases, it was inserted after the exterior clapboards had been nailed to the frame.[19] In *briquette entre poteaux* construction, bricks were laid up between the vertical posts. With both techniques, the surface was usually covered completely, frequently with plaster on the interior and stucco or wood clapboards on the outside. New Orleans, with its number of brickyards, preferred brick nogging, but the rural preference was for *bousillage,* even when bricks were made on the place. Only rarely did a Creole house have masonry construction for both stories.[20]

The Tuscan column was the established form for late-eighteenth-century plantation houses. As early as the sixteenth century, Palladio especially recommended the Tuscan column for "rustic" buildings. Colonnettes however were far more typical for the galleries of the principal floor. Turned on a lathe, colonnettes were a robust vase shape with brackets often forming a graceful transition to the roof. Typically, chamfered posts took the place of columns and colonnettes on lesser buildings and rear galleries. Square balus-

19. Aillet House, West Baton Rouge Parish, *ca.* 1830. Sid Gray observed this technique in his restoration. The house is now located at the West Baton Rouge Parish Museum, in Port Allen.

20. Samuel Wilson, Jr., *The Architecture of Colonial Louisiana* (Lafayette, La., 1987), 378. Only the ruins of the house at De la Ronde plantation, in St. Bernard Parish (*ca.* 1805), survive, but both stories were brick.

ters were common for the railings, but more fanciful and stylish geometric designs sometimes created the effect of chinoiserie.[21]

Little is known about the builders and architects of the plantation houses, including the French engineer-architects. Building methods were rooted in tradition, and master builders, many of mixed heritage, constructed houses whose model was so clearly understood that only a few words described a major contract. The building contract of 1787 for Destrehan survives and states that a mulatto named Charles, a free man of color, was the builder-contractor for the owner, Robin de Logny:

> Charles, carpenter, wood worker, and mason by trade, obligates himself to construct for the said Sieur Robin de Logny, a house of sixty feet in length, by thirty five in width . . . semi-doubles, raised ten feet on brick piers with a surrounding gallery of twelve feet in width, planked top and bottom, five chimneys which shall be contracted in the said house, two of which double and one single. The gallery piers shall be of wood or of brick pier, with doors, windows, sash and panelled doors inside, balustrade all around the gallery, casings at the doors of communication inside; three dormers above the three principal doors of the front, and one on the rear, with the roof in full over the body of the building and finally all the wood-work necessary for the said house. . . . Sieur Robin de Logny has given to the said Charles on account on the said enterprise, one untrained Negro from his plantation named l'Eveiller (Rouser) with a cow and her calf . . . Sieur Robin de Logny obligating himself besides to the said Charles, fifty quarts of rice in chaff, and fifty quarts of corn in husks, half this year and the other half next year, one hundred piastres at the end of the said work. The said Robin de Logny obligates himself besides, to furnish to the said Charles, two Negro wood squarers [hewers], three other Negroes from his plantation, who are those named Francois, Louis and Jean Louis, and one other Negro to help him with the masonry and to furnish him all the materials necessary for the construction of the said house, the wood squared, the rafters moulded, and the shingles dressed, the whole delivered on the place, and the said Negroes listed at his disposal, until the finishing of the said work.[22]

The inventory made in 1792 at the planter's death further describes the house as "raised ten feet in masonry containing six rooms on the ground floor and six on the upper, the main floor twelve feet between sills, built in *colombage, . . .* having a twelve foot wide surrounding gallery and roofed in shingles."[23]

21.   Andrea Palladio, *The Four Books of Architecture* (1738; rpr. New York, 1964), I, 14 (translated from *I quattro libri dell'architectturo* [Venice, 1570]). Pitot House, facing Bayou St. John in New Orleans, has a balustrade reconstructed to match the X-shaped originals.

22.   Building Contract of Charles, Free Mulatto, with Robin de Logny, in St. Charles Parish Notarial Book, 1787, January 3, 1787, No. 750, folios 89–91, translated by Wilson in *The Architecture of Colonial Louisiana,* 370–71.

23.   Inventory of the Estate of Antoine Robert Robin de Logny, December 14, 1792, in St. Charles Parish Notarial Book, 1792–1793, No. 376, folio 373. William de Marigny Hyland transcribed and translated the French in "Destrehan Manor House, St. Charles Parish, Louisiana," II, 194; a translation appears as well in *The Architecture of Colonial Louisiana,* by Wilson, 371.

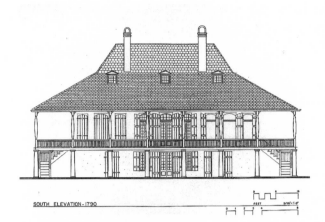

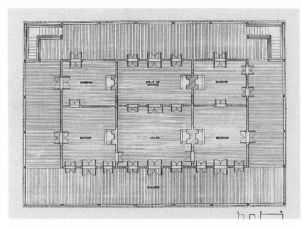

FIGURE 18   Destrehan, St. Charles Parish, 1790, facade and principal floor plan
HABS, 1989, Louisiana State Archives

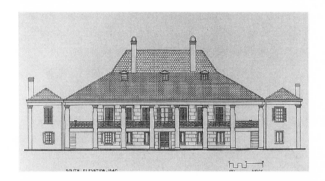

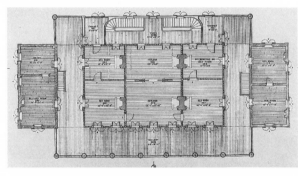

FIGURE 19   Destrehan, *ca.* 1840, facade
and principal floor plan.

HABS, 1989, Louisiana State Archives

Built between 1787 and 1790, the house and plantation were purchased in
1802 by Jean Noel Destrehan, who in 1786 had married Robin de Logny's
daughter.

As completed in 1790, Destrehan was a stylish house, and much of the
eighteenth century structure remains (Figure 18). The double-pitched roof
with its Norman trusses survives intact, but the bracketed colonnettes, marbleized around 1800 like Mon Plaisir's, are encased in the columns and walls
of the 1840s remodeling (Figure 19). The arched openings of french doors
and casement windows survive in the frame, and the beaded beams and
board ceilings are covered by the lower Greek Revival ceiling. A pair of sash
windows between the center rooms on the upper floor is hidden in the walls.
The masonry and *bousillage* remain. There were exterior stairs on the
peripteral gallery and tile in the ground-floor rooms. Destrehan is the largest
and earliest surviving Creole plantation house to be documented, but it is
only in the HABS drawings that its eighteenth-century appearance is apparent. The nineteenth century effected a major reworking in the Greek Revival
style. Colossal columns covered the single-story piers and colonnettes, the
rear gallery became an enclosed stair hall, the center rooms were changed

FIGURE 20   Magnolia Mound, Baton
Rouge, 1790s, *ca.* 1815.

*Courtesy of Magnolia Mound Plantation,
Baton Rouge. Photograph by Otis B.
Wheeler.*

FIGURE 20   Magnolia Mound, Baton
Rouge, 1790s, *ca.* 1815.

*Courtesy of Magnolia Mound Plantation,
Baton Rouge. Photograph by Otis B.
Wheeler.*

FIGURE 21   The parlor of Magnolia
Mound. The present ground and border
wallpapers are reproductions of the
original wallpapers used around 1815 and
found below later millwork.

*Courtesy of Magnolia Mound Plantation,
Baton Rouge. Photograph by Otis B. Wheeler.*

into a double parlor with pocket doors, and all the doors, mantels, and
moldings were replaced.

In Creole plantation houses most openings onto galleries were french
doors, but windows came into frequent use in the parlors at an early date.
The earliest windows were single or double casements, which hung like shutters from the side of the frame and opened in, whereas the shutters opened
out.[24] By 1800, double-hung sashes in the American manner replaced most
casement windows. The great majority of the Creole plantation houses
demonstrated a disinclination toward bilateral symmetry, with door and
window openings not lining up with the colonnettes. Dormers were evenly
spaced and admitted light and air only to large attics, not living space. Exposed beaded beams supported both wooden ceilings and the decking of the
galleries. Mantels were often as well made as furniture and expressed the
owner's aspirations to style.

As more and more Americans settled in Louisiana after the Louisiana
Purchase, the local architecture felt the imprint of neoclassical Federal and,
later, Greek Revival influences. Houses were built at once squarely in the
Creole world and squarely in the American world. Older houses were remodeled and enlarged in the latest styles.

Magnolia Mound, the present appearance of which dates from a remodeling around 1815 of a house of the 1790s, is a particularly fine example
of the wedding of Federal and Creole design (Figure 20). As part of the remodeling, the owners, the Duplantiers, literally raised the roof to install a
cove ceiling in the parlor (Figures 21, 22). It is the earliest ceiling of this type

24.   Madame John's Legacy has double casements, as did Destrehan as originally built. Maison
Chenal had single glazed casements (Figure 15).

FIGURE 22   Magnolia Mound, roof and
cove-ceiling framing. The truss system
was raised above the cove ceiling and
helped support the single-pitched
replacement roof. The octagonal
chamfered posts helped support the
new frame.

HABS, 1989, Louisiana State Archives

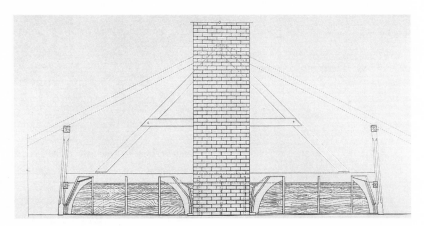

FIGURE 23   Magnolia Mound, side
elevation of mantels and overmantels in
parlor and bedchamber. The cove ceiling
of the parlor replaced a beaded beam
ceiling like that still in the bedchamber.

HABS, 1989, Louisiana State Archives

in the lower Mississippi River valley, and unlike most that came later, it and its elaborate cornice are entirely of wood, with the cove and ceiling originally wallpapered. The parlor's wraparound mantel with its paneled sides and overmantel is clearly Federal, as is that in the main bedroom on the other side of the double chimney (Figure 23).[25]

The fasces, or reeded, molding on the cornice comes from the Federal vocabulary, but the lozenge design on the overmantel is a Creole favorite that is repeated on the dining room cornice. Even with the Duplantiers' additions, Magnolia Mound clearly remains the sort of Creole house Robin described. Initially, the influence of the Federal style was principally in design motifs.

Another obvious innovation of the remodeled Magnolia Mound that later restorations and research have uncovered is the brilliant colors of the wallpaper and millwork. The wallpaper and border are of vivid yellows and ochers in a brocade pattern printed on a vermicelli ground. The subdued gray and ivory of the millwork is enhanced by subtle shadows of prussian blue, and the doors are grained. This vibrant scheme is in distinct contrast with the more traditional white plaster walls and gray moldings and beaded beam ceilings of the house of the 1790s. The exterior is white, with green solid paneled shutters.[26] With few exceptions, surviving Creole plantation houses were painted white on the exterior, and interior plaster walls were left unpainted or limewashed white.

The other prominent American Federal influence on Creole architecture, the central hall, with its insistent bilateral symmetry, found less favor in Louisiana plantation houses than design motifs did. For another generation, Louisianians preferred not to sacrifice living area for the privacy the hall provided. The traditional *en suite* plan prevailed into the 1830s, even in such a model of new tastes as Shadows-on-the-Teche, in New Iberia. There were

25.   Only the parlor and bed-chamber mantels are original to the house; the other two are early-nineteenth-century replacements of the lost originals.
26.   George Fore, *Magnolia Mound* (Raleigh, N.C., 1994), 16–23.

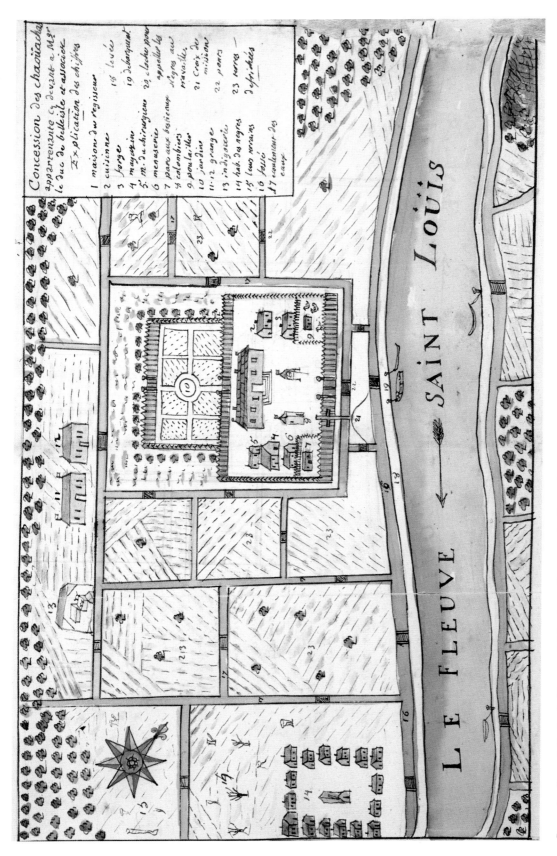

PLATE A François Benjamin Dumont de Montigny, *Concession des Chaouaches, ca.* 1737. Concession indigo plantation, in Orleans Parish, was established about 1721. KEY: 1, overseer's house; 2, kitchen; 3, blacksmith shop; 4, storehouse; 5, doctor's house; 6, carpenter shop; 7, cattle pen; 8, pigeon houses; 9, chicken house; 10, garden; 11, 12, barns; 13, indigo manufactory; 14, dwellings for blacks; 15, land for blacks; 16, ditches; 17, water drainage; 18, levee; 19, boat landing; 20, plantation bell; 21, mission cross; 22, bridges across ditches; 23, cleared fields.

Photo courtesy of Edward E. Ayer Collection, The Newberry Library, Chicago

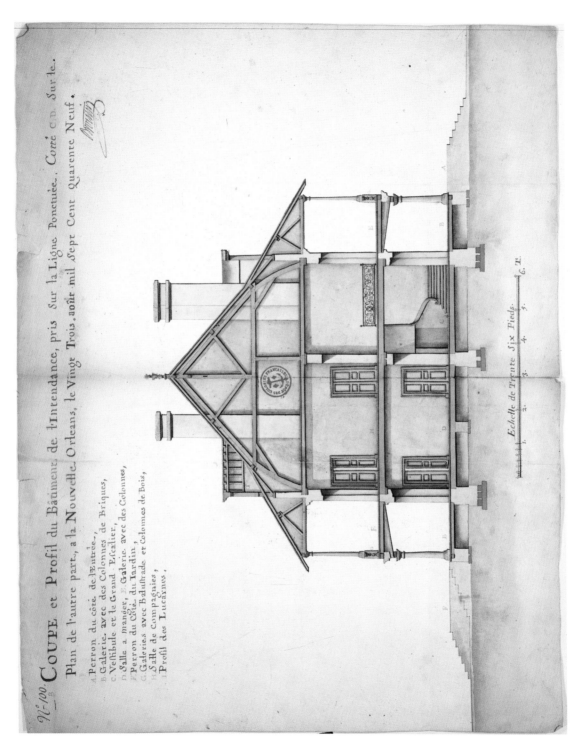

Nᵒ ⁄100.

COUPE et Profil du Bâtiment de l'Intendance, pris sur la Ligne Ponctuée. Côté C.D. sur le
Plan de l'autre part, a la Nouvelle Orleans, le Vingt Trois, août mil Sept Cent Quarente Neuf.

A.Perron du côté de l'Entrée.,
B.Galerie avec des Colonnes de Briques,
C.Vestibule et le Grand Escalier,
D.Salle a manger, E.Galerie avec des Colonnes,
F.Perron du Côté du Jardin,
G.Galeries avec Balustrade et Colonnes de Bois,
H.Salle de Compagnies,
I.Profil des Lucarnes,

Echelle de Trente Six Pieds.

PLATE B   Ignace François Broutin, *Coupe et Profil du Bâtiment de l'Intendance*, 1749. Broutin's cross section for administrative offices in New Orleans, a plan never executed, is the earliest known drawing for a Louisiana building with two-storied galleries and a double-pitched roof. The gallery roofs were to connect to a traditional Norman truss.

Archives Nationales, Paris

PLATE C   Cottages on Villere Street
between Bienville and Custom House
(now Iberville) Streets, in New Orleans.
Built in the 1830s, this short row included
three two-room cottages, each with its own
entrance, yard, attic stairway, kitchen, and
privy. There was some sharing of cistern
and well, and an opening between two of
the rear rooms provided rental flexibility
by allowing two units to serve together as a
typical four-room Creole cottage.

*Drawing signed Cosnier, dated 1845, New
Orleans Notarial Archives, Plan Book 16,
folio 1.*

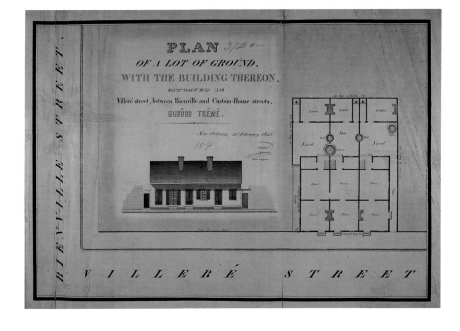

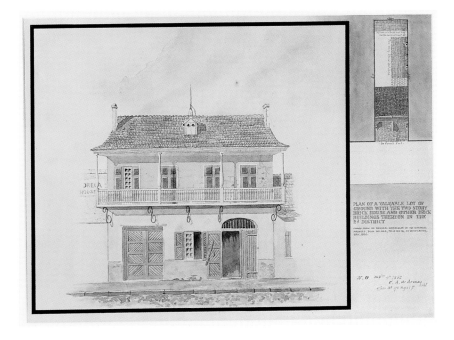

PLATE D   A watercolor by A. Boyd Cruise
of 722 Toulouse Street, New Orleans, 1955.
Louisiana was the only state in which the
HABS program engaged an artist to record
colors and details difficult to photograph.
This watercolor, however, is a copy of one
by C. A. de Armas in the New Orleans
Notarial Archives. Cruise painted it after
his work for the HABS program ended.
The Creole town house reflects its period,
the Spanish colonial era, in its tile roof and
projecting gallery supported by wrought-
iron brackets.

*Courtesy of the Historic New Orleans Collec-
tion (accession no. 1955.38).*

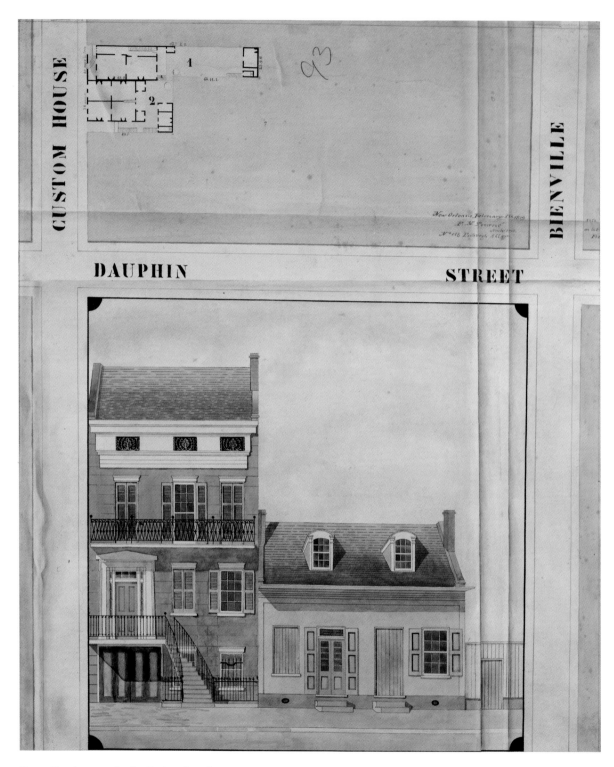

PLATE E A watercolor by Cruise of two houses on Custom House Street (now Iberville Street), in New Orleans, 1952. This rendition of a drawing from 1859 by F. N. Tourné in the New Orleans Notarial Archives contrasts a Greek Revival town house with a traditional Creole cottage. The larger, three-story red brick building had a stairway curving up to the entrance, a feature frequently encountered upriver in the American sector.

Courtesy of the Historic New Orleans Collection (accession no. 1988.107)

PLATE F   A watercolor by Cruise of Belle Grove, in Iberville Parish, 1938. Henry Howard, the architect, chose colors still visible here: lavender washed with pink for the walls, off-white for the columns, and olive green for the trim. The collapse of the rear wing revealed the white color scheme of the upper and lower central halls and the stair hall to the left. The small piazza to the right opens off the dining room.

Courtesy of the Historic New Orleans Collection (accession no. 1971.68)

PLATE G   Marie Adrien Persac, *Hope Estate Plantation, ca.* 1857. The house, in East Baton Rouge Parish, was built on a Creole plan with Federal details. Appearing here is a later ornamental fence of wooden pickets on a masonry base extending from the wrought-iron carriage and pedestrian gates to the octagonal *pigeonniers.*

Courtesy of Louisiana State University Museum of Art, Baton Rouge.

PLATE H   A watercolor by Cruise of one of the pair of *pigeonniers* that stood to the rear of the house on Uncle Sam plantation, in St. James Parish, 1938. The brick was painted, but not stuccoed and scored, to match the house.

Courtesy of the Historic New Orleans Collection (accession no. 1994.1.2)

PLATE I   A watercolor by Cruise of the Gauche House, on Esplanade Avenue, in New Orleans, *ca.* 1938. The cast iron balustrade and ornamentation of the eaves are notable in this Italianate villa.

Courtesy of the Historic New Orleans Collection (accession no. 1971.115).

PLATE J   A watercolor by Cruise of the Sixth Precinct Station House, in New Orleans, 1952. Designed by James Gallier in the early 1840s as the Jefferson Parish Courthouse Annex and Jail, the building recalls Egyptian temples. The lotus capitals resemble those on the United States Custom House, in New Orleans.

Courtesy of the Historic New Orleans Collection (accession no. 1952.31).

PLATE K   A watercolor by Cruise of the United States Custom House, in New Orleans, 1952. Brick ware-houses on Clinton Street frame the central section facing Iberville Street. The building occupies a full city block bounded by Canal, Decatur, Iberville, and North Peters Streets. All four elevations include Greek temple forms and Egyptian lotus capitals. The warehouses are typical of those from the mid-1800s, with granite piers supporting a granite lintel or brick arches at street level, doors completely opening the ground floor during business hours, and upper levels for storage.

Courtesy of the Historic New Orleans Collection (accession no. 1990.63.3)

PLATE L   A watercolor by Cruise of a mansion on Dauphine Street, in New Orleans, 1938. Still standing amid Creole cottages, this Greek Revival house possesses the elegance of a projecting portico and double return stairways.

Courtesy of the Historic New Orleans Collection (accession no. 1971.69.3)

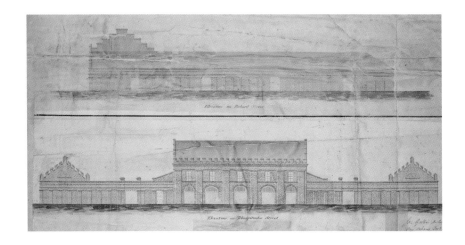

PLATE M   James Gallier, *Mississippi Cotton Press,* 1843. Gallier was commissioned to draw elevations and plans for this structure and an adjacent warehouse when the property, on Tchoupitoulas Street, in New Orleans, was sold to a consortium of cotton brokers in Liverpool. The press and four warehouses had been built between 1831 and 1838 in an area bounded by Tchoupitoulas, Market, Religious, and Richard Streets. Gothic crenellations turned what were otherwise plain brick buildings into a seeming castle compound.

New Orleans Notarial Archives, Plan Book 24, folio 5.

FIGURE 24 Wartelle (Moundville), St. Landry Parish, 1827–1829, facade and principal floor plan. The elliptical arches are an American feature, as is the central hall.

HABS, 1985, Louisiana State Archives

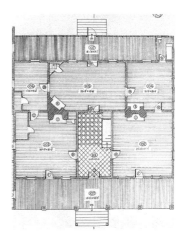

few truly Federal plantation houses, even in parishes heavily settled by Americans. Wartelle, built between 1827 and 1829 (Figure 24), has Federal elliptical arches between the posts of the front gallery, a fanlight over the entrance, and high-style mantels with paterae, that is, sunbursts. But it also has a Creole umbrella roof and french doors opening onto the gallery. The plan is transitional, with a short central hall leading to a dining room rather than directly to a rear gallery.

The number of Creole houses surviving from the first decades of the nineteenth century, as against the very few truly colonial examples, stems in part from the increased prosperity of those years and the number of plantations created from earlier French and Spanish land grants. The increasing population and prosperity created a whole new generation of houses built "like my father's" with respect to construction and plan.[27]

By the 1830s in south Louisiana, some great American plantation houses were beginning to rise. Louisiana planters embraced the Greek Revival style with the same enthusiasm as the people in other states. They rationalized it as the one most appropriate for a new and glorious republic, the true heir of Athenian democracy. In Louisiana and the Deep South, the era of the Greek Revival was from 1830 to 1860. This was also the period of great gains in population and wealth in the state. The profits from cotton and sugar, land transactions, and shipping appeared to grow, like the population, by leaps and bounds. Despite the insalubrious climate, Louisiana was a state where fortunes could be made. It was a land of opportunity for craftsmen, merchants, and professional men, and of even greater opportunity for those who could afford to purchase land. New immigrants and new money built in the new style.

27. Building Contract Between Despanet de Blanc and the brothers Joseph Terence Bienvenu Devince and Alexandre Bienvenu Devince, 1827, in St. Martin Parish Conveyance Records, No. 5975. De Blanc's plantation was later known as Lady of the Lake. Jack Holden and Pat Chapoton Holden located and transcribed the contract.

Across the South, buildings reminiscent of Greek temples became much the rage. The Grecian low triangular pediment and rows of monumental columns (Chapter 5, Figure 12) appeared on everything from sugarhouses to privies, from kitchens to tombs. Like the rest of the South, Louisiana has plantation houses with monumental temple facades and pediments, as at Madewood, in Ascension Parish, and with projecting temple porticoes, as at Hickory Hill (Front endpaper). In Louisiana, however, the pedimented form was not preeminent, and it was not the first choice for residences. Instead, many of the typical grand Greek Revival mansions in Louisiana had colossal two-story columns on three or four sides of an almost square, two-story masonry building with a central hall. The columns supported a heavy entablature and a low hip or pyramidal roof with dormers. The colonnade of this distinctively southern adaptation of Greek temple architecture was not limited to Louisiana, but there it was a logical evolution from the Creole peripteral galleries.

By the nineteenth century the vivid colors of Greek temples had washed away. While marble was the stone of choice for the Greeks, so white was the color of the Greek Revival. In colored pictures of mid-nineteenth-century plantations, almost all the houses and fences are white, whether new or just newly painted. Persac's gouache watercolors of Shadows-on-the-Teche show the house, originally red brick with white trim, entirely white in 1861.[28] Built from 1831 to 1834 by David Weeks, Shadows has eight colossal Tuscan columns across the facade. The frieze above the columns, with Doric triglyphs, metopes, and guttae, correctly replicates Greek models. The house has one of the earliest monumental galleries in the state (Figure 25). With it, the Greek Revival had arrived in rural Louisiana, but the Creole had by no means been forsaken. The exterior stairs, the open loggias between two rear rooms, the central dining room on the ground floor, and the parlor above are all Creole legacies (Figure 26). The loggias, today once again open, were enclosed in 1860 to create two additional rooms. The millwork includes both Federal and Greek Revival details. This combination of styles represents the encounter of Weeks's English and American heritage with local building practices. The Shadows, now facing Main Street, originally faced its plantation, which was not the Weekses' principal landholding. In grandeur and style it was definitely the big house for the family plantation and not simply a main house in town. The situation was different in Franklin, farther down Bayou Teche, where a number of main houses were clustered in the town.

One of the best-known peripteral houses was Uncle Sam, built for the

28. Marie Adrien Persac, *Shadows-on-the-Teche (Facade)* and *Shadows-on-the-Teche (Bayou Elevation),* both signed and dated 1861, in Shadows-on-the-Teche, New Iberia. All the paintings of plantations that Persac completed between 1857 and 1861 show white houses, as do all but one of the twenty-eight watercolors that Father Paret painted of plantations during his stay in St. Charles Parish between 1850 and 1859.

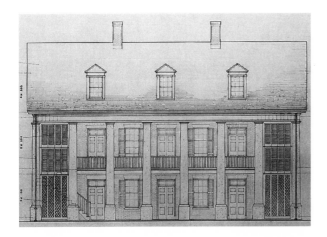

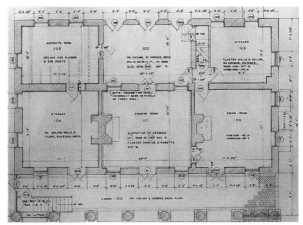

FIGURE 25   Shadows-on-the-Teche, New Iberia, 1831–1834, facade and principal floor plan. The colossal colonnade and entablature are in the manner of the Greek Revival style. The plan is Creole, and the main stairs are on the front gallery. The small enclosed service stairway led from the open loggia to the upper bedrooms.

HABS, 1963, Library of Congress

FIGURE 26   The parlor at Shadows-on-the-Teche. The central second-floor parlor is typical of Creole houses on a high basement.

Courtesy of Shadows-on-the-Teche, New Iberia, La., a museum property of the National Trust for Historic Preservation. Photograph by Ron Blunt.

French-born sugar planter Samuel Fagot and popularly called by his name (Figure 27). The house and its immediate dependencies defined the Greek Revival style for Louisiana. The house was a ninety-three-foot square, including twelve-foot-wide galleries on all four sides. On each side, eight Tuscan columns supported a heavy entablature. The hip roof had a pair of dormers on the front and rear and a single dormer apiece along the other two sides. Each dormer was framed by a pair of Tuscan columns supporting an entablature and a pediment. The house was flanked by a pair of small buildings, which HABS architects in 1940 described generally as offices, the one upriver most likely being the kitchen, since it had a large fireplace and stood where kitchens are often situated. These two dependencies had four Tuscan columns and pediments with heavy entablatures, giving them the effect of

FIGURE 27   Uncle Sam, with upriver *garçonnière,* St. James Parish, 1840s. The colonnade of the house is repeated on a smaller scale in the dependency. The balustrade is similar to those found on a number of Creole houses, such as Labatut (Figure 16).

Library of Congress. Photograph by Frances Benjamin Johnston.

FIGURE 28   Office and *pigeonnier* at Uncle Sam. The temple front of the office continues the classical order of the main house. The hexagonal *pigeonnier* stood to the rear of the downriver *garçonnière.*

Library of Congress. Photograph by Frances Benjamin Johnston.

small temples (Figure 28). Also flanking the main house, but farther away, were a pair of *garçonnières*. Each possessed an entablature supported by six Tuscan columns, and a hip roof with a pair of dormers both front and rear of the same design as those on the main house. In addition, a pair of decorative hexagonal *pigeonniers* with high hexagonal roofs defined the rear corners of the yard. Tall cisterns were placed at the rear corners of the house and the *garçonnières* to collect rainwater.

The line of five buildings with colonnades facing the river gave Uncle Sam a feeling of Classical grandeur (Figure 29) that was unequaled by most plantations, where the Classical order of the house was repeated on only two pairs of outbuildings. All five buildings were masonry, stuccoed and scored to look like stone, and limewashed or painted buff or yellow ocher. The columns were also stuccoed and set on plinths. The detailing at the entrance doors and on the interior was Greek Revival, with projecting architraves and tall four-paneled doors. As in other houses of substance, Uncle Sam had two parlors. These were separated by a monumental opening with a pair of sliding pocket doors. Only in Louisiana would all the downstairs windows be french doors. French doors functioned too as the side entrances to the *garçonnières* and the entrances to the offices. All the other buildings on the plantation were beyond this formal layout. The lower Mississippi frequently changes its course and now flows over the site. The house was demolished in 1940. Other houses represented the American Greek Revival style with greater purity, and Duncan Kenner's Ashland (Belle Helene), in Ascension Parish, is probably at the apogee of the style (Front endpaper). A house with the elements of Uncle Sam could have been found only in Louisiana.

The more typical midcentury plantation house was the raised Greek Revival cottage, traditionally a story-and-a-half house framed and clad in wood and raised on piers. The gallery was undercut, that is, sheltered under the length of the gable roof for the full width of the front. There could be an undercut gallery at the rear, as well, sometimes with *cabinets* at the ends, or a smaller porch could be attached to the body of the house. Onto the front gallery there opened a center door with sidelights and a transom, between a pair of sash windows to the right and another pair to the left. The five openings defined the five-bay facade and testified to a plan in which a central hallway opened into two rooms on either side. The typical rectangular box columns varied from the highly adorned to the very plain, and there were sometimes round columns.

Palo Alto, built around 1850, is fifty feet by sixty feet with a twelve-foot-wide gallery and six paneled box columns supporting a deep cornice (Figure 30). The front door and two pairs of french doors on either side are framed by Greek Revival moldings with the traditional ears, and each of the five openings is topped by a pedimented lintel (Figure 31). The Greek Revival moldings repeat in the interior, where, in addition, all the mantels feature

FIGURE 29   Uncle Sam, elevations and plans of the upriver *garçonnière,* kitchen, house, office, and downriver *garçonnière.*

HABS, 1940, Library of Congress

FIGURE 30   Palo Alto, Ascension Parish, *ca.* 1850. The box columns and pilasters are paneled. The double-return stairway is relatively rare.

Photograph by Jim Zietz

FIGURE 31   The front door of Palo Alto. The octagonal sidelights and transom windows are an unusual refinement, as is the amber glass of the panes.

Photograph by Jim Zietz

Greek motifs and the four paneled doors have elongated upper panels. Marking the building as one designed for Louisiana are the french doors, the stairway in the rear *cabinet,* and the construction of timber frame with brick between the posts. The frame is clad in flush boards on the facade and clapboards on the sides and rear. Despite its size, it is called a raised cottage. In Louisiana, *raised cottage* universally refers to single-story residences of some size and refinement elevated on piers.

The smaller Armitage, built in 1852 facing Bayou Terrebonne, is a similar five-bay raised cottage with box columns supporting a heavy entablature that continues around the gable ends (Figure 32). The central door is between one pair of sash windows and another, the frame of each window supporting an entablature, as the pilasters do at either side of the door (Figure 33). The configuration of the windows, with six panes in a sash, is typical of the midcentury. The interior detailing is strictly Greek Revival for the door frames and the mantels (Figure 34). Although small, the house is very fine,

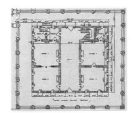

FIGURE 32 Armitage, Terrebonne
Parish, 1852. The raised cottage is in the
Greek Revival style with box columns.
The chimneys are set in the end walls
and gable.

Photograph by Jim Zietz

with close attention to detail, including the decorative leader head on the
downspouts and the exquisite bird's-eye-maple and flame-mahogany graining on the interior doors (Figure 35). The plan reflects the Creole preference
for a short central stair hall leading to a central dining room in the rear instead of extending the full depth of the house.

Although less common in the more sparsely settled areas of north
Louisiana, the Greek Revival raised cottage occurs wherever plantations were
established or houses rebuilt in the middle of the century. The Oaks, built
around 1855 in De Soto Parish, is a particularly distinguished example (Figure 36). The facade of this pyramidal galleried structure is enhanced by a
handsome entrance with an entablature and pilasters, and pedimented windows with panels below.

Much more elaborate and in the high Greek Revival style is Magnolia,
built near midcentury facing Bayou Black in Terrebonne Parish (Figure 37).
The house has five bays with box columns and full galleries across the front

FIGURE 33   The front gallery of Armitage. The simple balustrade with square balusters is a typical feature.
Photograph by Jim Zietz

FIGURE 34   The parlor mantel of
Armitage. The box pilasters and deep
entablature combine to make a typical
Greek Revival mantel. Mantels were
always painted, often to resemble slate or
marble.

Photograph by Jim Zietz

FIGURE 35   Parlor door at Armitage.
The door is grained in a pattern of bird's-
eye maple and, on the panels, flame
mahogany. This is the finest *faux bois*
remaining in the state. Grained doors
were the norm, but few survived.

Photograph by Jim Zietz

FIGURE 36   The Oaks, De Soto Parish,
ca. 1850. Paired front doors are fairly
unusual in Greek Revival raised cottages,
but the tall panels of the doors and the
rectangular glazing in the sidelights and
transom are typical.

Photograph by Jim Zietz

of both stories. It is on a far larger scale than the raised cottages. The galleries
project forward from the horizontal eaves of the gable roof, and a large ell extends to the rear. As in many urban houses, the galleries have cast iron
balustrades, and monumental windows open to the floor on the ground
story. The construction is frame, but the front walls are stuccoed and scored
to resemble stone. On the interior a graceful stairway curves down to the
wide rear hall, which an arch supported by plaster consoles visually divides
from the front hall. The mantels downstairs are white marble in the Rococo
Revival style, which was in vogue for furnishings at the time. The exterior architecture of Greek Revival plantation houses was usually serene and severe,
but interior decoration in these houses ran to the ebullient, elaborate, con-

FIGURE 37   Magnolia, Terrebonne
Parish, *ca.* 1850. The projecting two-story
gallery and the cast iron balustrades are
more common on houses in New
Orleans and on those with Italianate
details.

Photograph by Jim Zietz

voluted, and colorful. Plantation houses in Gothic Revival and Italianate styles were far fewer than Greek Revival houses. But even before the war, southerners, including Louisianians, were responding to new ideas. Two notable plantation houses were built in the Gothic Revival style, Afton Villa, in West Feliciana Parish (Chapter 5, Figure 70), and Orange Grove, in Plaquemines Parish (Chapter 5, Figure 67), but those houses were of extraordinary grandeur. From before the Civil War, the only Gothic plantation house to survive is Greenwood, in West Feliciana Parish (called Butler-Greenwood to distinguish it from another Greenwood in the parish). As built between 1810 and 1813, it was a simple raised cottage with an *enfilade* plan and french doors. Harriet Flowers Mathews, who inherited the property in 1816, added a new wing, now demolished, around 1855 to accommodate her son's growing family. Abreast of progressive fashions, she cloaked the house in Gothic raiment (Figure 38). The prominent central gable with its Palladian window and the wraparound gallery with ornate sawed balusters transformed the cottage into the kind of rural residence popularized by pattern books. The remodeling produced a spacious parlor with three floor-to-ceiling windows that open directly onto the gallery (Figure 39). The convenience of a front door made way for the elegance of an entire wall of windows. Rococo Revival conceptions of elegance dictated the white marble mantel with sculptured ornament and arched opening. The original furnishings survive—fitted strip carpeting, curtains, cornices, gilt pier looking glasses, and a Rococo Revival parlor suite of settees and chairs—exhibiting "all that artifice aided by wealth" could devise.

FIGURE 38   Butler-Greenwood, West
Feliciana Parish, 1810–1813, remodeled *ca.*
1856.

Photograph by Barbara SoRelle Bacot

FIGURE 39   The parlor of Butler-
Greenwood. A Connecticut firm
supplied the furniture, which was billed
in January, 1861. The upholstery and
draperies were red but have now faded to
rose.

Photograph by Barbara SoRelle Bacot

Few Louisiana planters developed a taste for true Italianate designs, despite their availability in plan books and from professional architects. In
Louisiana, it was the wealthy entrepreneurs and the high society of New Orleans who favored the Italianate, for their urban villas. Italianate villas were
the largest, the grandest, and the most elaborate of all plantation houses, but
there were not many of them. The style came late to rural Louisiana, and the

FIGURE 40   Belle Grove, Iberville Parish, 1852–1855. By the architect Henry Howard, this, the most splendid plantation house to have the form of an Italianate villa, suffered damage from fire in 1952 and was later demolished.

Library of Congress. Photograph by Frances Benjamin Johnston.

Greek Revival alternative remained in fashion. Henry Howard was the preeminent architect of the Italianate, but even he designed plantation houses in both styles. His designs for Belle Grove, constructed from 1852 to 1855 in Iberville Parish, gave the appearance of a vast and greatly expanded villa facing the Mississippi (Figure 40). The irregular and complex plans were a greatly expanded variation on the plans favored for stylish residences in Uptown New Orleans (Figure 41; Chapter 5, Figure 20). The ornamentation of its massive porticoes and spacious interiors elaborated upon the monumentality and details of Greek Revival architecture. The arches on the ground level and the irregular massing were Italianate, as was the use of brackets on both the interior and the exterior. The color palette for the stucco walls, which were painted lavender with a pink wash, and for the off-white columns and the olive green trim was Italianate (Plate F).[29] This plantation house owes as much to Greece as to the Italian picturesque (Figure 42). Here the Italianate appears to be a florid interpretation of Grecian forms.

The new taste of the postwar era is evident at the big house of Poplar Grove, in West Baton Rouge Parish (Figure 43). Designed by the renowned New Orleans architect Thomas Sully, the house was built as the Banker's Pavilion for the 1884 World's Industrial and Cotton Centennial Exposition in New Orleans. The New Orleans *Daily Picayune* of February 8, 1885, described it as "one of the handsomest structures on the Exposition Grounds. . . . The building is surrounded on three sides by a gallery; the

29.   Building Contract, for George Wheldon of Natchez to Build According to the Plans of Henry Howard, May 1846, in Iberville Parish Courthouse.

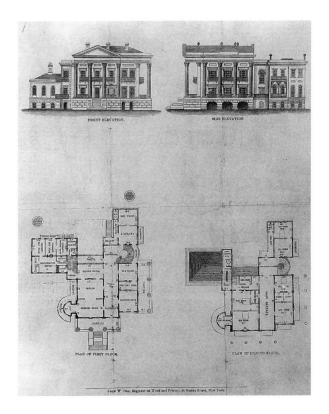

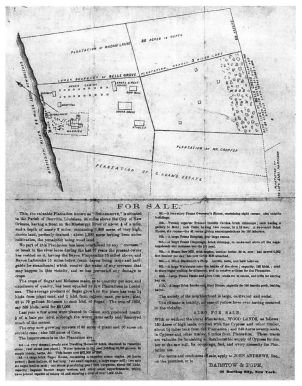

FOR SALE.

FIGURE 41   Belle Grove, first floor plan. The advertisement from 1867 or 1868 offering Belle Grove for sale shows plans, elevations, and plantation layout.

The Historic New Orleans Collection, 1970.13.1,2.

structure is in an ornate and substantial style of architecture, the walls are elegantly decorated, the windows are filled with fine stained glass, . . . and the building is complete in every detail."[30] "Every detail" covers jigsawed Chinese dragons as gallery brackets, and architectural elements in the Italianate, Eastlake, and Queen Anne Revival styles (Figure 44). In 1886, the pavilion was moved upriver by barge to its present site. The original two parlors and two retiring rooms were altered to allow for a central hall, and two chimneys for four fireplaces. Despite the adjustments for residential living, many of the features of the original interior remain. This unique house was moved into an altogether traditional plantation context.

Both the Greek Revival and the Italianate styles lingered after the Civil War, but there was little new building in rural areas. Constructed in 1882 in St. John the Baptist Parish, Emilie, a five-bay raised cottage with cupola, is clearly Greek Revival and except for its cupola looks very like the Oaks. The earlier traditions of the open loggia flanked by two *cabinets* on the rear, of *briquette entre poteaux* construction, and of french doors continued. The only remaining example in the postwar Gothic idiom is at Ardoyne, in Terrebonne Parish (Chapter 7, Figure 13). Southdown, also in Terrebonne Parish, became a Queen Anne house when it was remodeled and enlarged in 1894 (Figure 45). Despite the symmetry the original central-hall plan im-

30.   New Orleans *Daily Picayune,* February 8, 1885.

FIGURE 42   The foyer and stair hall at Belle Grove.

Collection of the Louisiana State Museum. Photograph by Robert W. Tebbs, 1926.

FIGURE 43   Poplar Grove, West Baton Rouge Parish, 1884. The house was built as the Bankers' Pavilion for the New Orleans Cotton Exposition. The cupola and spire were removed before the house was floated upriver.

Photograph by Jim Zietz

posed, the house assumed many of the decorative characteristics of the new style, including its color palette. The owner painted the masonry dark rose, the posts and balustrades dark green, and the shingled gables dark red. Early in the twentieth century the house was painted white, to suit the color preference of the newer Colonial Revival style. As at Poplar Grove, the style of the house was exotic but the plantation layout remained traditional.

Begun in the late nineteenth century, Oak Hall exhibits both a change in the concept of a plantation and a change in house style (Figure 46). Although sited in the middle of extensive sugarcane acreage, the house feels more like a country house than the seat of a working plantation. The owner sent his cane to a sugar mill nearby, and the workers lived elsewhere. The house today shows extensive remodeling in several stages. After the completion of renovations in 1923, the frame house looks like an exotic Colonial Revival, with Tuscan columns across the front and down the side galleries and a porte cochere at the front entrance. The tiled hip roof flares at the eaves, as do the gable roofs of the central upper porch and the pairs of dormers, which are further decorated with jigsawed bargeboards. French doors with transoms are the only windows for rooms looking out onto the porch, in continuation of the Creole form. On the interior, the central hall's mantel and wainscoting are in the Craftsman style (Figure 47).

The demolished Belle Grove is generally thought to have been the grandest, and the largest, of all Louisiana plantation houses. It was a paradigm of the wealth and high style of the 1850s. But there was an opposite end to the spectrum. Many more of the plantation houses in Louisiana were of modest proportions. Near the other extreme from Belle Grove is the Epps

FIGURE 44 The front gallery of Poplar Grove. Dragon brackets support the grilles, with their heavy spindles, and sawed brackets connect the square posts of the railing.

Photograph by Jim Zietz

FIGURE 45 Southdown, Terrebonne Parish, 1894. Built for the Minor family, the present house is a remodeling of a single-story house built about 1860.

Courtesy of Terrebonne Historical and Cultural Society. Photograph by Leonard Hingle.

FIGURE 46   Oak Hall. An open pergola
connects the octagonal gazebo to the
gallery of the house. The gazebo was
built in the twentieth century as a
summerhouse.

Photograph by Jim Zietz

House, built in Avoyelles Parish in 1852 (Figure 48) and famous because
Solomon Northup, the illegally enslaved free man of color and author of
Twelve Years a Slave, helped build it. The acreage attached to it was small, and
the house is only twenty-six by thirty-six feet, including the porch. Some log
houses were bigger, and indeed, a log cabin might be a plantation house.
When A. A. Parker traveled along the Red River in 1834 and 1835, he visited
a planter who after nineteen years on a large plantation still lived in a "log
house without a glass window in it." The planter said "that the house was
well enough; if the hole cut out for a window did not make it light enough,
he opened the door." Parker marveled, "It was not just such a house as I
could be contented in for nineteen years, and possessing the wealth he
had."[31] This planter had eight to ten slaves and raised cotton, cattle, and

31.   Solomon Northup, *Twelve Years a Slave* (New York, 1857), 263; A. A. Parker, *Trip to the West
and Texas* (Boston, 1836), 5.

FIGURE 47   The central hall at Oak Hall, 1923. The mantel, overmantel, and eight-foot wainscoting are crafted of oak and stained. Wrought-iron strap hinges support the sawed baluster doors of the overmantel, and wrought-iron mounts trim the glazed-tile surround.

Photograph by Jim Zietz

FIGURE 48   Epps House, Avoyelles Parish, 1852. Removed from its original site, this four-room house is one of the simplest and smallest plantation houses in the state.

Photograph by Jim Zietz

corn, but his dwelling was among the smallest of plantation main houses. It was little better than many a house occupied by slaves. Those who came to Louisiana with the wealth to buy land, slaves, and equipment could often afford a fine house as well. Others enlarged earlier houses or built new ones in more current styles once they gained a modicum of success. But the more conservative continued to live in raised cottages, and some in the northern and the Florida parishes chose not to abandon their log cabins, although they often added refinements such as clapboards and even wallpaper. But Parker had no doubts: only an eccentric would be content to live in housing built of logs without a single glass window.

THE QUARTERS

The houses of the slaves formed the rows and "villages" that distinguished plantations from country estates (Figure 49). In Louisiana, these houses were the quarters, as they continued to be called even after the Civil War. In the United States, because providing the quarters was the responsibility of the planter, the basic designs proceeded from those of the early settlers from Europe. The small houses on cotton and sugar plantations were much the same, with the wealth and character of the owner, not the crop, determining variations from one plantation to another. Sometimes on the sugar plantations of the Caribbean slave housing was the responsibility of the slaves themselves, who followed the building practices of their tropical homelands. The harsher

MUGNIER.   QUARTERS, BELLAIRE PLANTATION   N. O. LA.

FIGURE 49 The slave quarters at Bellaire plantation as they appeared around 1890. Cabins in rows were the traditional housing for plantation workers before and after the Civil War.

Louisiana Division, New Orleans Public Library. Photograph by François Mugnier (Quarters, Bellaire Plantation).

climate of Louisiana, however, required more substantial housing on even the earliest plantations.[32]

Across the South, few slave lodgings equaled those Thomas Jefferson built at Monticello, which were the envy of the county and better than the dwelling of the average frontier settler. The quarters at Monticello were of brick, "with real floors, doors that shut tight, and windows with glass panes." Still, they were small for a family. At Mount Vernon, a Polish visitor in 1798 judged that the slaves lived in "huts, for their habitations cannot be called houses. They are far more miserable than the poorest of the cottages of our peasants."[33] When the French traveler Robin visited Louisiana after the Louisiana Purchase, he described houses for both owners and slaves constructed of *poteaux en terre*, posts in the ground, with dirt floors. These were the "quick and cheap" equivalent of log cabins for Creole settlers: "Cypress posts about three inches square and about ten to fourteen feet long . . . dri-

32.   Roderick A. McDonald, *The Economy and Material Culture of Slaves: Goods and Chattels on the Sugar Plantations of Jamaica and Louisiana* (Baton Rouge, 1993), 92–94, 95. In *Back of the Big House* (Chapel Hill, N.C., 1993), John Michael Vlach describes the differences in quarters and dependencies in each of the slaveholding states.

33.   Julius Lester, ed., *To Be a Slave* (New York, 1968), 62–63.

ven into the ground to a depth of about two feet formed the shape of the house, approximately twelve feet square. The roof tree and joists were pegged to these posts and held the house together." The space between the posts was *bousillage* on laths. The poorer houses had roofs of cypress bark and batten doors hung with leather hinges. Like many of the chimneys on the more familiar log cabins, those on the Creole counterpart had four posts tilted inward that were secured by slats covered with a thick coat of mud. Robin observed that the "most miserable and poor" of such houses were "those of the Negroes which are called *cabanes* or *casas* à Niger." He added,

> On most plantations where the masters take care of things, all the cabins are aligned and spaced regularly. It looks like a little village and is usually called a camp. . . . Not all the Negro cabins are constructed with the same care. . . . One finds them sometimes scattered in confusion around the principal house and instead of a tight mud wall, the walls may consist of only badly made slabs, leaned against the posts through which the winds and rains penetrate at will. It is not astonishing to learn that there are indifferent and lazy masters who are almost as badly housed.[34]

The inventory of Duvernay plantation, in St. James Parish, that was conducted in 1737, described a "negro cabin with cypress posts in earth about 15 feet long by twelve wide [roofed] partly with bark and the rest with palmetto in very bad condition enclosed with mud walls." It had fallen to ruin in less than twenty years. In 1745, the planter Claude Joseph Dubreuil "undertook to begin sugar cane growing on a large scale" at his plantation just downriver from New Orleans. Twelve years later, after his death, the inventory included a cabin near the house, of "posts in the ground, surrounded with stakes and [the floor] bricked inside, roofed with shingles, planked top and bottom, brick chimney." Listed among the outbuildings of the sugarhouse was a "negro cabin in poor repair thirty-two feet long, fourteen wide, posts in the ground, bricked between posts, roofed half with rotted planks and half with pieces of stakes, chimney, wood mantel, two doors with hardware, one of which locking with a key, the other with a bolt, five windows with their shutters with hardware with their hooks."[35] Dubreuil's cabins followed a consistent plan. The twelve-by-fifteen-foot room in the single cabin and the approximately fourteen-by-sixteen-foot rooms in the two-room cabin mark out the narrow range of room sizes. Planters continued to build such one and two-room dwellings up to the Civil War.

The *poteaux en terre* cabins of the eighteenth-century Creole frontier,

---

34. Robin, *Voyage to Louisiana,* 122–23, 237.
35. Walter Prichard, ed., "Inventory of the Paris Duvernay Concession in Louisiana, 1726," *Louisiana Historical Quarterly,* XXI (1938), 979–94; Succession of Claude Joseph Dubreuil de Villars, Records of the Superior Council, October 17, 1757, in Louisiana State Museum, translated by Samuel Wilson, Jr., in "Architecture of Early Sugar Plantations," in *Green Fields: Two Hundred Years of Louisiana Sugar,* by René J. Le Gardeur, Jr., *et al.* (Lafayette, La., 1980), 56–58.

when almost everything inland from the river, even in the outskirts of New Orleans, was still the frontier, were certainly cheaper and easier to build than the other two types of structures in use by both settlers and slaves. Those two had timber frames, one with the sills on the ground, and the other raised on piers. Given Louisiana's almost tropical climate, with its high rainfall and ravenous insects, cabins with posts either in the ground or on sills touching the ground were difficult to maintain and did not last. Constructing a timber frame required considerable skill and time, but a cabin raised on piers could last for generations. By the nineteenth century, as what had been the frontier enjoyed improved access, almost everyone building cabins in Creole Louisiana erected them on piers.

Louisiana's frontier in the nineteenth century was not a simple line moving with western expansion; it was any area back from the waterways. The Weekses' house on the bank of the Teche was brick and sawed timber, but the first quarters built on their plantation in St. Mary Parish, in the 1830s, were log cabins, the best that could be built "under the circumstances," without access to sawmills and brickyards. In Natchitoches Parish, beyond the Creole settlement along the Cane River, log cabins continued to go up to house slaves. And in north and east Louisiana, the areas settled by Americans from the Upland South, both slaves and planters lived in log buildings. After establishing the plantation, some planters built frame houses, as on the Epps plantation, but the slaves frequently remained in log cabins. Slave quarters were not the snug cabins of the idealized frontier. Northup, the black chronicler, described his "log mansion" in the 1840s: "The cabin is constructed of logs, without floor or window. The latter is altogether unnecessary, the crevices between the logs admitting sufficient light. In stormy weather the rain drives through them, rendering it comfortless and extremely disagreeable."[36]

The earlier or more conservatively designed timber-frame dwellings in the quarters had hip roofs, with porches sometimes added later. By the middle of the nineteenth century the most common form of slave dwelling was the gabled house of one or two rooms, with a full undercut gallery across the front and only clapboard siding on the timber frame. The doors were single batten shutters, and single or double batten shutters closed over the unglazed window openings. In two-room cabins the two fireplaces with a shared chimney provided the only heat and a place for some cooking. The central brick chimney enabled a saving in construction costs. The double row of twenty-two cabins at Evergreen (Figure 50) is the largest row to survive in Louisiana. Built between 1830 and 1860, each line of eleven cabins includes ten two-room houses and a four-room house at the midpoint. The frames are pegged, with wide clapboards on the exterior and no interior siding. At Oak-

36. McDonald, *The Economy and Material Culture of Slaves*, 129–30; Northup, *Twelve Years a Slave*, 170–71.

FIGURE 50 Cabins at Evergreen plantation, *ca.* 1850. Two rows of frame cabins with central chimneys survive. Corrugated galvanized roofing was added over the wooden shingles in the early twentieth century.

Photograph by Donna Fricker

land, the quarters built in the 1830s were in the same style and similarly covered by clapboards, but the *bousillage* between the posts of the frame provided insulation mere clapboard could not.

At Welham, in St. James Parish (Figure 51), the two-room frame cabins had no porches. John Roy Lynch, the first black congressman from Mississippi, described a similar cabin at Tacony plantation, in Concordia Parish, across the river from Natchez. In his autobiography, Lynch recalled a visit in 1865 to his aunt and uncle, who lived with their son in a two-room frame cabin. At Magnolia, in Jefferson Parish, the quarters were well-constructed frame buildings eighteen feet by twenty-two feet, including the porch, and were raised two feet off the ground, with clapboard siding and shingled roofs. Each house, which was meant for but one family, had closely joined floors, glazed windows, and a large fireplace in each room.[37]

Rear rooms were sometimes added on to the basic two-room cabin, and others had two smaller rooms to the rear from the start, affording some privacy. The rear rooms had no fireplaces, however. At St. Louis plantation, in Iberville Parish, the one cabin that still stands, possibly from as late as the 1870s, has its two rear rooms separated by an open porch. Its plan is that of the smallest Creole cottage: two large rooms with two *cabinets* and an open loggia.

Cabins were at times four rooms across. At Hermitage, in Ascension Parish, twelve cabins appear to have housed most of the plantation's 116

37. *Reminiscences of an Active Life: The Autobiography of John Roy Lynch,* ed. John Hope Franklin (Chicago, 1970), 31–32 (from a MS produced between 1937 and 1939); J. C. Sitterson, "Magnolia Plantation, 1852–1862," *Mississippi Valley Historical Review,* XXV (1938), 199. William Postell refers to this article, in *The Health of Slaves on Southern Plantations* (Baton Rouge, 1951), 47.

FIGURE 51   A cabin from Welham plantation, St. James Parish, *ca.* 1850. The cabin is now on the grounds of the Louisiana State University Rural Life Museum and Windrush Gardens.

Photograph by Jim Zietz

slaves. If the cabins there were standard double cabins, that would have put four or five to a room, not unusual within a family group but exceptionally crowded conditions for the quarters as a whole, where a family might occupy a two-room cabin. It is certain that downriver, at Monroe plantation, several of the cabins were four rooms across. Roughly forty-eight feet by twenty feet, including a seven-foot gallery, each house had two brick chimneys, one between the first and second and one between the third and fourth rooms. Each room was approximately twelve feet square, the same size as the cabins Robin described. Given the economies possible, four-room construction may have been more common than there is evidence to suppose.[38]

38.   It is difficult to calculate the average, or even the typical, number of slaves on a plantation. Duncan Kenner, one of Louisiana's largest slaveholders, owned 117 slaves at Ashland in 1840, and 169 in 1850. At the outbreak of the Civil War, he owned 473 slaves on his three plantations. See *Sixth Census of the United States, 1840,* Microfilm of Enumerator's Report, Louisiana; *Seventh Census of the*

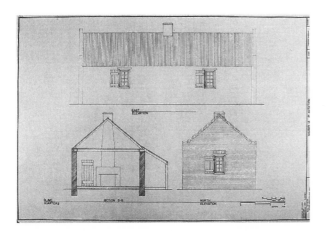

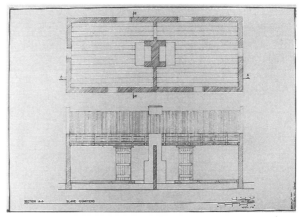

FIGURE 52 Magnolia plantation, Natchitoches Parish, cabin cross section and plan, *ca.* 1830–1850. Brick quarters were relatively rare.

HABS, 1986, Louisiana State Archives

FIGURE 53 Cabins at Magnolia
Photograph by Jim Zietz

Masonry construction was uncommon. Many plantations, like Palo Alto, had sawmills. In any case, lumber was readily available, and generally there were carpenters among the slaves. At Palo Alto, the main house, sugarhouse, and cabins were all framed with timber. But there was no dearth of brickyards. By the mid–nineteenth century, brick main houses and brick sugarhouses were familiar, but not brick quarters. Judge P. A. Rost, who owned Destrehan in the mid–nineteenth century, numbered among the planters who believed brick cabins were damp and caused sickness.[39] Nonetheless, some planters built their quarters of brick. At Magnolia, in Natchitoches Parish, the standard two-room plan was executed in brick (Figure 52). Eight houses survive there, in two rows facing the river. Each has molded gable ends, a central chimney, wooden floors, batten doors and window shutters, and an underground cistern at the side (Figure 53). A shed-roof porch was a later addition across the front, and the twentieth century saw the placement of corrugated roofing over the wooden shingles.

At least one plantation in Louisiana possessed quarters as fine as any in the country. Woodland, in Plaquemines Parish, had two-story brick quarters, with four rooms to a floor, a central chimney, and glazed windows. A sugar plantation, not named by its nineteenth-century visitor, had twenty-four buildings, each forty feet square and divided into four rooms, to accommodate 215 people. That plan recurred at Myrtle Grove, also in Plaquemines Parish, where an agriculturist visiting from Indiana in 1849 reported that the "negro houses built of brick, with elevated floors, 32 feet square, di-

United States, 1850, Microfilm of Enumerator's Manuscript Reports, Louisiana; and *Eighth Census of the United States, 1860,* Microfilm of Enumerator's Report, Louisiana. In 1856, St. Louis plantation had 167 slaves living as forty-nine families in twenty-five double cabins, with one vacant, giving each household a space about sixteen feet square. Ten single men shared one cabin. See McDonald, *The Economy and Material Culture of Slaves,* 135. Relocated to Hermitage, two of the cabins from Monroe survive with modifications.

39.   Judge P. A. Rost, *Sugar, Its Culture and Manufacture: Discourse Before the Agricultural and Mechanics Association of Louisiana, May 12, 1845* (Hahnville, La., 1876). McDonald refers to Rost's address in *The Economy and Material Culture of Slaves,* 130–31.

FIGURE 54   Quarters for field workers
around 1890.

*Collection of the Louisiana State Museum.
Photograph by François Mugnier
(*Plantation Quarters*).*

vided into four rooms with chimney in the centre," housed 139 slaves, 80 of
them field hands, in twelve cabins.[40]

The unnamed quarters the noted New Orleans photographer François
Mugnier photographed around 1890 testify to an even more unusual development (Figure 54). Each of eight masonry cottages had, as at Myrtle Grove,
four rooms and a central chimney, like urban cottages in New Orleans
(Chapter 2, Figures 8, 10, 11), but only party walls separate the cottages,
which occupy just two buildings of four row houses each.

The shotguns so popular in New Orleans and other Louisiana cities appeared on the plantation in the last quarter of the century. The bungalow, an
urban form ubiquitous in the United States, also found its place on the plantation, as both manager's and laborers' housing.[41]

Ordinarily, each house in the quarters stood at some distance from its
neighbors, allowing the slaves to keep kitchen gardens and some livestock. In
1853, T. B. Thorpe wrote, "In the rear of each cottage, surrounded by a rude
fence, you find a garden more or less in order, according to the industrious
habits of the proprietor. In all you notice that the 'chicken-house' seems to
be in excellent condition." The gardens and poultry houses supplemented
the staple fare the master provided. Slaves also sold for cash what they raised
there, either to the big house or off the plantation. On the sugar plantations,

40.   William D. Overdyke, *Louisiana Plantation Homes: Colonial and Ante Bellum* (New York,
1965), 204; T. B. Thorpe, "Sugar and the Sugar Region of Louisiana," *Harper's New Monthly Magazine,* VII (1853), 759; McDonald, *The Economy and Material Culture of Slaves,* 131–32. Postell refers to
Thorpe's account, in *The Health of Slaves,* 47.
41.   Rehder, "Sugar Plantation Settlements," 171–83.

FIGURE 55   The largest and only remaining dependency of Southdown plantation, Terrebonne Parish, *ca.* 1850. The photograph of Spot taken around the turn of the century shows the rear of the house and the dependency with a later one-story addition.

Courtesy of Terrebonne Historical and Cultural Society.

the slaves usually also cultivated, on their own time, allotments at some distance from the houses, which yielded cash crops, particularly corn.[42]

One planter said, "Interest as well as duty ought to prompt every master to the erection of comfortable cabins, for his slaves."[43] Still, the quarters that came closest to achieving the goal of comfort were as a rule those of the house servants. In the inventories after Dubreuil's death, the snug and well-maintained single-room cabin with the brick floor near the house was indubitably the abode of the house servants. The cabin for field hands, near the sugarhouse, was less well maintained. House servants could be quartered all together or dispersed among several cabins. The cook often lived at the kitchen, especially if it was designed with a second room, as at Oakland, but sometimes even if there was just one room. At Southdown (Figure 55), there was a single large building for all the house servants. Located to the rear of the main house, the two-story masonry structure built in 1847 and 1848 still stands. It has galleries facing away from the big house on each floor, with outside stairs, and each floor has three rooms approximately twelve feet by twelve feet with fireplaces. A dairy, a laundry, and a kitchen occupied the three ground-floor rooms.

The advice to planters was to equip a hospital on every plantation, with experienced nurses and rooms for women recovering from childbirth, as well as nurseries for infants and infirmaries for the sick and injured. Successful

42.   Thorpe, "Sugar and the Sugar Region," 129; McDonald, *The Economy and Material Culture of Slaves,* 50–91.
43.   Postell, *The Health of Slaves,* 44.

FIGURE 56   The chapel at Live Oaks
plantation, Iberville Parish, *ca.* 1840. The
local Episcopal congregation met here
until completing its church in 1859, as
did the first school in the area.

Photograph by Donna Fricker

planters made provision for nursing the sick, even in their own homes, and
many did have hospitals. A hospital might be just a one-room frame cabin,
but many plantations had larger facilities. At Magnolia, in Natchitoches
Parish, the hospital was a raised cottage with one large room, three small
rooms across one end, and 12-foot galleries on the other three sides.[44] At Parlange, in Pointe Coupee Parish, the hospital was a two-story brick building
with four rooms on each floor; it stood halfway between the house and the
quarters. The hospital at Uncle Sam was approximately 40 by 120 feet, including the galleries. It was along the road at the side of the house that led to
the quarters. The two hospitals at Destrehan were in the side yard of the
house (Figure 79). A plantation's interests dictated that the hospital be near
the big house or the overseer's house, and it was frequently under the supervision of the mistress, with a doctor calling when needed.

Not only the physical but also the spiritual health of slaves concerned
the early Louisiana governments and the planters of good character. The
colonial governments of Louisiana were Catholic, and the law required masters to accord their slaves religious instruction. A Spanish decree in 1789 required planters to provide chaplains on their plantations, but the need for
the decree lends credibility to one priest's lament that the masters "cared not
a whit about the salvation of these poor wretches." By about 1727, a mission
with its cross was part of Concession plantation. Despite the rarity of mission and chapel buildings, the missionaries of the church were zealous in
ministering to the slaves, and they laid a firm foundation for Catholicism

44. *Ibid.,* 129–36; Barbara A. Yocum, "Magnolia Plantation: Building Materials Assessment
and Analysis: Cane River Creole National Historical Park and Heritage Area, Natchitoches, Louisiana" (Typescript of report prepared for National Park Service, 1996), 43–44, 60.

among them. In Catholic churches, masters, slaves, and free people of color worshiped together. That was in contrast to the Protestant denominations, which generally relegated slaves to a remote corner or balcony. Conscientious and prosperous Christians built chapels on their plantations. In 1853, one wealthy master left instructions in his will that "there be a house erected on each plantation for a church." Another built the only plantation chapel still standing, the brick church erected at Live Oaks plantation, in Iberville Parish, around 1840 (Figure 56). Positioned near the main house, it is a simple structure with the entrance on the gable end facing the bayou, and three windows along each side. In south Louisiana, the sugarhouse often served as the church, or services were at the big house. Northup wrote kindly of the Baptist minister and planter who owned him for a brief time: "Seated in the doorway of his house, surrounded by his man-servants and his maid-servants, 'the master' read and expound[ed] the Scriptures."[45]

THE OVERSEER'S HOUSE

A necessary adjunct to the quarters was the overseer's house, which was generally more regular in its location, in some proximity to the quarters, than in its form. In the 1720s, the overseer's house at the absentee-owned Concession plantation had the siting and aspect of a main plantation house, but where both owner and overseer lived on the plantation, the overseer's house was smaller than the big house and its placement was different. At Oakland, on the Cane River, the overseer's house is between the big house and the quarters. On the Mississippi River, the overseer's house was often at a remove from the main house but still facing the river, in front of rows of cabins along a road leading away from the river. At Palo Alto, on Bayou Lafourche (Figure 6), the siting was similar, reflecting the overseer's anomalous position in the social hierarchy, somewhere between planter and slave. In most plans, the overseer's house was outside the fencing of the big house. At Magnolia Mound, in Baton Rouge, the overseer's house was at the end of the row in the quarters nearest the sugarhouse. But even when close to the rows of cabins, the overseer's house was always separate. It generally had a different orientation, and it was at least somewhat larger than a two-room cabin. Apart from the settings, the larger overseer's dwellings are indistinguishable from small plantation houses, and the smaller ones appear on the outside to be little more than commodious cabins. Those that have survived, however, are finished inside, with walls and millwork similar to what is in small plantation houses.

The overseer's house at Oakland, built probably between 1820 and 1830, has the umbrella roof and asymmetrical *en suite* plan of Creole tradition (Figure 57). In a house about thirty-six feet wide, the side rooms and rear rooms

45. Joe Gray Taylor, *Negro Slavery in Louisiana* (New York, 1963), 135, 149–50; Northup, *Twelve Years a Slave,* 97.

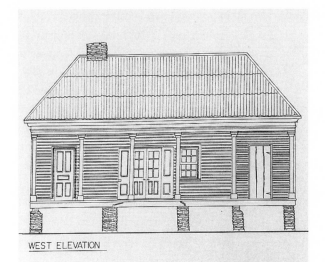

WEST ELEVATION

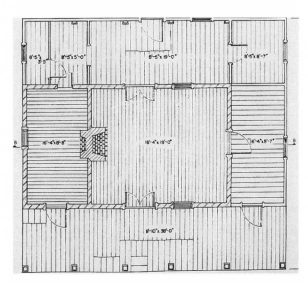

FIGURE 57 Oakland plantation, overseer's house, *ca.* 1825, facade and plan. The box columns on the gallery are a Greek Revival feature, but the construction is *bousillage* and timber frame and originally there were just two rooms with two *cabinets*. The galleries were enclosed later.

HABS, 1987, Louisiana State Archives

FIGURE 58 The overseer's house from Welham plantation, *ca.* 1850. The house is now on the grounds of the Louisiana State University Rural Life Museum and Windrush Gardens.

Photograph by Jim Zietz

are the same width as the gallery—eight feet, ten inches, including the exterior walls. The extent of the timber framing indicates that this was originally a two-room dwelling with galleries on three sides. *Bousillage* filled the frame of the initial two rooms, both served by the same chimney. At Welham, the overseer's house was likely of later construction, maybe around 1850, though possibly it was as early as 1836. Yet the fabrication was only frame (Figure 58). The overall size is about the same as at Oakland, but the plan is that of the four-room cottage, with interior chimneys serving the pair of front rooms and the smaller rear rooms. The house has side gables, and a gallery with the

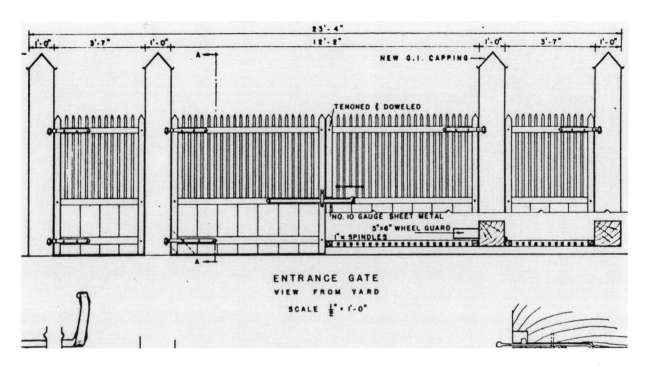

FIGURE 59   Homeplace plantation, St. Charles Parish, fence, *ca. 1850*. The gates led to the house.

HABS, 1937, Library of Congress

simplest Greek Revival box columns extends across the front. Plantation managers' residences regularly followed such Creole plans until well after the Civil War: the frame house built about 1880 at Magnolia Mound for the manager has two large rooms, an interior chimney, and a loggia flanked by *cabinets.*

Some plantations, Oakland among them, had a house that served as both lodging and dispensary for the doctor when he visited the plantation.

FENCES, DITCHES, AND LEVEES

Fences enclosed and defined the yard of the main house and its dependencies. They separated private land from public right-of-way and kept stock in pens and pastures and out of fields. Typically there was a decorative fence across the front of the yard enclosing the house and its outbuildings, and simpler fences, either wide palings or post and rail, along the sides and back of the main house's compound and elsewhere on the plantation. Early HABS drawings of Homeplace show a carriage entrance flanked by a pair of gates for pedestrians (Figure 59). The fence was of square pickets set in rails that were hung on twelve-inch posts seven feet, ten inches high. The fence at Homeplace was among the simplest. Aesthetic flourishes could be limited to just the gate, but they were rarely ignored completely. Some very modest houses had highly ornamental fencing, and the taste for embellishment continued into the late nineteenth century (Figure 60).

Each parish prescribed fencing heights by law. An ordinance East Baton Rouge Parish passed in 1819 reads, "No fence in this parish shall be consid-

FIGURE 60   Fence with sawed posts, late nineteenth century.

Library of Congress. Photograph by Frances Benjamin Johnston.

FIGURE 61   Marie Adrien Persac, *Hope Estate Plantation,* 1857, detail. The highly ornamental carriage and pedestrian gates and fences connect the *pigeonniers.* Those structures, with cupolas, frame the house, built in the period from about 1795 to about 1810.

Louisiana State University Museum of Art, Baton Rouge.

FIGURE 62   *Pieux* fence, in Paulina, St. James Parish.

Farm Security Administration, Library of Congress. Photograph by Russell Lee, 1938.

ered lawful, or entitle the proprietor to any damages for having been broken down, or overleaped by animals of any description, unless it be five feet, and, if of posts and rails, the three lower rails not more than three inches apart, and the posts two and a half inches thick." [46] Hope Estate, in East Baton Rouge Parish, had one of the grandest (Plate G; Figure 61). Along the River Road, masonry bases supported wood picket fencing with highly decorated wrought-iron carriage and pedestrian gates. On either side, however, were *pieux* fences. *Pieux* fencing, found throughout south Louisiana and on the Cane River, employed long cypress planks as palings (Figure 62). It was quick and easy to build and took advantage of cypress' resistance to rot. The upper ends of the planks were shaped in points, the lower ends were set in a shallow trench. Posts and a single upper rail supported the palings, which were seven to ten inches wide or wider. *Pieux* made a sturdy fence, albeit one that became shorter over the years as the bottoms of the planks rotted and the fence was remade.

The *pieux* fence was limited to areas where the initial settlement was under Creole influence. On the other hand, the zigzag snake fence, or worm fence, came to Louisiana with Americans from the Upland South and was found in areas of log houses and barns. The ordinances of St. Helena Parish

46.   *Digest of the Laws and Ordinances of the Police Jury of East Baton Rouge Parish* (Baton Rouge, 1821), 12–13 (July 7, 1819).

in 1813 required that "each inhabitant or planter shall be compelled to keep a fence of the height of five and a half feet either post and rail or if a worm fence well stacked and 'ridered' or braced."[47] The post-and-rail fence was ubiquitous until the advent of cheap barbed wire.

All houses facing the Mississippi were separated from the river by a fence, a ditch, a public road, and a levee. The East Baton Rouge compendium of ordinances, published in 1821, records requirements typical of the river parishes:

> A good and sufficient levee shall be made and kept in repair . . . to be made of earth taken . . . raised one foot above the highest water mark of the river, and presenting on the top, when finished, a surface of three feet; the width of the base being four times the height . . . of the levee; . . . a road . . . 30 feet wide . . . [and] on each side of the road, adjacent to the said levee, then shall be a good and sufficient ditch: . . . ditches shall also be made across the road, at a distance from each other not exceeding three arpents; . . . and the said cross ditches shall be continued at least five arpents back from the river, or so far as may be sufficient to discharge at all times, the waters which may pass the levee.[48]

The need for levees became immediately apparent above and below New Orleans. Although the system could work only if everyone maintained his section of the levee, not everyone was equally diligent. As early as 1727, rebuilding the levees and draining the ditches were obligations attached to leases of land. Along the bayous, private maintenance was largely successful, but on the Mississippi every flood was apt to open a crevasse, a breach in the levee. To the twentieth century, the levees of the two preceding centuries seem ludicrously small, for the great levees constructed by the U.S. Army Corps of Engineers, especially after the flood of 1927, now completely isolate the river from the land.[49]

Draining the land was absolutely necessary for growing indigo, sugarcane, or cotton. Because in low-lying south Louisiana, normal drainage was to the back swamp and away from the high ground near the river or bayou, small levees were sometimes built along the swamp as well. Concession plantation had a system of ditches draining away from the river (Plate A), and that arrangement was repeated throughout the eighteenth and nineteenth centuries. Sugar plantations had both irrigation and drainage ditches. De

47. Walter Prichard, ed., "Minutes of the Police Jury of St. Helena Parish, August 16–19, 1813," *Louisiana Historical Quarterly,* XXIII (1940), 15.

48. *Digest of the Laws and Ordinances of the Police Jury of East Baton Rouge Parish,* 30–32.

49. Walter Prichard, ed., "Lease of a Louisiana Plantation and Slaves, 1727," *Louisiana Historical Quarterly,* XXI (1938), 996; Lease Between M. Delachaise and M. Hugot, January 18, 1727, in Louisiana State University Libraries; Albert E. Cowdrey, *Land's End: A History of the New Orleans District. U.S. Army Corps of Engineers, and Its Lifelong Battle with the Lower Mississippi and Other Rivers Wending Their Way to the Sea* (New Orleans, 1977), 1–15.

FIGURE 63   A wooden draining wheel with its masonry machinery house. Its size indicates that it was on a large plantation. It drained water from low-lying fields across the rear levee and into the back swamp.

*Collection of the Louisiana State Museum. Photograph by François Mugnier (*Plantation Draining Wheel*).*

Boré irrigated his crop with river water whenever the rains failed. By the middle of the nineteenth century, new steam-powered engines could turn large wheels that moved water over the rear levee (Figure 63).[50]

Property holders were responsible for building and maintaining the road along the levee, and they discharged this responsibility as variably as they tended their levees. The Mississippi was the great highway, its tributaries and distributaries the feeder roads. Today the river is a divider, but earlier it unified. Before and during the era of the steamboat, no other transport offered the ease and affordability of travel by water.

GARÇONNIÈRES

It was customary in French Louisiana to have separate housing for the young men of the family as they grew older. Always within the house grounds and sometimes actually connected to the house, a *garçonnière* was a way of adding living space without the inconvenience or necessity of modifying the original plan. If sizable, it could include a kitchen and other service rooms on the first floor. A *garçonnière* is the only building to survive from the Barbera plantation, in St. Charles Parish (Figure 64). It was one of two, similar in size, that framed the approach to the house. The umbrella roof and the gallery extending around three sides transformed the design of a four-room urban cottage with central chimneys into a building for a rural setting. Here, as at Uncle Sam plantation, Tuscan columns were thought to suit rural

---

50.   Victor Collot, *A Journey in North America* (2 vols.; Paris, 1826), II, 169–74. This is a translation of Collot's *Voyage dans l'Amérique septentrionale*.

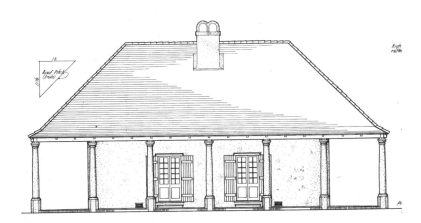

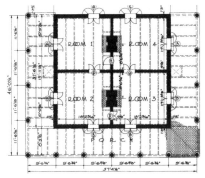

FIGURE 64   Barbarra plantation, St. Charles Parish, *garçonnière, ca.* 1810–1820, facade and plan.

HABS, 1934, Library of Congress

FIGURE 65   *Garçonnière* and rear elevation of Oaklawn, St. Mary Parish, *ca.* 1850. The photograph, taken around 1900, shows that the popularity of cross-pattern balustrades continued in Greek Revival buildings.

Private collection

FIGURE 66 *Garçonnière* at Houmas House (Burnside), Ascension Parish, *ca.* 1840. A pair of ornamental *garçonnières* stand in the front yard, one on either side of the house.

HABS, 1936, Library of Congress. Photograph by Frances Benjamin Johnston.

buildings. The two story *garçonnière* at Oaklawn plantation, in St. Mary Parish, was a masonry building that had six monumental Tuscan columns repeating those of the double galleries at both the front and the rear of the big house (Figure 65). Sometimes the *garçonnière* was constructed along with the house, as a way of giving additional space without impairing Greek Revival forms or the integrity of the peripteral gallery. At Houmas House, in Ascension Parish, where the style is Greek Revival with a monumental colonnade on the front and both sides, the *garçonnières* are ornamental, adding little space (Figure 66). The pair of two-story hexagonal *garçonnières,* with a hexagonal ogee roof ending in a plain finial, stand thirty feet high and ten feet to a side. They are masonry covered with stucco and whitewashed. Other plantations had monumental masonry garden houses, and here the *garçonnières* served also as garden houses. The pair of two-story rectangular *garçonnières* added to Destrehan off the side galleries around 1820 are in harmony with the big house's remodeling in the Greek Revival style twenty years later.

PIGEONNIERS

Domestic pigeons had value not only as ornamental birds and a delicacy but as a source of fertilizer. In the eighteenth century, the eggs and fowl held an important place in many people's diet, particularly in areas of new settlement. Concession, one of the first plantations in the colony, had a pair of dovecotes (*colombiers*) to complement its chicken houses and cattle pens (Plate A). The square, two-story structures framed the front of the main house. A century later, similar pigeon houses, by then called *pigeonniers,* framed the plantation house at Riverlake, on False River in Pointe Coupee Parish (Figure 67).

Pigeonniers went beyond the utilitarian even at Concession, where only the manager, not the owner, was in residence. Even the two simpler square *pigeonniers* that a watercolor from about 1794 shows at Chapdu plantation, in St. James Parish, were an adornment. Four posts in the ground lifted each of the pyramidally roofed *pigeonniers* a full story above ground, and the structures still framed the house aesthetically (Figure 68).[51] It was less a taste for squab than for status that exalted the pigeonnier. In France, only landowners had the right to keep pigeons under the Old Regime, and some of the landed gentry chose to frame their houses with pairs of dovecotes. In Louisiana, *pigeonniers* were rare outside the areas of French settlement. Only in Louisiana did commanding and decorative *pigeonniers* continue as a fashion well into the nineteenth century.

Placing a matching pair of *pigeonniers* to frame the big house as it was approached created the most baronial and decorative effect. But it was

---

51. Frank W. Wurlow and Trent L. James have told me that a similar *pigeonnier* stood near Thibodaux until the mid-1980s. In France, *pigeonniers* appear most commonly to have been round or square and made of stone. It is comparatively rare to find one raised on piers. Some polygonal structures appear to date from the late eighteenth century.

FIGURE 67   The *pigeonniers* at Riverlake, Pointe Coupee Parish, *ca.* 1830. In the vista toward False River, the oxbow formed by the cutoff from the Mississippi in 1722, only the building in the foreground survives.

Library of Congress. Photograph by Frances Benjamin Johnston.

FIGURE 68 Ink-and-watercolor representation of Chapdu plantation, St. James Parish, *ca.* 1794. Square dovecotes rose on piers in the area in front of a plantation house totally French in character. A row of slave quarters faced the rear of the house.

The Historic New Orleans Collection, 1971.66.

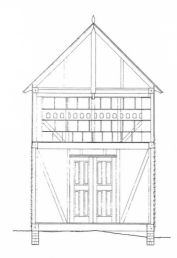

FIGURE 69 Oakland plantation, rear (north) *pigeonnier, ca.* 1825, facade and cross section. A ladder gave access to the second floor and to the eggs and squab there.

HABS, 1987, Louisiana State Archives

equally common to put a pair to the rear of the house, as at Uncle Sam, or to build a single *pigeonnier* either to the front or to the rear, as at Homeplace. Typically the building was square, of two stories, and its timber frame was raised on low brick piers (Figure 69). Clapboard siding covered the frame, which a wood-shingle pyramidal roof capped. At Oakland, the timber frames of both *pigeonniers* are filled with *bousillage* at the lower level and covered with clapboard at both levels. Unusually, both are at some distance from the house, one set forward and one to the rear. At Riverlake and Homeplace the lower story is brick and the upper clapboard over a timber frame. At Whitney, where only one of what was originally a pair survives, the construction is brick.

On some plantations the *pigeonniers* could be strikingly ornamental. The pair at Uncle Sam were hexagonal, eight feet to a side (Figure 28). The masonry walls were lime-washed the ocher color of the main house, but they were apparently not stuccoed and scored to resemble stone, although the house itself and its Greek Revival dependencies were (Plate H). The two-story *pigeonniers* had hexagonal steeply pitched curved roofs surmounted by finials. Forty-two feet high at the top of the weathervanes, a feature added later, they were a romantic and French touch in an otherwise Grecian setting. A similar pair of hexagonal *pigeonniers* that stood at Angelina, in St. John the Baptist Parish, were also eight feet to a side and had a comparable roof but rose only thirty-two feet (Figure 70). At both plantations, storage rooms were below and the pigeon loft above, and at both the pair were some distance from the rear of the main house.

The pair of octagonal *pigeonniers* at Parlange are the only polygonal ex-

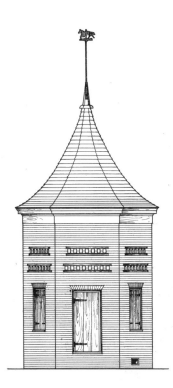

FIGURE 70   Angelina plantation, St. John the Baptist Parish, *pigeonnier, ca.* 1830–1850.

HABS, 1937, Library of Congress

FIGURE 71   *Pigeonnier* and house at Parlange plantation, Pointe Coupee Parish, *ca.* 1820. A pair of pigeon houses stand well forward, one to either side, framing the house.

Photograph by Jim Zietz

amples to survive (Figure 71). Seven feet to a side and thirty-eight feet tall with two full masonry stories, these have high-pitched octagonal roofs crowned with turned finials. Even more elaborate were the *pigeonniers* framing the house in the painting Persac did of Hope Estate around 1860 (Plate G). Octagonal, they were red brick on the first floor and white stucco on the second. Octagonal cupolas with weathervanes topped the high octagonal roofs.

To be secure from rats, cats, and other enemies, pigeons had to be housed high off the ground. Most pigeons inhabited the lofts of barns and carriage houses, even in the early nineteenth century. At Lady of the Lake plantation, in St. Martin Parish, where the house was built in 1827, the pigeons nested in the gable of the carriage house. By the latter part of the century, pigeons had few options among man-made shelters except for such lofts. The most elegant must have been the "castle" in the gable of the barn

FIGURE 72   Barn and pigeon loft at Elmwood plantation, near New Orleans, *ca.* 1860. The castellated dovecote in the barn gable is a whimsical and elaborate variation on post–Civil War cotes. Pigeons were now relegated to the barn.

Farm Security Administration, Library of Congress. Photograph by Russell Lee, 1938.

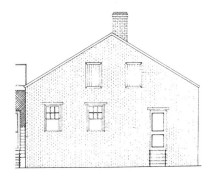

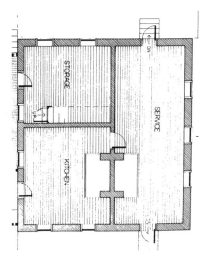

FIGURE 73   Wartelle, kitchen,
1827–1829, facade and plan.

HABS, 1985, Louisiana State Archives

at Elmwood, near New Orleans, photographed in the 1930s (Figure 72). During the final decades of the nineteenth century, owners were apt to follow the advice to make pigeon houses contribute, like the birds, to the decor of the grounds.[52]

KITCHENS

Pigeonniers and *garçonnières* were truly Creole, but they were not indispensable for a plantation. Other dependencies were true necessities. Every house had to have a kitchen, a privy, and a source of water. Wartelle still possesses its original kitchen and midcentury cistern and privy. That kitchen (Figure 73), like every other in eighteenth- and nineteenth-century Louisiana was separate from the house. It is unusual for its large size, approximately thirty feet to a side, its all-brick construction, and its three rooms, two of them with fireplaces. No evidence suggests that the simple pitched-roof building had a porch, though most drawings and photographs of other kitchens show porches across the front. It was the danger of fires, more than the heat of cooking, that dictated placing kitchens separately. At Magnolia Mound, at least one kitchen went up in flames, requiring a replacement, which was built on the same site.[53] Brick was safer but more costly.

The kitchen at Butler-Greenwood plantation also survives, and it is also brick (Figure 74). A unique component of that building is the open arcade set into the corner closest to the house for use as the well house. As at Wartelle, two of the rooms include fireplaces. The second of these may have been the cook's quarters, but a two-room kitchen building in Pointe Coupee Parish houses a kitchen and laundry. In an era when clothes were as a rule washed in the yard in a cast iron kettle, a laundry indoors, adjacent to the room for cooking, was a great convenience. Putting the well under the same roof made things even handier.

PRIVIES

The privy—or in the twentieth century's popular usage, the outhouse—at Wartelle faces the side of the house, the bedroom wing (Figure 75). Its three batten doors open into a single space with two carved seats, but only one with a lid. Three louvered windows open to the rear, and corrugated metal covers the original wood-shingle roof. A privy also sits behind the big house at Magnolia plantation, on the Cane River. It too rests on low brick piers and has a wooden floor and a low-pitched roof, but there is only a single batten door at the front. A louvered window ventilates from either side. The structure measures ten and a half by seven feet and rises twelve and a third feet at

52.   Byron D. Halsted, ed., *Barns, Sheds, and Outbuildings* (1881; rpr. Brattleboro, Vt., 1977), 43.

53.   Eileen K. Burden and Sherwood M. Gagliano, "Archaeological Excavation at Magnolia Mound: A Search for the 1830 Kitchen" (Baton Rouge, 1977), 29, 75–94. Kitchens with a porch across the front survive at Palo Alto, at Rosedown, in West Feliciana Parish, and at Maison Chenal, relocated from its original site to another, both in Pointe Coupee Parish.

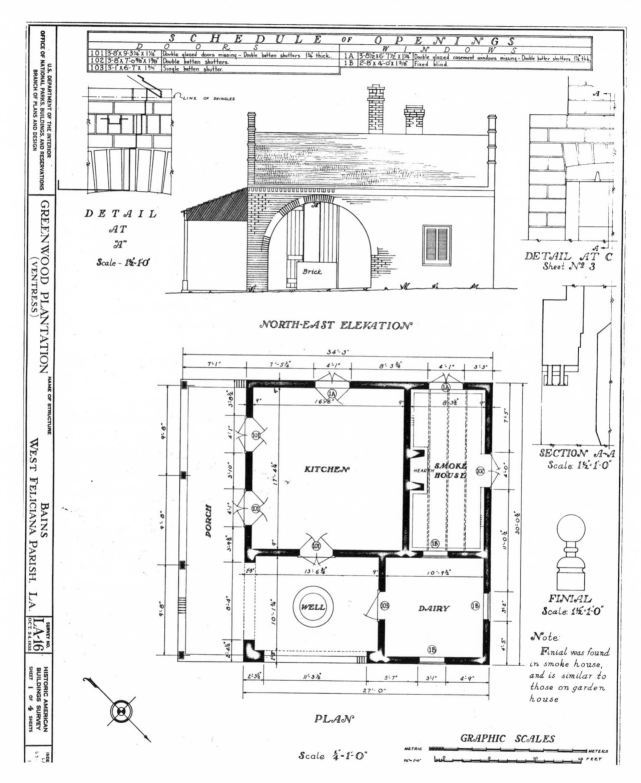

FIGURE 74 Butler-Greenwood, kitchen, *ca.* 1810–1830

HABS, 1938, Library of Congress

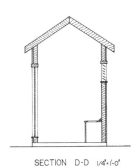

SECTION D-D 1/4"-1'-0"

FIGURE 75 Wartelle, privy, *ca.* 1850, facade and section.

HABS, 1985, Louisiana State Archives

FIGURE 76 A privy at Evergreen plantation, after 1832.

Photograph by Donna Fricker

the ridge of the roof. Until recently, a narrower privy with one door survived at Oakland plantation. There were three carved seats, two for adults and a lower one for children.

Few privies have long outlasted the need for them. Very few were brick, but the fine Greek Revival privy at Evergreen plantation has both brick walls and brick floors (Figure 76). It is situated in the rear yard and faces the house. Its four pilasters support a pediment, creating a miniature temple. The brick is stuccoed and scored to simulate stone on the front and sides. A pair of louvered windows flank the two center pilasters of the facade, and doors on either side of the building open onto private seats. The structure covers an area of seven and a half by thirteen feet, and it stands ten and a quarter feet tall on the side, thirteen and a half feet to the cap on the parapet. But far more customary, even for people of taste and refinement, was an almost square clapboard privy having a seat with just one hole.

Planters and their families could have the luxury of a commode, or commode chair—the *necessaire* of French Creoles—in their rooms. There was a removable pot beneath the carved seat, which was covered by a lid when not in use. Just about everybody had a chamber pot under the bed.

The best privies from after the Civil War are at Laurel Valley plantation, where rows of them, almost square and of frame construction, were installed on low piers behind rows of small frame tenant houses. Built in the late nineteenth and early twentieth centuries, many are still standing.[54] Their existence testifies to improved standards of sanitation after the war, since almost no privies paralleled antebellum slave quarters. Although there may have been pots, everyone had a yard. The earliest settlers and small agriculturists of the seventeenth and eighteenth centuries also did without privies.

WELLS AND CISTERNS

Any Louisianian could stand on the banks of the Mississippi and lament, "Water, water everywhere, nor any drop to drink." One of the last people to consider the water potable was probably Captain Philip Pittman in 1770, who allowed that the water was remarkably muddy but, "notwithstanding, extremely wholesome and well tasted." He added that the "inhabitants of New Orleans use no other water than that of the river, which, by keeping in a jar, becomes perfectly clear."[55]

In the eighteenth and nineteenth centuries water was mostly drawn from wells, but for those near the river or bayou, well water was scarcely an improvement. In 1822, the *New Orleans Directory and Register* recorded that wells were from five to fifteen feet deep, and although the water was clear, it

54. Neither the HABS drawings of 1978 nor the architectural inventory of 1975 included the privies, although there were rows of them at that time. The number is now much reduced.

55. Philip Pittman, *The Present State of the European Settlements on the Mississippi: A Facsimile Reproduction of the 1770 Edition* (Gainesville, Fla., 1973), 5.

was unpleasant to taste and unfit for drinking and washing clothes. Water from the river was preferred by the commentator for washing, cooking, and drinking, but only after it was filtered through a porous stone or allowed to settle in a large jar or cleared by alum. In 1847, *De Bow's Review* described a well in New Orleans as ten feet in depth and lined with boards but said that the water was "not adapted for washing in consequence of the presence of iron combined with carbonic acid: clothing, upon being washed or boiled in it, acquired a permanent yellowish hue." It judged even more objectionable the organic matter, which required careful filtering and still left a fetid aroma. Nineteenth-century wells at Lucy plantation, in St. John the Baptist Parish, had cypress lumber placed along the sides to prevent the soil from caving in. Those wells were as deep as thirty feet, with steps nailed to the sides for access. Larger wells up to eight feet square provided water for drinking and washing, and smaller ones watered the livestock.[56] On plantations, there was a well in the yard of the big house. A well house could protect the water from debris and the user from the elements. The round brick structure standing at the side of Hope Estate (Plate G) shelters the well. By the 1850s, well houses with lattice sides and hip roofs presented the appearance of summerhouses or gazebos. The well house for the Brame-Bennett House, in Clinton, repeats the Greek Revival style of the dwelling. It is a circular classical temple, small and rustic, with a conical roof and entablature complete with triglyphs and metopes, recapitulating the house's Doric order (Figure 77).

Planters in the lowlands of Louisiana may have wished to dig artesian wells, but the geology of the lower Delta for the most part precluded that. Still, there was usually plenty of rain, and rainwater was pure. The rain barrel, however, was a prime breeding ground for mosquitoes. Underground cisterns were built early in the nineteenth century. The one at Shadows-on-the-Teche was contemporary with the house (Figure 78). Built of brick, it was six feet deep and eleven feet in diameter, and it could hold over four thousand gallons. Its domed top extended almost three feet above the ground. Many of the neighbors were not equally well supplied. Mary C. Moore, of the Shadows, wrote in 1860, "I have found it very dry and many with cistern nearly dry." But underground cisterns were not limited to large houses. A set of underground cisterns served the quarters at Magnolia plantation, in Natchitoches Parish, possibly as early as the 1830s. On some plantations the cisterns were constructed of cast iron plates, which were available by the 1830s from Louisiana foundries. Building brick cisterns was a normal part of the building trade.[57]

56. John Adens Paxton, "Notes on New Orleans," *The New Orleans Directory and Register* (New Orleans, 1822), 41; "The Lowlands of Louisiana," *De Bow's Review,* I (1847), 455; Ervan G. Garrison *et al., Archaeological Investigations at Two Nineteenth Century Well Sites, Lucy, Louisiana* (College Station, Tex., 1980), 24.
57. Weeks Family Papers, Louisiana State University Libraries, from the research of Pat Kahle. The cast iron plates of the cistern at the Hermann-Grima House, in New Orleans, bore the mark

FIGURE 77   Brame-Bennett House, Clinton, well house, after 1840.

HABS, 1936, Library of Congress

FIGURE 78   Underground cistern at Shadows-on-the-Teche, 1831–1834.

Courtesy of Shadows-on-the-Teche, New Iberia, La., a museum property of the National Trust for Historic Preservation. Photograph by Pat Kahle.

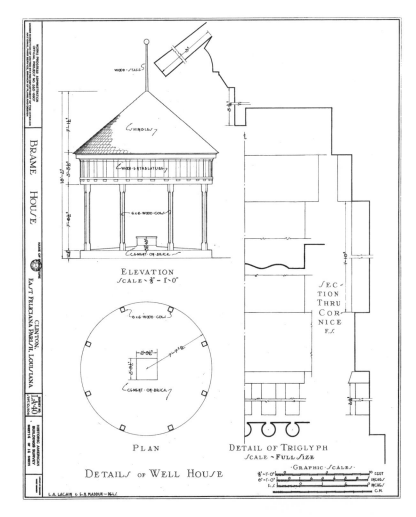

By far the most popular cistern, certainly the least expensive and most efficient, was assembled from cypress staves and iron hoops. It was in effect a large barrel, within the abilities of any good cooper. On October 10, 1853, William O. Diboll advertised in the New Orleans *Crescent,* "Carpenter & Builder, Cisterns made & repaired." In 1858, *Mygatt's Business Directory* listed fifteen cistern makers in the city. That is the earliest tabulation of cistern makers as artisans offering their services, but cisterns were common by the middle of the century. Those made of cypress were put on short piers or raised on a timber trestle or circular brick base (Figure 79). The cover was typically metal, whether flat with a decorative rim, conical, or ogee with a finial. The cistern that was at Gold Mine plantation, in St. James Parish (Fig-

E. E. Parker, N. Orleans, 1831. The original cistern was dismantled in 1935; the reproduction dates from 1973. A privately owned photograph shows that at least one plantation had cast iron cisterns on either side of the house.

FIGURE 79   The cistern at Destrehan, *ca.* 1850. Mrs. George Don Luce photographed her daughter Berthe and Destours LaRue, the plantation overseer, in 1893. The use of a great barrel supported on a trestle, here hidden by latticework, to supply domestic needs may have been inspired by the water towers that supplied the new steam locomotives. The two single-story buildings in the side yard were hospitals.

Courtesy of River Road Historical Society

FIGURE 80   The cistern that was moved from Gold Mine plantation, St. James Parish, to the Gallier House, New Orleans. The cistern was probably constructed around 1850.

Courtesy of the Gallier House, a museum property of Tulane University. Photograph by Frank Masson.

ure 80), but is now moved to the Gallier House, in New Orleans, rests on a round brick base four and a half feet high and is ten feet tall with a base diameter of seven and three-quarters feet. The height of the cistern's base produced sufficient water pressure for internal plumbing. The metal cover rises another four feet. The tallest cisterns, the height of which was limited by the length of the staves, ran to about fourteen feet. The broadest were about nine feet. At times one cistern sat atop another.[58]

In the second half of the nineteenth century, Louisiana cistern makers shipped cypress cisterns all over the South. After that, advances in indoor plumbing lessened the need, and the discovery of Walter Reed, during the Spanish-American War, that the mosquito is the carrier of yellow fever sparked questions about their safety, since stagnant bodies of water were breeding grounds for mosquito larvae.[59]

GARDENS AND GARDEN HOUSES

By the mid–nineteenth century, true garden houses and not just decorative well houses, cisterns, and outbuildings were gracing plantation grounds. Fanciful garden houses with lattice walls and ornamental roofs provided comparatively cool and breezy retreats and a focus for garden design. The fa-

58.   A newspaper clipping of an advertisement for P. A. Murran, a cistern maker at 183 Magazine Street, in New Orleans, is illustrated with a tall barrel cistern on a low brick base and a cover like Gold Mine's. The clipping is in the Historic New Orleans Collection (1982.127.191).

59.   *Twenty-Second Semi-Annual Report of the Sewerage and Water Board of New Orleans* (New Orleans, 1910), 35.

miliar American yard with grass and ornamental trees was already much in favor, although planters and their wives with more formal tastes lined the plantation approaches to their front doors with rows of trees and exotic specimens. Today the magnificent double row of live oaks, along the approach to Oak Alley, in St. James Parish, is the most beautiful and monumental record of the eighteenth- and nineteenth-century partiality to bordered drives. A love of the formal French gardens of the seventeenth and eighteenth centuries had been transposed to Louisiana and continued into the nineteenth, alongside the more contemporary preferences in landscape architecture.

The French arrived with designs for both buildings and gardens. As drawn around 1737, Concession plantation had a yard encircling the house and a formal garden laid out in parterres at the rear of the yard. Both yard and garden were enclosed by their own fences (Plate A). A circular bed defined the central cross axis of the garden, and radiating paths separated the beds. The drawing by Dumont de Montigny in the 1730s of probably the only plantation of the Jesuits in Louisiana shows a row of trees leading to the door, past two beds on each side.[60] Traditional Continental formalism of that sort continued through the eighteenth century. As drawn around 1794, Chapdu plantation had a fenced rear garden, with paths defining four rectilinear beds (Figure 68). The beds were tray shaped, with a quarter circle clipped from each corner and a circular bed placed neatly in the center. The chief dependencies stood on either side of the garden, which in all likelihood included herbs and vegetables as well as some purely ornamental plants.

Two different depictions of the de Marigny plantation, immediately downriver from New Orleans in the Faubourg Marigny, the neighborhood adjacent to the French Quarter, show four rectangles, each extending from the house to the front fence.[61] Separated by wide paths, these appear to be only turf. If so, de Marigny was perpetuating an especially austere seventeenth-century Continental formalism. The predilection for parterres continued into the nineteenth century. At Oakland, a formal garden still stands at the front of the house (Figure 81). On both sides of the brick path to the main steps are long narrow beds, and beyond them parterres: upriver is a square divided by diagonal paths with a star-shaped bed surrounded by a wide circular path at the crossing; downriver is a narrower rectangle with the single path, on its vertical axis, opening into a wide circular path around a small circular bed at the middle. Laid out probably after 1822, the garden is not bilaterally symmetrical; but then neither is the house: the square corresponds to the wider upriver section of the building. There are also beds between the front of the house and the other beds—rectangular, heart shaped,

60. Wilson, *The Architecture of Colonial Louisiana*, 105–107.
61. J. L. Bouquet de Woiseri, *Plans de la ville Orleans et des environs*, 1803, Vinache, *Map of Marigny Plantation*, 1801, both in Historic New Orleans Collection.

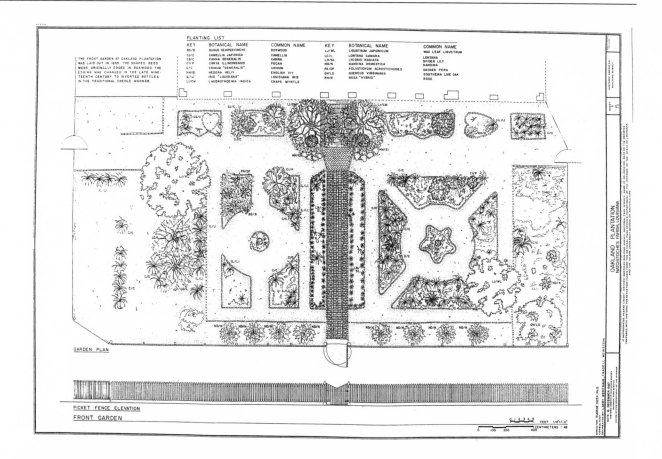

and rectangular with curved fronts. Paths outline these and separate them from the foundations. Oakland has the only surviving bottle garden, in which wine bottles pushed upside down into the soil edge every bed.

Formal plans and parterres were popular in England and its American colonies as well. The geometry of the garden at Butler-Greenwood plantation was much more intricate than at Oakland, but it followed the familiar pattern of a circular bed at the crossing of the principal walks (Figure 82). In the 1930s, remnants of the boxwood hedges still revealed the complex patterns of the formal design, which continued at a lower elevation on either side of the main parterre. Some plantings remain today, as do the steps and garden house of the north garden, on the edge of a deep ravine.

The focal point of the north garden is the octagonal summerhouse (Figure 83). Erected on a low mound, it has an ogee-arched roof in eight sections and an urn-shaped finial. The elegant framing of the roof is exposed to view on the interior. Elaborate lattices with pilasters between them provide shade and privacy without impeding the breeze. Entry is through arched openings, complete with keystones. Whether called garden houses or summerhouses, structures like this were the nineteenth century's charming addition to the garden. The one at Butler-Greenwood is likely from the 1850s, when the

FIGURE 82 Butler-Greenwood plantation, parterre, 1850s. The midcentury garden may have expanded an early-nineteenth-century design.

HABS, 1938, Library of Congress

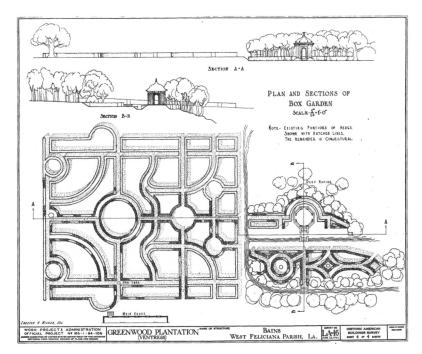

FIGURE 83 The summerhouse at Butler-Greenwood plantation, *ca.* 1850. The exotic summer house was a fanciful foil to the formality of the boxwood parterre.

Photograph by Barbara SoRelle Bacot

house was remodeled and enlarged, and it is similar to three at Rosedown plantation, nearby in West Feliciana Parish.

Much of the recent ancestry of these octagonal follies remains obscure. Their ultimate provenance is China, which was the inspiration for the octagonal pagodas of Anglo-Chinese gardens in France in the late eighteenth century, and earlier in England. A wide variety of antique and exotic structures punctuated the picturesque landscape of those gardens, which were considered particularly appropriate for urban settings, both large and small. Latticed pagodas had been suggested as "buildings for the ornamentation of the garden" by 1820.[62] By the mid–nineteenth century, they were a focus of gardens, irrespective of size, and whether rural or urban.

In Louisiana, Valcour Aime created a notable Anglo-Chinese garden at his plantation on the west bank in St. James Parish. An enthusiast for both high style and horticulture, he devised a garden that earned from its admirers the name Le Petit Versailles. As a young lady visiting in 1847 described it,

> There was a miniature river, meandering in and out and around the beautifully kept parterres, the tiny banks of which were an unbroken mass of blooming violets. A long-legged man might have been able to step across this tiny stream, but it was spanned at intervals by bridges of various designs, some rustic, some stone, but all furnished with parapets, so one would not tumble in and drown, as a little Roman [cousin] remarked. If it had not been before Perry's expedition to Japan, at any rate before his re-

62. Monique Mosser and Georges Teyssot, eds., *The Architecture of Western Gardens* (Cambridge, Mass., 1991), 19.

FIGURE 84   The carpenter shop, stable (outside the fence), setting pen for hens, and chicken coop at Oakland plantation, *ca.* 1820–1850.

Photograph by Jim Zietz

port was printed and circulated, one might have supposed M. Valcour received his inspiration in landscape gardening from the queer little Eastern people. There were summer houses draped with strange, foreign-looking vines; a pagoda on a mound, the entrance of which was reached by a flight of steps. It was an octagonal building, with stained-glass windows, and it struck my inexperienced eye as a very wonderful and surprising bit of architecture. Further on was—a mountain! covered from base to top with beds of blooming violets. A narrow, winding path led to the summit, from which a comprehensive view was obtained of the extensive grounds, bounded by a series of conservatories. It was enchanting. There I saw for the first time the magnolia frascati, at that date a real rarity.[63]

Others were equally entranced by the prospect. The site, now without house, pagoda, or exotic flora, survives with its river, which is usually dry, and its stone bridges and mountain—the mound of the icehouse.

Not every planter visited Versailles, as Aime did, or traveled to Italy, as the Turnbulls did, whose extensive garden may still be visited at Rosedown, where in addition to exotic flora, winding paths, a greenhouse, and gazebos, there are marble sculptures on high plinths lining the straight paths beside the live oak allée. The classical gods are copies, smaller in scale, of some of the statuary any educated tourist to Italy would see.

UTILITARIAN STRUCTURES ENCLOSED
WITHIN THE FENCES AROUND THE HOUSE

Most planters were more likely to have chicken coops than marble gods and goddesses, however. Even at Rosedown the dairy is close to the back door. Oakland has a formal parterre enclosed by its own fence in front of the house, and the house and garden and surrounding yard are enclosed by an

63.   Eliza Ripley, *Social Life in Old New Orleans* (New York, 1912), 188–89.

FIGURE 85   Oakland plantation,
carpenter shop, setting pen, chicken
coop, storage shed, fattening pen, and
washhouse, elevations along the rear
fence line, facing the house.

HABS, 1987, Louisiana State Archives

FIGURE 86   Enterprise plantation, Iberia
Parish, wine house, facade and section.
The buttery at Oaklawn plantation
looked very similar, and both served the
same purpose: keeping things cool.

HABS, 1994, Louisiana State Archives

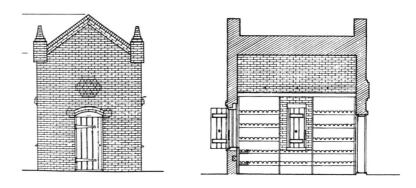

outer fence. Along the rear fence line and opening into the yard are a number of utilitarian structures: carpenter's shed, setting pen for hens, chicken coop, storage shed, and washhouse (Figures 84, 85). The necessities for living were thus close at hand, and Oakland's plan, of which there are today no other examples, may have been common. At Faye-Webster plantation, on Bayou Teche, a similar set of small buildings lined the side fence in the front yard.[64] The Hickeys, at Hope Estate, had peacocks, and the Lemanns, at Palo Alto, pet deer, but everybody had chickens and needed a place for them to roost, and few planters were willing to consider a tree, like Concession's willow, adequate protection.

The Yankee trader Ingraham remarked that "planters always have a separate building for everything," and a complete enumeration is impossible, even just around the house.[65] The yard and garden could include a cold frame for tender plants, a schoolhouse, a playhouse, a doghouse, a buttery for cool storage, and a building outfitted for storing wine (Figure 86). The planter de Boré had a billiard house and distillery near his residence. Outside the yard, but still close-by, were usually stables, barns, and corncribs.

STABLES AND CARRIAGE HOUSES

Even the earliest plantations numbered stables among their outbuildings. The inventory of Duvernay in 1726 records a stable twenty by thirty-two feet made of cypress posts in ground, most likely with *bousillage* between the

64.   Marie Adrien Persac, *Faye-Webster Plantation* (1857–61), in Louisiana State University Museum of Art.
65.   Ingraham, *Travels in the Southwest by a Yankee,* II, 242.

FIGURE 87   The stable at Oakland plantation, *ca.* 1820–1850. The rear *pigeonnier* stands to one side, and the carpenter shop is behind.

Photograph by Jim Zietz

posts. In form and material it differed only in size from other dependencies at the Duvernay concession. At Oakland, the timber-frame stable is forty by thirty-six feet, with two rows of stalls or loose boxes opening onto an off-center passage and a third set of boxes opening to the exterior (Figure 87). The double-pitched roof has exposed gable ends. In appearance it is the plantation's barn reduced in size, and both buildings were most likely constructed around or after 1820. The carriage house at Homeplace was the ground floor of the *pigeonnier.* The derelict building remains with brick walls at that level and frame above, with a pyramidal shingle roof. Possibly it dates from about 1800, but the same type recurred at Lady of the Lake, built in 1827 and 1828.[66] The two-story frame *pigeonnier* there had carriage doors the full width of the square. By 1860 it was painted white and had one-story shed-roof additions on two of its sides.

   Far more substantial and elaborate was the brick stable at Uncle Sam, with parapets at the gable ends (Figure 88). It stood in a pasture just upriver from the house and was roughly thirty feet by sixty feet. Its great height al-

66.   Prichard, "Inventory of the Paris Duvernay Concession," 986; Contract Between Despanet DeBlanc and Joseph Terence Bienvenu Devince and His Brother Alezandre Bienvenu Devince, 1827, in Conveyance Records, No. 5975, St. Martin Parish Courthouse. The house was completed the following year.

FIGURE 88   The stable at Uncle Sam
plantation, 1840s.

HABS, 1940, Library of Congress

lowed for the storage of hay on the upper level; the hay was brought in
through the upper opening in the gable end. Some plantation owners bred
racehorses. Among them, Kenner, of Ashland Plantation, was foremost, and
apparently his stabling was as extensive as his stock.

At times, plantation stables and carriage houses were as highly styled as
the plantation houses. The house at Germania, on the west bank in Ascension Parish, is in the Queen Anne style. The carriage house (Figure 89) and
the stable (Figure 90) more than match its high ornamentation. An ogee arch
frames the doors of the carriage house, with a broad ramp leading to them,
and a roundel and scalloped vergeboards decorate the gable. A tall octagonal
cupola crowns the roof over the entry, its louvers allowing good ventilation.
A watercolor by A. Boyd Cruise in the 1930s shows the building as ocher
with white trim. The stable must have been painted to match. It too has
ogee-arched doors, a roundel in the gable, and scalloped vergeboards. A
modest square cupola rises from the center of the elevated central bay. These
two structures are the unique surviving instances in Louisiana of intricately
decorated late-nineteenth-century dependencies.

BARNS

Sugarhouses and cotton presses and gins may have been the most evident ap-
purtenances of the plantation as a factory in the field, but barns, stables,
chicken houses, and fattening pens were part of the factory complex, as well.

Everywhere barns reflect the traditions of those who build them, and the
early barns of Louisiana exhibited the techniques of French Creole construc-

FIGURE 89 The carriage house at Germania plantation, Ascension Parish. A watercolor by A. Boyd Cruise in the 1930s shows what are very likely the original colors—ocher with white trim.

The Historic New Orleans Collection, 1983.47.4.1274. Photograph by Clarence John Laughlin, 1947.

FIGURE 90 The stable at Germania plantation, *ca.* 1890. Like the carriage house, the stable is in the Queen Anne style of the house.

The Historic New Orleans Collection, 1983.47.4.1275. Photograph by Clarence John Laughlin, 1947.

FIGURE 91   The barn at Homeplace plantation, *ca.* 1800. The HABS photograph—a copy of a photograph from around 1890—shows the original long shingles under the twentieth-century metal roofing. The original photograph does not survive.

HABS, 1940, Library of Congress

tion. Nearly every farm or plantation in colonial America needed a place to store grain. Where the winters were severe, the animals too had to be sheltered. The colonists' very survival hinged on their granaries and animal husbandry.

In 1737, at the time the early plantation Concession was sold, eighteen years after being established, it had two barns (*granges*) and an animal pen (*parc aux bestiaux*) with an enclosed shed. The pen stood within the palisaded stockade surrounding the house; the barns were to the rear, outside the stockade. The relatively crude drawing from around the time of the sale shows both barns with high hip roofs like the one on the house. They were not dissimilar from the barn built at Whitney plantation almost a hundred years later. Unlike northern barns, which stored grain and fodder and housed livestock, the barns at Concession appeared to be for storage only, and the animals, which required no shelter much of the year, had only a shed. No barns survive from the colonial era, but traditional Creole building methods continued well into the nineteenth century. The barn at Homeplace lasted into the twentieth century (Figure 91). Difficult to date, but possibly erected sometime around 1800, or earlier, it had timber-frame construction—mortised, tenoned, and pegged—that repeated earlier ways of building (Figure 92). The barn, seventy feet long and forty-eight feet wide, had a raised central area about fifty feet by twenty-seven feet. As in other timber-frame construction in Louisiana and barn building in other parts of the country, lateral frames (bents) were assembled on the ground and raised. The uprights of the central area and the roof trusses supported the vast umbrella roof, which extended out over a gallery ten and three-quarters feet wide on all four sides. Packed earth constituted the floor of the gallery, but the floor of the central area was planked. The HABS drawings of 1940 show no stalls, but animals, wagons, and equipment could have been

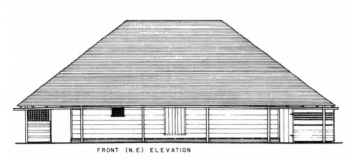
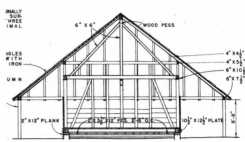

FIGURE 92   Homeplace plantation, barn, elevation and cross section
HABS, 1940, Library of Congress

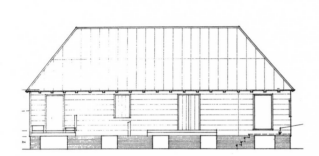
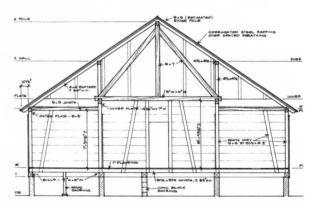

FIGURE 93   Whitney plantation, St. John the Baptist Parish, barn, *ca.* 1810–1820, facade and cross section.

Courtesy of William Brockway, LSU School of Architecture.

sheltered on the galleries. The plan is typical for Louisiana, as are the long Creole shingles, measuring over three feet.

The early-nineteenth-century barn at Whitney is smaller and has a less dramatic umbrella roof (Figure 93). Like the central section of the barn at Homeplace, this structure has a mortised, tenoned, and pegged timber frame elevated on piers, plank floors, and flush horizonal weatherboards. It too appears to have been a granary or a repository for fodder and equipment.

Another variety of Creole barn is found at Oakland (Figure 94). There a raised peeled-log crib with a plank floor and gable roof has a gallery on all four sides. The crib is thirteen feet by fourteen and a half feet, and the galleries are ten feet deep on one end and side and thirteen feet on the other end and side. Nonetheless, the roof appears symmetrical, and the barn roof is similar in construction, although without the double pitch, to those of typical small Creole houses with peripteral galleries. Across the Cane River at Magnolia the small barn used for a blacksmith shop has the same plan and roof, but the central section is timber-frame and *bousillage* (Figure 95).

The barns in Natchitoches Parish may embody a meeting of cultures. Without the galleries on the front and rear, the log crib barn with shed roofs

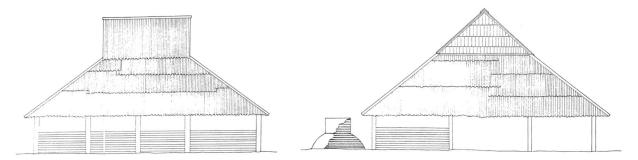

FIGURE 94   Oakland plantation, barn, *ca.* 1820–1850, north and east elevations. The upper section of an underground cistern stands at the corner.

HABS, 1987, Louisiana State Archives

FIGURE 95   A *pigeonnier* and barn at Magnolia plantation, Natchitoches Parish, *ca.* 1820–1850. The barn is timber frame and *bousillage.* It is known as the blacksmith shop, doubtless from the smith's setting up shop on the earth floor under the gallery, which extends on all four sides of the raised central section. The *pigeonnier* stands near the barn.

Photograph by Jim Zietz

on either side would be scarcely distinguishable from the single-crib barn familiar across the South.[67] Wherever settlers built log houses, they also built their barns and other outbuildings of logs. Log construction was common in the Florida parishes and in north Louisiana.

The mule barn commanded special attention on the plantation, for it was mules, not oxen or horses, that drew the plows and carts. The midcentury barn at Evan Hall plantation, in Iberville Parish, was unusual in being brick (Figure 96). With its stepped gables, it is a larger counterpart to the stable for fine horses at Uncle Sam.

After the Civil War, the United States became more unified both culturally and politically. The advent of better sawmills and extensive railroads in

67.   Stanley Schuler, *American Barns: In a Class by Themselves* (Exton, Pa., 1984), 54, 56–57. Schuler includes examples of typical southern barns in Louisiana: the gable-end, center-aisle barn with shed-roof side aisles, and the less common four-crib cross barn at Rosedown.

FIGURE 96 Stockyard in front of mule barn, Evan Hall plantation, Iberville Parish, as it appeared around 1890. The stepped gable of the mule barn repeats that of the sugarhouse.

Collection of the Louisiana State Museum. Photograph by François Mugnier (Stock Yard, Evan Hall Plantation).

FIGURE 97 Mule barn at Cinclare plantation, West Baton Rouge Parish. This was one of two large barns on the plantation.

National Register File, Louisiana Division of Historic Preservation. Photograph by Donna Fricker.

Louisiana in the postwar years meant the introduction of the balloon frame. Agriculturists became aware of the importance of ventilation, sanitation, and safety in barn design. The editor of the *American Agriculturist* in 1887 took farmers and planters to task for their outmoded habit of building small barns, and then "sheds, pigpens, corn houses, and such minor structures as might seem desirable. . . . In the course of a few years the group of roofs, big and little, span and lean-to, in the rear of a large farmer's dwelling, would present the appearance of a small crowded village." In an era of "good sense and enlarged ideas," he recommended replacing with a single well-arranged barn the crowd of inconvenient buildings that were expensive to keep in repair.[68]

The most conspicuous feature of late-nineteenth-century barns is the cupola or lantern providing ventilation. Ventilation was necessary for both the sanitary housing of livestock and the safe storage of hay. Drying hay generates heat and can result in spontaneous combustion, which the draft from doors and windows up through the cupola could make less likely. A gigantic cupola distinguished the mule barn at Cinclare, in West Baton Rouge Parish (Figure 97). At St. John plantation, in St. Martin Parish, the well-arranged barn of two cupolas—the building now demolished—complied with the recommendations of the late nineteenth century. By the end of the century, Louisiana barns were American in both plan and decoration.

OTHER PROCESSING FACILITIES

In the eighteenth century, the processing of wax myrtle for candles and indigo for blue dye required little in the way of buildings. Making wax and candles occupied only part of the rear ell at de Pradel's Mon Plaisir. Sheds, such as at Concession around 1737, were usually sufficient for extracting indigo. In 1758, Le Page Du Pratz, who had traveled from France to Louisiana in 1718 and spent sixteen years there, published a volume on the region in which he included a description of one indigo manufactory. That was a "shed at least twenty feet wide, without walls or flooring, but only covered. The whole is built upon posts, which may be closed with mats, if you please: this building has twenty feet in depth and at least thirty in length."[69]

With the large-scale planting of sugarcane made profitable in Louisiana by the successful granulation of sugar in 1795, the sugarhouse began to dominate the agricultural landscape. In the nineteenth century every sugar plantation had nearby access to a grinding mill and a boiling house, even if it was a joint operation with one or two neighbors. Like de Boré, planters continued to experiment. Steam power came in 1822, and by 1828 it drove 67 of Louisiana's 705 mills. By 1850, the state had 1,495 sugarhouses, 907 of them run by steam. In 1869, after the Civil War, the number of sugarhouses had declined to 817, but by 1882 there were 910.[70] In the twentieth century the decline resumed, first owing to the mosaic disease of the 1920s, and then because of the greater efficiency of larger operations. The last quarter of the twentieth century has seen a great reduction in the growing of sugarcane in the state. Only a few sugarhouses are still in use.

No early sugarhouses survive, but a building contract of March 12, 1799, between the civil architect Marie Godefroi Du Jarreau and the planter Alexan-

68. Halsted, ed., *Barns, Sheds, and Outbuildings*, 13.
69. De Pradel, *Le Chevalier*, 184, "Correspondence of the Chevalier de Pradel," 24; Le Page du Pratz, *The History of Louisiana* (1774; rpr. Baton Rouge, 1975), 190–91.
70. Rehder, "Sugar Plantation Settlements," 205, 199.

FIGURE 98 The sugarhouse built for Alexandre Bodin on his plantation in Metairie, Jefferson Parish, elevation. The right end is curved to accommodate the cattle mill.

New Orleans Notarial Archives. Acts of Narcisse Broutin, Book 42 (formerly Book 10). The elevation is bound in front of folio 1.

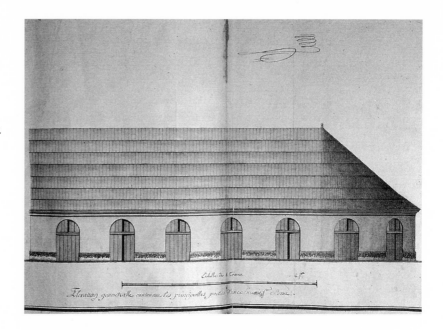

dre Bodin calls for the "establishment of a sugar mill, situated on his land called 'La Metairie.'"[71] The mill, or sugarhouse, was a long, brick structure with a steeply pitched roof; its floor plan was squared at one end and semicircular at the other, and large arched doorways opened into the interior (Figure 98). In addition to the elevation, there are drawings of construction details such as the roof truss, which was similar to that of the Ursuline Convent (Chapter 1, Figure 20). The rounded end of the building housed the cattle mill to crush the sugarcane and extract the juice. Whether, as in the eighteenth century, oxen or horses powered such mills, or as in the nineteenth, mules propelled them, they were always called cattle mills (Figure 99).

The French general Victor Collot described de Boré's sugar works, which he had visited: "His establishment consists of a mill, drying room and shed (the whole built of bricks and covered with tiles)." The inventory of de Boré's estate after his death in 1820 mentioned details about the sugarhouse, a mill for grinding, and a purgery for draining molasses from the barrels of crystallized sugar. The sugarhouse and contiguous mill had a shingle roof and galleries on three sides; the building was sixty feet long by forty feet

---

71. Court Proceedings, January–August, 1800, Narcisse Broutin notary, Book 42 (formerly Book 10), folios 1–123, in New Orleans Notarial Archives. See Samuel Wilson, Jr., "Architecture of Early Sugar Plantations," in *Green Fields,* by Le Gardeur *et al.,* 68–69. The elevation is presumed to be Du Jarreau's, but it is not dated, signed, or attached to the contract. Since it is bound with both the contract and the subsequent lawsuit, it may be by another hand. Bartholomey La Fon, who was called as an expert witness, testified that the building was not constructed according to the plans he was shown. This document is one of the earliest drawings in the New Orleans Notarial Archives and one of the few from the Spanish period.

FIGURE 99   An eighteenth-century cattle mill. A team of two horses turned the sweeps; larger mills had four teams.

Private collection. From a loose page from an edition of Encyclopédie; ou, Dictionnaire raisonnée des sciences, *ed. Denis Diderot, that was published around 1850.*

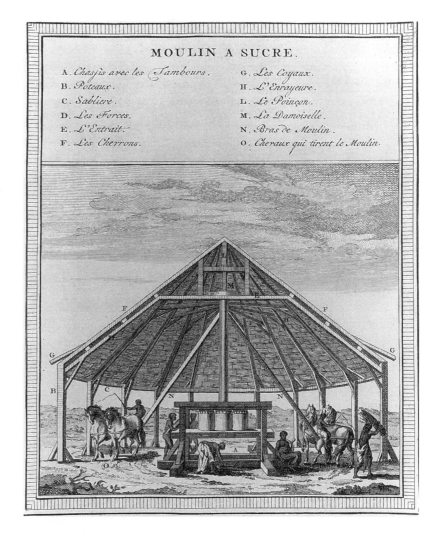

wide, not including the galleries, which were twelve feet wide on one side and nine feet wide on the other two.[72]

Robin described the first sugar mills in Louisiana as hexagonal or octagonal, and told of seeing the then-new circular mill of a Creole named de Gruise. That may have been the domed mill the engineer John Latrobe sketched in 1834. There the syrup was boiled in a long brick building adjacent to the mill. Latrobe recorded that the circular mill had been erected some years before and had been powered originally by horses. He added that the buildings put up since were very different in appearance.[73]

72.   Collot, *A Journey in North America,* II, 169–74; "Estate of Jean Etienne de Bore," in Probate Inventories, 1819–1820, p. 199, New Orleans Public Library. The inventory is also in "Architecture of Early Sugar Plantations" by Wilson, 72–73. Collot's description is also in "Translation of General Collot's Description of de Boré's Sugar House, *Louisiana Historical Quarterly,* I (1918), 327–29; and in "Architecture of Early Sugar Plantations," by Wilson, 72.

73.   Robin, *Voyage to Louisiana,* 107–109; Latrobe, *Southern Travels,* 56. Latrobe's father had also sketched a domed mill near New Orleans. See Samuel Wilson, Jr., ed., *Impressions Respecting New Orleans by Benjamin H. B. Latrobe, 1819* (New York, 1951), following p. 166.

The nineteenth-century sugarhouse was in its basic form a long rectangular building, either frame or brick, with tall square chimneys. The sugarhouse at St. John plantation, on Bayou Teche, was typical, although its high clerestory between the main roof and the lower roof made it better lighted than many (Figure 100). Some planters, however, went far beyond the basic. They built sugarhouses with a Greek temple front or with scrolled gables reminiscent of the Jacobean period and the British colonies in the Caribbean. At least one preferred a Gothic sugarhouse.[74] Of more lasting influence were technical advances in the processing of sugar, although epochal changes did not come to the sugarhouse until the twentieth century and the industry's consolidation in huge mills, as at Meeker (Chapter 6, Figure 16). In the twentieth century, sugarhouses came to be of steel-frame construction with corrugated metal roofing and siding, and they are the only ones still in use.

In addition to wax myrtle and indigo, eighteenth-century planters grew rice and tobacco. In the nineteenth century, small farmers continued to cultivate tobacco, and almost everyone, including slaves, grew corn. But when a hundred acres planted in sugarcane had the value of five hundred acres planted in rice, the allure of rice as a crop faded except, occasionally, on acreage away from the river.[75] In nineteenth century Louisiana, sugarcane in the south and cotton in the north were the principal crops. But the mosaic disease that attacked sugarcane in the 1920s and the boll weevil that infested cotton in the 1930s led to experimentation with other crops and the reduction of acreage for historic ones. Sugarcane plantations combined into great corporate holdings, and in the second half of the twentieth century farm products like soybeans became ascendant in south Louisiana. Along the Mississippi from New Orleans to Baton Rouge, petrochemical plants and barge facilities now loom where once there were fields of cane.

Timber brought in significant revenue for plantations in the eighteenth and nineteenth centuries. When the Mississippi was high, the flow of water through a channel at the top of the levee to the back swamp turned waterwheels and powered the sawmills. With the introduction of steam, any plantation with a good stand of timber could have a sawmill. Sawed timber was sold, and wood fired the boilers for the sugarhouse and the sawmill, which stood in a separate large shed, either open or enclosed.[76]

74. A. D. Lytle's photograph C-92, of Homestead, in West Baton Rouge Parish (Louisiana State University Libraries), shows a temple front on the long side of the sugarhouse. Paret's watercolors include the best example of scrolled gables. A photograph by Robert W. Tebbs from 1926 (Louisiana State Museum) shows a polygonal Gothic tower.

75. Rehder, "Sugar Plantation Settlements," 91. Whitney plantation, which grew rice in low-lying areas of the back swamp, was the only plantation to grow rice into the 1970s. The ditches were still clearly visible in the 1970s.

76. Pittman, *The Present State of European Settlements,* 24; D. B. Warden, *A Statistical, Political, and Historical Account of the United States of North America* (2 vols.; Edinburgh, 1819), II, 46. Warden had visited the United States in 1801–1802. For an illustration of water power, see Bouquet de Woiseri, *Plan de la ville Orleans.*

FIGURE 100 Marie Adrien Persac, *St. John Plantation in St. Martin Parish*, 1861, detail. The sugarhouse at Lizima plantation (St. John plantation after 1880) was typical of brick sugarhouses. All had tall brick chimneys, which were usually square. The windows along the edge of the upper roof helped light the interior. The gable-end wagon sheds sheltered both sugarcane and equipment.

Courtesy of Louisiana State University Museum of Art, Baton Rouge

FIGURE 101   The cotton gin at Magnolia plantation, in Natchitoches Parish, *ca.* 1830–1850. There were originally a greater number of dormers. The slave quarters are visible to the rear.

Photograph by Jim Zietz

Cotton needed less extensive processing on the plantation than sugar. The cotton gin removed the seed from the boll, and the press compacted the cotton into bales for shipping, both processes taking place in a building called a cotton gin across the South. The cotton gin at Magnolia plantation, in Natchitoches Parish, is a timber-frame building thirty-seven feet by eighty-five feet on low brick piers. The building has a high gable roof that continues down to a ten-foot overhang supported by posts (Figure 101). It is covered with clapboards and originally had a shingle roof. A wooden screw press from about 1830 is now inside the building (Figure 102). Originally it was out in a field, where it was turned by mules like a cattle mill. A late-nineteenth-century steam-powered gin and a hydraulic press also survive. The timber-frame gin and the wooden press are comparable to those on almost every cotton plantation of the time, but they are the only ones still existing in Louisiana.

FIGURE 102 The screw press at Magnolia plantation. Built of wood, it was turned by sweeps like the cattle mill. When it was moved inside the gin, it was likely powered by steam. The gin still has much of its late-nineteenth-century equipment.

Photograph by Jim Zietz

FIGURE 103 The store at Oakland plantation, converted sometime between 1870 and 1890 from a building that served another purpose.

Photograph by Jim Zietz

After the Civil War, when sharecropping replaced gang labor on cotton lands, the cotton house was added to the plantation's buildings. At Inglewood plantation, in Rapides Parish, the cotton house built around the turn of the century is still there—a long, narrow one-story frame structure with doors along each side opening to separate compartments for storing each tenant's crop. Other twentieth-century outbuildings at Inglewood were corrugated metal on wooden frames. Later in the twentieth-century, gins and their ancillary structures were to be steel frame with metal siding.

Another postwar addition to cotton and sugar plantations was the commissary, the plantation store. The commissary was the most convenient supplier of just about everything the new rural wage earners needed. Although at Oakland the commissary was adapted from an earlier building, it has the gable front and porch of most (Figure 103). Some large two-story commissaries looked like prewar country stores run by families. Some of the largest, like the one on the Ovide La Cour plantation, in Pointe Coupee Parish, served surrounding plantations (Figures 104, 105). It was frame, with the Italianate details favored for commercial buildings in the late nineteenth century.

Around the turn of the century, boardinghouses were erected for migrant workers.[77] But with increased mechanization and improved transport,

77. Cinclare had two boarding houses, segregated by race.

FIGURE 104   Ovide La Cour plantation, Point Coupee Parish, store, *ca.* 1880. The HABS architects employed photogrammetry to capture the structure shortly before demolition.

LSU School of Architecture. Photograph by Barrett Kennedy.

FIGURE 105   Ovide La Cour store

HABS, 1992, Louisiana State Archives

and with the rise of conglomerate landholdings, fewer gins, sugarhouses, and other structures related to processing were necessary. The advances that gas, electricity, plumbing, and refrigeration brought into the house meant that most of the outbuildings around the house were no longer necessary. What was no longer needed fell into disrepair and vanished from the landscape. The houses might still be used, but many spared by hurricane and fire were abandoned by families relocating to towns and cities and lost through neglect. Others were razed to make way for industry. The surviving houses and even rarer surviving outbuildings unite as the best document of Louisiana's plantation past.

5

Urban Growth, 1815–1880
Diverse Tastes—Greek, Gothic,
and Italianate

Joan G. Caldwell

In the 1830s, New Orleans was one of the fastest-growing cities in America. In the 1820s, the population grew from 17,000 to 46,000, and by 1840 it had reached 102,000. By 1835, New Orleans was the second port in America, exporting more than New York by several million dollars' worth of goods each year. By 1839, the banks in New Orleans had a larger capitalization than those in New York. Vigorous steamboat traffic had given rise to a cosmopolitan atmosphere by the late thirties, and the interplay of travelers, actors, merchants, planters, tradesmen, and immigrants made for an exciting urban milieu. The appetizing mixture of bustling activity and abundant wealth attracted architects from the East Coast and Great Britain to settle permanently in the city, which gradually outgrew its original colonial plan.

When, in 1721, John Law commissioned the surveyor Adrien de Pauger to lay out the streets of New Orleans, the result was a rectangular plan, similar to that of Detroit, another French settlement in America. In 1731, the city extended only to the river side of Dauphine Street, and everything beyond that was described as woods (Back endpaper). Development was slow during the eighteenth century. Barracks, Burgundy, and Iberville Streets were not developed beyond the city fortifications until the very end of the eighteenth century. Pauger based his street widths on the French foot, a measurement three-quarters of an inch greater than the English foot. Thus an ordinary street in the original town, now the French quarter, or Vieux Carre, when laid out to Pauger's specification of a width of 36 French feet, was 38 feet, 4 3/8 inches wide, and the streets bordering the Vieux Carre were considerably broader. The attraction of the Mississippi and the difficulties in draining swampy lands restricted the populace in the Vieux Carre to the natural levee along the river. Construction was on a relatively small scale, with two- and three-story buildings dominating until about 1820, when the American

FIGURE 1 Jacques Tanesse, *Plan of the City and Suburbs of New Orleans,* 1815, published 1817. The illustrations in the border include Latrobe's Custom House (*douane*) and waterworks (*pompe à feu*), the Spanish Colonial Cabildo (*hôtel de ville*), the church (*église Paroissialle*) and Presbytère, and the French Colonial Ursuline Convent (*convent des religieuses*) and government house. The original rectangular section of the city, the Vieux Carre, is defined by Canal Street upriver, Esplanade Avenue downriver, and Rampart Street—all shown here as boulevards with trees. Known now also as the French Quarter, it is at the apex of the river's crescent. Because of the curve in the city's layout as it follows the river's course, directions in New Orleans are given not by reference to the compass but as uptown and downtown, and lakeside and riverside. Upriver is to the left, downriver to the right. Lakeside is in the direction toward Lake Pontchartrain, that is, as the streets point away from the crescent of the river. The Central Business District and the Garden District are upriver from the French Quarter, Faubourg Marigny is downriver. Rampart Street is named for a fortification that was designed but never built.

The Historic New Orleans Collection, 1971.4.

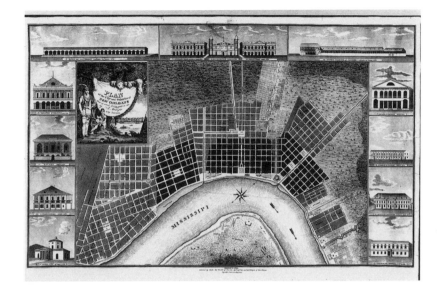

influence came to complement the earlier French-Spanish, or Creole, traditions and the city expanded both up and down the river.

Benjamin Henry Latrobe, the well-traveled architect and engineer who first came to the United States from England in 1796, brought with him a familiarity with Europe's architectural heritage and an awareness of architectural styles, ideas, and tastes. He established an office in Philadelphia, but his contacts soon grew well beyond that city. His various early designs in this country reflected popular neoclassical taste, as well as the beginning of the interest in Greek and Gothic forms. Latrobe sent designs south for two important early buildings in New Orleans: the Custom House, in 1807, and the engine house of the New Orleans Waterworks, in 1811–1812. He applied a temple front to the rectangular block of the engine house and surmounted it with an octagonal tower reminiscent of the Tower of the Winds, of ancient Athens. Latrobe sent his son Henry S. Latrobe to oversee construction of the waterworks. In 1814, the younger Latrobe collaborated with the architect Arsène Lacarrière Latour to design the Thierry House, at 721 Governor Nicholls Street, possibly the earliest surviving example of Greek Revival architecture in the city.

Both those buildings, now demolished, were among the structures illustrated in the margins of the map of New Orleans that Jacques Tanesse produced in 1815 (Figure 1). The engravings there show the changing taste of the period, when the Federal style, well established as the American interpretation of late-eighteenth-century English neoclassicism, was still strong. This style responded to the new awareness of ancient Roman buildings, such as the Palace of Diocletian, in Split, and to new discoveries, as at Pompeii. Ground arcades, delicate fanlights over doors and windows, carved cornices with simple bellflowers or garlands along the frieze, and wrought-iron bal-

FIGURE 2 Louisiana State Bank, 409 Royal Street, New Orleans, 1819, Benjamin Henry B. Latrobe architect, cross section and front elevation. The display windows on either side of the main entrance originally had heavy batten blinds.

HABS, 1934, Library of Congress

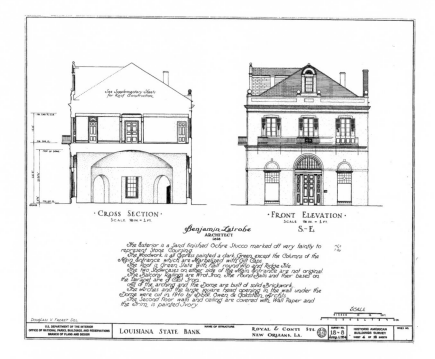

conies were all part of the Federal style. Elements of the newer Greek fashion sometimes accompanied the neoclassical.

When Latrobe visited New Orleans in 1819, he designed the State Bank of Louisiana (Figure 2), a discreet urban structure fronting directly on Royal Street, with arched windows at street level, a curved room at the back, and a delicate wrought-iron balcony at the second level. His design renders a subtle interpretation of the neoclassical, with the objective of fitting the bank into the New Orleans cityscape. In the interior, brick vaulting and dome arc over what were the ground-floor banking quarters, demonstrating Latrobe's proficiency as an engineer. Originally the roof was almost flat; the dormers and hip roof were added later. The plan (Figure 3) is reminiscent, on a smaller scale, of Latrobe's Bank of Pennsylvania, built in Philadelphia in 1800. The State Bank of Louisiana was the architect's final building. He died in 1820 of yellow fever, the plague that regularly devastated New Orleans in the nineteenth century.

The years from 1820 to 1835 were formative for both the Vieux Carre and the new neighborhoods (*faubourgs*). Row houses like those in Philadelphia and Boston went up in twos and threes and then in blocks of a dozen or more. Among the architects and builders active in this period were William Brand, J. N. B. de Pouilly, and A. T. Wood, as well as Claude Gurlie and Joseph Guillot, who were in partnership. The very number of architects practicing was an index of the growth and sophistication of the city. Brand, the architect of the Grima House, built in 1831 at 820 St. Louis Street with modest Federal motifs, began designing in the neoclassical style as early as

FIGURE 3   Louisiana State Bank, first
floor plan.

HABS, 1934, Library of Congress

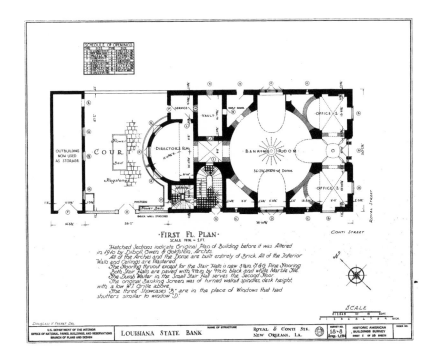

FIGURE 3   Louisiana State Bank, first
floor plan.

HABS, 1934, Library of Congress

1810. Gurlie and Guillot employed bellflowers and garlands in their friezes in
the Tricou House, at 711 Bourbon Street, and the Vignie House, at 713–715
Royal Street. Other Federal details that began to recur were wrought-iron
balconies, arcaded ground stories, and dormer windows. De Pouilly included ground-level arcades in several of his buildings, among them
Dufilho's Pharmacy, at 514 Chartres Street, a building at 618–620 Conti
Street, and Exchange Passage. Exchange Passage was a harmonious set of
three-story buildings developed to provide an approach to the St. Louis Exchange Hotel, then in competition with the St. Charles Hotel, across Canal
Street in the American sector. Property owners along the street agreed to
build according to the architect's plans for a uniform effect, setting a precedent for later city-planning efforts. Although there is much variation in the
structures in the Vieux Carre, the scale of the buildings at its core—most are
two or three stories—and the frequent appearance of wrought-iron galleries,
and then of cast iron in the mid–nineteenth century, impart an impression
of unity.

By the late eighteenth and early nineteenth century, while the French
and Spanish continued governing New Orleans, domestic architecture had
developed four repeating forms. The French or Creole cottage had four in-
terconnecting rooms—and no hall—on a single floor. The raised cottage was
also a one-story cottage but on tall piers. The Creole town house had a side
passage to a rear courtyard. The galleried pavilion was above a raised basement or first floor. (Because of the high water table, virtually no New Orleans structures of the eighteenth or nineteenth century had underground

FIGURE 4   Julia Row, 600 block of Julia Street, New Orleans, 1833.

Photograph by Jim Zietz

FIGURE 5   608 Julia Street, detail of original entrance.

Photograph by Jim Zietz

basements.) Construction modeled on these four types persisted through the nineteenth century, and later in the century a fifth type gained acceptance, since it could occupy a narrow lot: the so-called shotgun house, with rooms arranged one row behind the other (Chapter 7, Figures 17–24).

After the Louisiana Purchase, American ideas about layout brought the sidehall house—which was also called the London-plan house. Acceptance of sidehall layouts drew a sharp comment from Latrobe, who wrote that houses without halls, in the French manner, were superior to English houses in their use of space: "But so inveterate is habit that the merchants from the old United States . . . have already begun to introduce the detestable, lop-sided London house, in which a common passage and stairs acts as a common sewer to all the necessities of the dwelling."[1]

In the 600 block of Julia Street is a row of thirteen houses with common side walls (Figure 4), as in Philadelphia and Baltimore. According to Arthur Scully, James Dakin may have been the architect of the row houses, erected in 1833. Still residing in New York at the time, Dakin was connected with a New Orleans contractor and sent drawings for the houses.[2] Each of the three-story units is two rooms deep and has a side stair hall. The width of a dwelling is 26 feet. A one-room-deep service wing stands at right angles to the rear of each house, with galleries facing a narrow courtyard. Including the wing, the depth of a house is 135 feet. The elegant fanlights above the doors and the slender Ionic columns alongside are neoclassical details (Figure 5). The transom fanlights radiate from a central nodal point, and six floral torches or spikes separate them. The door's sidelights are articulated as

1. Samuel Wilson, Jr., ed., *Impressions Respecting New Orleans by Benjamin H. B. Latrobe, 1819* (New York, 1951), 42.

2. Arthur Scully, *James Dakin: His Career in New York and the South* (Baton Rouge, 1973), 13–14.

FIGURE 6   A Greek Revival town house, one of a row of three on Rampart Street, near Bienville Street, in New Orleans, 1834, James Gallier architect.

Richard Koch Collection, Southeastern Architectural Archive, Tulane University. Photograph by Richard Koch for HABS.

elongated garland shapes, three to the right and three to the left, and these are linked by carved bows. On the facade, only the deep entablature has the robustness of a Greek style. On the main floor—the second story—the black marble mantel with Ionic columns supporting the shelf and the heavily undercut acanthus leaves of the ceiling medallions are typically Greek. The reeded moldings are reminiscent of earlier neoclassical motifs. Like many buildings of the 1830s, the row houses of Julia Street are transitional in style. The transitional coexisted with the full-blown Greek Revival. In a row of three townhouses built on North Rampart Street, at the edge of the Vieux Carre, in 1834, each unit had a monumental portico, with four columns supporting a heavy entablature and a pediment (Figure 6). Yet temple fronts were rare for town houses. Numerous multiple-unit residential buildings followed the row on Julia Street. The sidehall plan, with its two major rooms, was extremely well received in the city, particularly for more expensive houses and apartments. Two- and three-story brick town houses with second-story balconies still stand not only in the upriver American sector but also in

FIGURE 7   A Greek Revival town house with side stair hall on Clio Street, between Prytania and St. Charles Streets, in New Orleans, *ca.* 1850, elevation and plan.

New Orleans Notarial Archives, Plan Book 27, folio 54, n.d.

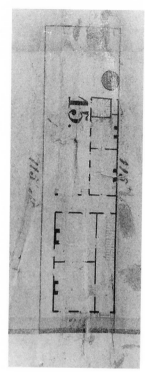

FIGURE 8   Lower Pontalba Building, 500 block of St. Peter Street, New Orleans, 1850–1851. The spacious residences on the second floor continue the traditional Creole town-house plan.

Collection of the Louisiana State Museum

the French Quarter, along Esplanade Avenue, and downriver in the Faubourg Marigny. Similar buildings in wood can be found upriver from the American sector. Drawings in the New Orleans Notarial Archives, frequently including both plan and elevation, offer copious evidence of the prevalence of this plan in the city (Figure 7).

The most notable town houses in the city are the two parallel and facing rows of brick buildings, the upper and lower Pontalba buildings (Figure 8). These stand on opposite sides of Jackson Square, defining the aspect of one

FIGURE 9   Double Greek Revival town houses with rear stairs on St. Peter Street between Perdido and Poydras Streets, in New Orleans, 1854, elevation and plan.

New Orleans Notarial Archives, Plan Book 6, folio 14, dated 1854.

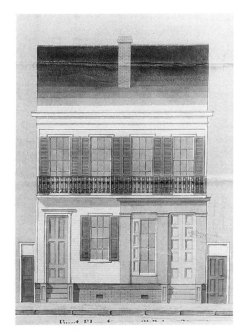

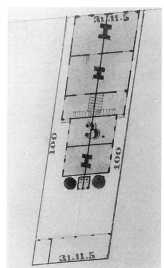

of the finest urban squares in the United States. Erected in 1850–1851 at what in colonial times had been the Place d'Armes, the buildings heralded the next generation of urban planning. The owner was Micaela Almonester, baroness de Pontalba, daughter of Don Andrés Almonester y Roxas, who had helped pay for the Cabildo, cathedral, and Presbytère. She lived part of the time in France and commissioned buildings on her properties in both countries. The Pontalba buildings are typically French, in putting stores on the ground floor and residences above, as around squares like the Place des Vosges and the Place Royale, in Paris. James Gallier was the original architect; Henry Howard did the final plans. The florid cast iron galleries, made in New York, are the first known instances of their kind in New Orleans. Madame Pontalba designed the AP monogram on them by connecting her and her husband's initials. Like earlier buildings in New Orleans, these too come to the edge of the street. The refurbishing of the Cabildo and Presbytère with third-story mansard-roof additions in 1847, as well as de Pouilly's enlargement and rebuilding of the cathedral between 1849 and 1851, effectively harmonized the scale of the buildings surrounding Jackson Square.

When cost control was a high priority, however—in small two-story rental houses, for instance—the staircase was generally positioned behind two ground-floor rooms of equal size, allowing a narrower lot (Figure 9). Promoted by Creole architects and builders, that economy continued to be practiced through the 1840s and 1850s. Two-story columnar houses also had their stairs at the rear. De Pouilly's famous row of five double two-story pillared Greek Revival houses in the 1200 block of Chartres Street were constructed as rental housing, and the rear stairs maximized the use of the land (Figure 10).

FIGURE 10   1206–1208, 1210–1212, 1216–1220, 1224–1226, 1232–1234 Chartres Street, New Orleans, 1845, J. N. B. de Pouilly architect.

Photograph by Susan Gandolfo

Kitchens in rental units were a fire hazard to tenants and neighbors alike, and until midcentury they were invariably detached from the houses to allow a backyard zone of safety around them. Cisterns, which collected rainwater from the house gutters, supplied water for each unit of a row, and the privy was at the far end of the yard.

Surviving outbuildings with kitchens, as well as plans recorded in the New Orleans Notarial Archives, confirm that until 1835 or 1840 all cooking was done in fireplaces, and probably brick ovens. Although advertisements for stoves appeared in the 1830s—one ran in the *New Orleans Commercial Bulletin* for 1836—the stove remained a luxury until the late forties. The daily routine of tenant life during the period must have included marketing, carrying groceries for a number of blocks, and cooking over an open hearth, with food served either in a dining room above the kitchen or in the house. As a rule, the kitchen had a projecting shed roof that covered an upper-level balcony and allowed sheltered passage on rainy days. Only around 1850 did rental units begin to be offered with the kitchen an attached appendage of the house.

The optimum in small housing was the single Creole cottage, two rooms wide and two deep, for a total of four rooms, with two smaller rooms, or *cabinets,* attached to the rear (Figure 11). By the third decade of the nineteenth century, American contractors building rental units had adopted the Creole practice of employing one *cabinet* for the stairwell and leaving the other for storage. In single-story or one-and-a-half-story houses, builders also put *cabinets* to the usual French end of providing extra space.

The usage of the word *tenement* has undergone a change between the nineteenth and the twentieth century. In building contracts of the 1850s the word referred to any unit that renters, or tenants, were to occupy in a build-

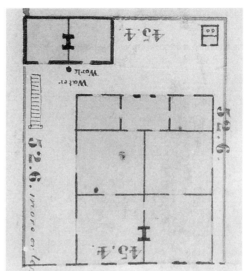

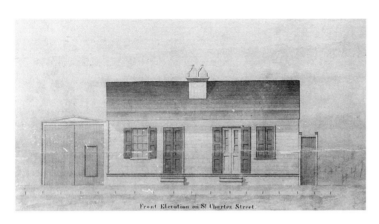

FIGURE 11   A Creole cottage with loggia and *cabinets* on St. Charles Avenue between St. Joseph and Julia Streets, in New Orleans, 1852, elevation and plan.

New Orleans Notarial Archives, Plan Book 83, folio 47, drawn 1852.

ing. A building contract of 1853 reads, "Abraham Howell builder for Bernard Cohen for two story frame house, three tenements at Bacchus and Euterpe, $6,965."[3] In the twentieth century, *tenement* has become a synonym for *slum dwelling.* Too many of the remaining Greek Revival apartment buildings now fit the second usage.

THE GREEK TASTE, 1807–1850

Architecture in the Greek Revival style prevailed between 1830 and 1850 from Maine to Texas, and not least throughout the Deep South. Americans of the Romantic era idealized the moral authority of the classical past, desired to identify themselves with the best in Greek civilization, and attempted to emulate the ideals of Greek democracy. They gave tangible expression to their outlook in a revival of Greek architectural forms. The taste for Greek culture and art erupted in mid-eighteenth-century England, France, and Germany. British publications such as James Stuart and Nicholas Revett's *Antiquities of Athens,* published between 1762 and 1816 and then republished with a fourth volume in 1830, familiarized Europeans, and then Americans, with ancient Greek buildings (Figure 12). Acquaintance with the Greek vases in the Hamilton Collection amounted to a revelation for architects, who copied the details. Those who had known Greek artistry only through Roman and Renaissance interpretations learned the true measure of the ancient creations.

Archaeological correctness was a preoccupation of the style. The paradigm was the rectangular temple raised on low steps. Monumental columns supported a deep entablature and a low pediment, and deep porches stood at each end, and colonnades on each side. The heavy, fluted Doric column with a cushion capital, the relatively slender fluted Ionic column with a base and

3. Contract between Abraham Howell and B. Cohen, July 9, 1853, A. Barret notary, Vol. 13, No. 548, in New Orleans Notarial Archives.

FIGURE 12   Erechtheum, east elevation, fifth century B.C.

From Antiquities of Athens, *by James Stuart and Nicholas Revett (1825), Vol. I, Plate XXI.*

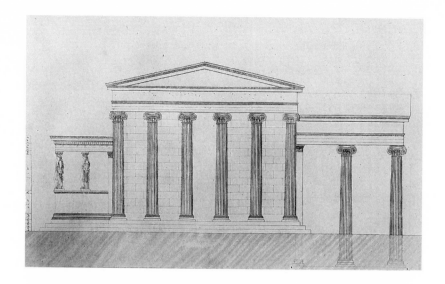

a volute capital, and the similar Corinthian column with a foliate capital were the Classical orders. But the unfluted Tuscan column of Roman architecture continued in use.

Shorn of Roman forms and neoclassical interpretations, Greek architecture at first appeared plain and ponderous. It was soon recognized as monumental and dignified, however—as an appropriate and desirable model for a democratic nation whose political antecedents lay in Rome and Athens. But as in every Classical revival, the antique forms had to be reinterpreted to suit existing conditions. Stone temples were translated into brick and stucco or frame. Windows and fireplaces were added, and the buildings were designed with utilitarian floor plans. Architects replicated small octagonal and round buildings as garden houses. Greek models enabled them to use the correct Classical vocabulary, but Romantic attitudes allowed them to do so in innovative ways. One wag has said that the farther removed from the source, the more archaeological was the architecture produced in imitation of the Greeks.

Ancient Greek buildings were an inspiration and instrument for the new profession of trained architects, who created a new style. Latrobe's design for the Bank of Pennsylvania, in Philadelphia, introduced Greek Revival impulses to America. But despite the building's innovations, it was several decades before the style was established and popularized.

Only the next generation of architects truly brought the new style to Louisiana. Like Latrobe, they knew about archaeology and correct proportion. Still, their designs, like his, were new creations. Gallier trained in the architectural office of William Wilkins, a prominent architect in London as well as the author of the *Antiquities of Magna Graecia* and the *Atheniensia;* Dakin was a professional associate in the firm of Town and Davis, in New York. Before they settled in New Orleans, around 1834, Gallier drew the frontispiece for Minard Lafever's—his employer's—*Beauties of Modern Architecture,* published in 1833, and Dakin designed ten plates for that work. Lafever's books were among the most important pattern books of the Greek Revival for American architects and builders. Like the authors of many other pattern books, Lafever never saw Greece but reinterpreted Greek design and decoration in the service of modern architecture. Thorough familiarity with Greek design through pattern books gave local architects the confidence to experiment on their own. Even in country towns and rural parishes, Classical forms received a much more accomplished execution than a submissive fidelity to carpenter's patterns could have produced. The Greek style insinuated itself into houses, banks, churches, offices, courthouses, warehouses, and college buildings. Greek Revival tendencies found a ready reception in the South on two accounts: the style was revered for its Classical antecedent, and it lent itself to the region's climate. Columns, porticoes, and porches were practical features that met the need for shade and were provisions that let leisure be taken and conversation enjoyed as a natural part of living. In Louisiana, where galleried houses were an entrenched tradition, the Greek colonnade became an easy graft. The aesthetic and utilitarian combined seamlessly in Greek Revival architecture.

The Greek Revival style is most apparent in buildings closely following the temple form. In Louisiana, the old New Orleans City Hall, now Gallier Hall, created to serve a second municipality, the American sector, conveys the monumental character of the style (Figure 13). One of the first designs by Gallier, it demonstrates the architect's thorough understanding of the principles of Greek architecture. The state's most intact structure of Grecian temple form is in Clinton, though, where, working from pattern books, a country builder erected a small residential temple, the Brame-Bennett House (Figures 47, 48). Built between approximately 1825 and 1833, the unpretentious dwelling typifies the Greek Revival style. The six-column porch supports a low pediment. A classic frieze continues around the house. A Grecian door with two long vertical panels stands in a doorway with a wide, flat molding decorated with rosettes and a projecting lintel. A frieze of anthemia, the most popular of Grecian designs, decorates the parlor. The high baseboards and deep cornice and the mantels are characteristic reinterpretations of Greek motifs.

The Victor David House, better known as the Petit Salon (Figure 14), a three-story town house on a raised basement in the Vieux Carre, is a typical sidehall urban house of the 1830s and has an urban New York house as its model. Built in 1838 to specifications calling for a "good Doric cornice in front" and a Greek entrance door, it has wrought-iron railings that differ in pattern at each of its three levels above the high basement. The crossed-arrow motif of the third floor is noteworthy. Some of the details, among them the anthemion motif in the frieze of the doorframe, were distinctly influenced by Lafever's *Beauties of Modern Architecture.* The tall house with its curved

FIGURE 13 Gallier Hall, 545 St. Charles Avenue, New Orleans, 1850–1851, James Gallier architect
Photograph by Jim Zietz

FIGURE 14   Victor David House (Petit Salon), 620 St. Peter Street, New Orleans, 1838.

Photograph by Jim Zietz

staircase leading to the first-floor entrance eight and a half feet above the sidewalk is an anomaly in the French Quarter.

There are still a number of large houses in the Greek Revival style on the once-fashionable Esplanade Avenue, at the downriver edge of the French Quarter. These were the homes of Creole families who had moved from the interior of that part of the city. The Gauche House, built in 1856 on a central-hall plan, is a two-story square structure of plaster-covered brick (Plate I; Figure 15). Simple moldings surround vertically proportioned windows, the planes of which provide an interesting contrast to the second-story balcony and the elaborate cast iron overhang and brackets beneath the plain cornice. The distinguished granite portico has Doric columns.

With population growth and the influx of Americans into New Orleans, Canal Street turned into the boundary, the so-called neutral ground, between the French in the Vieux Carre and the new arrivals who spread out up-

FIGURE 15   Gauche House, 704
Esplanade Avenue, New Orleans, 1856.

Photograph by Jim Zietz

FIGURE 16   Toby-Westfeldt House, 2340 Prytania Street, New Orleans, 1838–1842. In
1858, the house was remodeled for Thomas Smithfield Dugun in the Greek Revival
idiom by the builder Robert I. Lilly and a carpenter named J. H. Behan.

Photograph by Betsy Swanson

river toward the suburb of St. Mary. The brash push of the Americans for
influence and power created a new suburb with large lots, mansions, and gardens that became known as the Garden District in acknowledgment of the
Edenic lushness supported by the alluvial deposits left in 1816, when the levee
broke and the land flooded. The earliest house of consequence in the Garden
District, which was carved from the Livaudais plantation, was for Thomas
Toby, a Philadelphia wheelwright. Between 1838 and 1842, when the house
was built, sugarcane fields still surrounded the property (Figure 16). The
Toby House started as a large raised wooden cottage with servants' quarters
at ground level and porches only at the front and rear. The house acquired its
present form in 1858, when it was remodeled in the Greek Revival style for a
new owner. The addition of a Classical cornice and entablature was part of
that renovation.

Anglo-Saxon conservatism of taste limited the variety of house types
constructed. One of the favorites was the raised cottage with a simple five-
bay front. The Susan Hackett House, erected in 1854 according to the usual
central-hall plan, is one of the least complicated houses of this genre, with its
square columns, handsome entrance door with sidelights, and low crisscross
wooden railing (Figure 17). The John A. Adams House, at 2423 Prytania
Street, which is attributed to Frederick Wing, has an exceptional semicircular colonnade facing the garden. Facades could be stretched to seven bays
and be as capacious as the large cottage James Freret built at 1525 Louisiana
Avenue.

FIGURE 17   Susan Hackett House, 2336
St. Charles Avenue, New Orleans, 1854.
Photograph by Betsy Swanson

The sidehall house also had admirers. Possibly the best known of these is the Lavinia Dabney House, at 2265 St. Charles Avenue, built in 1856 and 1857 by Gallier and Turpin (Figure 18). It is of brick, though the contract specified wood. The ell of the service wing—like the main part of the house, two stories, but lower—extended to the rear, almost to the full depth of the lot (Figure 19). Houses following the three-bay plan might also gain space by communicating with a setback two-story addition behind a balcony on one side of the house. The Albert Hamilton Brevard House, on First Street, designed by James Calrow in 1857, does that (Figure 20). The hall there shows the monumental scale and elaborate Greek detailing these urban mansions could achieve (Figure 21). The dining room possesses the refinements of fashionable taste: Greek motifs at the windows, a plaster center medallion, a deeply molded plaster cornice, and a Rococo marble mantel with carved roses (Figure 22). Toward the end of the fifties, such houses had become truly massive.

In 1850, Howard designed a house for the cotton broker Robert A. Grinnan that broke all the rules (Figure 23). He grouped the three main ground-floor rooms at right angles one to another, separated them by halls and a staircase, and opened interesting views to two columnar porches (Figures 24, 25). Outside, on the street facade, the mass of the end parlor contrasts with the open, slightly recessed one-story entrance portico (Figure 26). Cast iron anthemia decorate the facade. The carved wooden capitals are exact replicas of those for the Choragic Monument of Lysicrates, in Athens, and the Greek door, with its acroterion and inset rosettes, reproduces precisely earlier pattern-book designs.

Still one of the most underappreciated architects in the city is Lewis E. Reynolds, who designed the commercial block known as Factor's Row, as

FIGURE 18   Lavinia Dabney House, 2265 St. Charles Avenue, New Orleans, 1856–1857
HABS, 1963, Library of Congress

FIGURE 19   Dabney House, side elevation.

HABS, 1963, Library of Congress

FIGURE 20   Albert Hamilton Brevard House, 1259 First Street, New Orleans, 1857, James Calrow architect, elevation.

HABS, 1963, Library of Congress

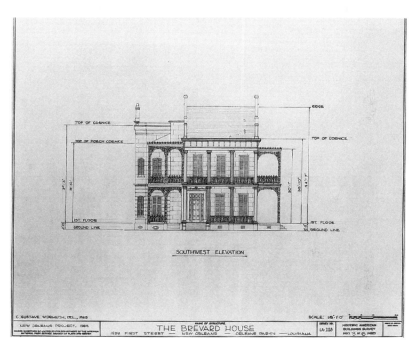

FIGURE 21   Brevard House, entrance hall.

HABS, 1964, Library of Congress

well as three significant houses in the Garden District, two on Jackson Avenue and one on Prytania Street. Jackson Avenue was the Americans' equivalent of the Creoles' Esplanade Avenue, and Lewis endowed it with two great mansions facing each other. One he designed for Henry Sullivan Buckner, and it went up rapidly, between April and December, 1856 (Figure 27).[4] The house rises two stories above a full above-ground basement, and it is nearly surrounded by columnar porches, Ionic on the first story and Corinthian on the second. The front and both sides have pediments above the second story.

4.   John Ferguson, "History for Sale: The Buckner-Soule Mansion," *Preservation in Print*, May, 1988, pp. 8–9.

FIGURE 22   Parlor of Brevard House, unchanged from the 1870s.

Richard Koch Collection, Southeastern Architectural Archive, Tulane University. Photograph by Richard Koch for HABS.

FIGURE 23   Robert A. Grinnan House, 2221 Prytania Street, New Orleans, 1850, Henry Howard architect.

HABS, 1963, Library of Congress

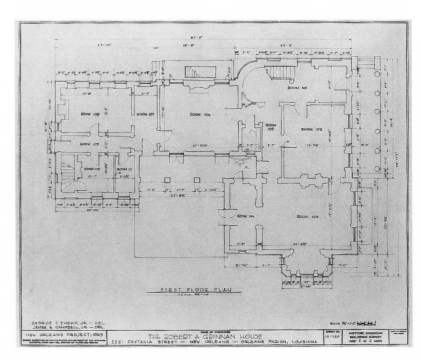

FIGURE 24   Grinnan House, first floor plan.

HABS, 1963, Library of Congress

The portico under the pediment on the Jackson Avenue facade, which advances toward the street with an added row of columns, emphasizes the entrance to the great center hall inside. In the Buckner House, Lewis successfully wedded the raised plantation cottage with the urban dwelling.

Across the street, the William Perkins House bears a family resemblance to Athenaeum buildings in London and Manchester, with heavy door and window surrounds, scored first-story plasterwork, and a roof balustrade (Figure 28). A pair of gigantic Corinthian antas stretch two stories high and in

FIGURE 25   Grinnan House, first floor hall.

HABS, 1963, Library of Congress

FIGURE 26   Grinnan House, main entrance.

HABS, 1963, Library of Congress

FIGURE 27   Henry Sullivan Buckner House, 1410 Jackson Avenue, New Orleans, 1856, Lewis E. Reynolds architect.

Photograph by Betsy Swanson

company with the two Corinthian columns between them support a massive pediment. The street facade includes progressive setbacks, first to a covered double portal, then to a side wing. What on entering seems an almost standard center-hall house opens on the left into a wing of three additional rooms, wider than half the core house and longer than the whole core house. The mood of the facade is at once elegant and heavy, and this house differs in its plan and aspect from any other in the Garden District.

The influence of Stuart and Revett's and Lafever's books is palpable in

FIGURE 28   William Perkins House, 1411 Jackson Avenue, New Orleans, 1850–1851, Lewis E. Reynolds architect.

FIGURE 29   Jacob U. Payne House, 1134 First Street, New Orleans, *ca.* 1842–1850
Photograph by Betsy Swanson

FIGURE 30   Arsenal (State Armory), 600 block of St. Peter Street, New Orleans, 1839, James Dakin architect.

Photograph by Jim Zietz

the exceptional quality of architectural details throughout the Garden District. Column capitals with fine Tower of the Winds motifs occur frequently, usually in cast iron, but sometimes in wood. In two-story houses, Tower of the Winds columns with two rows of foliage in bas-relief can appear either on the first story, as at the Bosworth House, at 1126 Washington Avenue, which has Corinthian columns on the second story, or on the second, as at the Jacob U. Payne House, at 1134 First Street, which has Ionic columns on the first story (Figure 29). At the one-story Bogart House, at 1020 Fourth Street, the columns are placed *in antis* between square pilasters. William Freret was to position them *in antis* also in designs for the five buildings he constructed in the 1700 block of Second Street in 1860 and for the five he built at 2700–2726 Coliseum Street in 1862.

Although architects relied heavily upon pattern books, they were by no means inhibited by them. Dakin's arsenal in New Orleans, built in 1839, is a lesson in design: a facade created to fit the unique function of the building (Figure 30). Bold and simple, the four massive and deep square pilasters are backed by vertical windows, crossed with iron straps. The heavy door, covered with rivets, reinforces the feeling of strength. Flags and cannons decorate the entablature, and flaming bombards top each of the giant pilasters. According to Dakin's drawings, the building was at one time capped with a pelican, an emblem of the state.

At the downriver side of the French Quarter is the United States Mint, completed in 1838 following designs William Strickland sent to New Orleans

FIGURE 31 United States Mint, 400 block of Esplanade Avenue, New Orleans, 1838, William Strickland architect.

Collection of the Louisiana State Museum. Photograph by François Mugnier (The Mint).

(Figure 31). It is the oldest mint building standing in the United States. At the time New Orleans was selected as a site for coining money, its strategic location was drawing much foreign gold through the port. The facade on Esplanade Avenue incorporates a projecting Ionic columnar portico, with two flanking wings similar to those of the mint Strickland designed for Philadelphia. Strickland seems to have favored the Ionic order. The mint is huge, with walls three feet thick in some places. At a length of 282 feet, it occupies the better part of a city block. Granite steps lead to the templelike portico, but the rest of the building is of brick plastered and scored to simulate the stone blocks of antiquity. An analysis of old paint, along with historical descriptions, has disclosed that the original color was reddish brown, to resemble sandstone, and the building is that color once again.

The New Orleans Barracks—the Jackson Barracks after 1866—is a Greek Revival complex in which all the buildings bear features related to the

FIGURE 32 Jackson Barracks, New
Orleans, first buildings, 1834.

*The Historic New Orleans Collection,
1979.65.1. Photograph* ca. *1880.*

Doric order (Figure 32). Few sets of nineteenth-century American military buildings are today as complete as this one, on the east bank of the Mississippi three miles below New Orleans. Had the nearby military hospital installation, built in 1848 on a site parallel to and upriver from the barracks, survived, the grouping would be even more remarkable.

In 1833, the War Department had approved plans for barracks outside the city that were to house the troops stationed in the area, letting them move from the downriver end of the French Quarter where they had been quartered for generations. Lieutenant Frederick Wilkinson, the architect, was only twenty years old. He was later to design the Egyptian-style Cypress Grove Cemetery. The barracks, which occupy a parallelogram some three hundred feet by nine hundred feet, were built to garrison four companies of infantry. Heavy brick walls enclose the compound, and two of the original four round corner towers survive. These are fitted with slits for rifles and embrasures for cannons, and battlements surmount them. Quarters for the officers and surgeons were along the length of a rectangular parade ground. Behind the rectangle the four barracks form a square, and beyond them were the kitchens, prison, commissary, and ordnance depot. Some roofs are hip

FIGURE 33   Union troops in front of Pentagon Barracks, Baton Rouge.

Andrew D. Lytle Collection, Louisiana and Lower Mississippi Valley Collections, LSU Libraries. Photograph by A. D. Lytle, 1862–1865.

and others gabled. Deep Doric porches are part of the facade of what was the officers' housing along the quadrangle. Each of the officers' apartments consisted of a kitchen and mess downstairs, and a two-room living area above, reached by an outside stairway. In the buildings' present use as housing, the only concession to the twentieth century is the screens on the porches.

In 1825, long before the Pentagon was built in Washington, the Pentagon Barracks rose in Baton Rouge on the site of an earlier riverside fort (Figure 33). That fort had originated as a western outpost of the United States. Only four sides of the pentagon were buildings; the fifth side was open to the river. The arsenal was some distance away from the barracks on the river bluff, on the fifth side. The commanding Doric colonnades are somewhat heavier and more grandiose than those at Jackson Barracks, and the columns stand on enormous plinths. The colonnades are an addition of the early 1830s, and it is possible that the new barracks below New Orleans inspired them.

Louisiana joined the rest of the South in establishing institutions of higher learning in the 1830s. One of several new colleges founded, Jefferson College, was on grounds along the Mississippi, in Convent, St. James Parish, that the Manresa Retreat House now owns (Figure 34). The college was purposely situated a four-hour boat ride upriver from the tempting distractions of New Orleans. Although the legislature helped with preliminary funding for the college in 1831, most of the financial support after its founding, in 1833, came from wealthy Creole sugar planters, the *ancienne population* that had decided it wanted to ensure its sons' education in the United States.

Jefferson College's first main building, constructed in 1833, was lost to fire in 1842. The replacement building, completed in the same year, has been described as an "imposing structure, three stories high, built in the style of pure Greek architecture."[5] It has twenty-two Doric columns and a six-column central portico. Two fine Greek Revival porter's lodges and the president's house, constructed in 1836, escaped the 1842 fire. Given the heavy concentration in Greek and Latin studies at the college, the institution's architecture and its education were in extraordinary agreement.

5.   Vaughn Glasgow, "Beautiful Building with Varied History," Baton Rouge *Sunday Advocate,* April 16, 1967.

FIGURE 34   Main Building, Jefferson College (Manresa Convent), 1842.

Library of Congress. Photograph by Frances Benjamin Johnston.

Greek Revival architecture was thought especially apt for government office buildings at every level. James Gallier described the old city hall (Figure 13), proposed in 1836 and completed to his design in 1850: "The portico and ashlar front of the City Hall are of white marble procured from quarries near New York; the basement and steps are granite. The style of the structure is Grecian Ionic, and the portico is considered a very chaste and highly finished example of that style." Although the building was still incomplete in 1845, when *Norman's New Orleans and Environs* appeared, the book conveyed the effectiveness of the facade: "At the top of the steps, at an elevation of fourteen feet, is a platform extending along the whole front, twenty-five feet deep, sustaining, by a range of six pillars in front, and four in the rear, a massy pediment, all of which is of Ionic construction."[6] The eighty-four-foot lyceum, or meeting hall, which soared twenty feet from the third floor

6.   *The Autobiography of James Gallier, Architect,* intro. Samuel Wilson, Jr. (New York, 1973), 41; B. M. Norman, *Norman's New Orleans and Environs* (New Orleans, 1845), 127–28.

FIGURE 35 Third District Courthouse, Jefferson Parish, 719 Carrollton, New Orleans, 1854–1855, Henry Howard architect.

Photograph by Jim Zietz

into the attic, was particularly impressive, and the building remains one of Gallier's finest works in the city.

In 1853, when New Orleans annexed the city of Lafayette, the town of Carrollton became the seat of Jefferson Parish. For the new Third District Court, Howard designed a courthouse, which was completed in 1855 (Figure 35). The original drawings have been lost, but not the specifications, dated and signed by the architect on January 16, 1854. They called for a two-story brick-and-plaster building in the Greek Revival style, the columns of which were to have cast iron bases and Ionic capitals based on those of the Erechtheum. The walls were to be scored, and granite steps, a slate roof, and good-quality marble for the stonework were specified. The details of the Ionic columns and the portico compare favorably with the Greek model.

When the courthouse, which is now a school, and Gallier's City Hall are considered together, the conclusion is usually that Howard had the heavier

FIGURE 36 Jim Blanchard, *St. Charles Hotel*, 1996. The hotel was built between 1835 and 1838 to a design by James Gallier and Charles Dakin. Fire destroyed the building in 1851. Drawn to scale.

Courtesy of the artist

hand; he paid less attention to decoration and, unlike Gallier, included no sculpture on the facade. But there is little to the supposition that Howard's four-column Ionic portico, with its flat pilasters, is just an unfortunate abbreviation of the six-column portico Gallier rendered. Rather, it is probable that Howard took the northern facade of the Erechtheum, with its four columns and attached pilasters, as his model. Gallier, on the other hand, turned to the more common model, the six-column eastern facade.

When the St. Charles Hotel was completed in 1838 (Figure 36) it rivaled Boston's Tremont Hotel in size. The firm of James Gallier and Charles Dakin received the original commission. Although Gallier was finally retained as architect, Dakin is credited with the dome. The capacious structure, sited on a trapezoidal lot—as incidentally was the Tremont—vitalized the American side of Canal Street. The entrance portico of six Corinthian columns rested on an above-ground granite basement, and a large pediment topped it. The hotel was crowned by a handsome dome raised on a rooftop drum with a circular colonnade around it. Inside the building were restaurants, an enormous barroom, baths, a wine cellar, a saloon, spiral staircases, a gallery, and parlors. The bar was decorated with Ionic pilasters, and the more refined saloon with Corinthian. Both were centers of social and business activity. The gentlemen's dining and sitting rooms occupied an entire side of the building, and the upstairs guest rooms numbered 350. Shops selling tobacco, wine, and sundries opened onto the corridors along the street. The hotel was destroyed by fire in 1851.

Masculine amenities like those the hotel provided were available in many of the city's public facilities. Banks, exchanges, hotels, restaurants, and public baths all catered to the businessman's needs and comfort.

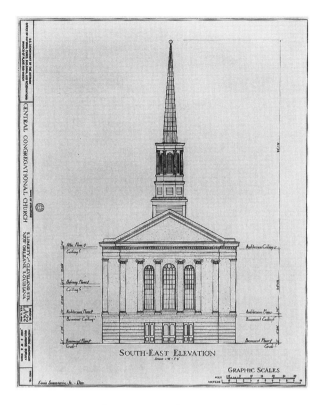

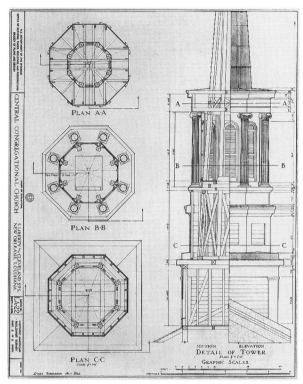

FIGURE 37   Central Congregational Church, South Liberty and Cleveland Streets, New Orleans, 1846, now demolished.

HABS, 1938, Library of Congress

FIGURE 38   Central Congregational Church, tower detail. The church was built in 1859–1860 by the architects and builders Samuel Jamison and James McIntosh. It was originally the Fourth Presbyterian Church.

HABS, 1938, Library of Congress

The Greek Revival temple front was easily adapted to churches, which were usually rectangular with the facade and entrance conveniently at one end. The building Gallier and Dakin designed for Christ Episcopal Church, on Canal Street, to replace an octagonal Gothic Building by Latrobe, had a temple-front facade with six Ionic columns in the portico. This edifice, erected in 1835, was demolished after its congregation moved uptown to a less commercial location. Central Congregational Church, formerly Fourth Presbyterian Church, at South Liberty and Cleveland Streets, was built by the architects and builders Samuel Jamison and James McIntosh in 1859 and 1860. Above its Ionic facade a centered octagonal tower with Ionic columns supported the entablature from which the steeple ascended (Figures 37, 38). The Ionic order recurred in the side elevations. The fondness for the Classical extended even to funerary monuments, of which the Peniston-Du-plantier tomb, in St. Louis Cemetery No. 2, is an excellent example (Figure 39). Egypt also made an appearance in tombs, like the Grailhe tomb, in the same cemetery. Egyptian temples inspired the architect of the Jefferson Parish Courthouse Annex and Jail, with its facade of pylon gates (Plate J).

The massive United States Custom House that stands on Canal Street near the river was begun, with Wood as its principal architect, in 1849, but the Civil War and postwar problems, as well as architectural fractiousness, delayed its completion until 1881 (Plate K; Figure 40). Capitals with a lotus-blossom motif impart an Egyptian flavor to the four facades. The Egyptian trait may have seemed appropriate for the large structure, since the massing

FIGURE 39   Peniston-Duplantier tomb,
St. Louis Cemetery No. 2, New Orleans,
1842, J. N. B. de Pouilly architect.

HABS, 1965, Library of Congress

FIGURE 40   United States Custom House, 400 block of Canal Street, New Orleans,
1848–1881, Alexander Thompson Wood architect.

*Richard Koch Collection, Southeastern Architectural Archive, Tulane University. Photograph
by Richard Koch for HABS.*

of Egyptian temples far exceeded that of the Greek. Inside, the building is
more detailed, and the monumental central section, the Marble Hall, or
main business room, is an immense space, three stories tall, that is daringly
lit by a huge skylight capable of showing off its marble lining and fourteen
colossal Corinthian columns (Figure 41). The capitals on those columns feature male and female faces in relief—Mercury, the god of commerce, and
Luna, the moon of the Crescent City.

The influence of Greek Revival architecture reached beyond New Orleans (Plate L) to other areas of new wealth and expansion. East Feliciana
Parish, where people of Anglo-Saxon lineage acquired holdings in the eighteenth century through Spanish land grants, became a countryside dotted
with plantation houses in the style. Its two towns, Jackson and Clinton, possess some of the most remarkable buildings in the state. The rich farmland
assured prosperity, and Clinton, the parish seat, was the terminus of the
Clinton and Port Hudson Railroad.

Until 1847, the mentally ill of Louisiana shared the general facilities of the
Charity Hospital, in New Orleans, but in that year the legislature decided to
build an institution at Jackson specifically for them. G. N. Gibbens was the
architect of the asylum, now known as East Louisiana State Hospital (Figure
42). Gibbens began with two three-story wings, each having a Doric facade at

FIGURE 41 Marble Hall in Custom House.

Richard Koch Collection, Southeastern Architectural Archive, Tulane University. Photograph by Richard Koch for HABS.

FIGURE 42 East Louisiana State Hospital, Jackson, 1853, G. N. Gibbens architect.

Andrew D. Lytle Photograph Collection, Louisiana and Lower Mississippi Valley Collections, Louisiana State University Libraries. Photograph by A. D. Lytle, 1870–1890.

FIGURE 43   East Feliciana Parish Courthouse, Clinton, 1840, S. J. Savage architect.

Library of Congress. Photograph by Frances Benjamin Johnston.

the extremity farthest from the other wing. By 1853, he had completed a center structure linking the wings. For this four-story building, he designed a remarkably fine Ionic temple front with pediment, and he filled the pediment with bas-relief sculpture. Except for the sculpture, the buildings have endured to the present day, and they continue to serve the mentally ill.

Dominating the center of Clinton is the parish courthouse, constructed in 1840 on a small rise (Figure 43). A monumental peripteral Tuscan colonnade accords eight columns to each side of the square building. S. J. Savage, the architect, adapted the multicolumn Louisiana plantation house into a public structure, covered it with a hip roof, and capped everything with an outsize octagonal drum and dome. Unlike the columns on plantation houses in the Felicianas, those on the courthouse do not support a second-story gallery. The omission of the gallery puts emphasis on the monumental columns and confers a clean, stark look upon the structure. All the exterior surfaces are painted white, and ornamentation is severely restricted to a stringcourse between floors and a cast iron balcony in the center of the second story of both the north and south facades.

On the north side of the square occupied by the courthouse is Lawyers' Row, five small Greek Revival buildings in file (Figure 44). Despite manifest differences in the five facades and construction at different times between 1840 and 1865, a harmonious effect is realized through the retention of a consistent porch depth and strict columnar alignment. The Lyon-Ligon building and the Dart building (Figure 45) are the only ones with a Classical temple pediment. They also have Doric columns. Together the courthouse and

FIGURE 44   Lawyers' Row, Clinton, 1825–1829.

Collection of the Louisiana State Museum. Photograph by Robert W. Tebbs, 1926.

FIGURE 45   Lawyers' Row, Dart building, plan and elevation.

HABS, 1936, Library of Congress

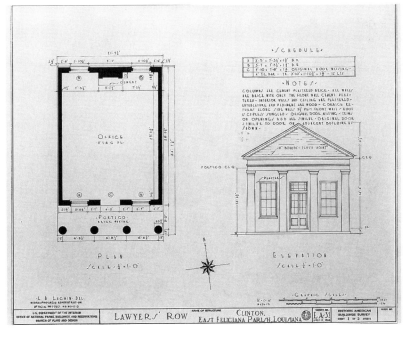

Lawyers' Row constitute a small Greek Revival parish-seat hub, unique in the state.

Several private residences in the parish exhibit the same combination of accurate Classical detailing and irregular emphases as the courthouse. Rose-neath, in Jackson, is a large in-town house built between 1830 and 1832 with a two-story Doric temple front (Figure 46). The four fairly slender fluted

FIGURE 46   Roseneath, Jackson,
1830–1832.

Photograph by Jim Zietz

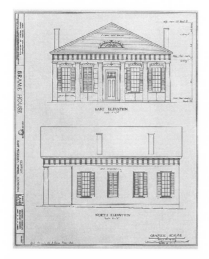

FIGURE 47   Brame-Bennett House
(formerly Brame House), Clinton,
1839–1842, facade and north elevation.

HABS, 1938, Library of Congress

columns rest on the stylobate, or platform, in conformity with the Greek ideal. In a departure from Classical conventions, however, there are guttae at both the top and the bottom of the metopes instead of only at the top. The base of the frieze receives extra emphasis because of the busy detailing. But the frieze, true to the norms for Greek temples, continues around the house, and the entrance portal is airy and delicate, flanked by slender Doric colonnettes.

The Brame-Bennett House, built for David Davis between 1839 and 1842, is small in scale and finely articulated (Figure 47). The six columns of the Doric porch support a low pediment, and as at Roseneath, an ample Classical frieze continues around the house. Another frieze, of still larger dimensions, appears around the cistern. A Greek door with inset rosettes leads into a four-room interior with a center hall (Figure 48). At the rear end of the hall a curved staircase leads to three upstairs rooms.

St. Mary Parish, another area of Anglo-American settlement, has been left with a full array of Greek Revival buildings. Franklin, a center of sugarcane production for over a century, is a town of notable mansions. Some would not be out of place in the Garden District of New Orleans; others resemble plantation houses on generous urban lots. The buildings, like those in Clinton, are mostly in the high style of Greek design. In De Soto Parish, the small community of Keatchie, south of Shreveport, has numerous Greek Revival buildings of a vernacular nature. The town was founded in the 1850s and 1860s, during the heyday of Greek Revival architecture, by settlers from the upper South. Among its Greek Revival buildings are a store,

FIGURE 48   Brame-Bennett House, plan.

HABS, 1938, Library of Congress

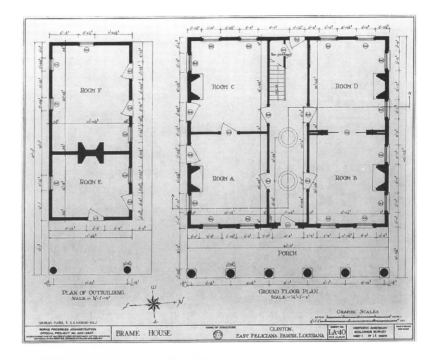

FIGURE 49   Keatchie Store, De Soto Parish, *ca.* 1855.

Photograph by Jim Zietz

churches, and some houses close to town (Figure 49; see also Chapter 4, Figure 36).

The Greek Revival style in Louisiana was indicative of the enthusiasm throughout the nineteenth-century South for Classical associations. The irony is how so Classical a style eventually created so Romantic a legacy.

FIGURE 50   St. Patrick's Catholic Church, 724 Camp Street, New Orleans, 1837–1840, James Dakin and Charles Dakin initial architects, James Gallier completing architect.

Photograph by Mike Posey and Michael P. Smith.

THE ROMANTIC GOTHIC

The momentous changes that occurred in aesthetics, history, and literature with the beginning of Romanticism affected architecture by opening choices between historical styles. The Gothic style became a live option, a reminder of feudal times and the High Middle Ages, when great cathedrals towered over daily life. Writers like Sir Walter Scott romanticized the period, sparking in the late nineteenth century a partiality to Gothic designs both archaeological and fanciful.

Archibald Alison's *Essay on the Nature and Principles of Taste,* published in 1790, maintained that forms are not beautiful in themselves but come to be considered beautiful because of the thoughts they engender in the mind of the observer. The associationism Alison championed had a pervasive effect on aesthetic attitudes in both Britain and America. The Gothic Revival movement originated in England, where it was first associated with a respect for ruins, then with the construction of large Gothic houses, and finally, after 1820, with a religious revitalization and the re-creation of Gothic forms in churches.

In England, the religious revitalization received impetus from the impassioned writings of the architect A. W. N. Pugin. Pugin argued for a conservative liturgy as it had been conducted in the Gothic cathedrals of the thirteenth century and the parish churches of the fourteenth and fifteenth centuries. He produced brilliant designs to underpin his conviction, and they went far toward popularizing the Gothic style in church architecture.

The tall and handsome St. Patrick's Catholic Church was constructed for New Orleans' Irish population between 1837 and 1840 (Figure 50). Designed by James Dakin and Charles Dakin in 1837, it was meant to be built to specifications that called for taking that "unrivaled example of splendored majesty, York Minster Cathedral," as a guide. The windows were to be in a florid Gothic style, and the ceiling to be modeled after Exeter Cathedral's. The tower was to be 185 feet high, on heavy foundations reaching into the city's muddy soil. According to surviving plans, the Dakins intended an interior space totally open and unsupported by columns. To support the weight, they planned a scissors truss supported by large cast iron members. When structural problems became evident, after the building was two-thirds complete, the congregation dismissed the Dakins and engaged Gallier to find remedies and complete the project. Gallier was responsible for the simplicity of the exterior and the present appearance of the interior (Figure 51). He added the clustered Gothic piers leading upward to the rib vaulting over the nave. His piers also support galleries that he introduced into the plans. As completed, the gigantic four-stage bell tower nearly spans the whole facade, drawing the worshiper inward toward a rib-vaulted apse with light streaming through stained glass. Few of the state's church buildings of the time were as elaborate as St. Patrick's, nor did others have so checkered a history.

FIGURE 51   St. Patrick's Catholic Church stained-glass vaulting in apse.
HABS, 1963, Library of Congress

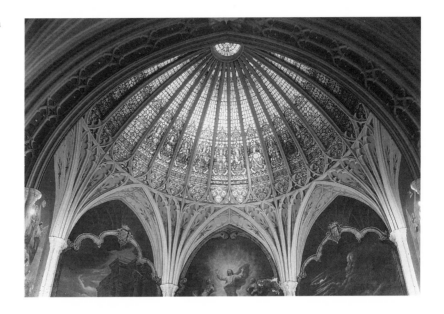

The Ecclesiological movement within the Protestant Episcopal Church in America aligned itself with the Anglicans who concurred with Pugin in favoring a return to a more conservative liturgy and to simple Gothic designs for parish churches. Three churches in Louisiana were designed by Frank K. Wills, a British-born architect who became the official architect of the New York Ecclesiological Society. Wills had been trained to work with and from medieval originals in England and to accoutre his buildings both internally and externally with clear indicators of their function. Of the three, Christ Episcopal Church, erected in Napoleonville in 1853 and 1854, is the one that most closely resembles a thirteenth- or fourteenth-century English parish church (Figure 52). It is clearly divided into chancel and nave, with a side portal and a single chapel. At St. Mary's Episcopal Church, near St. Francisville, nave and sanctuary are differentiated, as well. On the west end there is a fine tower. This church has been deconsecrated and is today in poor condition. Wills's third building, St. Stephen's Episcopal Church, at Innis, in Pointe Coupee Parish, went up in 1857 and 1858. It has a tripartite brick tower and buttresses.

Grace Episcopal Church, in St. Francisville, is a cruciform red-brick church constructed between 1858 and 1869 by the builder Charles Nevitt Gibbons (Figure 53). The large bell tower on the north side is asymmetrically joined to one of the transepts. On the entrance facade, a combination of enclosed vestibule, heavy buttresses, rose and lancet windows, and heavy stringcourses reinforces the resemblance to English parish churches. In a setting of live oaks and abutted by a cemetery with handsome marble tombstones and iron fences, the church forms part of a picturesque scene.

Carpenter Gothic churches, executed by craftsmen who looked to pattern books or made up their own designs, were usually one-room frame struc-

FIGURE 52   Christ Episcopal Church, Napoleonville, 1853–1854, Frank K. Wills architect.

Photograph by Jim Zietz

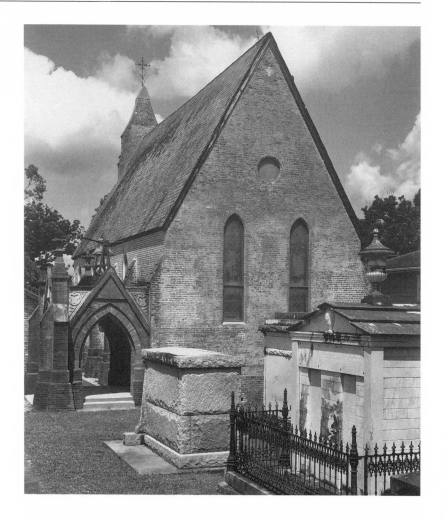

tures resting on piers. They had gabled facades, with an emphasis on the entrance portico, and steeply pitched roofs. The windows could be plain or lancet, and the exterior siding was often board-and-batten. The vertical emphasis of the Gothic was sustained through the use of barge-boarded gables, bell cots, and pinnacles. Most of the many Carpenter Gothic churches in Louisiana were constructed after the Civil War. Among those still in use are St. Andrew's Episcopal Church, built in Clinton about 1871 (Figure 54), St. Mary's Episcopal Church, built in Franklin in 1871, and Grace Memorial Episcopal Church, built in Hammond in 1876 (Figure 55). All churches in the style may owe something to pattern books; the tower of Grace Memorial Church bears a particularly strong resemblance to the one in Plate 6 of Richard Upjohn's *Rural Architecture*. Unpretentious wooden Gothic churches were appropriate for rural communities: they were inexpensive and required only a modest effort to construct.

The Gothic taste for ecclesiastical architecture continued after the Civil War. Rayne Memorial United Methodist Church, in New Orleans, com-

FIGURE 53   Grace Episcopal Church, St. Francisville, 1858–1869, Charles Nevitt Gibbons architect.

Photograph by Jim Zietz

pleted in 1876, is a postwar urban brick Gothic Revival church (Figure 56). Its bell tower, dominating the facade, is broad enough to embrace the side entrances as well as the central portal.

Since the Gothic was associated with medievalism, higher inspiration, and the afterlife, it was natural to apply the style to funerary monuments. Medievalizing details, crockets, finials, and pointed arches came to adorn tomb sculpture. About 1835, New Orleans passed ordinances requiring that tombs be above ground. Whether it was the boggy soil or something else that prompted the legislation, the result was conspicuous cities of the dead. The Caballero tomb, constructed in 1860 in St. Louis Cemetery No. 2, received a strong architectonic character from its designer, de Pouilly (Figure 57). The Gothic regard for picturesque ruins is evident in the late-nineteenth-century tomb of Bentinek Egan, in Metairie Cemetery (Figure 58).

In America, the castellated Gothic style is thought of primarily in con-

FIGURE 54   St. Andrew's Episcopal
Church, Clinton, 1866.

Photograph by Jim Zietz

nection with large institutions and university campuses. Ironically, the
British paradigms for it were eighteenth- and nineteenth-century domestic
structures, like Luscombe Castle, designed by John Nash and completed in
1804. By the mid-1830s, American architects, among them the partners Ithiel
Town and Alexander J. Davis, had evolved a Neo-Gothic castellated style for
both domestic and institutional buildings in New York.

In 1837, the castellated mode got its first foothold in Louisiana, in the
winning design for the United States Marine Hospital. The federal commission for this facility, which would be built in McDonoughville, across the
Mississippi from New Orleans, was awarded after what may have been the
first large architectural competition in the state (Figure 59). Robert Mills, an
architect for the United States Treasury Building, in Washington, submitted
the plans that the jury selected. His hospital was a four-story castellated
Gothic structure with an inner court. A decade later, in 1847, James Dakin

FIGURE 55 Grace Memorial Episcopal Church, Hammond

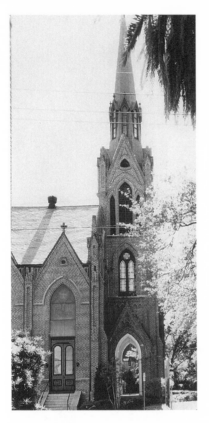

FIGURE 57   Caballero tomb, St. Louis Cemetery No. 2, New Orleans, 1860. J. N. B. de Pouilly architect.

Collection of the Louisiana State Museum

FIGURE 56   Rayne Memorial United Methodist Church, 3900 St. Charles Avenue, New Orleans, 1876.

Photograph by Susan Gandolfo

completed a design for a capitol in Baton Rouge, where, according to a decision of two years before, the seat of state government was to move (Figure 60). The architect justified the choice of castellated Gothic on two grounds: first, its novelty would differentiate the building from other state capitols in the Greek Revival style, and second, since much of the ornamentation of the structure would be prefabricated cast iron, it would be economical to assemble. Dakin visited the Pittsburgh foundry of Knapp and Toten, suppliers of the 350,000 pounds of cast iron needed. Brick came from a local source, and marble and granite from a New Orleans firm. Dakin had the rest of the capitol painted white to match the white marble curtain walls between the towers.

The capitol is dramatically located on a commanding bluff along the Mississippi, the first high ground upriver from New Orleans. Surrounded by spacious grounds, it became a romantic focus for steamboat travelers. It is one of the most finely articulated secular Gothic buildings from the first half of the nineteenth century in America. The ninety-foot octagonal towers along the river side flank pointed-arch doorways and windows. Square corner towers are perforated with lancet-arch windows. The brick is stuccoed, with the stucco scored to simulate stone, but on the three street sides the walls between the towers are marble. The Gothic fence along the perimeter of the grounds is of cast iron, like many of the building's Gothic features, in-

FIGURE 58   Bentinek Egan tomb, Metairie Cemetery, New Orleans, 1881.

Photograph by Jim Zietz

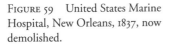

FIGURE 59   United States Marine Hospital, New Orleans, 1837, now demolished.

The Historic New Orleans Collection, 1949.8.

cluding the crenellations and the window hoods. Large cast iron eagles perch as finials on the gateposts (Figure 61).

The building was partially destroyed in 1862, when it was under Union occupation. Only in 1882 was Freret's plan for restoration and a new cast iron interior with a monumental spiral staircase carried out (Figure 62). The stairs rise three stories under a fan vault, between the members of which are panes of stained glass (Figure 63). The eye is led to the vault by the octagonal rotunda's composite columns on the first floor and the cast iron Gothic arcades on the upper level (Figure 64). To accommodate the vault, Freret added a fourth story to the building. He also installed tall cast iron turrets above the towers, and bartizans on the tower corners (Figure 65). Today, except for the central fourth-story area, all the later appendages have been removed.

In 1851, James Gallier, Jr., and John Turpin presented two designs for the New Orleans and Carrollton Railroad depot, built at the point where St. Charles and Carrollton avenues meet. Here Gallier's father's British experi-

FIGURE 60   Old State Capitol, Baton Rouge, 1847, James Dakin architect.

The Historic New Orleans Collection, 1981.247.1.1631. Photograph by Clarence John Laughlin, 1949.

FIGURE 61   Gate and fence of the Old State Capitol, 1856.

The Historic New Orleans Collection, 1981.247.1.1638. Photograph by Clarence John Laughlin, 1951.

FIGURE 62   Spiral stairway of the Old State Capitol, 1882, William Freret architect. The Historic New Orleans Collection.

The Historic New Orleans Collection, 1983.47.4.1638. Photograph by Clarence John Laughlin, 1949.

FIGURE 63   Fan vault of the Old State Capitol, 1882.

The Historic New Orleans Collection, 1983.47.4.1637. Photograph by Clarence John Laughlin, 1950.

ence was demonstrably present. The design that was accepted featured irregular massing, playing the large square corner tower and a pair of smaller towers against each other. The building had crenellated parapets. Triple Gothic windows with finials and quatrefoil panels decorated the second story. According to the Carrollton *Star* of April 24, 1852, the clock tower was a wel-

FIGURE 64   Old State Capitol, rotunda, 1882.

HABS, 1944, Library of Congress

FIGURE 65   Old State Capitol as it appeared prior to about 1900

LSU Libraries

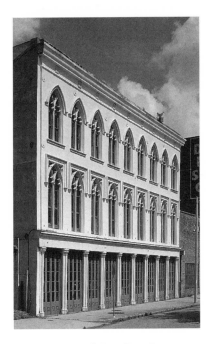

FIGURE 66   Leeds Iron Foundry, 923 Tchoupitoulas Street, New Orleans, 1852, Gallier and Turpin architects.

Photograph by Jim Zietz

come addition: "They are to put up a clock, which is very much needed here, and, when placed in the depot will be little else than a private donation to the town." This medieval-inspired structure was supported by cast iron. The window surrounds and arches on the first floor were also of cast iron. The building has been demolished.

In one of the most extensive applications of cast iron technology in New Orleans, Gallier and Turpin also designed the Leeds Iron Foundry, completed in 1852 (Figure 66). Its Gothic Revival details were all cast by the Leeds Foundry itself as a spectacular display of the firm's capabilities and included clustered columns, pointed windows, and heavy drip moldings.

The Gothic Revival style did not win wide acceptance for domestic architecture in Louisiana. It suffered from its association with the British: New Orleans had undergone its own battle with Great Britain some twenty years before. The Gothic Revival houses in English and American pattern books were perceived as an architecture for eccentrics, not the ordinary man. They struck Louisianians as expressing an antidemocratic cultural pretension. Besides, they were difficult to build.

The earliest documented Gothic Revival residence in the state was very probably at Orange Grove plantation, near Braithewaite, in Plaquemines Parish (Figure 67). Built for the sugar planter Thomas Ashton Morgan over the years from 1847 to 1853 according to plans a Philadelphia architect, William Johnston, drew up, this Tudor Gothic house achieved its picturesqueness through large-scale gables, decorated bargeboards, and asymmetric chimney clusters. Rectangular in plan, it had an attached service wing with bath, sewing room, and kitchen. The house has been referred to as a cottage-villa-style dwelling, and it resembles a "cottage-villa in the Rural Gothic style" that the American architecture theorist A. J. Downing included in *The Architecture of Country Houses*. The house was technologically

FIGURE 67 Orange Grove Plantation, Plaquemines Parish, 1847–1853, destroyed by fire 1984, William Johnston architect.

The Historic New Orleans Collection, 1976.132.45.

advanced in its sanitary facilities and, above all, in having a basement and heating system, both novelties for the Deep South.[7] It was destroyed by fire in 1984.

In 1849, Nathaniel Newton Wilkinson, an Englishman, elected the Gothic style for his unique Maltese-cross-plan house in Carrollton (Figures 68, 69). Orleanians sometimes located their summer homes here, where they could travel easily by rail. Lots in Carrollton were huge, and the Wilkinson House retains a sizable portion of its original grounds, preserving its distinctive rural character. Designs from William Ranlett's pattern book *The Architect,* published in two volumes, one in 1847 and the second in 1849, may lie behind some features of the Wilkinson House, from its cruciform plan to its casements and other exterior details. Inside, large rooms open onto an octagonal hall with a finely carved Gothic staircase. The nineteenth-century diamond-pane windows and carved Gothic bookcases still remain in the

7. A. J. Downing, *The Architecture of Country Houses* (New York, 1852), Design XXIV; William R. Cullison, "Design and Construction of Orange Grove" (M.A. thesis, Tulane University, 1969).

FIGURE 68   Nathaniel Wilkinson
House, 1015 South Carrollton Avenue,
New Orleans, 1849.

Photograph by Jim Zietz

FIGURE 69   Vergeboard of the
Wilkinson House.

Photograph by Jim Zietz

house. The brick exterior walls were once covered with stucco scored and painted to imitate stone.

The most romantic Gothic residence in the state was Afton Villa, near St. Francisville (Figure 70). It belonged to the tradition of eclectic British Gothic residences typified by that of Horace Walpole. Afton Villa resulted from David Barrow's enlargement of his old house when he remarried, in 1849. The forty-room house was wider across the front—taking in the entrance hall, sun porches, and parlors—than across the rooms behind, which were probably part of the original house. The two-story groined arches of the terrace allowed light to fall into the sun parlors and communicated a feeling of irregular massing as the sun traversed the facade during the course of the day. Interior finishes were rich: fluted columns, real marble (*faux marbre* for the sun parlor's walls), carved stairways and moldings, and modeled plaster ceilings. Outside, the bargeboards were carved in Masonic designs—Barrow was a Mason—and the cornice in an egg-and-dart motif. A twenty-acre garden included a maze, and the approach to the dwelling was by a serpentine driveway half a mile long.

Like the Wilkinson House, the Briggs House, on Prytania Street in the Garden District of New Orleans, was built for an Englishman (Figure 71). In 1849, Cuthbert Bullitt, a Kentuckian who had moved to New Orleans, had commissioned James Gallier to design a Gothic house. Gallier based his plans for the two-story cottage on a plate in Downing's *Cottage Residences*. The pointed arches of the second floor and the flat hood moldings of the first were in widespread use in the central part of the United States. Bullitt, in

FIGURE 70 Afton Villa, West Feliciana Parish, 1849, destroyed by fire in 1963.

Library of Congress. Photograph by Frances Benjamin Johnston.

financial difficulties, rejected Gallier's design, but Charles Briggs, from London, apparently accepted it with modifications. The clustered chimneys were kept, the center gable was enlarged, the second-story dormer was omitted, and Tudor arches were chosen for the porch of the house, which was completed in 1851. Wooden Gothic servants' quarters in the side yard echo the lines of the main building of stucco-covered brick. The architect Thomas Wharton described the Briggs landscape as a "sweet spot—with a garden such as you seldom meet outside of England—walks, lawn, shrubbery and flower beds exquisitely arranged."[8]

The John Howard Ferguson House in uptown New Orleans, built around 1870 and designed by an architect whose name is not recorded, has

8. A. J. Downing, *Cottage Residences* (London, 1842), Plate II; Thomas Kelah Wharton Diary (MS in New York Public Library), cited by Samuel Wilson, Jr., in *A Guide to Architecture of New Orleans, 1699–1959* (New York, 1959), 36.

FIGURE 71   Briggs House, 2605 Prytania Street, New Orleans, 1851, James Gallier architect.

Photograph by Betsy Swanson

FIGURE 72   John Howard Ferguson House, 1500 Hurst Street, New Orleans, *ca.* 1870.

Photograph by Jim Zietz

traits reminiscent of campground cottages at Wesleyan Grove, on the island of Martha's Vineyard, in Massachusetts, in its large Gothic bargeboard on the narrow street facade and its setback porch (Figure 72). Ferguson was born on Martha's Vineyard in 1838 and could have seen cottages of this kind go up in the years before the Civil War. Trained as a lawyer, he came to New

FIGURE 73   Toby Hart House, 2108
Palmer Street, New Orleans, 1873.

Photograph by Jim Zietz

Orleans about 1867, where he became a legislator and judge. Renovations
and an enclosed porch on the Hurst Street side may date from the 1890s.

The Toby Hart House, on Palmer Street, in New Orleans, is not strictly
a Gothic Revival structure but rather a *cottage ornée* with Gothic touches
(Figure 73). The original cottage consisted of four rooms. There were also
outbuildings on the lot, which stretched several blocks in 1873, when the cottage was built. Queen Anne wings were added on the two sides in 1889, and
a kitchen was added around 1910. The facade combines Italianate round-
headed windows, a Gothic-inspired porch with flat balusters, and a second-
story Queen Anne balcony. The wooden basket weave of the balcony remains in excellent condition, and the balusters of the porch have been
restored. In keeping with associationism, it was felt that modest homes,
given the right ornamentation, could summon up ideas less of economic
constraint than of cozy domesticity.

The role the Mississippi River steamboat played in acquainting ordinary
people with the Gothic Revival must also be acknowledged. Persac's painting
Interior of the Steamboat "Princess" (Figure 74) conveys an impression of a
long, resplendent Gothic tunnel filled with light and vaulting, a true floating
palace designed, as most Gothic Revival structures were, to create awe and
wonder in the beholder.

FIGURE 74   Marie Adrien Persac,
Interior of the Steamboat "Princess."
Louisiana State University Museum of Art,
Baton Rouge.

PICTURESQUE ITALIANATE

What is now called Italianate architecture developed out of the concept of the picturesque, which involved a way of looking at a landscape as though at a painting. The Italian word *pittoresco* means "painterlike," and in England, where receptivity to the concept first flourished, the word *picturesque* has the sense of "like a painting" or "as in a picture." The concept invoked painterly concerns with the sublime and painterly exploitations of asymmetry and irregularity. The pursuit of the picturesque was one of the effects of the grand tour and the exposure of the English aristocracy from about 1700 onward to Italy and the painters of the Italian landscape, especially Claude Lorrain, Salvator Rosa, and Gaspard Dughet. The pursuit occurred first in landscape gardening, then was theorized, and finally was extended to architecture.

Architectural pattern books reinforced the sway of the picturesque. The first villa to be designated Italian in the plan occurred in Robert Lugar's *Architectural Sketches for Cottages,* of 1805. Four years later, Pierre Clochard's *Palais, maisons et vues d'Italie* set itself the task of making available to untraveled architects Italian views to excite their imagination. Picturesque pattern books culminated in John Claudius Loudon's *Encyclopedia of Cottage, Farm, and Villa Architecture and Furniture,* justly called the bible of the villa style. Its thirteen hundred pages include a history of the villa, analytical discussion, commentary by the author's contemporaries, landscape details from Old Master paintings, patterns for villas and cottages, and explicit instructions for construction. The *Encyclopedia* was one of the archetypes for the pattern books by Downing. In *A Treatise on the Theory and Practice of Landscape Gardening,* Downing defined and characterized the Italianate style and recommended it for domestic architecture. The following year, in *Cottage Residences,* he again commended the Italianate but declared it best adapted to warm climates. At the beginning of the next decade, when he published *The Architecture of Country Houses,* he still found the Italianate style suitable, but primarily for the South and Midwest. He also promoted Italianate designs for suburban construction. In 1852, Samuel Sloan, a Philadelphia architect, observed in *The Model Architect* that the Italian style was compatible with level country. That provided an impetus for regular and symmetrical Italianate architecture, creating the condition for the sort of aesthetic of regularity that the Italianate style of architecture was to manifest in Louisiana.[9]

The acceptance of the Italianate style in America coincided with a shift in attitudes toward art and luxury. To Americans of the early nineteenth century, art and ornament were wasteful extravagances. But the notion that art was executed at the "expense of food for the poor" softened as America approached the middle of the century. The fine arts came to be recognized as a source of genuine pleasure. Traveling in Europe, Ralph Waldo Emerson expressed a glowing sensuous delight in beauty, declaring, "Rome is a grand town and works mightily upon the senses and upon the soul."[10]

Toward the late 1850s, New Orleans became noticeably more hospitable to ornamentation. In 1856, the New Orleans *Daily Crescent* mentioned the rising tide of Italianate taste: "We may remark that the plain fashion of building has almost entirely gone out of vogue. Not only the public buildings display the finest designs of the architect, but residences and stores are also elegantly ornamented; the residences being put up in different styles of fanciful architecture."[11]

New Orleans residential interiors were even more elegantly ornamented and appointed, and they grew increasingly elaborate. Behind what was hap-

9.   Robert Lugar, *Architectural Sketches for Cottages* (London, 1805), Plates 27, 28; Pierre Clochard, *Palais, maisons et vues d'Italie* (Paris, 1809); John Claudius Loudon, *An Encyclopedia of Cottage, Farm, and Villa Architecture and Furniture* (London, 1833); A. J. Downing, *Theory and Practice of Landscape Gardening* (New York, 1850); Samuel Sloan, *The Model Architect* (2 vols.; Philadelphia, 1852), I, 32.

10.   Joan G. Caldwell, "Italianate Domestic Architecture in New Orleans, 1850–1880" (Ph.D. dissertation, Tulane University, 1975), 51; *The Letters of Ralph Waldo Emerson* (New York, 1939), I, 373.

11.   "City Improvements," New Orleans *Daily Crescent,* October 21, 1856, p. 6.

FIGURE 75 A page in the catalog of Roberts and Co., New Orleans, 1891.

Southeastern Architectural Archive, Tulane University.

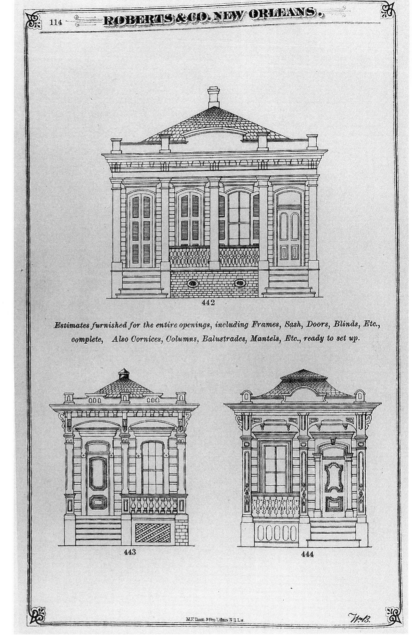

FIGURE 76 Elements of Italianate facades offered by Roberts and Co. in their catalog.

Southeastern Architectural Archive, Tulane University.

pening was technical innovation as well as a change in tastes. After the Civil War, mills produced an ever wider range of architectural components (Figures 75, 76). Millwork increasingly substituted for cabinetwork even in the specifications for the finest houses. Marble mantels became the focal point of many a double parlor, and interlaced or foliate plaster center medallions decorated the ceilings. James Gallier, Jr., designed rich plaster cornice moldings of grape leaves and lion's heads for his own house, and other elaborate plaster heads for the Luling Mansion, in New Orleans. Aside from the superbly carved wooden columns and woodwork, one of the most interesting features of New Orleans interiors was the unusual number of "frescoes," which were actually painted on plaster in oil. The city's artists were extremely familiar with the technique. Millwork might also be marbleized or imitate fine wood (*faux bois*). Orleanians sought whatever was enriched by texture, pattern, and ornament for their rooms.

Segmented-arch windows, round-headed windows, heavily molded windows, segmented-arch pediments, and segmented-arch doors are all characteristic of Italianate architecture in Louisiana. Brackets are usually paired and frequently have a console or volute shape. Italianate houses in New Orleans, where the greater part of the state's Italianate domestic architecture was built, are seldom asymmetrical. The massing is regular, and small but heavy three-dimensional Baroque detailing provides the multiformity that asymmetry does in other topographies. The visually preferred front view on a small city lot and local building traditions also translated into a receptivity to the symmetrical picturesque.

The Italianate style had attained a measure of popularity by 1857 and continued popular until the late 1880s. The major spurts in Italianate construction were between 1857 and 1860 and in 1869 and 1870. New Orleans was perhaps three to five years behind the rest of the nation, but in both the city and the state there was enough of an overlap with the national trend to suggest that Louisiana traveled the same trajectory of enthusiasm for the style as other regions.

Until the end of the century, the four colonial house types—the French or Creole cottage, the raised cottage, the Creole town house, and the galleried pavilion—along with the London-plan urban house type, prescribed the internal layouts of new residential construction in the state.

In the 1850s, Louisiana's steady commercial success lured businessmen from the Northeast and Midwest. These were the patrons for local architects like James Gallier, Jr., and for architects attracted from elsewhere, like Howard, who came from Ireland, and Reynolds, who had worked professionally in Baltimore and St. Louis. Except for Latrobe, no major nineteenth-century American architects based elsewhere traveled to New Orleans to carry out commissions. Strickland and Thomas U. Walter sent designs to the city. Pattern-book architecture was much less prevalent in the area than in most places, largely because a group of talented and well-schooled architects who settled in the state worked within locally accepted norms for domestic and commercial architecture and nurtured a New Orleans look that had no parallel anywhere else in the country. The New Orleans look endured into Italianate architecture.

In New Orleans, the combination of narrow lots, high ceilings, and full-length windows yielded a persistently vertical architecture, whether the style

FIGURE 77 James Robb Mansion,
Washington Avenue, New Orleans,
1853–1855. A second story was added after
the building became the H. Sophie
Newcomb Memorial College in 1891.

*Louisiana Landmarks Society Collection,
Southeastern Architectural Archive, Tulane
University Library.*

was Italianate or not. The vertical emphasis was reinforced by the columns on the galleries or balconies, sometimes at two levels. The insistent symmetry of the city's architecture was carried to the interiors of Italianate houses. The space is nearly cubic in the average-size nineteenth-century room, as high as it is broad. Room entrances are always aligned, not only for better circulation and ventilation but also because such an arrangement was aesthetically preferred. This constant symmetry seems to have been inherent, and was not surrendered.

Among New Orleans' earliest structures in the Italianate style were several palazzo houses built in the city from about 1854. Inspired by British and East Coast interpretations of urban Italian Renaissance palaces, these were large in scale, cubic in form, and ponderous in detail. All were of stucco-covered brick. The James Robb Mansion, now demolished, was a one-story palazzo that, with the gardens, occupied an entire city block (Figure 77). The balustrade and classic window surrounds were influenced by Sir Charles Barry's Athenaeum, in Manchester. Robb, a brilliant self-made banker, made his millions financing technological developments like gas lighting and railroads. Not exempt from the boom-and-bust cycles of his era, he went bankrupt in the financial crisis of 1857.

FIGURE 78   Forstall House, 920 St. Louis Street, New Orleans, 1860s.

The Historic New Orleans Collection, 1950.5.33.

The only palazzo house still standing is the Forstall House, in the French Quarter (Figure 78). The building, with colossal two-story pilasters, rests upon a high raised basement, making it unusual for the area. The structure above its base is reminiscent of the palazzo design of the Brooklyn Savings Bank by Lafever in 1847. The palazzo style in New Orleans has to be considered an aberration, a brief flirtation with East Coast and British influences. It may have started as an attempt to transplant a style, but the necessary grafting to the local tradition failed and no building of this type was constructed after 1859.

FIGURE 79   Augustus J. Tardy House,
1305 Jackson Avenue, New Orleans, 1869.
Photograph by Jim Zietz

The double-galleried sidehall, or London-plan, residence developed some time in the decade of the 1830s. Typically it was of frame construction with four columns to each of the two floors, usually fluted and finished with capitals in one of the Classical orders. A raised-box parapet or its round-head variant usually capped the center pair of columns. In New Orleans, Italianate segmented-arch windows and doors were sometimes incorporated into Greek Revival facades. The Augustus J. Tardy House is in this native genre (Figure 79). A wing has a setback, and the columns at both levels are of the Corinthian order. The residence of E. A. Tyler, built in 1859 and now demolished, had Doric columns on the second story and Ionic below.

A Garden District residence perhaps as famous for its cornstalk fence as for itself was the one Howard designed for a Kentucky colonel, Robert Henry Short, in 1859 (Figure 80). The large Italianate masonry house has an Italianate exterior and a Classical transitional interior. The detailing of the

FIGURE 80   Robert Henry Short House, 1448 Fourth Street, New Orleans, 1859, Henry Howard architect.

Photograph by Jim Zietz

exterior ironwork galleries is different for the two stories. Like the Tardy House, the dwelling built for Short is irregular, its setback creating asymmetry. The scale is deceiving. From the street the house seems fairly modest, but the interior is of unsuspected grandeur (Figure 81). The interior plasterwork and millwork are pure Greek Revival, but the white marble fireplaces betray a definite Italianate heaviness. Apparently the first cast iron fence in a cornstalk pattern was designed by Downing for Lafayette Square, in Washington, D.C., in 1852.

Union troops occupied New Orleans during the Civil War, and the city suffered economically, but it was not devastated like Atlanta or Columbia. River trade resumed by 1863, and the railroads and levees were restored. By 1864, old and new money and ambitious Yankees were building some of the largest mansions in the city. By the end of the decade, there were the Robinson House, in the Garden District, completed in 1864; the Luling Mansion, at 1426 Leda Street, in 1865; the Rice House, at 1220 St. Philip Street, in 1866;

FIGURE 81   Parlor of the Short House

Richard Koch Collection, Southeastern Architectural Archive, Tulane University. Photograph by Richard Koch for HABS.

FIGURE 82   Walter Grinnan Robinson House, 1415 Third Street, New Orleans, 1864.

Photograph by Jim Zietz

the Palacios House, at 5824 St. Charles Avenue, in 1867; and the Joseph C. Morris House, at 1331 First Street, in 1869.

After the Civil War, round-headed windows and doors appeared more frequently. Moldings of different designs appeared, quoins received more emphasis, porches became deeper, wooden railings became more common, and central-hall plans gained acceptance. The Walter Grinnan Robinson House, constructed around 1864 at 1415 Third Street, combines notably heavier detailing, massive proportions, and a central-hall plan (Figure 82).

Another type of double balcony residence—with chamfered pillars— came later. In the August Tete House, by the architectural firm of Howard and Thiberge and erected in 1882, the chamfered columns have capital details that derive from a pierced-balustrade motif much repeated by the Robert Roberts Company, a millwork firm active in the city (Figure 83). The available catalog components—arches between porch columns, heavy double brackets, diamond designs on the column faces, dentils with a double profile—meant that Italianate departures from buildings' basic styles observed fixed limits.

Acceptance of the London town-house plan grew in this period. That plan combined a long hall with a straight stairway on one side of the house, running the full length of two major rooms, usually contiguous parlors, on the first floor. The younger Gallier and, after him, Samuel Jamison, sometimes added a third room with a large polygonal bay at the end of the two

FIGURE 83   Auguste Tete House, 1914
Esplanade Avenue, New Orleans, 1882,
Howard and Thiberge architects.

parlors. Although the London plan may have originated in conditions where row housing was advantageous, as adapted to New Orleans it was possible for any site, crowded or not, and usually was found in freestanding housing. The younger Gallier used the town-house plan in several dwellings: in his own residence, at 1132 Royal Street; the J. J. Warren House, at 1529–1531 Jackson Avenue; and the Michael Heine House, now demolished. Built around 1860, the Warren House has double parlors backed by a dining space with a three-sided bay at the end.

Although Jamison was the architect for only three Italianate mansions in the city, he managed to be one of the most delightful designers of the second half of the century. In 1869, he designed a two-story masonry town house for Joseph C. Morris, a brickmaker (Figure 84). Jacob Baumiller, a local ironworker, executed the cast iron galleries that add a touch of lightness to the facade and side elevation. The Blaffer House, completed in 1869 and designed

FIGURE 84   Joseph C. Morris House, 1331 First Street, New Orleans, 1869, Samuel Jamison architect
Photograph by Jim Zietz

234

FIGURE 85   Montgomery-Reynoir
House, 1213 Third Street, New Orleans,
ca. 1869.

Photograph by Jim Zietz

by Charles Lewis Hillger, possesses a partial tower facade, something common enough in Italianate houses in the eastern part of the United States but
practically unknown in Louisiana.

In the Montgomery-Reynoir House, completed about 1869, the
influence of a pattern book is evident (Figure 85). The house may have been
indirectly influenced by Calvert Vaux's *Villas and Cottages,* which appeared
in two editions.[12] The Italianate houses Sloan designed may also have been
an influence. The deep gables, heavy brackets, and one-story, double-
columned porch are all unusual for the area though common in the rest of
the country.

The imposing Luling Mansion, designed by James Gallier, Jr., for Florence A. Luling, a German merchant, required several years of construction
(Figure 86). The central building is sixty-seven feet by fifty-two feet and rises
two stories above a high rusticated terrace. The whole structure is capped by
a square central tower. Galleries with low balustrades extend around three
sides of the building at the first and second stories. The second-floor balcony
is protected from the weather by extremely deep eaves. Two wings were originally attached to the sides of the building, but they have been destroyed.
Arched bridges led from the second floor of the wings to the first level of the
main house. One of the appendages contained a bowling alley, the other a
conservatory. The attaching of appendages to a central building is a Palladian
device, and this particular arrangement, placing wings close to the house that

12.   Calvert Vaux, *Villas and Cottages* (New York, 1857; 2nd ed., New York, 1864).

FIGURE 86 James Gallier, Jr.'s drawing of the Florence A. Luling Mansion, 1436 Leda Court, New Orleans, 1864–1866. The flanking bridges and pavilions do not survive.

Sylvester W. Labrot Collection of James Gallier Sr. and Jr., Southeastern Architectural Archive, Tulane University.

rose about a story and a half, is reminiscent of Sloan's Joseph Harrison House, in Philadelphia, built from 1855 to 1857.

The raised villa evolved in part from climatic necessity. Besides clearly separating the living and service areas, tall brick piers kept the upper floors away from dampness and floods. The area in which this type of building was common stretched along the Gulf Coast from East Texas to Florida. In New Orleans, there are about a dozen important examples in the Italianate style, dating from 1856 to 1883. All follow a central-hall plan, which is not found in French or Spanish colonial raised-pier structures. Howard is credited with designing the best-known raised villa in the city. In 1867, Daniel Fraser, a builder, constructed a one-story frame house over a brick raised basement for Antonio Palacios at an address in Hurstville, then part of Jefferson Parish but now 5824 St. Charles Avenue, in New Orleans (Figure 87).

The Rice House, completed nearby in 1866, is a suburban Italianate villa (Figure 88). Typically late details of the style give definition to the front elevation: the six columns of the porch are surmounted by a heavy entablature and topped by a deep rusticated cornice with double brackets over each column capital.

Nottoway, along the River Road at White Castle, is the largest surviving plantation house in the South (Figure 89). Built according to plans by the architectural firm of Howard and Dittel for John Hampden Randolph, a sugar planter, between 1849 and 1859, it is a frame three-story mansion with massive cypress porch columns. The style is Italianate, skillfully combined with some Greek Revival details on the exterior. Inside, an incredible variety of

FIGURE 87 Antonio Palacios House,
5824 St. Charles Avenue, New Orleans,
1867.

Photograph by Jim Zietz

FIGURE 88 Rice House, 1220 Philip
Street, New Orleans, 1866.

Photograph by Jim Zietz

rich plasterwork adorns the ballroom and parlors. The plan is irregular, and
the bold extrusion of the curved porch contributes to the picturesque effect.

Two commissions by the younger Gallier demonstrate his mastery of the
palazzo mode applied to large public buildings. In 1854, he designed the Mechanics Institute for an artisans' benevolent society in New Orleans (Figure 90).
The building, completed in 1858, had a giant two-story Corinthian columnar front and rested on a rusticated base. A balconied attic story topped the
structure, and the ends of the facade were rounded. The complex plan served
the many functions of the society: there were lecture rooms, a library, meeting rooms, reception rooms, retiring rooms, and offices. This building, now
demolished, was the state capitol during Reconstruction. In 1859, Charles

FIGURE 89 Nottoway, White Castle, 1849–1859, Howard and Dittel architects.

Photograph by Jim Zietz

FIGURE 90 Mechanics Institute, New Orleans, 1854, now demolished, James Gallier, Jr., architect.

The Historic New Orleans Collection, 1988.134.19.

FIGURE 91   James Gallier, Jr.'s drawing of the French Opera House, Bourbon and Toulouse Streets, New Orleans, 1859. The building was destroyed by fire in 1919.

Sylvester W. Labrot Collection of James Gallier Sr. and Jr., Southeastern Architectural Archive, Tulane University.

Boudousquie, a notary and theater manager, acquired property for a new opera house at Bourbon and Toulouse Streets in the French Quarter (Figure 91). De Pouilly lost the commission because of other commitments, and Gallier designed and built the theater in incredible haste. The structure was begun in May and completed in November, in time for the opening of the fall opera season. The elliptical building seated about 1,600 patrons, some in a capacious dress circle and latticed boxes, and it housed a bar, a greenroom, a rehearsal theater, offices, and a huge stage. There were a covered carriage way and commercial space for seven shops in the raised basement. The exterior resembled that of the Mechanics Institute, but it was plainer, with pierced parapets and rounded corners. Gallier had produced a building exactly suited to its purpose: the presentation of French opera to Creole audiences. Performances continued to be staged in it until the fire that destroyed it almost sixty years after it opened.

Much of the commercial construction of the 1850s was in the form of the store row, usually with the Italianate features of molded window hoods, bracketed cornices, and high parapets. Bold Italianate window treatments dress the stores and office buildings erected on Canal Street, in New Orleans, in 1871 (Figure 92). In 1866, the firm of Gallier and Esterbrook constructed a commercial building with a cast iron facade and the remarkable height of five stories (Figure 93). The upper-floor windows are completely in the

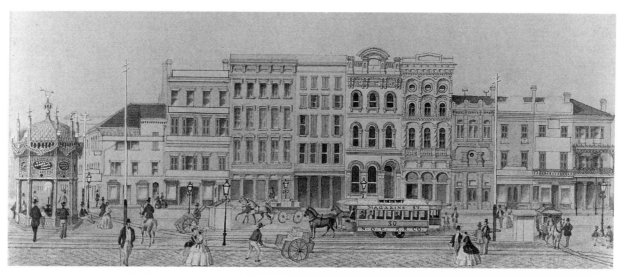

FIGURE 92 Marie Adrien Persac, Drawing from *Illustrated Guide of New Orleans, Canal Street, 1873.* This depiction of the upriver side of the 600 block shows the Belknap Fountain at the corner of Camp Street and a number of commercial buildings with Italianate facades. The third building from Common Street is typical, but both buildings in the middle of the block employ exotic motifs on basic Italianate forms. A foundry in New Orleans cast the iron facade at 622 Canal Street, which survives with its upper stories intact. The sophistication of its eclectic design, especially the spiraling rope columns on the second story, illustrates the great plasticity and variety of form that the new medium of cast iron made possible.

The Historic New Orleans Collection, 1958.78.2.4.

FIGURE 93 James Gallier's drawing of an addition to the Bank of America, on Exchange Place, in New Orleans, 1866. The building is also known as the Cavaroc Building, and the five-story section was originally occupied by the wine-importing business of Charles Cavaroc, the bank's chief officer.

Sylvester W. Labrot Collection of James Gallier Sr. and Jr., Southeastern Architectural Archive, Tulane University.

PLAN, SECTION AND ELEVATION OF STORE DOORS, ETC.

FIGURE 94   Talley's Bank (Spring Street Museum), 525 Spring Street, Shreveport, 1866.

Photograph by Barbara SoRelle Bacot

Venetian Renaissance style, and the first-story columns are Corinthian. This remains one of the state's handsomest commercial buildings in the Italianate style.

Commercial buildings constructed in the Italianate style appeared in several Louisiana cities. Donaldsonville had a few, notably the Lemann Store, attributed to James Freret. Views of Monroe around 1905 show late Italianate buildings on DeSiard and South Grand Streets. In the heart of downtown Shreveport, later Italianate stores jostled with mid-nineteenth-century buildings. On Texas Street, an interesting assortment of stamped metal and cast iron cornices, window moldings, pilasters, and columns ornament brick buildings (Chapter 7, Figure 1). Among Shreveport's remaining nineteenth-century architecture in the Italian mode is the Harrison Building, at 515 Spring Street, from around 1880. Less typical but distinctively Italianate is Talley's Bank, built in 1866, with a fine cast iron balcony and segmented-arch windows on the second floor (Figure 94).

In Louisiana, both the Greek Revival and the Italianate style remained solidly traditional and were chiefly turned to finding the optimum local solutions to architectural problems. In particular, New Orleans' Italianate architecture evolved into peculiarly local forms.[13]

13.   In addition to what is mentioned above, several sources listed under References (pp. 391–94) have been useful in the preparation of this study: the volumes of *New Orleans Architecture,* which appear under their authors' names; *Gibson's Guide and Directory of the State of Louisiana and the Cities of New Orleans and Lafayette* for 1838; Mills Lane's *Architecture of the Old South: Louisiana;* S. Frederick Starr's *Southern Comfort;* Betsy Swanson's *Historic Jefferson Parish from Shore to Shore;* Samuel Wilson, Jr.'s *The Vieux Carre, New Orleans;* Wilson and Leonard Huber's *Landmarks of New Orleans;* and Laura A. Wooldridge's M.A. thesis on Greek Revival buildings in Clinton. Circular No. 4 (December 5, 1870) of the Surgeon General's Office, U.S. War Department, a report on barracks and hospitals, has also provided important information. The New Orleans Notarial Archives are a remarkable resource. During the middle years of the nineteenth century it was customary for architects or surveyors to prepare drawings when property was put up for sale, often including watercolor renderings of plans and elevations. Although the original purpose was to advertise the properties, the drawings became part of the legal record. The Notarial Archives are in the City Hall of New Orleans. Photographs of some of the records are at the Historic New Orleans Collection and the New Orleans Public Library.

6

THE COMING OF MECHANIZATION
Jonathan Fricker

AS THE CULTURAL GEOGRAPHER MILTON B. NEWTON HAS OBSERVED, THE term *revolution* "falls too easily from the lips and pens of those trying to describe the important changes that have altered the historic landscape."[1] Nonetheless, it is indisputable that the face of Louisiana changed dramatically between the antebellum years and the eve of World War II. The broad, mainly technological changes during that time affected the look of the landscape, the way people lived and worked, and not least, the architecture. Many of the buildings we owe to advancing technology are utilitarian at best and rather the reverse of distinguished. Nevertheless they are very important for the history they represent. A surviving steamboat warehouse or Louisiana's last remaining sawmill may rank very low on an aesthetic scale, but each amounts to a compelling part of the record of what has happened to the state—of the life and work that have gone before. Together, such vestiges stand for the historical forces that have made Louisiana what it is today.

Beginning with the arrival of steamboats in 1812, machine technology was a force for change in the state. Then, after the Civil War, the frenetic construction of railroads opened many previously remote areas to settlement and resulted in railroad towns like Ruston and Leesville. The railroads also made it feasible to harvest the vast virgin forests, in what has come to be known as the great Louisiana lumber boom. Sugar processing changed too, from the small antebellum sugar mills run by individual planters to large, centralized mills and refineries operated as factories. In the early twentieth century, the automobile age arrived, with the most far-reaching effect of all. And each technological innovation has left us an architectural legacy.

1. Milton B. Newton, "The Historical Settlement of Louisiana" (Typescript of report prepared for Louisiana Division of Historic Preservation, 1980), 54.

The steamboat era has probably left least in recognizable standing buildings. There were not that many steamboat-related structures to begin with. Plantations generally had no special docking and loading facilities; steamboats merely pulled up at a convenient point on the riverbank and took on and discharged passengers and cargo. Anyway, what steamboat wharves and loading platforms there were have long since vanished. In addition, as steamboating declined in the late nineteenth century, other facilities, such as the dry docks needed for boat repair and the warehouses that sheltered steamboat cargo, tended to disappear. The working steamboats themselves are all gone, their average life being about thirty years.

In our own day waterways are regarded as barriers to transport that must be bridged, but in the antebellum period they were the very arteries of commerce. Louisiana's fabled plantation system developed along a network of rivers and bayous penetrating many miles into the interior. Without cheap and available water transport, cash crops would not have been easily brought to market nor consumer goods brought home.

The first steamboat appeared on the Mississippi in 1812. Named the *New Orleans,* it operated successfully between the Crescent City and Natchez, but in the summer of 1814 a boiler explosion caused it to sink.[2] Steamboats gained tremendously in numbers and commercial dominance in the 1820s, as the vessels displaced more primitive craft like flatboats, barges, and rafts, which could not travel upstream. By the 1840s, steam-powered craft dominated river and bayou traffic, becoming the principal link between the plantation and the world marketplace in New Orleans. Cotton was picked, ginned, and compressed into bales on the plantation; then it was shipped out by steamboat. Of course, the underwriters wanted the maximum profit per trip, and cotton bales often covered the entire boat, giving it the appearance of an enormous cotton bale with chimneys on top and a massive paddle wheel at the rear. Once the cotton reached New Orleans and was sold through factoring houses, it was compressed into smaller bales by massive steam-powered presses and loaded onto ocean-going ships (Plate M).

Most of the riverine commerce passed through New Orleans' Warehouse District, a good portion of which is preserved. Commodities were often bought and sold directly on the wharves, but because the city required cargoes to be moved from the river levee within a week of arrival, there was much warehousing.[3] The building at 800–848 South Peters Street, in New Orleans, is typical of warehouses in the 1830s and 1840s (Figure 1). Vaguely Greek Revival, it has two stories and party walls, and wide entry doors on the ground level accommodated large wagons. The bay spacing is very regular, and the roof line is finished off with a more or less full brick entablature. The

2. Edwin Adams Davis, *Louisiana: A Narrative History* (Baton Rouge, 1971), 323.
3. Patricia Duncan, "New Orleans: Port of Distinction," *Preservation in Print,* February, 1989, pp. 5–6.

FIGURE 1   A brick warehouse of the 1830s
Photograph by Jim Zietz

FIGURE 2   A steamboat warehouse, Washington, St. Landry Parish, *ca.* 1850.
National Register File, Louisiana Division of Historic Preservation.

metal canopy is a later addition. Although a wide variety of commodities could have been stored here, cotton and sugar were the most likely, given the plantation economy.

Warehouses also had a purpose in smaller towns, the so-called interior ports. Towns were established at the head of navigation of this or that bayou or bayou system, often serving plantations far in the interior. The steamboat warehouse in Washington, on Bayou Courtableau, is perhaps the only one to survive from the antebellum period (Figure 2). Its construction is very straightforward, and lacking in architectural refinement. Its thick brick walls and heavy timber make only a utilitarian statement. In this it is probably typical.

What superseded such buildings were the structures associated with railroads. Railroad tracks could go anywhere, not just along navigable waterways. What is more, railroads were three or four times as fast as even the fastest steamboats. Nine short pioneer rail lines were built in Louisiana in the decades prior to the Civil War, but the Louisiana railroad boom was almost entirely a post–Civil War phenomenon. Between about 1880 and 1910, some five thousand miles of mainline track were laid, opening sparsely populated areas to settlement and creating, besides Ruston and Leesville, railroad towns like Oakdale and De Ridder.[4]

In the late nineteenth century, every small town awaited the great day when a rail line would reach it. Towns bypassed by the railroad ceased to thrive, becoming economic backwaters with small populations. Incorpo-

4.   Newton, "The Historical Settlement of Louisiana," 61–62.

FIGURE 3   Vicksburg, Shreveport and Pacific depot, Arcadia, Bienville Parish, 1910.

Photograph by Donna Fricker

FIGURE 4   Texas and Pacific depot, Natchitoches, 1926.

Photograph by Donna Fricker

rated in 1855, the town of Arcadia, in Bienville Parish, was a thriving community and a busy stagecoach stop before the Civil War. But in 1883 the Vicksburg, Shreveport and Pacific Railroad skirted the town some miles to the south, causing a migration to the rail line and producing a "new" Arcadia. The nucleus of the town's railroading history is its historic Vicksburg, Shreveport and Pacific depot (Figure 3). Constructed in 1910, this long, low frame building is fairly representative of small-town depots across the state. Like most, it combined passenger and freight service. The freight area has a loading platform, and exposed roof trusses inside. The passenger area includes a ticket office and what were separate waiting rooms for whites and blacks. The exterior is of board-and-batten siding, and there is a wide skirting roof supported on plain struts. The depot is almost entirely unadorned, although it features a decoratively shingled gable at each end, a legacy of the Victorian Queen Anne Revival style. Like almost all other depots still standing in the state, the one at Arcadia does not date from the arrival of the line in the region—which in this case was 1883.[5] Depots were usually replaced after a generation or so. Very few, if any, depots from before 1900 remain.

Small-town depots tended to be generic and relatively unadorned, but those in larger towns and cities often featured distinctive architectural treatment. Handsome downtown depots went up in a variety of architectural styles ranging from the neoclassical, in Baton Rouge, to Mission, in De Quincy, and Jacobean Revival, like a demolished station in Alexandria. These buildings were individually designed. The Texas and Pacific depot built in Natchitoches in 1926 is a consummate work, even if the architect is unknown (Figure 4). The building takes its cue from the Italian Renaissance, and it might be described as an Italian villa in miniature. In 1931, a promotional publication of the city extolled the new depot: "President Lancaster of the 'TP' has the knack of putting beauty and dignity into structures built for useful purposes, without adding materially to the cost of them. The Natchitoches station is a notable example." At the center of the depot is a two-story lobby and waiting room that was originally for whites and is reached through a grand arcaded loggia. The loggia is flanked by a pair of towers with pyramid-shaped red-tile roofs. Single-story side wings house a freight area, a ticket booth, and what was a waiting room for blacks. The building is richly ornamented with Persian columns, panels of stylized leaves, and bull's-eye panels, among other details.[6]

Perhaps fifty historic railroad depots survive in Louisiana, although few of the grander stations. Railroads also constructed other facilities, among them machine shops, roundhouses, and train sheds, but they too have virtu-

5.   Vicksburg, Shreveport and Pacific Depot (Arcadia, Bienville Parish) National Register File, Louisiana Division of Historic Preservation.

6.   Texas and Pacific Depot (Natchitoches, Natchitoches Parish) National Register File, Louisiana Division of Historic Preservation.

FIGURE 5 Jefferson Hotel, Shreveport, 1922.

National Register File, Louisiana Division of Historic Preservation.

ally disappeared. A few railroad hotels survive. These were not in the grand Beaux Arts style of hotels across the square from city hall. They were functional, mostly unpretentious buildings that filled a role much like that of motels at interstate interchanges today. Those still standing tend to be ample, straightforward brick buildings with hesitant touches of neoclassical or commercial Italianate ornamentation. They usually have their rooms along long corridors, and each door is surmounted by a transom for ventilation. Bathrooms are generally down the hall. Such places catered above all to people whose livelihood demanded travel, such as salesmen, or "drummers," as they were sometimes known during the gaslight era. These were not clients who shunned a hotel because it lacked personality. But though railroad hotels are not likely to catch the eye, they are part of an exceedingly important historical phenomenon.

The Jefferson Hotel (Figure 5), one surviving example, stood directly across the street from Shreveport's mammoth Union Depot, which was razed in 1972. Designed in 1922 by H. E. Schwartz, the blocky 106-room brick structure is sparely ornamented with shop-ordered Classical features. The lobby entrance, marked by an arched canopy, is placed without any bow to symmetry. The entrance door is set within a Classical frame with panels containing sunbursts. During the hotel's heyday, the portions of the ground floor not taken up by the lobby went to shops, including a café, drugstore, bar, restaurant, ice cream parlor, and barbershop. Each of the upper windows in the facade features a jack arch with a prominent concrete keystone. At the top of the facade is a brick parapet inset with cast concrete panels on which there are bas-relief urns. When the Jefferson opened, a local publication hailed the event: "Sheveport's transient population, especially 'shall rise up and call her blessed,' for in the building here of another mammoth up to date hotel, the traveling public will indeed be adequately cared for."[7]

Scarcely anyone could have imagined that railroads would decline almost as quickly as they arose. But as the twentieth century progressed, increasing competition from cars and trucks and a publicly funded highway system left railroads at a disadvantage. By 1970, mainline trackage in the state was down to fewer than two thousand miles from the high of five thousand in 1910. With retrenchments, physical plant began to disappear. In the early years of the century, Ruston possessed a roundhouse, a railroad foundry and shops, two small buildings in which traveling salesmen could display their wares, four depots, and several railroad hotels. Today two small depots and a single railroad hotel are all that remain, a bare trace of the pivotal force railroading had been for the city.[8]

In addition to having an effect on cities and towns, railroads played a critical role in opening the state to timber harvesting. The lumber boom lasted from about 1880 to 1930, and to a fair extent it rebuilt Louisiana. It also denuded the state, leaving between 1904 and 1927 a stumpscape of cutover timberland where there had been some 4.3 million acres of virgin timber.[9] It was another manifestation of the familiar boom-and-bust cycles of the state's economy.

Through much of the nineteenth century, a local, mainly folk forestry industry existed in many parts of Louisiana. It did not consume more than a negligible part of the timber resources of the state. All that changed toward the end of the century, when the nation, having exhausted lumber stands in the northeastern and midwestern states, turned to the South and West. The United States, more than any other advanced nation, showed a preference for building with wood. Indeed, a United States Department of Agriculture survey in 1910 disclosed that more than 94 percent of the country's homes were constructed primarily of wood.[10]

The most harvested wood in Louisiana was pine and red cypress, most of it virgin and thus very old. After a time a tree's growth slows and its wood hardens and becomes saturated with natural preservatives, making it almost impervious to insects and decay. Consequently, the wood from virgin forests

7. Jefferson Hotel (Shreveport, Caddo Parish) National Register Nomination File, Louisiana Division of Historic Preservation.

8. Newton, "The Historical Settlement of Louisiana," 63; Sanborn Fire Insurance Maps, City of Ruston, 1902, 1908, 1914; Vicksburg, Shreveport and Pacific Depot (Ruston, Lincoln Parish) National Register File, Louisiana Division of Historic Preservation.

9. Alexander State Forest Headquarters Building (Rapides Parish) National Register File, Louisiana Division of Historic Preservation. My research includes personal communication with Anna Burns, a historian of Louisiana forestry and a librarian at Louisiana State University at Alexandria.

10. Newton, "The Historical Settlement of Louisiana," 58.

is highly prized by builders.[11] The use of such wood in buildings of the period explains why houses erected then are often in much better structural condition than their more modern additions.

Industrial lumbering spread into Louisiana from Florida around 1880, first to the pine forests of the Florida parishes and the cypress swamps around New Orleans. It soon spread to other parts of the state. The prosperity it brought was an exception to the relatively weak post–Civil War economy. Both the lumber and the money lumbering earned impelled Louisianians to begin building furiously. A great many of the buildings today counted as historic date from the boom times of lumbering.[12] The Queen Anne Revival cottages and the Colonial Revival houses and bungalows scattered in almost every town in Louisiana are the boom's most widespread architectural legacy, though not its most instructive.

More instructive are the relatively small number of historic properties directly linked to the industrialized production of lumber: mills, company towns and mill workers' neighborhoods, owners' and managers' houses, and company-built facilities such as schools, commissaries, and churches. Scores of sawmills once existed in the state, but only one historic mill is known to survive.[13] The Crowell Sawmill, in Longleaf, in southern Rapides Parish, was built in 1892 and modified about 1910, again in 1920, and again in the 1950s (Figure 6). The Crowell Sawmill carries the twentieth-century dictum that "form follows function" to the extreme of making function the sole determinant of form: there is no concession to aesthetics at all. The heavy timber-frame building, once mainly open, was sheathed in corrugated metal siding during the 1930s. On its principal floor is the sawing area, a broad open space, where a succession of rollers and chain conveyors moves logs along the journey that turns them into trimmed planks. At the north end of the space is a murderous looking circular saw that cuts incoming logs to specific lengths. Originally there were two additional large circular saws, one set on each side of the space, which cut the logs into planks. Adjacent to each of the plank cutters was a cart, set on tracks, on which the logs were placed for sawing. Large pistons called shotguns that were mounted on the floor propelled the carts back and forth under the saw, each passage cutting off another plank. Rollers conveyed the freshly sawed planks to an edger saw and then out of the building to a sorting shed. In the 1950s, the plank-cutting circular saws were replaced with a large band saw. At one time the mill operated on steam power generated by burning sawdust. An elaborate system of conduits with internal chain conveyors transported sawdust beneath the principal

11. *Ibid.,* 59.

12. *Ibid.*

13. The staff for the National Register in the Louisiana Division of Historic Preservation knows of no others. The staff's experience comprises thirty-one man-years of National Register field work in the state.

FIGURE 6 Crowell Sawmill, Longleaf, Rapides Parish, 1892, axonometric drawing that includes later modifications.

HABS, 1992, Louisiana State Archives

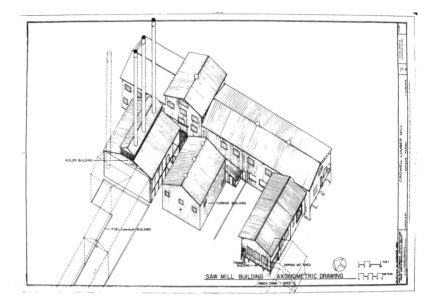

floor to the two boiler buildings, which were near the north end of the mill. Originally there was only one boiler building, a metal-frame structure covered with corrugated metal, occupied by two pairs of boilers, each pair with a stack. In 1920 a third pair was added, with a third stack. In the 1930s, the second boiler building became necessary. The buttressed brick structure includes a hold for sawdust and a larger boiler than the others, with its own somewhat taller stack. An imposing brick fire wall shields the sawmill from the boilers, conflagration being a constant concern in lumber plants. The stacks at Crowell must have been a prominent visual landmark, visible from afar, particularly when they were belching smoke.

Getting timber to the Crowell Sawmill was a feat in itself. Temporary, or "dummy," rail lines ran deep into the forest. These were often casually built, with rails resting on felled trees at irregular intervals. The trains that went out over the dummies were equipped with specialized cars for the task to be performed. First were the pony cars. When the train reached a camp, boys the mill employed rode ponies out into the woods, pulling steel cables with them. Each cable was fastened to a freshly cut log, and steam-powered winches on so-called skidder cars then dragged the logs to the train, where they were hoisted onto special flatcars by a log loader. This was a curious piece of rolling stock indeed. It consisted of a large steel frame that could plant itself firmly on the ground and hoist its carriage and wheels high in the air, permitting the flat cars literally to pass through it. As they passed, a boom at one end of the loader lifted the logs into place. The Crowell complex retains two loaders and one skidder (Figure 7), all in reasonably good condition considering their age. After the flatcars returned to the mill, the logs were unloaded into the millpond. The pond was a regular provision at

FIGURE 7   Crowell Sawmill, Clyde Skidding Machine, 1911, axonometric drawing.

HABS, 1993, Louisiana State Archives

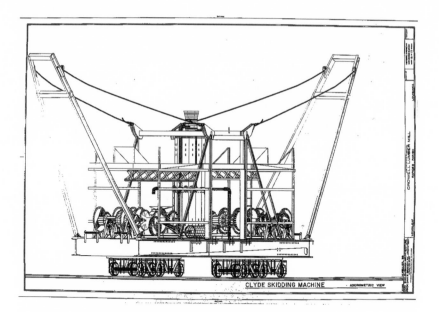

CLYDE SKIDDING MACHINE · AXONOMETRIC VIEW

sawmills, because it enabled large quantities of cut trees to be stored, cleaned, and handled easily. At Crowell, the millpond has been filled in, but HABS has recorded its location. The Crowell pond was like others in lying roughly in the middle of the works, with railroad facilities, machine shops, lumber sheds, the sawmill, and a planing mill arranged around it.[14]

Also surviving at Crowell are a few remnants of the company town. Lumber company towns, with their company-built stores, churches, and houses, once dotted the Louisiana landscape. None of these sawmill communities remain intact, but a half dozen or so have been sufficiently well-maintained to show what a lumber boomtown looked like. Garyville, in St. John the Baptist Parish, was founded in 1903 by the Lyon Cypress Lumber Company, reputedly the second largest industrial operation in the parish's history.[15] At the company's height, it owned acreage of virgin cypress swamp that stretched far into neighboring Livingston Parish. Garyville was laid out in an orderly grid, as was fairly typical for lumber company communities. At the north end was the industrial area with its mill, millpond, and the like. The middle was for commercial purposes, with stores, a bank, a livery stable, and not least, the Lyon headquarters building. The commercial zone was anchored by a railroad corridor, and of course, there was a depot. Farther to the south were long residential streets reaching toward the Mississippi. Here were the company-built churches and schools. Early-twentieth-century pho-

14.   Crowell Sawmill Historic District (Rapides Parish) National Register File, Louisiana Division of Historic Preservation. Much of the information in the Register nomination file is based on interviews with Allen Crowell, whose family has owned the Crowell Sawmill since it was built. He remembers the property from the 1920s onward.

15.   Jean M. Eyrau, *A History of St. John the Baptist Parish, with Biographical Sketches* (Marrero, La., 1939), 49.

FIGURE 8   Garyville streetscape, St. John the Baptist Parish, 1903.

Garyville Timbermill Museum

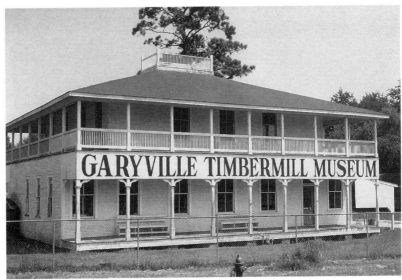

FIGURE 9   Lyon Company headquarters, Garyville, 1903.

Photograph by Jonathan Fricker

tographs reveal a bleak treeless townscape with muddy streets and wharflike plank sidewalks (Figure 8).

Undoubtedly, the most historically significant building remaining at Garyville is the company headquarters (Figure 9). It is a plain two-story galleried building with vaguely Italianate brackets on the downstairs columns. The only other noteworthy exterior feature is the balustrade atop the hip roof. The lower story was given over to offices, with narrow-gauge beaded board walls. The upper story contained bedrooms for use by visiting dignitaries. Overall, the building has an unpretentious character that belies its importance in the scheme of the town. Here was the place from which Garyville was run, both its industrial side and its municipal side. Lumbering was, after all, a highly centralized and controlled business; furthermore, like

FIGURE 10   A typical house for workers in Garyville, 1903.

Photograph by Patricia Duncan

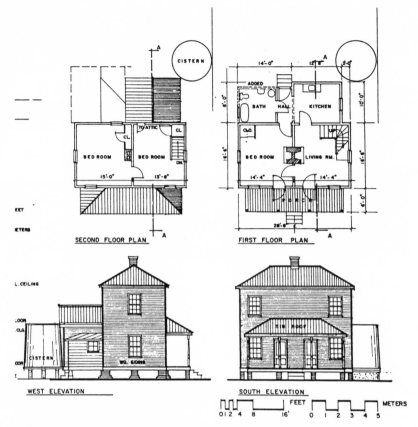

FIGURE 11   Garden City worker's housing, St. Mary Parish, 1890s, facade and plan
HABS, 1990, Louisiana State Archives

most other lumber towns, Garyville was not incorporated: the company was the government.

It is by repetitiveness that Garyville's housing stock makes its strongest impression. Company-built houses were limited to a small number of plans. The most common model in this town, though relatively few remain, was a narrow two-story frame dwelling with a single-story porch (Figure 10). It is uncomplicated, with two rooms downstairs and two rooms on the second floor. Some have a one-room rear wing, for five rooms in all. The location of the stairway is no secret from anyone who sees the windows along the side. Like most of the other buildings in Garyville, the houses are starkly devoid of ornamentation. The workers' row must have had a decidedly dismal feel: the line of identical clapboard boxes just stretched on.[16]

There is a similar type of worker's house in the old lumber community of Garden City, in central St. Mary Parish (Figure 11). Two rooms are set side by side on each floor, with a one-story wing at the rear and a shallow front

16.   Garyville Historic District (St. John the Baptist Parish) National Register File, Louisiana Division of Historic Preservation.

porch. Houses such as these are more characteristic of the industrial North than of turn-of-the-century Louisiana. A more typical small house in Louisiana during the period was a one-story cottage with horizontal lines and a generous gallery. The mill houses at Garyville and Garden City are, by contrast, two stories high with fairly vertical lines. In addition, their galleries are a less salient feature than galleries are in Louisiana houses of indigenous design. The northern flavor shows where so many of the lumber companies came from and visually reiterates the often-heard theme of outsiders exploiting the state's resources.

Not all lumber companies adopted the northern model. Some, as at the towns of Elizabeth, in Allen Parish, and Fisher, in Sabine Parish, built galleried cottages for mill workers. And lumber companies often built larger and somewhat more distinctive residences for higher-ranking employees. The archives at the Garyville Timbermill Museum contain some company drawings for houses for this or that executive. A fairly boxy fourteen-room house is labeled "Mr. Bloss' Two Story Residence." Another plan for an eleven-room house is labeled "Mr. Derby's Two Story Residence."[17] As far as anyone can tell, these houses no longer exist.

Undoubtedly the grandest company-built house in Louisiana is the one the Great Southern Lumber Company erected in Bogalusa for William Henry Sullivan, its vice-president. (Figure 12). The building has the look of a villa, which certainly bespeaks Sullivan's position as virtual ruler of his community in both civic and business affairs. The city of Bogalusa was begun in 1906 by Great Southern, a Pennsylvania-based corporation. According to Amy Quick, Sullivan is justly known as the Father of Bogalusa. Quick states that Sullivan "had instructions at all times to build the largest and best equipped plant in the world; to make the town a good town in which to live; to give the people good schools, churches, well arranged homes with electric lights, pure water, sewerage and all modern conveniences; to build good streets, good sidewalks, and to make the town so attractive that men who worked in lumber enterprises would be glad to live in Bogalusa." Once the town was built and incorporated, Sullivan served simultaneously as both company manager and mayor, positions he held until his death in 1929.[18]

Sullivan's house is one of the few distinguished buildings remaining from Bogalusa's halcyon days. It is thought that Sullivan and his builder designed the house in 1907, the year after Great Southern founded the city.[19] Like many early buildings there, the Sullivan House is of longleaf yellow pine. Its two-and-one-half story central block is flanked by three-story wings, each of which has its own hip roof. A massive two-story, three-bay,

17. Copies of architectural drawings in Garyville Historic District National Register File.
18. Amy Quick, "The History of Bogalusa, the 'Magic City' of Louisiana," *Louisiana Historical Quarterly,* XXIX, (1946), 96, 185–90.
19. William Sullivan House (Bogalusa, Washington Parish) National Register File, Louisiana Division of Historic Preservation.

FIGURE 12   William Henry Sullivan
House, Bogalusa, 1907.
Photograph by Jim Zietz

columnar gallery juts out from the front of the central block. Three dormers pierce the roof above the gallery, the one in the middle topped by an unusual English swan-neck pediment. The dominant style might be called Colonial Revival, though it is a vernacular version. The Sullivan House is one of the area's best examples of the trend away from the irregularity of the larger Queen Anne Revival houses at the turn of the century, toward a more rigid, ordered, and mannered style.

In Bogalusa, as in other planned lumber towns, the company provided for most aspects of its employees' lives. This, of course, included groceries and dry goods. The company commissary—essentially a company-run department store—was often the commercial heart of a lumber community.

George A. Stokes writes,

Such stores were ordinarily superior to anything seen in other small communities, since they were so large and well-stocked. Without leaving the building one might buy a pound of bacon, a box of shotgun shells, a gal-

FIGURE 13   Fisher Commissary, Sabine
Parish, 1900, enlarged 1914.

Photograph by Donna Fricker

lon of kerosene, a rocking chair, and a pair of overalls. In many cases the
commissary building housed other facilities as well. It was not uncommon
for the barber, the doctor, the deputy, and others to occupy office space
under the same roof. Almost everything sold in the commissaries was
brought in by rail, including foodstuffs. Local farms made practically no
contribution to the economy of the town.[20]

Only a handful of lumber-company commissary buildings survive in
the state. Probably the best-preserved is the Fisher Commissary (Figure 13).
The Louisiana Longleaf Lumber Company founded Fisher in 1899 and continued to own and operate the town until 1966. According to John Belisle,
an early chronicler of the area, the town "was laid out with a view of making
something more substantial than the ordinary sawmill town. The townsite is
among the prettiest in Sabine Parish and was platted with uniform streets
and avenues. Splendid homes have been built for the employees, and in numerous instances furnished with all conveniences of a city, including electric
lights and waterworks. . . . The town has a splendid public school for the
benefit of children of employees, and religious services by different denominations are held at stated periods." Today most of Fisher's buildings survive
and are in good repair, enabling the town to present an almost photographic
impression of lumber-town life at the turn of the century.[21]

20.   George A. Stokes, "Lumbering in Louisiana: A Study of the Industry as a Culturo-
Geographic Factor" (Ph.D. dissertation, Louisiana State University, 1954), 59–60.
21.   Fisher Historic District (Sabine Parish) National Register File, Louisiana Division of Historic Preservation; John Belisle, *History of Sabine Parish* (Many, La., 1912).

Built in 1900, the Fisher commissary is a broad, low frame building with a long chamfered-post gallery across the front. The original 1900 plate-glass storefront is surmounted by a three-stage shaped parapet. This design was repeated in the extension to the storefront when the building was enlarged in 1914. Narrow-gauge beaded board, the plywood paneling of the era, sheathes the interior.

Houses for the owners of timber mills are comparatively rare in Louisiana's company towns, inasmuch as the ownership was often northern. A few out-of-state timber magnates took up local residence, however, most notably the so-called Michigan Men, in Lake Charles. Among them were R. H. Nason and W. E. Ramsey. Nason, an Englishman, had thirty years' experience in the lumber industry in Michigan when he came on an exploratory visit to Louisiana in the early 1880s. He and his associates acquired the old Goos Mill property and formed the Calcasieu Lumber Company. In 1886, the company was reorganized in partnership with Ramsey, also a lumberman from Michigan. The company was a gargantuan operation, with two large mills, one of which was known as the Michigan Mill.[22]

Both Nason and Ramsey built impressive houses in the burgeoning residential area of lumber-boom Lake Charles (Figures 14, 15). Notwithstanding the large differences between the two houses, they both depart from local norms. In contrast to the broad, galleried cottages of late-nineteenth-century Louisiana, these houses are tall, vertical, and angular. They are also more richly articulated. They reflect the mainstream American taste of the late Victorian era and represent types apparent in any wealthy suburb in the East or Middle West.

Constructed in the 1880s, the R. H. Nason House is a transitional building from the era when the elaborate structural "honesty" of the late Stick style was giving way to the complex surface textures of the Queen Anne Revival style. The mix of styles, such as Gothic, Italianate, and Eastlake, and the somewhat ungainly transition from the second story to the tower suggest that it was probably builder-designed. The Colonial Revival porch is an early-twentieth-century replacement for the original smaller porch that featured turned Eastlake posts. The massing of the house is lively and adds dramatically to one of Lake Charles's principal thoroughfares.

The W. E. Ramsey House is reminiscent of the early American Colonial Revival style. It has a tall narrow mass with a massive early-colonial-looking chimney. It also has thin turrets front and rear as well as oversize colonial-style dormers. About 1910, the original delicate Eastlake front gallery was replaced with a massive gallery with two-story paneled pillars, a popular feature in Lake Charles at the time.

22. Lake Charles Historic District (Calcasieu Parish) National Register File, Louisiana Division of Historic Preservation.

FIGURE 14   R. H. Nason House, Lake Charles, 1880s.

Photograph by Donna Fricker

FIGURE 15   W. E. Ramsey House, Lake Charles, *ca.* 1890, renovated *ca.* 1910.

Photograph by Jim Zietz

Louisiana's loss of so many properties from the era of the lumber boom stems from the very nature of the boom. Virtually all timber companies pursued the same shortsighted policy of "cut out and get out." Reforestation was largely unheard of, and as a result, much of the state was reduced to a stump-covered wasteland. Most farmers considered the cutover timberland worthless. Some lumber companies tried to get rid of the land they had exploited by attracting settlers from out of state; others simply allowed parishes to take it for delinquent taxes. By the late 1920s, it was clear that the available timber had about played out.[23] The precipitous decline of the industry was accelerated by the Great Depression, and whole towns eventually disappeared. In some cases, companies dismantled their buildings and moved them to fresh timber resources farther west. In other cases, they simply abandoned facilities, leaving them to ultimate demolition. Probably well under 10 percent of Louisiana's lumber-boom buildings survive with any degree of integrity.

The momentous changes associated with the state's lumber industry had a parallel in the growth and post–Civil War recovery of the sugar industry. After the Civil War, Louisiana sugar producers continued the antebellum practice of having each planter process his sugarcane at his own mill. Early mills had for the most part been small, with mules powering the grinding machinery. Few of these survive, since remarkable developments that began in 1877 with the formation of the Louisiana Sugar Planters Association were to make such sugarhouses obsolete. The association, under the leadership of its first president, Duncan F. Kenner, who had served in the Confederate congress, sought to improve conditions for the industry by fostering scientific research and working for favorable legislation. Kenner himself experimented and made several technical innovations. He is thought to have been the first to use a portable railroad to carry sugarcane from the fields to the mill. Under the association's influence, Louisiana's first experiment station for sugar was established in 1885, and it conducted experiments into new breeds and on the width of cane rows, fertilization, and the like. Concurrently, shortages of both labor and capital in the post–Civil War years led some planters to favor central factories for processing the crop. In 1885, Harvey Wiley, of the United States Department of Agriculture, concluded that the production of sugar in Louisiana fell short both scientifically and economically and recommended central factories as the only solution. In the system that developed, large mills grew much of the sugarcane they processed, but they also purchased some from small planters and farmers. The owners of the mills wanted a reliable source, and thus they had a reason to buy more and more land. And as their harvest increased so did mill size and capacity. In 1880, a mill with the capacity to process 300 tons of cane a day was considered large; by 1900, mills with a capacity of 700 to 1500 tons were not unusual. Owing to the cost of building and operating the larger mills, single proprietorship became rare, and corporate ownership became the rule.[24]

Large steam-powered mills with their huge stacks were visible from a

23. Alexander State Forest Headquarters Building (Rapides Parish) National Register File, Louisiana Division of Historic Preservation. Here too my research includes communication with Anna Burns.

24. J. Carlyle Sitterson, *Sugar Country: The Cane Industry in the South, 1753–1950* (Lexington, Ky., 1953), 252–68.

FIGURE 16   Meeker sugar mill and refinery, near Lecompte, Rapides Parish, 1911.

Photograph by Jim Zietz

long way across the flat sugarcane landscape. One of the best known of these is the Meeker Sugar Refinery, located south of Alexandria and visible from U.S. Highway 71 (Figure 16). This plant, which was state-of-the-art in 1911, when it opened, was owned by a Chicago corporation. In its day, it had the full range of processing equipment, from cane crushers, with their heavy rollers, to juice clarifiers and filters, to sugar crystallizers, to centrifuges to separate grains of sugar from molasses. The factory processed its last sugarcane during the 1981 season. The machinery has now been removed, and the building shell has suffered severe deterioration.

At the time the mill started operating, the *Louisiana Planter and Sugar Manufacturer* made its importance for Rapides and Avoyelles parishes clear: "The territory from which this factory will draw its cane is one of the richest in Louisiana and the lack of adequate factory facilities has doubtless deterred many farmers in that locality from going into cane who will now do so." The publication explained that local growers had until then been forced to ship their product to "factories in the more southerly portions of the sugar district."[25]

Meeker's architecture is distinctive among sugar mills. The layout of the plant, with an elevated center section, originally provided for gravity feed of the cane juice from one step in the process to the next. Monumental buttresses divide the high exterior walls into bays, and bands of contrasting dark-colored headers are set every four courses in the brickwork. The round-arch doors and windows on the ground story are a surprising nicety in a utilitarian structure. Equally distinguished are the large round oculus windows that light the upper spaces. The mill was part of a larger complex of buildings once used as a syrup cannery, a chemist's office, an administrative office, a warehouse, and a privy.

The future appears bleak for the Meeker buildings. Sugar mills are a particularly intractable problem for preservationists, since the huge barnlike structures lend themselves poorly to adaptive reuse.

One sugar factory that has shown remarkable staying power and robust economic health is Colonial Sugars, in Gramercy. Like Meeker, Colonial was the doing of northern investors and illustrates Louisiana's status as an economic colony. The founders were the New York–based group of investors that owned the Yazoo and Mississippi Valley Railroad. The group's goal was to fill boxcars on their way north after delivering goods to New Orleans.

In 1895, the Y&MV Railroad syndicate constructed a mill and refinery, along with housing and other buildings for employees, at Faubourg Lapin. The small village became the town of Gramercy, named no doubt for Gramercy Park, in New York City, where apparently many of the investors lived. Colonial operated successfully as a mill and refinery for nearly twenty years. Then, in 1914, the company made the decision to discontinue milling and concentrate on refining—on converting raw sugar into white sugar. Today Colonial survives with an impressive array of historic refining buildings and equipment. The nine-story brick char house, where liquid raw sugar is filtered to remove the brown color, dates from 1902. It contains twenty-seven char filters—massive steel cisterns containing animal-bone char through which the liquid sugar is pumped. Over half the cisterns in current use date from 1908. Truly, this is an operating industrial museum.

Of special interest is the powerhouse (Figure 17), which contains steam-turbine generators that produce electricity for the plant and company housing. Constructed in 1929, this elegant brick structure in the style of a Roman temple was designed by the New York architectural firm of McKim, Mead and White and is thought to be one of only two buildings by the renowned firm in Louisiana. That the architects of Vanderbilt mansions and Columbia University designed a turbine shelter for an industrial plant in south

25.   Meeker Sugar Refinery (Rapides Parish) National Register File, Louisiana Division of Historic Preservation; *Louisiana Planter and Sugar Manufacturer,* December 9, 1911.

FIGURE 17   Colonial Sugars power
house, Gramercy, St. James Parish, 1929,
McKim, Mead and White architects.

Photograph by Donna Fricker

Louisiana can only be attributed to the New York background of Colonial.[26]

Most sugar mills that have continued to operate over the years have, by
acquiring wings and appendages, evolved into complexes with extraordinarily varying massing. The core of the Sterling Sugar Mill, near Franklin (Figure 18), was built in 1890, but there have been many expansions. The original section, designed by the New Orleans architectural firm of Sully and
Toledano, is a four-story brick building with a prominent gable and a roof
that rests on a corbel table. By about 1930, this building adjoined a boxy
four-story set of offices with wide metal windows separated by upward
thrusting brick piers.

Attached to the original section were also large side and rear additions of
corrugated metal over a steel frame. It was there that the manufacturing op-

26.   Colonial Sugars Historic District (St. James Parish) National Register File, Louisiana Division of Historic Preservation.

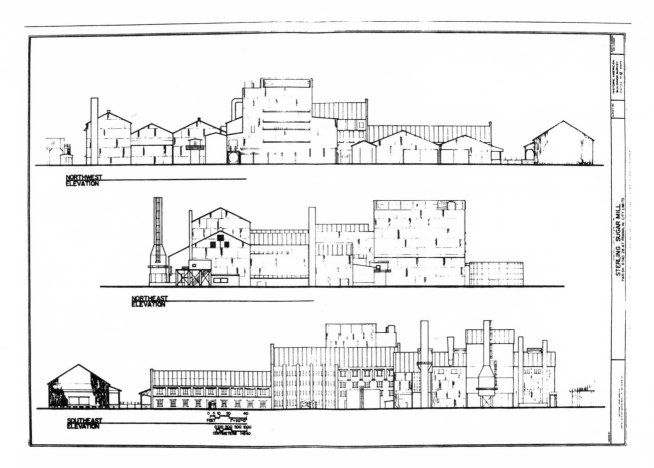

FIGURE 18   Sterling Sugar Mill, near Franklin, St. Mary Parish, begun 1890, elevation drawing, Sully and Toledano architects.

HABS, 1989, Louisiana State Archives

eration moved, the original mill having been converted mostly to storage.[27] The more or less random development of plants like Sterling has produced a result that can be enjoyed for its visual character as well as its historical associations. These buildings have achieved an unpremeditated but striking sculptural effect that feeds the imagination well.

Nothing else, however, has transfigured Louisiana so much as the automobile. There is no record of when the first motorcar appeared in the state. In 1909, though, a world's speed record of sixty miles per hour was set in New Orleans, and that event did much to popularize "horseless carriages." By 1916, almost nine thousand automobiles were registered with parish governments. But prior to about 1920, few hard-surface roads existed in the state outside its major cities. It was the progressive governor John M. Parker who moved the state squarely into the automobile age. His administration, which began in 1920, undertook an ambitious road-building program and inaugurated a state highway system. Governors Huey Long and O. K. Allen per-

27.   Sterling Sugar Mill (St. Mary Parish), Historic Structures Survey, form 51-535, Louisiana Division of Historic Preservation.

petuated the program and added to it, commissioning automotive bridges spanning the Mississippi at New Orleans and Baton Rouge. Despite the Great Depression, automobile ownership surged, so that by 1940 there were nearly 375,000 cars registered in the state.[28]

The automobile had a much broader effect than the technological innovations before it. Railroad towns had developed along rail lines, and beyond the towns, the landscape generally gave way to farmland. The automobile created a seemingly endless transitional zone between town and country in which development petered out. Unreined suburbia was a phenomenon of the 1920s and 1930s, as it is of our own time.

The automobile also brought with it some kinds of buildings that had not existed before, among them the tourist court, or motor hotel. Motor hotels developed from campgrounds at which travelers would pay to spend the night. A progression from pay camps to tourist cabins occurred in the mid- to late 1920s, marking the beginnings of the motel industry. The first tourist cabins were little more than shacks where people on the road could camp out for the night, with at least a roof of sorts over their head. Intense competition caused the cabins to be upgraded until they were homey cottages with flower boxes and picket fences. At first there were rows of freestanding cabins with a central building for bathroom facilities. Later the cabins were connected, perhaps by carports, and later still they were joined with a continuous roof line in the way of today's motels.

The 3 V Tourist Courts, in St. Francisville, which were built in 1938, consist of five small frame cabins connected by latticework carports, along with a duplex cabin and two larger single-unit houses (Figure 19). It is uncertain how many tourist courts once existed in Louisiana, but only four are thought to survive.[29]

Just as tourist cabins satisfied travelers' need for quick in-and-out lodging, cafés and diners provided them with quick, inexpensive food. Many of the roadside restaurants were in streamlined, modernistic structures with lots of glass blocks and brushed aluminum trim. The Airline Motors Inn, in La Place, is a combination filling station and restaurant built in 1939 (Figure 20). Its neon sign is designed to catch the eye of the passing motorist.[30]

As with tourist courts, few roadside diners still stand, but historic filling stations survive in fair number. The first filling stations were simply a pump or pumps outside a business place like a feedstore or drugstore. Next came separate drive-in buildings, often little more than makeshift sheds. In re-

28. Davis, *Louisiana*, 323, 361–62.

29. 3 V Tourist Courts (St. Francisville, West Feliciana Parish) National Register File, Louisiana Division of Historic Preservation.

30. Airline Motors Inn (La Place, St. John the Baptist Parish), Historic Structures Survey, form 48-456, Louisiana Division of Historic Preservation.

FIGURE 19   3 V Tourist Courts, St. Francisville, West Feliciana Parish, 1938.
Photograph by Jim Zietz

sponse to criticism of the unsightly buildings, oil companies began to erect more substantial stations. By the early 1920s, the companies were polishing their image by fashioning service stations to look like houses, perhaps taking a tack from the domestic imagery of the tourist courts. English cottages were favorites. An excellent example is at 803 Broad Street, in the Lake Charles Historic District (Figure 21). But by the end of the 1930s, stations such as that had given way to the gleaming white streamlined box service station. Louisiana's historic service stations tend to be either in a low-key Mission Revival style (Figure 22) or in a streamlined Art Moderne style.

It may seem odd to think of old filling stations as historic properties worth study and preservation. But the filling stations, motels, and diners of the past have recently received scholarly attention as icons of an era. Preserving those which remain is a challenge for the future. The problem is that commercial culture changes so fast that often the related buildings have all

FIGURE 20 Airline Motors Inn, La Place, St. John the Baptist Parish, 1939.

Photograph by Donna Fricker

FIGURE 21 Filling station, 803 Broad Street, Lake Charles, Calcasieu Parish, *ca.* 1930.

Photograph by Donna Fricker

but disappeared before even the informed observer recognizes them as historic.

Historians generally accord Louisiana's technological development less heed than they do political and military events in the state. Yet in some ways the technology has had the greater impact. The revival of the sugar industry

FIGURE 22   Filling station, Ruston,
Lincoln Parish, *ca.* 1930.

Photograph by Donna Fricker

in the late nineteenth century affected the average south Louisianian much
more basically than any choice of governor. Similarly, historic preservation
has traditionally focused upon patriotic landmarks and the homes of the
"best people." Only by enlarging perspectives to encompass properties associated with every influential aspect of Louisiana's history, growth, and development will it be possible to do justice to the state's heritage.

7

CITY AND COUNTRY, 1880–1915:
NEW IMPULSES AND NEW TASTES

Ellen Weiss

THE LOUISIANA ECONOMY, DEVASTATED BY THE CIVIL WAR, RECOVERED much of its buoyancy between 1880 and 1915. Sugar prices revived, and the lumber industry expanded, bringing some towns, such as Lake Charles, explosive growth and many new residents, especially from the Midwest. As the economy went, so went construction. The prosperity supported construction in the fashionable new architectural styles around the state—and even a few skyscrapers, an innovation from the booming industrial North. Railroads, which expanded throughout the state soon after the Civil War, connecting what had been remote areas with the rest of the country, including Texas and the West, also dispersed the merchant activity of New Orleans out into midsized cities and towns so that planters and those they employed could trade locally. Small Louisiana towns developed vibrant commercial cores—Main Street rows of brick party-wall buildings—surrounded by handsome neighborhoods of Queen Anne and, later, Colonial Revival houses embedded in greenery.

Because of the early occupation of the New Orleans port by Federal troops, the port continued to operate and the city mended from the war's economic destruction. In relation to other North American cities, the city never reachieved the preeminence in wealth and grandeur it had enjoyed before the war, when cotton and sugar were building fortunes in its hinterlands. But if northern cities soon surpassed it in growth, its postwar prosperity was real—and evident in the mansions and large commercial buildings going up. Fortunes now came from shipping, trading, and banking, as entrepreneurs replaced planters as the men of wealth. Commerce in New Orleans benefited particularly from the clearing between 1875 and 1879 of a deepwater channel at the mouth of the Mississippi that allowed larger ships access to its docks. A remarkable pumping system, built from 1900 on, drained the often-flooded city, rendering it significantly more healthful and turning marshes into areas suited to development. Some of the new construction was of shotgun cottages, nineteenth-century middle-class dwellings that make vast ranges of the city as magically different from the rest of the nation, and even the world, as the better-known French Quarter and Garden District are. New Orleans never developed the kind of large manufacturing base that fueled the spectacular growth of many northern cities. In one way, that was fortunate, for slow development protected the city's stunning building fabric—French, Spanish, Anglo-American, and possibly African-American— leaving a monument of nineteenth-century architecture and urbanism in zones that are now, and with continued protection could always be, a mecca for tourists, scholars, and city buffs from everywhere. The souvenirs of modest economic growth have proved greater treasures than those of urban booms.

THE GROWTH OF TOWNS

The building of a rail network across Louisiana from the 1880s stimulated the establishment and growth of lumber mills, brickyards, sugar and rice mills, and cotton gins in the state's towns. Parish seats, with their concentration of legal business, and river towns burgeoned, their good economic fortune lodged in solid construction. A typical town center at the turn of the century consisted of rows of common-wall brick business and shop buildings, one to three stories high, with plate-glass windows on the ground floor to let in light and display goods for sale. Many had visually engaging detailing at the cornice level in corbeled and patterned brick, as well as parapets, finials, or chimneys silhouetted against the sky and decorative window surrounds on the upper stories. By 1909, Shreveport had more than thirty blocks of fireproof brick buildings two to four stories high with wooden or metal canopies over the sidewalk to protect pedestrians from sun and rain. Old photos show lively streets with buggies, and later, cars, parked along the edge while their owners went about their business in the shops and offices (Figures 1, 2). Not only the commercial but the political and social life of the community was played out along these brick rows. Records of the 800 block of Texas Street show that there was a vital ethnic mix of Jewish, Syrian, Lebanese, African-American, and Chinese enterprises.[1]

Shreveport's dense commercial core was surrounded, except on the river side, by an outer town of wooden houses standing free on their lots—the lawns serving as natural firebreaks. The builders shaped many of the houses in the Queen Anne style, with projecting bays, towers, and verandas swinging out in several directions as if in celebration of domestic ease, in contrast

1. Sanborn Insurance Company Maps, Shreveport, 1909; Texas Avenue Historic District (Caddo Parish) National Register File, Louisiana Division of Historic Preservation.

FIGURE 1 Texas Street, Shreveport, in the 1880s.

The Historic New Orleans Collection, 1974.25.4.110.

FIGURE 2 Texas Street, Shreveport, in the 1920s.

Archives and Special Collections, Noel Memorial Library, Louisiana State University, Shreveport.

FIGURE 3   East Main Street, Franklin
City of Franklin

to the strictures of the business world. In small Louisiana towns, the basic division of both large and small American cities between the tightly packed business core and the loose, green residential zone around it is clearly fixed (Figure 3). It is the way Americans like to live: in one place a dense urban concentration for working, and in another leafy suburbs for relaxing. In 1904, tiny New Iberia had four blocks of one- and two-story common-wall commercial buildings, with canopies sheltering the sidewalk, and then a surrounding swath of wooden houses on large lots. The commercial buildings contained several barbershops, drugstores, confectionery shops, two music stores, many dry goods and clothing stores, a Chinese laundry, a harness dealer's shop, banks, and hardware, furniture, tailoring, and billiard establishments. Farther out from both the brick core and the wooden domestic ring were the industries: lumberyards, brickyards, a rice mill, and a sugar company. Bayou and railroads met in New Iberia, advancing businesses that transformed and transported the products of the countryside.[2]

In most Louisiana towns, much of the masonry commercial core remains, with numerous buildings escaping the ravages of both growth and decay. Hammond has one of the most complete town centers left in the state (Figure 4). The Boos Building, of 1898, has a particularly inventive and rhythmic band of parapets, the patterned and corbeled bricks stepping up and down. Some of the parapets may have incorporated chimneys.[3] Covington, Ponchatoula, Winnsboro, Monroe, Jackson, Homer, Franklin, and Donaldsonville also have solid enough collections of turn-of-the-century business buildings to justify historic districts.

2.   Sanborn Insurance Company Maps, New Iberia, 1904.
3.   Hammond Historic District (Tangipahoa Parish) National Register File, Louisiana Division of Historic Preservation.

FIGURE 4 East Thomas Street, Hammond, as it appeared around the 1920s, with the Boos Building, built in 1898, on the left.

Private collection

FIGURE 5 Oil and Gas Building (formerly Bank of Lafourche), Thibodaux, 1897, George Knapp architect.

Photograph by Jim Zietz

Occasionally party-wall business buildings had front elevations of special distinction. The Oil and Gas Building, in Thibodaux, built in 1897 as the Bank of Lafourche, has a sophisticated facade in varying textures of stone with an array of classical features (Figure 5). The entry, under an arch, together with the two side windows separated from it by Ionic columns, embodies the Renaissance architectural device of the *serliana,* or Palladian window. In Lafayette, a party-wall brick building constructed for the Bank of Lafayette in 1898, which later served as the city hall, presents a particularly creative composition of arches punctuated by projecting brick headers and an arresting curved balcony with a conical roof pointing up to a curved parapet (Figure 6). Designed by George Knapp, it manages to squeeze into a limited frontage the force and character of a dynamic Queen Anne suburban house.[4]

QUEEN ANNE, A DOMESTIC STYLE

Through the 1880s and 1890s and into the new century, more and more of the houses surrounding the brick commercial cores of Louisiana towns and cities were built in what was called the Queen Anne style. Such houses were broken apart in as many ways as possible, with projections, recessions, and other complications—towers, turrets, wings, gables, bays, dormers, and verandas pushed in and out or up and down. Often an upward-thrusting tower or turret on one side of the entry would asymmetrically balance the horizontal spread of a broad veranda on the other. Verandas—spaces that both belonged to the house and lay outside the house, and thus that were both of

FIGURE 6 Bank of Lafayette, Lafayette, 1898.

Photograph by Donna Fricker

4. Oil and Gas Building (Thibodaux, Lafourche Parish) National Register File, Bank of Lafayette (Lafayette Parish) National Register File, both at Louisiana Division of Historic Preservation.

the family and of the community—received special attention with turned balusters and posts, and screens of abacus-like spindles or jigsaw brackets. The impression the Queen Anne style left is that no one ever wanted a wall to be predictable and boring and that therefore every opportunity to break it up had to be taken. If a flat stretch remained, the builder usually gave it texture with patterns of shaped shingles or a wooden sunburst.

The decorative work—the brackets, spindles, turned posts, and shaped shingles—were easy to produce by the 1880s, since the specialized machines for making them had become inexpensive. Many sawmills, planing mills, and sash and blind factories manufactured them as prefabricated parts, so that any carpenter or builder with an eye for the picturesque could assemble them into configurations of his own choosing and have all the pleasure of being a designer. The name Queen Anne was something of a misnomer, since the architecture during the reign of this early-eighteenth-century English monarch was much simpler. To the English, the term conveyed an architectural vocabulary rooted in plain vernacular forms from before the more formal Georgian era. The towers and turrets in the American Queen Anne style actually came from sixteenth-century France, but that hardly mattered. The idea that some distant queen could be the mother—or sweetheart—of this cheerful, celebratory, and definitely domestic formal language seemed just right. Later, a younger generation of trained architects would complain that it was all too amateurish, lacking in learning, proportion, and restraint. But before their views took hold, architects and carpenters had thirty or forty years of satisfaction assembling their bits and pieces of wooden fancy to make cottages and mansions.

Every part of Louisiana has splendid Queen Anne houses, of both the multistory variety that is found throughout the nation and the spreading, one-story variety that held special appeal in the Deep South. Rose Lawn, built in 1903 in Natchitoches to designs of the Nashville architects George Barber and Thomas Kluttz, is a spacious dwelling that recalls English half-timbering in the front-facing gable and brings off the typical period caprice of an asymmetrical play of balconies and windows below (Figure 7). The Lewis House, in Shreveport, has an octagonal three-story tower with a conical roof that activates the skyline (Figure 8). It is in most ways representative of builders' Queen Anne across the nation. Most Queen Anne houses in Louisiana were simpler one-story cottages with hip-roofed blocks extending into gable-roofed wings (Figure 9). Rounded verandas often wrapped several sides of the building. A high hip roof over an unoccupied attic helped insulate the lower story from the summer heat. Sometimes behind the whimsical exteriors were traditional center-hall interiors. Some Louisiana Queen Anne houses reflect the owner's origins more than the place of construction. The Nason House, in Lake Charles, once occupied by one of the Michigan Men

FIGURE 7 Rose Lawn, Natchitoches, 1903, George Barber and Thomas Kluttz architects.

Photograph by Donna Fricker

who moved south for lumbering opportunities, declares an Upper Midwest provenance (Chapter 6, Figure 14). Most striking among transplants are the buildings of Jennings (Figure 10). Spare and austere, these two-story houses, with mere hints of the Queen Anne mood in small porches and bands of shaped shingles, must have been built by carpenters accompanying the Iowa farmers who came to revolutionize rice cultivation. Other late-nineteenth-century houses in the southern part of the state kept some local characteristics, for Louisiana builders did not always avail themselves of the most advanced possibilities. Classic center-hall raised cottages embellished with sparse Victorian detailing were built as plantation houses through the 1880s. Emilie, constructed near Garyville in 1882 with an antebellum Greek Revival–looking gallery (Figure 11), perpetuated the traditional with the merest nod to national fashions.[5]

Louisiana may be especially famous for its great plantation houses of earlier periods—in the Creole, Greek Revival, and Italianate styles—but grand country mansions were erected at the end of the century as well. The vast Glencoe, built from 1897 to 1903 near Jackson, is covered in patterned shingles and has three towers and extensive double galleries (Figure 12). Edgewood, constructed in 1902 in Union Parish, is a spreading one-story

5. Rose Lawn (Natchitoches, Natchitoches Parish) Tax Act File, Lewis House (Shreveport, Caddo Parish) National Register File, Funk House (Jennings, Jefferson Davis Parish) National Register File, Emilie Plantation House (St. John the Baptist Parish) National Register File, all at Louisiana Division of Historic Preservation.

FIGURE 8   Lewis House, Shreveport, 1898
Photograph by Jim Zietz

FIGURE 9   Queen Anne cottage, Franklin Historic District.

Photograph by Donna Fricker

FIGURE 10   Funk House, Jennings, *ca.* 1895.

Photograph by Jim Zietz

FIGURE 11   Emilie, near Garyville, St. John the Baptist Parish, 1882.

Photograph by Jim Zietz

Queen Anne raised cottage with a rounded gallery set off by a single turret. Inside are eleven rooms with fourteen-foot ceilings and chandeliers that were fueled by the estate's own gas plant. The oak and cypress for the building were cut on the owner's land but sent from the plantation's deepwater wharf to St. Louis for milling. Ardoyne, near Houma, is exceptional for being built as a very late Gothic Revival villa but with an asymmetrical integration of gable, tower, and veranda and decorative details that show the late-nineteenth-century Queen Anne aesthetic (Figures 13, 14). Designed by W. C. Williams and C. Milo Williams, of New Orleans, in the 1890s, Ardoyne has sixteen-foot ceilings on the ground floor, twenty-one rooms, and a range of Gothic

FIGURE 12   Glencoe (Westerfields), East
Feliciana Parish, 1897–1903.

Photograph by Jim Zietz

motifs at several scales on its wraparound gallery and its gable bargeboards.
A dramatic seventy-five-foot tower, with a steeply pitched and cross-gabled
roof, renders this a wholly memorable house.[6]

New Orleans is in many ways a late-Victorian city, with Queen Anne
structures of a host of sizes and shapes making up much of the housing
stock. There are one-story raised cottages with broad verandas and coni-
cally roofed pavilions. Uptown, in the rapidly developing sixth and seventh districts, grand and tiny houses cut to many different patterns were
going up from the 1880s through the 1910s. New Orleans builders even
figured out how to shape the city's vernacular house types—the shotgun,
the double shotgun, and the latter's cousin, the two-story party-wall
double—and make them speak to the taste of the time. Most freestanding
two-story Queen Anne houses are on narrow city lots, so the complica-
tion of turrets, towers, gables, and porches tends to be confined to their
facades (Figure 15). That imparts a quality of constraint, as well as an ex-
aggerated verticality, to which the Creole legacy of long narrow windows

6.   Glencoe (East Feliciana Parish) National Register File, Edgewood (Union Parish) National
Register File, Ardoyne (Terrebonne Parish) National Register File, all at Louisiana Division of Historic Preservation.

FIGURE 13   Ardoyne, Terrebonne Parish, 1890s, W. C. Williams and C. Milo Williams architects.

Photograph by Jim Zietz

on both lower and upper stories contributes. But there are also many full-bodied, spreading, large-lot Queen Anne residences like those in other parts of the state and the nation. Many of these were designed by Thomas Sully, who with Louis Lambert, an architect and builder of humbler dwellings, is credited with bringing the style to town. Sully grew up in New Orleans but trained in an architectural office in New York City. Orleanians perceived Queen Anne houses as progressive not only because they looked fresh and new, like New York or Boston, but also because they came with the latest mechanical conveniences. A newspaper in 1896 observed that a king's palace of twenty years before would not have had the amenities of the home of a progressive New Orleans businessman. Substantial houses at the end of the century often had hot and cold running water, hot-air or hot-water heating, gas service or electricity or both, and "sanitary closets." That was modernity (Figure 16). And it was confidence, counting on coming urban services, for the city did not yet have the drainage and pumping system that enabled sewerage lines and a public

FIGURE 14   Hallway at Ardoyne
Photograph by Jim Zietz

FIGURE 15   Row of apartments on
Prytania Street, New Orleans, as it
appeared around 1895.

*Collection of the Louisiana State Museum.
Photograph by François Mugnier.*

FIGURE 16   Sitting room in New Orleans around the turn of the century.

Collection of the Louisiana State Museum. Photograph by François Mugnier.

water supply. In 1896, most household water was still from private, above-ground cisterns.[7]

SHOTGUNS, A LOUISIANA BUILDING TYPE

The end of the nineteenth century saw the spread of the shotgun cottage into all parts of New Orleans. Shotgun houses, in their various forms, seem almost as special to viewers today as the French Quarter, though they are just middle- and working-class habitations of a particularly attractive kind. Engaging, architecturally enriched facades hug the streets, the houses' front galleries providing for social interaction between families, their backyards offering the privacy of a world apart. Most cities do not have anything comparable. Instead, they have row houses or multistory apartment blocks without inviting private outdoor space. Shotgun neighborhoods, with their urban streetscapes and often their tangle of subtropical plantings behind, seem to achieve the miracle of fusing city and country into a seamless whole. When shotguns are mixed with other New Orleans vernacular buildings—Creole cottages, balconied town houses, center-hall raised cottages, and corner stores—as in districts like Carrollton, Bywater, or the Irish Channel, the result is livability, variety, and formal complexity, not to mention historic interest and sheer exotic beauty.

The shotgun cottage is a long, narrow house with a single file of rooms running from front to back (Figures 17, 18). Single shotguns can be as narrow

7.   Uptown Historic District (Orleans Parish) National Register File, Louisiana Division of Historic Preservation; "Architects and Builders Hopeful," New Orleans *Daily Picayune,* September 1, 1896, p. 14.

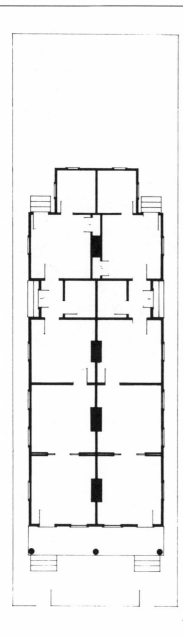

FIGURE 17   The shotgun cottage at 800–802 Henry Clay Street, in New Orleans, *ca.*
1880. The porch's posts were converted to posts on piers around 1915.

Photograph by Jim Zietz

FIGURE 18   A double shotgun cottage at
1017–1019 Fourth Street, in New Orleans,
ca. 1910, plan. The construction of
shotguns continued into the twentieth
century, with facades and decorative
details in the prevailing taste.

Drawn by Davis Lee Jahncke, Jr.

as twelve feet while stretching eighty or ninety feet to the rear. The most common type, the double, joins two shotguns side by side with a party wall between, each unit with windows on the front and rear and on the long outside wall. The double lets two units fit on one lot without building upward. A variation on the double or single, the camelback, puts a second story on the back part of the cottage (Figures 19, 20). Usually the shotgun's rooms are connected only by doors, without hallways. Sometimes the doors line up near the wall—an outside, windowed wall in the case of a double—so that there is an uninterrupted line of vision all the way through. As someone once said, "Standing at the front door, you could shoot the chicken in the backyard." But enough shotguns have partial hallways or open side galleries serving as passages that the absence of a hall cannot be considered a defining feature (Figure 21). All shotguns have the long ridge of the roof at right angles to the street, however, with a hip end or gable above the entry. Most of those in New Orleans flaunt high-style architectural displays on the front: Italianate segmented-arch openings and rusticated panels or Eastlake and Queen Anne bracketed overhangs and galleries with intricate turned and jigsaw work. Twentieth-century shotguns mix Queen Anne, Colonial Revival, and Craftsman Bungalow motifs, some with Louisiana Colonial Revival elliptical fanlights (Chapter 8, Figure 8). They may even finish up with stucco facades in a Mediterranean or Mission style. The accretion of styles over time testifies to middle-class fashion and more: the cottages reflect a scaling-up, both economically and in the fantasy they can sustain. The ambitious decor also distinguishes them from the plain shotguns that in the early part of the twentieth century served as workers' housing all through the South, from the Carolinas to Shreveport, where there is a large historic district of plain shotguns.

FIGURE 19 A camelback double shotgun cottage in New Orleans, *ca.* 1890.

Photograph by Jim Zietz

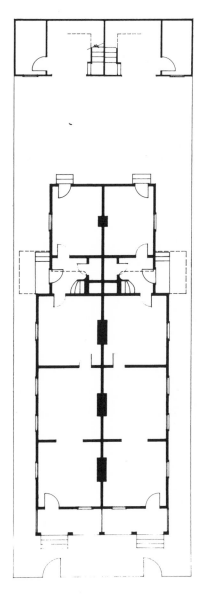

FIGURE 20 The double shotgun cottage at 3516–3520 Magazine Street, in New Orleans, *ca.* 1860, plan. This camelback double is among the most spacious of shotguns. The unusual curved stairs to the upper rooms are part of the high level of refinement.

Drawn by Davis Lee Jahncke, Jr.

Shotguns seem to have appeared in New Orleans by the 1840s as an import from French-speaking Caribbean islands or, perhaps, as a rearrangement of the standard New Orleans Creole cottage (Figure 22). John Michael Vlach has shown that similar cabins two or more rooms deep were common in West Africa and Haiti, which suggests an African origin of the form. But Sally Kittredge Reeves has argued that most West Indian immigrants built four-room *en suite* Creole cottages (Chapter 2, Figures 10, 11) and town houses when they got to New Orleans, not shotguns.[8] In France, a file of rooms connected by doors in a line, without hallways, was a common arrangement at

8. John Michael Vlach, "The Shotgun House: An African Architectural Legacy," in *Common Places: Readings in American Vernacular Architecture,* ed. Dell Upton and John Michael Vlach (Athens, Ga., 1986), 63–77; Sally Kittredge Evans [Reeves], "Free Persons of Color," in *New Orleans Architecture: The Creole Faubourgs,* ed. Roulhac Toledano, Sally Kittredge Evans, and Mary Louise Christovich (Gretna, La., 1974), 25–36.

FIGURE 21 A shotgun cottage at 2321 Coliseum Street, in New Orleans, *ca.* 1870, facade and plan. One of a row of eight designed by Henry Howard, this single shotgun has an open side gallery.

Photograph by Susan Gandolfo

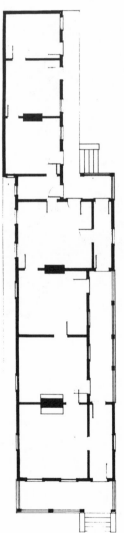

Drawn by Davis Lee Jahncke, Jr.

high social levels. If a sequence of rooms with a line of connecting doors next to the windowed wall is considered a shotgun, King Louis XIV was living in a shotgun in his grand apartment at Versailles. But shotguns may also have developed in New Orleans as an enlargement of Creole cottages, with a change of ninety degrees in the direction of the roof ridge from parallel to the street so that the Creole practice of extending rooms back from the street without halls could be carried farther. Since many early shotguns had hip roofs, as did many Creole cottages, the change is easy to imagine. With hip roofs, after all, it is often hard to say which way the ridge is running (Figure 23). Shotguns of the late nineteenth and early twentieth century appropriated other Creole building elements as well. The deep overhangs shading the front walls, the long front windows with the same dimensions as the doors, the louvered shutters, and the french doors all tinctured the farthest reaches of the growing, and now often Yankee, parts of the city with a Creole cast. The long windows onto the galleries are a luxurious gift from the past. Even humble cottages can have the mansionlike amenity of nine-foot-high double-hung windows opening onto a porch or gallery, giving a small building a monumental presence on the street. The camelback shotgun, with a two-story hump to the rear, which enjoyed a vogue late in the nineteenth century, may have had its origins in the two-story service wings behind one-story Creole cottages. Camelbacks often have second-floor projecting balconies on their sides—still another Creole element.

The late-Victorian shotguns, whether single, double, or camelback, lend a fine consistency to spread-out New Orleans, since the little house-blocks are alike in overall proportions and dimensions, materials, roof slopes, and the repetitive line of alternating chimneys and ventilators on the roof peak.

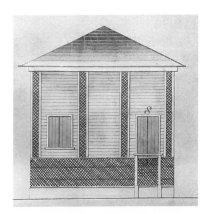

FIGURE 22   One of a row of four simple houses with lattice posts on St. Denis Street (now Loyola Street), in New Orleans. A matching row faced Second Street. Both were built on speculation as workers' housing. Only two main rooms deep, these early antecedents of the true shotgun were drawn in 1853.

New Orleans Notarial Archives, Plan Book 64, folio 5, dated 1853.

FIGURE 23   Shotgun with open side gallery on St. Bernard Street, in New Orleans. The plan is similar to that in Figure 21.

New Orleans Notarial Archives, Plan Book 78, folio 47, dated 1871

FIGURE 24   A row of camelback double shotgun cottages on Camp Street, in New Orleans, *ca.* 1880.

Photograph by Jim Zietz

Most have clapboard sides, which contrast with smooth, flush boarding on the front or, more often, wide dropleaf siding with square blocks, that is, quoins, at the corners to give a definite edge (Figure 24). Such a facade was described as rustic, in a shortening of the word *rustication,* the term for some ways of rendering the joints of stonework conspicuous that were employed during the Renaissance and imitated in the Italianate wooden facades of a

FIGURE 25   Wares offered in the catalog
of Roberts and Co., New Orleans, 1891.
*Southeastern Architectural Archive, Tulane
University.*

number of the great houses in Louisiana of the 1860s and 1870s. Rustic facades carried rustication on into the twentieth century and give the city one
of its characteristic textures. Many shotguns have dramatic overhangs—hip
roofs extending over the facades often five and sometimes seven feet. These
are supported by ornamental brackets of great sculptural character from the
several planing mills in the city. One mill, the Louisiana Steam Sash and
Blind Company, published catalogs of its wares—mantels, doors, blinds,
moldings, window frames, columns, and balustrades—in 1880 and 1891. The
catalogs offered one hundred different bracket designs. Another, Roberts and
Company, published catalogs in 1894 and 1904 (Figure 25).[9] The overhangs
sheltered the long front windows and doors from the sun and rain, allowing
residents to keep them open during cooling downpours. Other shotguns had
galleries with prefabricated decorative posts from mill yards. There are both
harmony and a wonderful variety in the arrangements of pierced spandrels,
brackets, spindle friezes, finials, gablets, and jigsaw panels that festoon the
galleries—a Queen Anne and Eastlake festival of assembled turned and
sawed bits that make New Orleans one of the country's great Victorian cities.

Shotgun interiors also show considerable variety considering the con-
straints. They can have partial or complete halls, or open galleries hidden
from the street, along the sides. Rooms vary from twelve to fifteen feet
wide—usually the same or slightly longer in length—and twelve to fourteen
feet high. Each room had its own coal-burning fireplace; thus the rhythmic
line of corbeled brick chimneys on the roof. Architectural drawings from the
late 1890s show some flexibility in the assignment of functions to the rooms.
The two front rooms were usually labeled as a parlor and dining room, with
one or two bedrooms between them and the kitchen at the rear. But there
could also be a parlor, then a bedroom or two, and then the dining room and
kitchen. One tiny double built for a widow had the front room of each unit
labeled as a bedroom with the second a dining room in front of a small
kitchen. Occasionally the builder specified gas heating and cooking. Sometimes the cisterns behind the cottages were connected by pipes to the kitchen
sink or a pantry bathtub. Outhouses were always placed at the rear of the
property. Victorian shotguns were built of pine, sometimes with stud walls,
sometimes with planks fixed vertically to sills and plates without posts.
Trim—doors, mantels, the quoins, and usually, the front dropleaf siding—
were of cypress. Builders and architects, such as Paul Broyard, Joseph Riley,
and Felix Rolland, often attached both elevation drawings and foundation
plans to their contracts. The foundation plans showed the brick piers, with a
slate damp course, raising the houses two or three feet to protect them from
vermin, moisture, and high water.[10]

9.   See also William C. Bell, *Illustrated Catalogue of Mouldings, Architectural and Ornamental
Woodwork* (New Orleans, 1880).

10.   Building Contracts, J. F. Meunier notary, in Acts No. 25 (July–December, 1895), No. 230,
Acts No. 26 (January–December, 1896), Nos. 1, 78, 142, both in New Orleans Notarial Archives.

FIGURE 26   Thomas Sully House, Carrollton Avenue, New Orleans, 1893, Thomas Sully architect.

Photograph by Jim Zietz

COLONIAL AND ANTEBELLUM MEMORIES EVOKED

By the 1890s, the Queen Anne style was shading into another, the Colonial Revival style, that employed an architectural language of greater restraint and more specific historical reference. Once again, Sully led the way in New Orleans. In 1893, he built a house for himself on Carrollton Avenue that, in massing, is a quiet Queen Anne with gentle asymmetries but that has discrete details from the American East Coast colonial past, such as a modillion cornice, Tuscan porch columns, and a segmental swan-neck pediment over the window of his own study (Figure 26). The swing to the Colonial Revival style, too, was a national movement, one born of the historical awareness the centennial of American independence excited. Sully was again introducing the latest and best from the North.[11]

With time, Colonial Revival designs became more "correct," more for-

11. Sully House Landmark Nomination Form, Historic District Landmarks Commission, New Orleans.

FIGURE 27   Castles House, 6000 St. Charles Avenue, New Orleans, 1895, Thomas Sully architect.

Photograph by Jim Zietz

mal and more closely based on the study of eighteenth-century houses, rather than simply the application of colonial details to Queen Anne buildings. Sully's Castles House, at 6000 St. Charles Avenue, which was built in 1895, has a symmetrical facade, like eighteenth-century mansions in New England and the middle colonies (Figure 27). The Castles House has Ionic pilasters at the ends of the facade and supporting the central pediment over the door, a clear reference to the colonial house in Cambridge, Massachusetts, that was the home of the poet Henry Wadsworth Longfellow in the nineteenth century. A remarkable but less scholarly Colonial Revival building, the Nicholas Burke House, at nearby 5809 St. Charles Avenue, succeeds in applying a full eighteenth-century or Georgian language—gooseneck dormer gables and classical urns as finials on the attic, as well as clusters of Ionic columns, the capitals draped in flower swags, supporting a wraparound veranda, its entablature festooned with still more swags—without giving up the Victorian assertiveness of an earlier architectural sensibility (Figure 28). The Burke House was designed by Toledano and Wogan in 1896 and today has one of the best-preserved interiors from the early twentieth century in the city.[12]

Colonial Revival buildings in the South also adapted forms of the southern plantation, with large columns and projecting porticoes marking the entrances and shading the walls. The McCarthy House, of 1903, at 5603 St. Charles Avenue, has a particularly handsome pedimented portico with six

12.   Uptown Historic District (Orleans Parish) National Register File, Louisiana Division of Historic Preservation; Nicholas Burke House Landmark Nomination Form, Historic District Landmarks Commission, New Orleans.

FIGURE 28 Nicholas Burke House, 5809 St. Charles Avenue, New Orleans, 1896, Toledano and Wogan architects.

Photograph by Jim Zietz

large fluted Ionic columns (Figure 29). This house has a Beaux Arts sense of control and monumentality and makes a clear reference to great southern Greek Revival plantations, such as Henry Howard's Madewood. The house built in 1907 to designs by Toledano and Wogan for William T. Jay at the corner of Audubon Place and St. Charles Avenue is less correct and more dynamic (Figure 30). Now used by Tulane University as a presidential mansion, it has deep verandas with large Ionic columns to shade the walls and to pro-

FIGURE 29   McCarthy House, 5603 St.
Charles Avenue, New Orleans, 1903.

Photograph by Jim Zietz

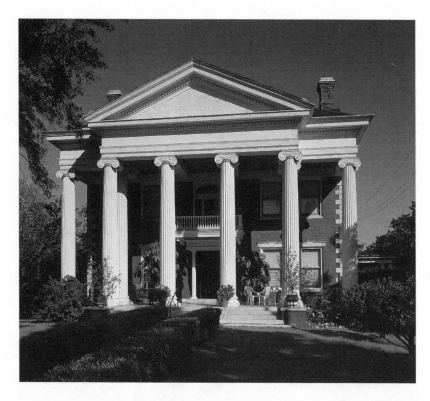

tect open windows during summer downpours.[13] Houses like this were built
all through the deep South in the early twentieth century, and they were
called Southern Colonial even though their model, big houses of the 1840s
and 1850s, were built long after the colonies had become a nation. They
might better be called Antebellum Revival, since they draw stylistically on
the period just before the Civil War.

There are a number of Colonial Revival houses outside New Orleans,
although there are not as many as in the Queen Anne style. The Cook
House, in Alexandria, built in 1910, is in massing a brick Queen Anne structure, complete with octagonal tower, but it has a variety of colonial decorative motifs: classical swags on panels on the tower, Palladian windows in the
gables, and verandas with Ionic columns, a full Classical entablature and
cornices, and balustrades of Classically shaped spindles (Figure 31). The
Cook House, like Sully's on Carrollton Avenue, shows the first phase of
Colonial Revival design: Classical or Georgian motifs sprucing up a Queen
Anne form. The Walter S. Goos Mansion, built in 1906 in Lake Charles, is
the handiwork of the academic phase (Figure 32). Its deep, wall-shading,
two-story portico has a great deal to do with George Washington's house at
Mt. Vernon, Virginia—as if a trained architect were tidying it up. The Gov-
ernor Luther E. Hall House, built in Monroe in the same year, is Southern
Colonial in its giant Ionic columns supporting a pedimented portico—the

13.   Uptown Historic District (Orleans Parish) National Register File, Louisiana Division of Historic Preservation; Malcolm Heard, Jr., and Bernard Lemann, *Tulane Places* (New Orleans, 1984), 12.

FIGURE 30   William T. Jay House,
Audubon Place, New Orleans, 1907,
Toledano and Wogan architects.

Photograph by Jim Zietz

FIGURE 31   Cook House, Alexandria,
1910.

Photograph by Jim Zietz

FIGURE 32   Walter S. Goos Mansion,
Lake Charles, 1906.

Photograph by Jim Zietz

early twentieth century's idea of what a plantation house ought to have
been, even if it seldom was (Figure 33). Also of interest are the local variants
of the Colonial Revival in Lake Charles in which builders adapted the tall
columns to informally planned wooden houses and interwove them with
second-story galleries, a traditional Louisiana building element (Chapter 6,
Figure 15).[14]

It is ironic that Louisiana's Colonial and Southern Colonial architectural
revivals should be so much like those of other states in the South and the nation when most of Louisiana did not share the English origins of the rest of
the region. But Louisiana builders, aligning themselves with progressive aspirations to business growth and national success, seldom looked to their
own colonial past. It took a couple of artistic New Englanders to attend to
that. In 1885, Ellsworth Woodward and William Woodward came to New
Orleans to teach art and architecture at Newcomb College and Tulane University. Along with northern tourists who were reading George Washington
Cable and seeking out picturesque Creole buildings in the French Quarter,
the Woodwards found themselves entranced by Louisiana's distinctive history as a colony of France and Spain. Ten years later, William Woodward
showed what he had learned, in a house he designed for the corner of Benjamin and Lowerline Streets that mimics, at tiny scale, a Creole raised plantation house, complete with gallery colonnettes and an elliptical fanlight

14.   Cook House (Alexandria, Rapides Parish) National Register File, Lake Charles Historic
District (Calcasieu Parish) National Register File, Governor Hall House (Monroe, Ouachita Parish)
National Register File, all at Louisiana Division of Historic Preservation.

FIGURE 33   Governor Luther E. Hall
House, Monroe, 1906.

Photograph by Jim Zietz

FIGURE 34   House at 443 Benjamin
Street, New Orleans, 1895, William
Woodward architect.

Photograph by Jim Zietz

over the door (Figure 34). Ellsworth Woodward inspired Rathbone De Buys'
design for the Crafts Building at Newcomb College, which was erected in
1903 (Figure 35). The architect melded motifs from Creole plantations and
French Quarter town houses to yield a truly Louisiana Colonial Revival
structure. But the Woodwards' message was one most Louisiana architects
and builders were not attuned to hear until much later in the twentieth century.[15]

There are also some buildings that are so integrated with Louisiana traditions that they seem as much a continuation as a revival. The sophisticated
design by General Allison Owen and Collins C. Diboll for the Academy of
the Sacred Heart on St. Charles Avenue, in New Orleans (Figure 36), is redolent of earlier institutions of Catholic Louisiana—the convents, monasteries,
seminaries, schools, and hospitals that give weight to city neighborhoods and
to sections of the state. The academy achieves a sense of timelessness even
though it was built in the twentieth century. Its core, constructed in 1900, is
an H-plan building, two stories high, that was completely encircled by a
colonnaded veranda. The knowing play on Louisiana galleries carried a subtle
academic edge by virtue of the pairing of Tuscan columns at selected points

15.   John Ferguson to author, June 13, 1991; Jessie Poesch, *Newcomb Pottery: An Enterprise for
Southern Women, 1895–1940* (Exton, Pa., 1984), 32; Bernard Lemann, Malcolm Heard, Jr., and John
P. Klingman, eds., *Talk About Architecture: A Century of Architectural Education at Tulane* (New Or-
leans, 1993), 19–23.

FIGURE 35   Crafts Building, Newcomb College, New Orleans, 1903, Rathbone De Buys architect.

Photograph by Betsy Swanson

FIGURE 36   Academy of the Sacred Heart, 4521 St. Charles Avenue, New Orleans, 1900, Allison Owen and Collins C. Diboll architects

Photograph by Betsy Swanson

of emphasis. That was the kind of refinement Owen may have learned during his two years of architectural studies at the Massachusetts Institute of Technology, which offered the best professional design training available to his generation. The academy's mottled beige brick walls contrast softly with the sandstone-colored plastered quoins and hood molds, increasing the illusion of age. In 1906, the architects extended the building toward St. Charles Avenue with two new wings, deepening the sense of embrasure and in another gentle historicism alluding to a long French tradition of courtyard entries for large structures. Ten years later, the same architects added a third story to the original block, increasing its volume and its presence on the avenue. In 1908, shortly after the academy's wings were built, a visitor from the North wrote a sharp criticism of some of the city's new buildings for *Architectural Art and Its Allies,* the city's new design magazine. In his view, the pretentious houses on St. Charles Avenue and the city's big new hotels seemed too much like New York and Chicago and were unresponsive to New Orleans' climate and to its French and Spanish cultural heritage. He did not discuss the Academy of the Sacred Heart. He must have passed it as he rode up the avenue, so perhaps he did not realize it was new and thought that it had always been there. That is how much it seems of its place.[16]

PROFESSIONALISM AND DISCIPLINED
ACADEMIC VOCABULARIES

The design vocabulary and grammar of the handsome masonry buildings Louisiana towns and cities were acquiring by the early years of the twentieth century had been invented in Renaissance Italy of the fifteenth and sixteenth centuries as a revival of ancient Rome. The Renaissance vocabulary consisted, in part, of the ancient Roman orders—Doric, Ionic, Corinthian, Composite, and Tuscan—for columns and entablatures, each order with its own proportions and definitions of parts. Ideas about the appropriate way to combine the orders with masonry wall construction changed during the four centuries after the Italian Renaissance, and the new possibilities were taught at the best school of architecture of the nineteenth century, the Ecole des Beaux Arts, in Paris, where many American designers studied. Louisiana-born Henry Hobson Richardson was the second American to go there, entering in 1859. After the Civil War and during the following decades Americans founded their own schools of architecture on the model partially of the Ecole des Beaux Arts. Tulane University started one in 1894, pioneering architectural education in the Deep South.

The new academic or Beaux Arts architectural language quickly became a trademark of the professionalization of design. In 1911, the year architec-

16. Dorothy G. Schlesinger, Robert J. Cangelosi, Jr., and Sally Kittredge Reeves, eds., *New Orleans Architecture: Jefferson City* (Gretna, La., 1989), 163; H. Hanley Parker, "New Orleans Architecture As Others See It," *Architectural Art and Its Allies,* III (January, 1908), 1–3.

tural licensing was introduced in Louisiana, established New Orleans architects organized a club with classes for young draftsmen who were learning architecture by the traditional apprentice system. They too needed history lectures, discussions of theoretical treatises, and the Beaux Arts design exercises
that would allow them to enter national competitions. Important institutional buildings were no longer to be designed by a carpenter-builder with
access to a pattern book and eyes to take a hard look at a nearby structure.
Academic architecture was to address a higher artistic purpose than the
building craftsman set himself. Beaux Arts design also provided principles
for organizing large, complex institutional interiors, which were to be symmetrical in plan, with rooms disposed according to a comprehensible system,
on axes, so that the users knew how to enter and where they were all the time
they were inside. The plans of buildings were to make plain the hierarchy of
importance of the activities they housed; they were to lay out meaning as
well as convenience, and the hierarchy had to be clear from the exterior too,
through the signals of massing and of aspects such as window size and decoration. It was possible to marshal not only the Doric, Ionic, Corinthian,
Composite, and Tuscan orders in this but also panels, pediments, cartouches, quoins, arches, piers, and moldings. Just the right play of shadows
could define the building's character. Designers needed to know architectural history so that they would have a wide repertory of Classical forms to
invoke when arriving at the best solution for complex design problems. Professional architects also needed to study music, literature, and all the visual
arts to become sensitive to the subtle adjustments that could make a building compelling. The more beautiful the design, the more ennobling it would
be for those who saw or used it. Architecture had become an art and a profession, and it bore the burden of doing justice to America's success. At least
that was the point of view of believers in the American Renaissance among
the country's governing elite, who by the 1890s were maintaining that the
United States was a great civilization, perhaps the finest since Rome, perhaps
the culmination of the entire Western tradition, rather than just an embar-
rassingly provincial extension of Europe. It was felt that the times demanded
the expression of this unifying and at times imperial grandeur, elevating the
population by the highest artistic means, and academic architecture accord-
ingly sought to embody the finest ideals and the loftiest visions of a heroic
civilization.

Today, Americans are likely to see not only the glorious ambitions
reflected in these often wonderful buildings but also the ironies and ambi-
guities of the actual historical situation. The great fortunes behind the supposed American Renaissance were built on the chilling poverty of the workers at the bottom. The era was one of new repressions for many minorities,
especially African Americans. The ideals of civic responsibility, good government, and a rationally organized society were at times mouthed by corrupt

politicians for whom the construction of expensive Beaux Arts buildings was an occasion for graft and pork-barrel politics. The present can do no better than to treasure these well-crafted buildings for themselves, as souvenirs of the era's aspirations, if not its realities, and to remind itself that human justice can always elude an unsteady grasp.

Louisiana has many fine examples of academic architecture. One of the earliest is the United States Post Office built in Baton Rouge in 1895 (Figure 37). With its sharp definition of basic building mass, its Roman Doric portico, its decorative frieze at attic level, and its open balustrade above the cornice, this building exhibits the best in advanced practice of the period. The federal government, which designed and built the nation's post offices, was allied with the American Institute of Architects, a national professional association, in placing a priority on the transmittal of an edifying Beaux Arts culture to small cities and towns. In Monroe, fluted Corinthian columns on pedestals, with a modillion cornice above and acroteria on the pediment, give the Ouachita National Bank building, of 1906, a scaled-down Roman grandeur (Figure 38). The Isaac Delgado Museum of Art, built in 1912 to designs of the Chicago architect Samuel A. Marx and now the central building of the New Orleans Museum of Art, has an Ionic portico and sculptural panels embedded in the walls (Figure 39). The interior, with a skylit atrium, a

FIGURE 37 United States Post Office (now City Club), Baton Rouge, *ca.* 1910. *LSU Libraries. Photograph by A. D. Lytle.*

FIGURE 38 Ouachita National Bank Building, Monroe, 1906.
Photograph by Jim Zietz

FIGURE 39 Isaac Delgado Museum of Art (now part of New Orleans Museum of Art), City Park, New Orleans, 1912, Samuel A. Marx architect.
Courtesy of New Orleans Museum of Art

FIGURE 40   Tensas Parish Courthouse, St. Joseph, 1906.

Photograph by Jim Zietz

grand stairway, and a border of galleries, was the right setting for citizens to meet the great art of earlier civilizations. In 1911, the *Architectural Record,* the leading national professional journal in the field, sent a correspondent through the South to report on the state of practice there. He admired, and presented photographs of, three New Orleans buildings that in his judgment were designed to the best Classical standards: the fifteen-story Whitney National Bank Building, by the New York firm of Clinton and Russell in association with the New Orleans architect Emile Weil; the smaller City Bank and Trust Company Building, by De Buys, Churchill, and Labouisse; and the city's main post office and courthouse, by the northern firm of Hale and Rogers.[17]

Parish courthouses were especially apt receptacles of the Beaux Arts impulse to give expression to a beneficent civic realm. The Tensas Parish Courthouse, built in 1906 at St. Joseph, has a becoming arrangement of wings projecting at angles to frame Corinthian porticoes (Figure 40). (Porticoes are the faces, so to speak, of ancient Greek and Roman temples.) The cupola on top has an English tone without being a slavish imitation. In Oberlin, the Allen Parish Courthouse, of 1914, was designed by Favrot and Livaudais, of New Orleans, with a definite French flavor. A comparison of the courthouses in

17. United States Post Office (Baton Rouge, East Baton Rouge Parish) National Register File, Downtown Monroe Historic District (Ouachita Parish) National Register File, both at Louisiana Division of Historic Preservation; Henry Hansen, ed., *Louisiana: A Guide to the State* (New York, 1971), 331; Russell F. Whitehead, "The Old and the New South," *Architectural Record,* XXX (1911), 1–56. The guidebook edited by Hansen was compiled by the Federal Writers Program, of the Work Projects Administration, in Louisiana.

FIGURE 41   Calcasieu Parish Courthouse, Lake Charles, 1912, Favrot and Livaudais architects.

Photograph by Jim Zietz

FIGURE 42   Old Federal Building, Shreveport, 1910, James K. Taylor architect.

Photograph by Jim Zietz

St. Joseph and Oberlin illuminates the wide range in character and allusion possible with academic buildings. The Calcasieu Parish Courthouse, built in 1912 at Lake Charles, also to the designs of Favrot and Livaudais, is an especially impressive demonstration of how academic imperatives can shape a large structure (Figure 41). Built of brick and terra-cotta on a cruciform plan, it has a Roman Doric portico entry and a low dome over the center crossing. The courtroom is under the dome and is lit by windows hidden from outside view. The building is on a podium, above the mundane aspects of daily life, but it also spreads horizontally, as if conforming to the landscape. It makes concrete the civic virtue it is its function to enforce.[18]

The paramount edifice of academic design in Shreveport is the Old Federal Building, once a post office and courthouse, now the city library (Figure 42). It is a single powerful block, given visual order and scale by treating the first floor as a single long arcade framed by pilasters and entablature. This story is rusticated, and the window frames, corner quoins, and cornice awakened memories of Italy in the many whom European travels were educating in architecture. But it is also a controlled, urbane design suited to bringing the grandeur of older countries to those who stay at home. James Knox Taylor, the supervising architect of the United States Treasury Department, was head of the large architectural team responsible for this structure and for other post offices and courthouses across the state and nation.[19]

18.   Carl A. Brasseaux, Glenn R. Conrad, and R. Warren Robison, *The Courthouses of Louisiana* (Lafayette, La., 1977), 32–33, 50–51, 162–63.

19.   Old Federal Building (Shreveport, Caddo Parish) National Register File, Louisiana Division of Historic Preservation.

FIGURE 43   Bentley Hotel, Alexandria, 1907–1908, George R. Mann architect.

Photograph by Jim Zietz

FIGURE 44   Bentley Hotel lobby

Photograph by Jim Zietz

In Alexandria, the Bentley Hotel, built by a Louisiana lumberman in 1907 and 1908 to designs by George R. Mann, is another instance of restrained academic taste in control of a large building mass (Figure 43). The Ionic columns at the entry give little hint of the dramatic surprise within: a long, two-story lobby (Figure 44). The Bentley Hotel has recently been restored, confirming the long life possible for good buildings when they are properly maintained. Small civic buildings too can show the elegance and dignity of Beaux Arts symmetry and the classical orders. The Bogalusa City Hall, of 1917, was built not of masonry but of wood, appropriately for the city the Great Southern Lumber Company contrived. The old B'nai Zion Temple, in Shreveport, built in 1915, deployed academic precepts to religious ends (Figure 45). Modeled on French houses from the eighteenth century, the temple is a particularly assertive design by the Shreveport architects Edward F. Neild and Clarence Olschner. Even traditional commercial blocks,

FIGURE 45   B'nai Zion Temple,
Shreveport, 1915, Edward F. Neild and
Clarence Olschner architects.

Photograph by Jim Zietz

FIGURE 46   Schepis Building,
Columbia, *ca.* 1916.

Photograph by Sharon Jones

FIGURE 47   Statuary of Columbus and
Washington crowning the Schepis
Building.

Photograph by Sharon Jones

FIGURE 48   Winnfield Hotel, Winnfield, 1908, John A. Colvin architect.

National Register File, Louisiana Division of Historic Preservation.

FIGURE 49   Entrance to Winnfield Hotel with Lykes glass transom and sidelights.

Collection of the Louisiana State Museum. Photograph by Wallace Voltz.

the kind that line the main streets of all Louisiana towns and cities, were wont to borrow the tenets of the Ecole des Beaux Arts, if only as a means to get noticed. The Schepis Building, in Columbia (Figures 46, 47), reverberates with traces of the subtle facade of Leon Battista Alberti's fifteenth-century Rucellai Palace, in Florence. It succeeds in connecting a small Louisiana city to a remote architectural past, but it also pleases the eye of those who do not recognize the reference. The Winnfield Hotel, built in 1908 by John A. Colvin, follows the formula for a Renaissance palace, something like Louis XIV's Versailles (Figures 48, 49). The rusticated base separates the lower story from those above, which are bound together by Ionic pilasters. An entablature and cornice top the building, giving it shape and dimension. The proportions of cornice to pilasters to rusticated base are carefully calculated to be memorable and convincing.[20]

RICHARDSON AND THE ROMANESQUE REVIVAL:
A LOCAL SON CREATES A NATIONAL STYLE

Henry Hobson Richardson, after training at the Ecole des Beaux Arts, worked out of New York and Boston from the middle 1870s to the middle 1880s. Richardson devised a way to combine early-medieval features—French and Spanish Romanesque and Syrian Early Christian—with the clearly articulated plan and massing that were at the heart of the Beaux Arts aesthetic. His style seemed unambiguously American to the many all over the country and even in parts of Europe who admired and emulated it. James

20.   Bentley Hotel (Alexandria, Rapides Parish) National Register File, Bogalusa City Hall (Washington Parish) National Register File, Old B'Nai Zion Temple (Shreveport, Caddo Parish) National Register File, Schepis Building (Columbia, Caldwell Parish) National Register File, Winnfield Hotel (Winn Parish) National Register File, all at Louisiana Division of Historic Preservation.

FIGURE 50 Howard Library, Lee Circle, New Orleans, 1886, Shepley, Rutan and Coolidge architects, from a design by Henry Hobson Richardson.

Photograph by Jim Zietz

F. O'Gorman has suggested, however, that he may have picked up one part of his powerful idiom as a boy in Louisiana. Richardson, whose childhood home was in New Orleans, spent his summers at Priestly plantation, next to Oak Alley, in St. James Parish. Something of Richardson's breadth of form, of the way he gathers his architectural elements under a simple spreading hip roof, may be due to his admiration of the handsome plantation house next door.[21]

Richardson died before reaching age forty-eight, in 1886, the year plans were under way for a library at Lee Circle, in New Orleans, a gift of Charles Turner Howard, the cofounder of the Louisiana Lottery Company. It may be that Richardson's sister in New Orleans persuaded Howard's heirs to hire Shepley, Rutan and Coolidge, the successor firm to Richardson's. As John Ferguson has shown, the firm's plans enlarged an unbuilt competition entry by Richardson for a library in Michigan (Figure 50).[22] The builders inscribed Richardson's monogram on the entry in honor of a famous Louisianian.

21.   James F. O'Gorman, *H. H. Richardson: Architectural Forms for an American Society* (Chicago, 1987), 5.
22.   John Ferguson, "The Howard Memorial Library: Renaissance of a Masterpiece," *Preservation in Print,* October, 1989, pp. 15–16.

FIGURE 51 *Ignorance Chained,* detail of the entrance arch of the Howard Library.

Photograph by Jim Zietz

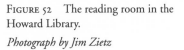

FIGURE 52 The reading room in the Howard Library.

Photograph by Jim Zietz

Richardson's posthumous building remains a masterpiece, though it has suffered on the interior. Rough-cut sandstone walls wrap smoothly around a powerful building mass in which secondary features, such as the dormer windows, the cross-gable sheltering the entrance and the stair tower, and the little turrets at the south end, are contained within the quieting whole of a simple silhouette. From the deep, darkened entrance arch, with its intricately carved detailing (Figure 51), to the band of high windows, each separated by clusters of medieval colonnettes, the whole strip riding over narrow, fortress-like slits, this is a building that gathers and protects. Some critics believe that Richardson wanted to console a society stressed beyond endurance by the Civil War and the anxieties of a devouringly competitive age, that he wanted to give succor. The Howard Library does just that. This comes across particularly forcibly in the recently restored reading room, a round space anchored by a massive stone fireplace and oak paneling which reaches up beyond the high hammer-beam rafters to an umbrella-like conical roof (Figure 52). Here is a room in which to find shelter and peace.

FIGURE 53   Tilton Memorial Hall,
Tulane University, New Orleans, 1901,
1907, Andry and Bendernagel architects.

Photograph by Jim Zietz

Louisiana built fewer structures in the Richardsonian Romanesque style than did other parts of the country, perhaps because less stone was available. But today there remains an excellent arrangement of seven such Romanesque buildings on the Tulane University campus, in New Orleans. The five round-arched stone buildings, and the two orange-brick buildings behind them, were constructed from 1894 to 1923 to designs by several local firms (Figure 53). Distinguished colleges and universities all through the North upgraded themselves with handsome new Richardsonian Romanesque campuses at the end of the nineteenth century. But as Alan Gowans has observed, Tulane now has the best-preserved remnant of this powerfully rooted vision of medievalizing academic stability. Other schools, such as Oberlin College and Princeton University, tore down much of their Romanesque plant.[23] The campus-as-a-park is an ingrained American theme: knowledge and community have often seemed most capable of advancement when placed far from urban ills and embedded in leafy nature. Tulane's Richardsonian structures surround a pool of deep shade—live oak, ginkgo, magnolia, and cypress—to make a place of great calm suited to nurturing the life of the mind.

Richardson often worked with the landscape architect Frederick Law Olmsted, who designed estates and parks throughout the country. Olmsted's Boston-based firm, led by his heir John Charles Olmsted, designed Audubon Park, which faces Tulane across St. Charles Avenue. Begun in 1898 on the site of the World's Industrial and Cotton Centennial Exposition of 1884–1885,

23.   Tulane University (Orleans Parish) National Register File, Louisiana Division of Historic Preservation; Alan Gowans, *Styles and Types of North American Architecture* (New York, 1992), 184–85.

FIGURE 54   Gravier Building, New Orleans, 1888.

The Historic New Orleans Collection, 1979.325.514.

FIGURE 55   Hennen Building (now Maritime Building), 204 Carondolet Street, New Orleans, 1894–1895, Thomas Sully architect.

The Historic New Orleans Collection, 1979.325.597.

the park is laid out at its center like the Meadow in Olmsted's Central Park, in New York, but this section was also planned as the golf course it is today. A meandering, picturesque watercourse and carriage way border the open part. More formal design principles organize the land near St. Charles Avenue: a symmetrical terrace of gardens and a fountain tie the watercourse's naturalistic irregularity to the boulevard in front and the crescent of the Romanesque face of Tulane, directly opposite. The older parts of Audubon Zoo, at the other end of the park, near the river, laid out by John Charles Olmsted much later, complete an agreeable composition of interlocking architecture and landscape that interweaves the formal and the unaffected.[24]

TALL BUILDINGS: TECHNOLOGY AND INCREASING URBANIZATION

Although New Orleans was hardly a center for the development of tall commercial blocks—skyscrapers—it did not lag far behind in using the technologies pioneered in New York and Chicago. The eight-story Gravier Building, built in 1888, showed clearly and elegantly how the need for daylight, and thus glazing, could result in a modern-seeming skin, even though the building was of a structurally traditional cypress "mill construction," not iron- or steel-frame (Figure 54). Large double-hung windows cover most of the Gravier Building's surface, as the visible structure is reduced to brick piers and multitextured brick spandrels. The piers are ornamented with the geometrical patterns of the iron anchors used to tie the masonry to the timber frame. The lintels over the windows and the entry are metal I-beams, frankly exposed to view. Austere and sophisticated, the building makes a frank exposure of structure and material its primary ornament. The I. L. Lyons Company, a wholesale druggist with outlets throughout Central and South America, commissioned the building.[25]

By 1891, architects and engineers in Chicago had fully developed the framed skyscraper, designed for daylight, flexible interiors, and speedy construction, out of steel I-sections with tile cladding for fire protection. And by 1893 Sully had provided drawings for the eleven-story, steel-framed Hennen Building (now the Maritime Building), which was built in 1894 and 1895 and clad with brick and terra-cotta (Figure 55). The foundations for such a heavy load were a set of concrete and iron rafts that rested on spreading brick pyramids, which in turn stood on cypress pilings thrust deep into the city's marshy soil. Built as a speculative office building, the Hennen Building also had some civic overtones: visitors could ride to its rooftop observation deck to view the city around them. The first two floors and the interior were re-

24.   L. Ronald Forman and Joseph Logsden, *Audubon Park: An Urban Eden* (New Orleans, 1985), 110–21.

25.   Mary Louise Christovich *et al.*, eds., *New Orleans Architecture: The American Sector* (Gretna, La., 1972), 115.

FIGURE 56   Hutchinson Building,
Shreveport, 1910.

Photograph by Jim Zietz

modeled by Weil around 1920, but the rest of the exterior remains as Sully designed it. It is a forceful block with three horizontal divisions—the base, the middle, and the top with a projecting cornice—and bands of vertically stacked bay windows (a Chicago motif) enlivening the surface and providing light and space for the offices within.[26]

The full story of Louisiana's tall business buildings of the early twentieth century must await the research this subject deserves. In New Orleans, the Norman Mayer Memorial Building, designed by the New Orleans firm of Andry and Bendernagel and erected in 1900, would surely figure in the story, as would the nine-story Denechaud Hotel (now Le Pavilion), which was built in 1906 to designs of Toledano and Wogan, with assistance from De Buys. Buildings elsewhere in the state, such as the particularly handsome Commercial Bank and Trust Company Building, in Alexandria, designed by W. L. Stevens, of New Orleans, and built between 1915 and 1916 (Chapter 8, Figure 1), the United Mercantile Bank Building, in Shreveport, designed by Mann and Stern, of Little Rock, and erected in 1910, and the Hutchinson Building, also built in Shreveport in 1910, and with a dramatic facade of terra-cotta and glass (Figure 56), would also enter the account.[27]

THE PRAIRIE STYLE AND OTHER INDIVIDUALISMS

Two railroad stations in New Orleans, both destroyed, were designed by well-known architects from Chicago, one by Daniel Hudson Burnham and the other by Louis Sullivan. Burnham's Beaux Arts Southern Pacific station, of 1908, was in many ways a small version of his Union Station, which is now the pride of Washington, D.C. Sullivan and his partner Dankmar Adler's Illinois Central station, of 1891–1892, was a low, hip-roof building with a garden in front and a belvedere on top to vent the railroad company's offices on the second floor (Figures 57, 58). The building of pressed and glazed brick and pine had the low arches that are one of Sullivan's trademarks both at the entry and in the belvedere. Its profile was similar to the later Prairie School houses around Chicago, which may not be coincidental, for Frank Lloyd Wright, the great Prairie School architect, worked on the design for the New Orleans building while he was an assistant to Sullivan.[28]

An important Prairie School house in Monroe, designed for Gilbert B. Cooley in 1908 by Walter Burley Griffin, a gifted young associate of Wright's,

26. *Ibid.,* 148. See also Maritime Building (Orleans Parish) National Register File, Louisiana Division of Historic Preservation; William R. Cullison III, *Architecture in Louisiana: A Documentary History* (New Orleans, 1983), 23; James S. Zacharie, *New Orleans Guide* (New Orleans, 1902), 195.

27. Christovich *et al.,* eds., *New Orleans Architecture: The American Sector,* 11, 13, 76, 109; Commercial Bank and Trust Company Building (Alexandria, Rapides Parish) National Register File, United Mercantile Bank Building (Shreveport, Caddo Parish) National Register File, Hutchinson Building (Shreveport, Caddo Parish) National Register File, all at Lousiana Division of Historic Preservation.

28. Mary Cable, *Lost New Orleans* (Boston, 1980), 30–31.

FIGURE 57   Illinois Central station, New
Orleans, 1891–1892 (now demolished),
Adler and Sullivan architects.
*The Historic New Orleans Collection,
1979.325.6091.*

FIGURE 58   Platform at Illinois Central
station.
*The Historic New Orleans Collection,
1979.325.6096.*

survives (Figures 59, 60). Nobody can be sure why Cooley chose a little-
known architect from a suburb of Chicago. Cooley's business was a laundry,
but his avocation was his steam yacht, and perhaps the steamship qualities of
Wright's houses—which he may have seen in architectural journals, with
their horizontal lines and forward-thrusting gables pointing like prows into
the prairie-sea—were suggestive to the river yachtsman. Cooley's retention of
his architect required perseverance that was equally out of the ordinary, for it
took almost twenty years for him to save enough money to build the house
and by then his architect had moved to Australia. In 1912, Griffin, with the
assistance of his wife, Marion Mahony, a graduate of Massachusetts Institute
of Technology and a longtime assistant to Wright, won an international
competition to design a capital city for Australia, Canberra. Before leaving
for the antipodes, he stopped by Monroe to see to the design of the Monroe
Country Club, of which Cooley was a director. The club was razed about

FIGURE 59   Cooley House, Monroe, 1926 (designed 1908), Walter Burley Griffin architect.

Photograph by Donna Fricker

1930 for a levee, but drawings show a fine Prairie School building, cruciform in plan, with window-filled projecting gables and a horizontal board-and-batten ground story. The Monroe Country Club had an eloquence, a freshness, and a sprightliness that are the best qualities of this inventive midwestern architecture. When, in 1926, Cooley finally purchased his lot on South Grand Street facing the river, Griffin had to send the working drawings, along with an Australian assistant to supervise construction. The Cooley House is now a nationally recognized Prairie School monument and an illustration of Griffin's late, highly original design manner as well. The faceted fireplace surround inside reflects Griffin's Australian work of the 1920s (Figure 61). The rest of the house—the plan, the banks of casement windows carefully placed for cross-ventilation, and the double-height balcony that encircles the living room—was all in Mahony's early renderings.[29]

There are modest strains of the Prairie School in many houses in New Orleans, but one house there synthesizes the Prairie School and the aspirations of the American Renaissance in a thoroughly original way. The Biaggio

29.   Cooley House (Monroe, Ouachita Parish) National Register File, Louisiana Division of Historic Preservation; Paul Kruty, "The Gilbert Cooley House—A Prairie Style Masterpiece in Monroe," *Preservation in Print,* June 5, 1994, pp. 10–12.

FIGURE 60   Sketch and plans for Cooley House by Walter Burley Griffin, drawn by Marion Mahony around 1910.

Mary and Leigh Block Gallery, Northwestern University.

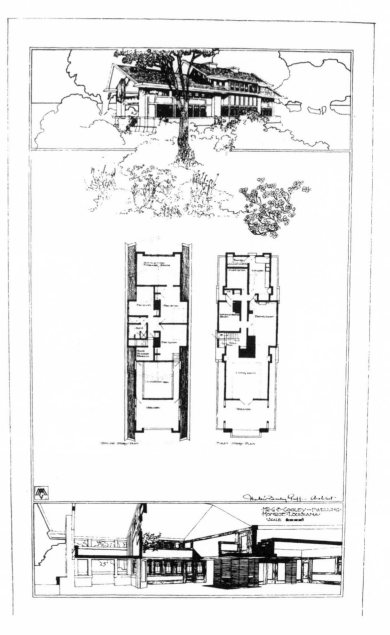

FIGURE 61   Living room of Cooley House, 1926.

Photograph by Donna Fricker

D'Antoni House, at 7929 Freret Street, designed around 1918 by Edward Sporl, of New Orleans, is a palatial bungalow the thin buff-colored Roman-like bricks and flat-edged cornices of which corroborate the lessons learned from McKim, Mead and White, until 1910 the largest architectural firm in the world (Figure 62). But Sporl combines the house's formal elegance with decorative motifs favored by Sullivan and a pronounced horizontality. Broad urns flank the entrance, alluding to Wright. The dwelling must have pleased its owners, for a family member ordered a similar house for 6 Newcomb Place.[30]

30.   D'Antoni House Nomination Form, Historic District Landmarks Commission, New Orleans.

FIGURE 62   Biaggio D'Antoni House,
7929 Freret Street, New Orleans, *ca.* 1918,
Edward Sporl architect.

Photograph by Jim Zietz

FIGURE 63   Doullut House, Egania and
Douglas Streets, New Orleans, 1905.

Photograph by Jim Zietz

Not every house of this period to gain national attention was planned by a professional architect. The two Doullut Houses, built in 1905 and 1913 in the Holy Cross District of New Orleans, were apparently designed by the occupant of the first, Milton Doullut, a Mississippi riverboat captain and shipbuilder, who built the second for his son, Paul (Figure 63). With the principal living level raised a full story above ground and encircled by deep, wall-shading galleries, the Doullut houses look as if they started as raised Creole cottages but turned into the owner's riverboats themselves as they acquired belvederes, or observation cupolas, that for all the world look like pilothouses with a Japanese accent. Both the main roofs and the roofs of the pilothouses have inward-curving slopes ending in pressed tin crestings, an orientalism possibly witnessed at the St. Louis Exposition of 1904. Doullut capped the lilting, celebratory mood of his creation with graduated cypress balls strung from post to post along the principal story, like a double strand of pearls on an exotic Mardi Gras queen. Pressed tin in a variety of patterns covered both the ceilings and the walls of the main rooms. Doullut was a folk artist with the talent to pull different ideas together into a witty and coherent whole. He was a poet of available materials, of the bits and pieces anyone could purchase in building-supply yards but only a rare imagination could use with such verve.[31]

31.   John Ferguson, "Captain Milton Doullut and His Fantastic House: 400 Egania Street," *Preservation in Print,* September, 1990, p. 20.

8

THE MODERN ERA, 1915–1940

Karen Kingsley

TWO SETS OF CIRCUMSTANCES WERE CRUCIAL FOR THE TRANSFORMATION that Louisiana underwent between 1915 and 1940. One was the discovery of oil in 1901 near Jennings and the development of the oil and gas industries that followed, and the other was the election as governor of Huey P. Long, Jr., in 1928, and the enactment of the populist programs he promoted. Both of these chains of events affected the state economically, politically, socially, and culturally. Louisiana experienced an unprecedented era of industrial and economic growth at the same time that Long's Share the Wealth programs spread the benefits broadly. During the period, some of the most radical changes in the history of American architecture occurred, and Louisiana played a significant role in producing new forms that expressed the modern age.

Most obviously, the skylines of the state's principal cities were changing. In the downtown commercial districts, tall buildings of steel and concrete replaced the older two- and three-story brick structures. In Alexandria, the seven-story Commercial Bank and Trust Company Building, designed in 1915–1916 by W. L. Stevens, of New Orleans, recapitulates the skyscraper form developed in Chicago in the 1880s in which the structural steel frame is clearly expressed by the exterior of the building and the interior is well lit by virtue of the large areas of glass (Figure 1). The repeating geometric brick and cast-concrete detailing on the ground-level piers and entrance portal of this structure is reminiscent of the work of Louis Sullivan.

By the 1920s, structural and functional candor in design had been firmly rejected in favor of historicized camouflage. In 1921, when the new building for the Cotton Exchange, in New Orleans, was constructed, the architects, Favrot and Livaudais, selected a classicizing style for it (Figure 2). They covered the eight-story steel-frame building with granite and emphasized its im-

FIGURE 1 Commercial Bank and Trust
Company Building, Alexandria,
1915–1916, W. L. Stevens architect.

Photograph by Jim Zietz

portance for the city's economy by siting it to command two major center-
city streets. They ennobled the corner entrance further through a consciously
nonstructural attachment of classical details, like the columns and pilasters
and the decorative pediment. During the 1920s, neither the public nor the
architects saw a problem about appropriating history: the past struck them
as a treasure of riches from which to select freely. Architects believed they
were creating something new from the old, and they regarded their tradi-
tionalism as different from revivalism, which they associated with nineteenth-century architects and with copying the past, not reinventing it.

While the Cotton Exchange was under construction, another classically
influenced building designed by the same pair of architects was going up
across the street. The twenty-three story Hibernia National Bank Building,
completed in 1921, was enriched at both its base and its top by giant
Corinthian pilasters and capped with a jaunty white lantern in the shape of

FIGURE 2   Cotton Exchange, Gravier and Carondelet Streets, New Orleans, 1921, Favrot and Livaudais architects.

The Historic New Orleans Collection, 1979.325.603.

FIGURE 3   Hibernia National Bank Building, 313 Carondelet Street, New Orleans, 1921, Favrot and Livaudais architects.

The Historic New Orleans Collection, 1979.325.312.

a circular temple (Figure 3). Besides enhancing the city's skyline with a lively silhouette, this lantern tower had the very practical purpose of housing a navigation beacon for ships on the Mississippi.

In the north of the state, the growth of Shreveport was dramatic. Oil was struck north of the city in 1903, and by 1910 it was being pumped in great quantities. The boom in the oil and gas industries attracted many people to the area, and by the early 1920s much of Shreveport reflected newfound prosperity. In addition to its new commercial buildings, the city expanded into exclusive new residential sections with palatial mansions, and subdivisions for the prosperous middle class. During this time the number of building permits multiplied so rapidly that the Shreveport *Times* heralded them on the front page in a regular feature entitled "Shreveport: See It Grow Day by Day."

Shreveport's seventeen-story reinforced-concrete-frame skyscraper, the

FIGURE 4   Slattery Building, Shreveport, 1924, Mann and Stern architects.

Photograph by Jim Zietz

Slattery Building, named after its owner, John Bernard Slattery, a businessman, was completed in 1924 (Figures 4, 5). The building, designed by the firm of Mann and Stern, from Little Rock, is in the Gothic style, allowing the emphasis of tall piers. The building followed a contemporary prototype in high-rise design, the celebrated Gothic-inspired Chicago Tribune Building, which was then under construction. Unlike the structure in Chicago, however, the Slattery building had Gothic elements applied to its facade rather than integrated into the expression of its structure. Still, the height of the Slattery and its careful detailing testified to Shreveport's vibrant economy and its desire to reflect fashionable tastes.

Nostalgic historicism is particularly apparent in the new residential areas that grew in step with the commercial downtowns. Most of the houses in Fairfield, a district of Shreveport where the oil community was settling, are of two stories with hip roofs, wood siding, and a porch running along the front, and all are set in well-planted lots and are spaciously laid out. Al-

FIGURE 5 Parapet detail of Slattery Building

Photograph by Jim Zietz

FIGURE 6 A house on Fairfield Avenue, in Shreveport, 1920s.

Photograph by Jim Zietz

though much simpler in configuration than the houses of the late nineteenth century in the Queen Anne style, the dwellings here display a rich and varied exterior treatment. The more palatial, on Fairfield Avenue itself, invariably assumed some revival style or other. There was a great eclectic freedom of selection, from among neoclassical, Colonial, Mediterranean, Italian Renaissance, French Renaissance, Tudor, and Gothic precedents (Figure 6). The owners spared no expense, for the intention was to demonstrate a wealth of pocket as well as of culture. Many of the houses were designed by architects.

Despite the self-conscious individuality of each house, the district as a whole possesses the quality of coherence. Even today it maintains an ambience of the 1920s, having changed little from the tree-lined suburb it was when it was built. The neighborhood's zeal for history is arresting in view of the part the residents were playing in an industry that was to reshape twentieth-century behavior.

The new residential districts in other Louisiana cities and towns were on a more modest scale than Fairfield, although they similarly followed the pattern of garden suburbs. For example, Roseland Terrace, in Baton Rouge, one mile east of the old center, was built to provide working people with a more bucolic domestic life. Developed between 1911 and 1930, the district consists mostly of bungalows, all similar in plan—two rooms wide and three rooms deep—but distinctive in their use of porches, dormers, gables, and exterior color (Figure 7). Roseland projects comfort and charm, and its lawns and tree-lined streets conjure a feeling of openness. The popularity bungalows

FIGURE 7   A bungalow on Park Boulevard, Roseland Terrace, in Baton Rouge, 1911–1930.

Photograph by Donna Fricker

FIGURE 8   A double shotgun cottage with bungalow features at 627–629 Barracks Street, in New Orleans, *ca.* 1925.

Photograph by Betsy Swanson

were winning in the state at this time was assured by their aptness for Louisiana's climate: the wide, spreading roof and capacious, shady porch protected the house from both heat and heavy rains. But a local variant emerged: bungalow features were grafted onto the traditional shotgun cottage (Figure 8). Both bungalows and houses of more traditional types for the state went up during this period in the suburban residential developments of South Highlands and Broadmoor, in Shreveport; Gentilly, in New Orleans; and Old Metairie.

The postwar spirit of progress and the state's new wealth fostered the formation of new cultural and educational institutions and enabled existing institutions to improve their physical accommodations. Schools, from elementary to high schools, were constructed throughout the state in styles that left no doubt about the architectural pluralism of the age. The city architect of New Orleans, E. A. Christy, designed schools ranging from Gothic to Renaissance and, by the 1930s, to the modern, like Art Deco, as at the Eleanor McMain School, in 1932, and the L. E. Rabouin School, in 1937.[1] Christy borrowed from the past and from current trends to give each school an identifiable style and character.

The architecture of colleges and universities, however, frequently had to satisfy more than a preference for variety. Another need was to provide specifically for groups that had held a marginal position in society and in the past had had few and inferior educational facilities. The educational opportunities for African Americans expanded in the 1920s, although always under conditions of segregation. Similarly, women's access to higher education increased, especially with the enlargement of the state university system and, in the private sphere, of H. Sophie Newcomb Memorial College for Women, in New Orleans.

James Gamble Rogers in 1911 designed a new campus for Newcomb College, although construction took place only after World War I, in 1918 (Figure 9). By then, Rogers' New Orleans Post Office Building was completed, after construction that lasted from 1909 to 1915, and his Harkness Tower and Memorial Quadrangle, at Yale University, for which the cornerstone was laid in 1917, had burnished his reputation. Newcomb College, founded in 1886 under a bequest by Josephine Louise Newcomb in memory of her daughter, had proved so appealing to young women that it had outgrown its space in a former mansion. The new college buildings were to stand on a tract of land adjacent to Tulane University, a men's institution. The trustees of the college wanted a design "fitting for a college for women in the south at a minimum of expense" that would have a "unity and harmony of the whole."[2] In striking contrast to the rugged Richardsonian Romanesque and heavy masonry of Tulane's buildings, the campus Rogers designed is in a more residential red brick inset with delicate patterns and enlivened with white trim. The combination of materials and the detailing on a domestic scale contributed to an appropriately gendered imagery and attained the required economy and southernness. Rogers produced a group of buildings that would reassure parents of the respectability of education for their daughters and render the new concept less alien.

1. John Ferguson, "The Architecture of Education: The Public School Buildings of New Orleans," in *Crescent City Schools: The History of Public Education in New Orleans, 1841–1991*, ed. Donald DeVore (Lafayette, La., 1991), 308–49.

2. Karen Kingsley, "Designing for Women: The Architecture of Newcomb College," *Louisiana History*, XXXV (1994), 183–200.

FIGURE 9   H. Sophie Newcomb Memorial College for Women, New Orleans, 1918 (designed 1911), James Gamble Rogers architect.

University Archives, Howard-Tilton Memorial Library, Tulane University.

The design of educational facilities for African Americans in the 1920s introduced different challenges for architects. Xavier University of Louisiana, founded in 1915 by Mother Katherine Drexel, moved into its new Gothic Revival buildings in New Orleans in 1935. The architects followed the precedent of earlier Xavier colleges, which had adopted Gothic as appropriate to their Catholic affiliation. More interesting is the design for Dillard University, in the neighborhood of Gentilly, a residential area that developed in the 1920s as New Orleans grew. Dillard resulted in 1930 from the merger of two black schools, Straight University and New Orleans University, and it buttressed its new identity by moving to a new campus that Moise Goldstein, of New Orleans, designed in 1935 (Figure 10). The master scheme, similar to that of Newcomb College, consisted of an elongated court, open at one end and terminated at the other by a porticoed structure. The pattern is reminiscent of Thomas Jefferson's design for the University of Virginia, which was influential in early-twentieth-century campus planning. The central building at Dillard, however, was not domed. Still, classical allusions

FIGURE 10   Dillard University, New Orleans, 1935, Moise Goldstein architect.

American Missionary Association Archives, Amistad Research Center, Tulane University.

abound in the symmetrical Beaux Arts–inspired planning, the templelike form of the buildings, the columned porticoes, and the uniform white of the color. Goldstein had presented three options regarding style to Dillard's board of trustees—Gothic Revival, Modern, and Classical—and the board selected the last of these. The avenue of trees leading to the columned central building is very much in the southern tradition, but the severe classical lines—a consequence, in part, of a limited budget—lack any trace of the residential, in direct contrast with Newcomb.

Louisiana State University held its first classes on its new campus south of Baton Rouge in the fall of 1925; its quarters in the Pentagon Barracks (Chapter 5, Figure 33) had long been inadequate for the number of students. Designed in 1922 by Theodore C. Link, of St. Louis, the new campus had its focus in a Latin-cross-shaped open quadrangle bordered by academic buildings in a Northern Italian style (Figure 11). A 175-foot bell tower of sixteenth-century Venetian inspiration anchored the shorter east-to-west axis of the cruciform quad at its eastern end (Figure 12). Link, who designed thirteen of the sixteen original buildings, gave them a unity through round-arch arcades along the quad and a repetition of pediments, Tuscan columns, red tile roofs, and an exterior surface of a honey-colored stucco over an aggregate of tiny pebbles. The textural quality of these walls, their soft color, and the harmony of the simple architectural features make the quad one of the most attractive university spaces anywhere, though the placement of a library at the center of its crossing in 1958 destroyed its spatial qualities and blocked what had been handsome vistas.

FIGURE 11 Louisiana State University, Baton Rouge, 1922, Theodore C. Link architect.

Photograph by Donna Fricker

FIGURE 12 Memorial Tower at Louisiana State University, 1922, Theodore C. Link architect.

Photograph by Jim Zietz

FIGURE 13   Madonna Manor and Hope Haven homes for dependent children, Marrero, Jefferson Parish, 1925–1941.

Photograph by Jim Zietz

FIGURE 14   Madonna Manor Chapel, 1925–1941.

Photograph by Jim Zietz

In striking and exuberant contrast to these universities is another institutional group of buildings, Madonna Manor and Hope Haven homes for dependent children, built between 1925 and 1941 in Marrero, across the river from New Orleans (Figure 13, 14). They form a unique ensemble in the Spanish Mission and Spanish Colonial Revival styles, which were very much in vogue in the 1920s, particularly in the southwestern United States. The main building of Hope Haven, the first one constructed and the least ornamented, is comparable to structures in the sparsely decorated Mission Revival style that emerged in California in the late nineteenth century. The more decorated Spanish Colonial Revival style of the majority of buildings in the complex was modeled on the ornamental architecture referred to as Churrigueresque, with which America at large made its acquaintance in the Spanish-inspired buildings of the Panama-California Exposition in San Diego in 1915. The Marrero buildings are of masonry over which there is cream-colored stucco. Arched arcades, curvilinear parapets, red tile roofs, and twisted columns are among the adornments. Each new building was more elaborate in appearance than its predecessors, and the chapel was the culmination, with an asymmetrically placed tower, contrasting ornamentation in slate-colored stone, engaged columns, niches with saints, and other curvilinear and floral decorative elements. The embellishments, concentrated most densely at the center of the facade, embroider a frame around the entrance portal, and the play of light and shade on the superimposed details is an essential ingredient of their drama. In this group of buildings the picturesque Spanish Colonial Revival style cheerfully negated the often drab ambience of institutional buildings for the needy.

FIGURE 15   Kansas City Southern depot, De Quincy, 1923.

National Register File, Louisiana Division of Historic Preservation.

FIGURE 16   Barksdale Air Force Base, Bossier City, 1931–1935.

Photograph by Donna Fricker

In Louisiana, Spanish-inspired architectural styles are in the main found in the southern parishes. Reminders of the Spanish heritage of the state, they were chosen especially for residences, elementary schools, and churches. St. Joseph's Catholic Church, in Gretna, dating from 1926, has a splendid entry facade in a Spanish Baroque idiom. More restrained and establishing an appropriate link with the Southwest in their design are the Colorado Southern Railroad depot constructed at Crowley in 1907 and the Kansas City Southern depot constructed at De Quincy in 1923 (Figure 15).

The idea of fitting buildings' styles to their localities sometimes had strange results. When the Barksdale Air Force Base, in Bossier City, was constructed, military policies required that a base conform architecturally with the particularities of its region. Barksdale ended up with distinctly French traits, notwithstanding its location a few hundred miles from the state's areas of French settlement (Figure 16). Nevertheless, it is indisputably handsome, with a Beaux Arts axial scheme. Residential streets fan out from a tree-lined boulevard that leads from the principal entry to the administration building.

FIGURE 17 Wray-Dickinson Building, Shreveport, 1917.

Photograph by Jim Zietz

More than 250 buildings, including hangars, barracks, and residences, share a style. When Barksdale was completed, in 1935, it was the largest military airfield in the world.

The 1920s were also a decade of new pastimes and greater permissiveness, and Louisiana's prosperity gave its people abundant opportunity to enjoy themselves. The private automobile came into its own as a form of transport. Automobiles spawned a whole line of roadside businesses to serve traveling Americans, from filling stations to diners, motels, and commercial tourist attractions. It is surprising, however, to find that an invention as revolutionary as the automobile was purveyed in rather traditional-looking showrooms. The Packard showroom in New Orleans was in a Beaux Arts–inspired building, where a sculpted winged wheel over the entry symbolized the arrival of the new age. The Wray-Dickinson Building, built in 1917 in Shreveport, was faced in white glazed terra-cotta and also employed winged wheels over the central portal (Figure 17). A richly ornamented cornice, Corinthian columns, and a balustrade frame the display windows.

FIGURE 18   Strand Theater, Shreveport, 1923, Emile Weil architect.

Photograph by Jim Zietz

Going to the movies turned into an especially popular form of recreation in the early twentieth century, and Shreveport gave birth to one of the largest theater chains in the United States. In 1911, the brothers Julian Saenger and A. D. Saenger, seeing the potential for profit, formed the Saenger Amusement Company, which eventually operated 320 theaters in eleven southern states and the Caribbean. The Saengers wanted the Strand Theater, which they built in their hometown in 1923, to be the finest palace of entertainment in the South. Emile Weil, of New Orleans, whom they chose as architect, made the theater's exterior a flamboyant synthesis of architectural styles and motifs that transcends any specifics of time and place (Figure 18). A corner entrance, marked by an openwork cast concrete dome reminiscent of Joseph Olbrich's Secession Building, which was erected in Vienna in 1899, led to a circular lobby. The theater's auditorium was even more opulent, with an encrusted and gilded ceiling inspired by the ducal palace in Venice.

FIGURE 19 Saenger Theater auditorium,
1101–1109 Canal Street, New Orleans,
1926.

*National Register Files, Louisiana Division
of Historic Preservation.*

By the 1920s, theater design had achieved a dizzying glory, and Weil surpassed the Strand with his design for the Saengers' theater in New Orleans, which opened in 1927. The Saenger Theater, which cost $2.5 million and accommodated 3,400 people, was one of the largest theaters in the South. Its rather restrained exterior gave little hint of the marvels within (Figure 19). Conscious of the atmospheric theater auditorium that John Eberson created in 1923 for the Majestic Theater, in Houston, Weil substituted for an ornate ceiling dome like the one in the Strand a smooth plaster shell painted deep blue and perforated by hundreds of twinkling pinpoint lights. At the sides, a

FIGURE 20 Municipal Auditorium, Shreveport, 1929, Samuel G. Wiener, of Jones, Roessle, Olschner and Wiener, architect.

Photograph by Jim Zietz

painted rising sun and setting sun framed these heavens, and across them billowed slowly moving clouds, projected from a hidden machine. The auditorium walls—building facades, towers, exotic plants and birds, rooftops crowned with classical statues—completed the illusion of an outside setting of romantic fantasy.

By the late twenties, many places of entertainment were in the new Art Deco style, which acquired its name from the Exposition des Arts Decoratifs in Paris in 1925. Smooth-surfaced geometric masses bearing bands and panels of abstract patterns, whether zigzag motifs, chevrons, arabesques, or stylized florals, embraced the modern without sacrificing ornament. Much in the way of the Spanish Revival style, the Art Deco concentrates most of its ornament at the entry of buildings, but in contrast with the Spanish Revival its ornamental forms are abstract and of shallow relief. Art Deco, a salute to the vitality of modern life, lent itself particularly to the new urban building types of the twenties: skyscrapers, cinemas, hotels. Art Deco was one of several modern styles of the late 1920s and the 1930s with a family resemblance; they have been described variously as Modernistic, Stripped Classical, and Classic Modern. The name Art Deco usually conveys an emphasis on decoration. The other names most often express a primary concern with three-dimensional form.

Art Deco, by that criterion, is unquestionably the right term for the style of the Municipal Auditorium, in Shreveport, built in 1929 and dedicated to the soldiers of World War I (Figure 20). The auditorium has accommodated a wide range of entertainments and public events, and from 1948 to 1960 it

FIGURE 21 Detail of Municipal
Auditorium.

Photograph by Jim Zietz

FIGURE 22 Municipal Auditorium,
light fixture.

Photograph by Donna Fricker

was the studio for the *Louisiana Hayride* radio program, which for a time rivaled the Grand Ole Opry in popularity. Elvis Presley first gained wide exposure on the program. The auditorium's designer, Samuel G. Wiener, a partner in the firm of Jones, Roessle, Olschner and Wiener, used simple blocky forms for the body of the building and combined brick, terra-cotta, and cast stone into intricate wall patterns (Figure 21). Wiener demonstrated an exquisite sensitivity to the ornamental potential of brick, varying its size, laying it in different courses, varying the width and depth of the mortar, weaving materials, color, and pattern so that each surface is by itself a work of art yet all are united and unified. This is a spontaneous, inspirational work that is celebratory in its richness. The Municipal Auditorium, in its rejection of historicism and historical style, hinted at the role Wiener was to play in the 1930s when a European architecture of basic geometric forms was welcomed by the more avant-garde designers of buildings (Figure 22).

As the 1920s drew to a close, Louisiana was moving from a predominantly agricultural and rural economy to an urban and industrial one, and its architecture reflected the change. In 1928, Huey P. Long, Jr., had been inaugurated governor, after running on a platform of progressive change and government attention to the poor. He improved highways (the 296 miles of concrete roads in the state highway system in 1928 grew to 2,446 miles by 1935), bridges (the three major bridges of 1928 were among more than forty by 1935), schools, and hospitals. His Every Man a King populism broke the hold of the old-money oligarchy with roots going back to the plantation system and created a new force in Louisiana politics. Long was at times ruthless in his methods, but the result was that in the 1930s Louisiana entered the industrial age. Long opened a new chapter in the state's history.

By the time Long was elected, the Old State Capitol, the Gothic castle

FIGURE 23   Louisiana State Capitol, Baton Rouge, 1930, Weiss, Dreyfous and Seiferth architects.

Photograph by Jim Zietz

of 1847 (Chapter 5, Figure 60), could no longer accommodate all it was meant to. Among Long's first projects were a new state capitol and a new governor's mansion. Nowhere is the endless tug between new ideas and traditional values more manifest than in those two buildings. The firm of Weiss, Dreyfous and Seiferth, formed as a partnership between Leon C. Weiss, a friend of Long's, and F. Julius Dreyfous in 1919 and expanded in 1923 to make Solis Seiferth a third member, designed both of the markedly different buildings.

The new capitol was commissioned not only to meet mundane needs for additional space but also to serve as a symbol of the new Louisiana (Figure 23). The steel-frame building consists of a soaring tower, thirty-four stories and 450 feet tall, flanked by two identical lower wings, everything faced in Alabama limestone. Bertram Grosvenor Goodhue's skyscraper capitol in Lincoln, Nebraska, constructed between 1916 and 1928, was clearly a model, but Long's—for this building is remembered as Long's, not the architects—has greater similarities to urban skyscrapers, with its stepped-back, almost needlelike top, which resembles that on the Empire State Building, in New York City.

Long insisted on a tower but otherwise allowed his architects a free hand. Weiss, Dreyfous and Seiferth, liberated from any subservience to the American tradition of portico, dome, and rotunda by the precedent of the old Gothic capitol, opted for a progressive design. Yet the Beaux Arts principles of symmetry and axiality, and the implied classicism of the forms, kept the new building within an architectural ambit that was respectably conservative.

FIGURE 24   Detail of entrance to
Louisiana State Capitol.

Photograph by Jim Zietz

The style of the capitol can be described as Classic Modern. The architects'
foremost concerns were three-dimensional: the tower, the flanking geometric wings, the setbacks, the ceremonial stairs, and the tall, deep entry portal.
The bas-relief sculptures around the entrance and along the top of the wings
and the almost fully sculptured figures near the top of the tower ornament
the otherwise streamlined exterior surfaces (Figure 24). The symbolic content of the sculpture is important: the friezes, crowded with geometrically
stylized figures, depict episodes from Louisiana's history, as well as mainstays
of its economy and resources and activities connected with the well-being of
the community. Certainly, images of riches and stability were a solace during
the depression. The sculptors numbered some of the most prominent in the
country: Leonardo Taft, Lee Lawrie, and from Louisiana, Angela Gregory.
The effect was a variety of sculptural treatments within the framework of an
abstract modern style.

FIGURE 25   Old Governor's Mansion,
502 North Boulevard, Baton Rouge,
1930, Weiss, Dreyfous and Seiferth
architects.

Photograph by Jim Zietz

The interior of the building combines a suitable grandeur of height with
sumptuous materials. The lobby, with its glistening gold and russet marbles,
golden ceiling, bronze-and-glass lighting fixtures, and murals, leads to a
bank of high-speed elevators, behind which is the corridor where Huey Long
was assassinated in 1935. Chipped spots in the marble-faced walls are said to
be the damage of the bullets the assassin and Long's bodyguards fired. To either side of the lobby, the assembly chambers for the state senators and state
representatives are more traditionally classical than the exterior of the building. Coffered ceilings, huge fluted Ionic columns, and walls faced in varie-
gated marble and travertine of golden and bronze hues contribute to an aura
of splendor and power.

The Governor's Mansion, constructed in 1930, is, on the other hand,
completely historicized in a Classical vein (Figure 25). The building, of brick
covered with plaster and painted white, is two stories high and has a slate
mansard roof to which are attached dormers and a balustrade. Four thirty-
foot Corinthian columns support a pedimented portico. The first floor of
the house held the state rooms, including a formal east room and a state dining room. The second floor, which was the living area, has an oval sitting
room. The many affinities between the Governor's Mansion and the White
House, in Washington, D.C., gave rise to the rumor that the politically ambitious Long patterned his mansion in a way that would let him "get in practice." The architects who designed a capitol that celebrated the transformation of the state produced a mansion evocative of the Old South.

The nation's general economic slowdown in the thirties, after the stock-market crash of 1929, left many businesses in Louisiana surprisingly healthy, and some even prospered. Shreveport continued to thrive. Deep wells tapped some of the largest pools of crude oil known to exist at that time, and in the 1930s the great East Texas Field revived the oil industry, providing employment for thousands.

Louisiana also benefited from the vast public works projects of the decade. Under President Franklin Delano Roosevelt, elected in 1932, the federal government took an increasingly active role in revitalizing and stabilizing the economy. During the first months of the Roosevelt administration, innovative legislation was enacted, including, in June, 1933, the National Recovery Act. The NRA provided for a comprehensive public works program directed toward the improvement of rivers and harbors and the construction of highways, public buildings, and low-cost housing. The act established a Public Works Administration (PWA) to coordinate the whole effort. In 1935, the WPA, or the Works Progress Administration—later renamed the Works Projects Administration—came into existence. It employed architects directly and allocated funds to construct the buildings they designed. Long was a political rival of Roosevelt's, and federal funds flowed slowly to Louisiana. But after Long's assassination, his successors made peace with the president and brought millions of dollars in WPA contracts to the state. Buildings, highways, bridges, and parks followed. In 1938, when the Huey P. Long Bridge was completed at New Orleans, the combined highway and railway span was both the first bridge across the Mississippi in Louisiana and the longest railroad bridge in the world.

Landscape projects, which required much manual labor but little expensive equipment, proved to be an economical way of dispensing federal financial assistance widely. By 1926, three years before the stock-market crash, City Park, in New Orleans, had expanded to 1,300 acres, doubling its size and becoming one of the largest urban parks in the nation. The park had acquired a number of recreation facilities: a swimming pool and expanded children's playground, as well as golf courses, football fields, and tennis courts. But the desirability of a master plan became evident, and in 1929 the Chicago firm of Bennett, Parsons and Frost was hired to draw one up. Almost nothing in the plan was implemented, though, until 1933, when the park received federal funding, first from the PWA and then from the WPA and the Civil Works Administration. After that, the park underwent a spectacular reshaping that cost $13 million, of which the City Park board paid only 5 percent (Figure 26). Landscaping the east golf course alone kept fourteen thousand men busy with hand tools for eighteen months. Then a chain of lagoons, mostly dug by hand, and eight new and three rebuilt bridges, along with eight major avenues, a rose garden and statuary, a golf course, a stadium and gates, a bandstand, a dance pavilion, fountains, and a collection

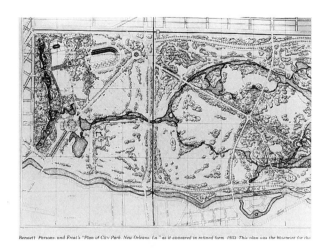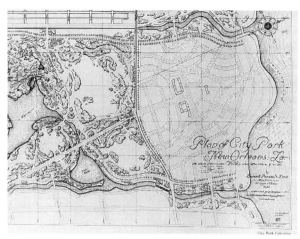

Bennett, Parsons, and Frost's "Plan of City Park, New Orleans, La." as it appeared in refined form, 1933. This plan was the blueprint for the

City Park Collection

FIGURE 26 City Park, New Orleans, 1933, Bennett, Parsons and Frost architects.

Courtesy of City Park Collection, New Orleans.

of sculptures by Enrique Alferez were added. These were the kinds of improvements advocated by those who saw urban parks as allowing a wholesome use of Americans' more plentiful leisure time and as deflecting youth from delinquency. Sports would replace the decadence of movie houses, dance halls, and saloons. The predilection for organized dances, however, was taken as a given, and open-air pavilions were soon provided for them. Women and girls began to go to the parks for athletics, but although by the 1920s mixed swimming was countenanced, segregation by age and sex was customary in most sports programming.

Fifteen parishes in Louisiana gained new courthouses through PWA and WPA funding. Approximately one-third of Louisiana's sixty-five parishes built courthouses between 1915 and 1940. Most of those constructed in the twenties, before the depression, adhere to Beaux Arts standards. One that is especially monumental, even bombastic, is the Caddo Parish Courthouse, designed by Neild and Somdal and completed in 1928. Of massive piled blocks adorned with columns and weighty cornices, it dominates its site in the center of downtown Shreveport. With the exception of a Georgian Revival structure in Madison Parish, all the PWA and WPA courthouses share the massive, blocky forms of their 1920s predecessors, though they are built on a smaller scale than the Caddo Parish Courthouse and subordinate the Classical elements to a streamlined, modernistic appearance. Despite the broad dimensions of all these buildings, the central section of each is much taller than the building is wide, and the vertical extent is emphasized through full-height pilasters, tall, narrow windows, and a monumental entry.

Perhaps the most remarkable of these rather uniform courthouses is the one in Natchitoches, designed by J. W. Smith in 1939 (Figure 27). The dominant feature of the otherwise fairly austere brick building is the pair of Natchitoches Indian chiefs sculptured in relief on the stone entrance. Many

FIGURE 27 Natchitoches Parish
Courthouse, Natchitoches, 1939, J. W.
Smith architect.

Photograph by Jim Zietz

of Louisiana's courthouses occupy the central square of their town, and although that has the disadvantage of preempting space that might be used for other public purposes, it also has the advantage of establishing a substantial physical focus for the town.

The modernity of these buildings proclaims the new spirit. But the classical consistently underpins the modern, reinforcing the public's perception of the strength and durability of democratic institutions. No such easily comprehended symbolism was requisite in buildings in the private sphere, and it was with those—houses, commercial structures, and some institutions—that the more adventurous architects and their clients could abandon convention.

During the 1930s, a number of the new buildings in Louisiana were in a pure and not merely streamlined modern idiom. Whether residences or commercial buildings or public buildings, these buildings, most of them in Shreveport, were regularly featured in the leading architectural journals of

FIGURE 28   Samuel G. Wiener House,
Shreveport, 1937, Samuel G. Wiener
architect.

*Archives and Special Collections, Noel
Memorial Library, Louisiana State
University, Shreveport.*

FIGURE 29   Wiener House, stairway
Photograph by Donna Fricker

the day. The buildings stand in startling—even shocking—contrast to what else was under construction in the United States during that decade. It is especially surprising that the earliest of Louisiana's modern buildings were designed before 1932 and the exhibition in New York of the International style, which was the formal introduction of Europe's geometrically modern architecture to American architects and the American public.

Samuel Wiener, the architect of Shreveport's Municipal Auditorium, and his brother, William Wiener, were the designers of most of these buildings, and most of the earliest ones were houses. The houses invariably caused a sensation in the exclusive neighborhoods where they were constructed. In 1937, Samuel Wiener designed a house for his own family that both epitomized the new style and showed his particular handling of it (Figures 28, 29). Located in one of the new residential neighborhoods of Shreveport, the structure appears to be a cluster of rectangular forms under a large overhanging roof plane. The two voids under the roof are a screened sleeping porch and an entrance porch, two traditional spaces in southern domestic architecture. The entrance, which is cut deeply into the body of the house, has a kinship with traditional porches, though Wiener replaced the usual Classical columns with a single, slender two-story-tall steel-pipe column painted a brilliant red.

Wiener designed the interior spaces to flow together (Figure 30). By placing room entrances at the corners, he connected the spaces diagonally. The communication between them, as well as the corner windows, lets breezes cross through the building. What is traditional in this house is in response primarily to its climatic environment, but its formal elements, such

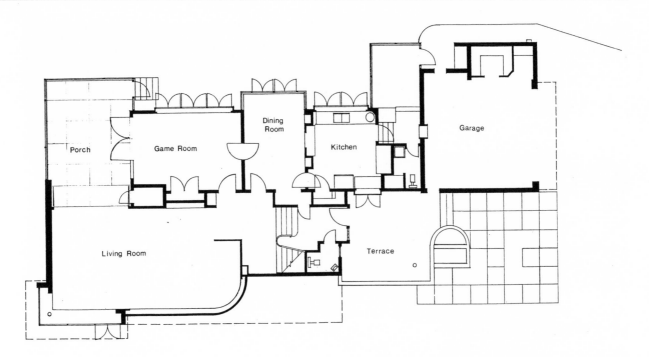

FIGURE 30   Plan of Wiener House
Redrawn by Diana Melichar

as the white stucco walls, strip windows, and overhanging flat roof, derive from the European avant-garde. Some features, like the white walls and the eight-foot overhang on the south side, provide comfort in Louisiana's weather at the same time that they follow European practice. The flat roof itself, a touchstone of modernism, is thickened to produce an insulating layer between the rooms and the hot sun overhead. The house gives the language of modern architecture a regional intonation. By the middle of the 1930s, the houses the Wieners designed were gaining in client appeal. Among these were the Wile-Schober House, dating from 1934, and the Flesch-Walker-Guillot House, dating from 1936 (Figure 31), both in Shreveport. There was also an extraordinary weekend house on Cross Lake, from 1933, that evidenced a strong influence by Le Corbusier. This was demolished in 1988. Other work by Samuel Wiener includes the El Karubah Club, on Cross Lake, from 1931, and several schools, including Bossier City High School, built between 1938 and 1940. The Big Chain Store, by Samuel and William B. Wiener, erected in Shreveport in 1940, has sweeping curves of the sort in buildings by Erich Mendelsohn in Germany (Figure 32). This is one of the nation's earliest supermarkets to dispense with exterior display windows and employ the solid wall for interior display and self-service. The building is without interior supports, for the steel-and-concrete construction allowed a sixty-foot span. A horizontal glass-block strip in the wall provides natural light inside in the daytime, and at night the interior lights help illuminate the parking lot. A deep overhang shades the windows and walls from the sun

FIGURE 31   Flesch-Walker-Guillot
House, Shreveport, 1936, Samuel G.
Wiener and William Wiener architects.

Photograph by Jim Zietz

FIGURE 32   Big Chain Store,
Shreveport, 1940, Samuel G. Wiener and
William Wiener architects.

*Archives and Special Collections, Noel
Memorial Library, Louisiana State
University, Shreveport.*

and protects shoppers from bad weather. The parking lot in front of the
building was considered unnecessarily large in its time.

The Shreveport Municipal Incinerator, designed by Samuel Wiener and
built in 1935 with PWA funds, was the first structure of its kind to be designed by an architect rather than an engineer (Figure 33). Photographs of
the incinerator were part of the exhibit of modern American architecture in
the United States Pavilion at the Paris International Exposition of 1937. The

FIGURE 33 Shreveport Municipal
Incinerator, 1935 (now demolished),
Samuel G. Wiener, of Jones, Roessle,
Olschner and Wiener, architect.

*Archives and Special Collections, Noel
Memorial Library, Louisiana State
University, Shreveport.*

photographs, published extensively in international architectural journals, brought Wiener much acclaim. In 1938, Lewis Mumford bestowed special praise on the facility in an article in the *New Yorker* magazine: "If I had any gold medals to distribute, I would quickly pin one on [the] Municipal Incinerator in Shreveport . . . an excellent design, with no vulgar attempts at prettifying a form that needs no additions."[3] The incinerator has been demolished.

The question arises why such buildings were erected in Louisiana so early in the development of American modernism rather than in an area having closer contact with the European avant-garde. Part of the reason lay with the architects. Fascinated by the illustrations of modern buildings he had seen in magazines, Samuel Wiener traveled to Europe in 1927 and again in 1931 to see this new architecture for himself. Like his younger brother William, he formed an intellectual and emotional commitment to the idea of the European avant-garde that it was up to architects to invent forms that symbolized the era. Both the Wieners came to their conviction in the context of a powerful regional tradition, and the Wieners' buildings of the thirties mark a radical break with their earlier designs and with contemporaneous building in the United States. But for these two architects there were no second thoughts. Their work discloses an aesthetic certainty informing their search for an authentic modern expression.

Their buildings looked as they did, too, because their clients wanted them that way. Almost all the residences and many of the commercial build-

3. Lewis Mumford, "The Sky Line: The Golden Age in the West and the South," *New Yorker,* April 30, 1938, pp. 50–51.

FIGURE 34 Rankin House (now Rankin-Wilson House), St. Tammany Parish, 1938.

Photograph by Donna Fricker

ings they designed were for family and friends, who, like the architects, were Jewish. To them, southern antebellum plantation motifs seemed both irrelevant and inappropriate; they wanted architectural forms that declared their attitudes and their vision of the times.

In other parts of the state, including New Orleans, a pure architectural modernism made few inroads. The Rankin House, by an unknown architect in St. Tammany Parish, is an interesting exception (Figure 34). Overlooking a bayou, this eleven-thousand-square-foot house was begun in 1938 for William Rankin, the state commissioner for the Department of Conservation. Harnett T. Kane has described the house: "It was to be a castlelike all-brick-and-glass mansion, planned for a large-scaled way of life; two-story gaming hall, partly roofed sun porch which gave commanding view of the countryside, wide passageways, new glass materials which had never been used in the Deep South, specially colored semi-transparent walls."[4] Rankin, found guilty in an oil scandal, was sent to the state penitentiary, and the mansion was completed only in the 1990s.

Weiss, Dreyfous and Seiferth were responsible for several severe, obsessively axial structures. The Charity Hospital, in New Orleans, built from 1937 to 1938, and the second largest hospital in the United States when it opened, has, like the attached school of nursing, a crisp, efficient, functional

4. Harnett T. Kane, *Louisiana Hayride: The American Rehearsal for Dictatorship* (1941; rpr. Gretna, La., 1971), 334.

FIGURE 35 Municipal Auditorium, Lake Charles, 1939, Weiss, Dreyfous and Seiferth architects. The building is now the McNeese State University Auditorium.

Southeastern Architectural Archive, Tulane University.

form that conveys an impression of progressive modernity. The same architects produced the Municipal Auditorium, in Lake Charles, dating from 1939, which now forms the focal point of the campus of McNeese State University (Figure 35). Curved vertical forms sweep upward from the triple-door entry to the roofline and are echoed inside in the oval-shaped piers and flowing forms. The Louisiana State Exhibit Building, in Shreveport, was designed to blazon how far Louisiana had come by 1937 (Figure 36). Designed by Neild and Somdal, the circular building is flanked by identical boxlike wings. The main entrance of this insistently symmetrical building includes a porch *in antis* with dark granite columns of the plainest design, without any hint of bases or capitals. All windows open upon a circular interior court-

FIGURE 36 Louisiana State Exhibit Building, Shreveport, 1937, Neild and Somdal architects, frescoes by Conrad Albrizio.

Photograph by Jim Zietz

yard, and the exterior, without fenestration, is a continuous smooth monochrome surface relieved only by horizontal molded strips. A set of Conrad Albrizio's frescoes illustrating the plentiful resources of Louisiana fills the porch with color, however. In architectural expression, the building is characteristic of the freewheeling, enthusiastic experimentation of the time.

9

WHY HISTORIC PRESERVATION?

Eugene Darwin Cizek

WHY HISTORIC PRESERVATION? I BELIEVE HISTORIC PRESERVATION, BY SUS-
taining environmental continuity, can underlie individual and communal
mental health. It provides the context for education and learning. It is the
foundation upon which sound planning and growth-change management
are based. It is the basis for the economic development that cultural tourism
supports.

Self-preservation is a drive of individuals and of societies. We try to preserve those things that are valuable to us. Sometimes what a society finds
valuable is not immediately obvious and only careful study and assessment
can uncover the values implied by the exquisite dynamics between our attitudes toward what we already have and our priorities regarding what we do
not have.

The selection process by which historic preservation occurs identifies
certain things as valuable to society. The life and culture of the ancients is
known to us through the things that have been preserved from their time:
paintings in caves, carved artifacts, writings, earthen mounds, buildings,
parts of cities. The civilizations that left documents and other writings in addition to monuments are the ones of which we have the fullest awareness.
Monuments by themselves give only part of the picture. When enough survives to let us see a society in its many facets, we gain an understanding of
ourselves and of the forces that have carried us to our present circumstances.

In 1978, the New Orleans Historic District Landmarks Commission
designated the French Hospital, at 1821 Orleans Avenue, a city landmark.
The structure had been built for the French Benevolent and Mutual Aid Association of New Orleans in 1860. Thousands of Orleanians had passed
through the hospital at birth or during a recovery from illness. Others had
experienced the death of a loved one there. The masonry building's air of

permanence had given many a sense of security. In 1951, the hospital had ceased operations, and the building had been sold to the Knights of Peter Claver, an African-American Roman Catholic benevolent society that had evolved into a powerful insurance company. Later on, the building had become an office building and the center for civil rights activities in New Orleans. In the 1960s and 1970s, the French Hospital had housed the offices of many prominent black attorneys, including Ernest Morial, who was to become the first black mayor of the city.

Despite the designation as a landmark, the structure was inadequately maintained, and it began to deteriorate. In the 1980s, the Knights of Peter Claver sought to have the landmark designation lifted so that they could demolish the old hospital. They had put up new facilities alongside it and had no further use for the old building. A host of people came forward at public hearings to discuss the fate of the building. People who had received hospital care in it spoke of its place in the city's collective memory. Others held that its time as the seat of the local civil rights movement made ending the designation unthinkable. The building gave concrete form to a momentous period for racial activism, sociopolitical discussions, and legislative remedies to injustice. It could easily have become a museum capable of keeping the freedom movement fresh for later generations. It might have become a magnet for black cultural and civil rights tourism. It could have been the catalyst for retrieving the historic Treme neighborhood, which only a few years earlier had been devastated by the construction of an elevated expressway that robbed the area of the great linear park an alley of live oak trees five trees across had been. But too few in the community saw all this. The building was demolished. Today there are only a vacant lot, a lone live oak tree, and the remnants of the elaborate granite-and-iron fence that once surrounded the site. The historic structure and all its associated memories were torn from the urban fabric of the city to the detriment of the current generation and all those to come. Historic preservation is a guardianship of more than timber, masonry, and steel. The health of our society depends on knowing who we are and how we got to where we are today.

Sound historic preservation is likeliest when policies exist for maintaining the quality and ambience of neighborhoods. In 1895, William Woodward, a founder of the Tulane School of Architecture, led a successful campaign to save the historic Cabildo, on Jackson Square, in New Orleans, from demolition. For him the building was an emblem of the city's soul and identity. He placed a high value on the picturesque structures of the old part of the city, since they illuminated the historical evolution of the place and constituted a repository with many tested examples of architecture that functions well. Although he believed that new architecture should speak to and represent its own time and place, he did not think that this should be at the cost of destroying the very roots of the new creations.

Two generations later, in 1964, John Lawrence (1923-1971), then dean of the Tulane School of Architecture, succinctly expressed much the same idea in talking to a local group:

> As one vitally interested in the contemporary world—one who welcomes living in the Twentieth Century and nourishes the hope of contributing to it—I have independently come to the conclusion that the preservation of that which is good, be it old or new, is absolutely essential to our sanity as well as our understanding of ourselves, and to our own progress. We make a mistake if we equate old with good, but when we do find these coexisting then there is the greatest imperative to preserve the old for only by doing so can we have a sense of time and a sense of place without which we have only a present, ever fleeting—which is an intolerable and unbearable state for man. When, therefore, I say that the preservation of the good and the old is essential for man's sanity, I do not overstate the case.[1]

Lawrence understood the worth of preserving individual buildings as well as the ensembles of which individual buildings are a part.

Lawrence encouraged his students to study the buildings of earlier times. The students who help in preparing HABS drawings hone their technical skills in measurement and drawing. They also learn an appreciation of the past: sometimes they fall in love with the old buildings. They learn how previous builders solved aesthetic and technical problems. By such experience they gain depth in their understanding of their own craft. A few become actively involved in historic preservation. Many more, in subtle and unpredictable ways, use what they have learned in their own creations.

The context of decisions about historic preservation is inevitably complex. When what is in question is an entire neighborhood, such as the Vieux Carre, in New Orleans, the context for sensitive decision making is even more complicated. Bernard Lemann (1905-), in *The Vieux Carre: A General Statement,* zeroes in on the source of much of the complexity:

> As an historic storehouse the Vieux Carre represents a cumulative effect, not an isolated moment of history, but a kind of mobile moment, ever receding into the background, or moving forward, depending on how one prefers to see it. Here we find a colorful kaleidoscopic blending, not only of many periods, styles and historic associations, but also the varied types and activities of hucksters and barkers, artists and shopkeepers, show girls, antique dealers, tourists, evening crowds. This very diversity is not only a true image of what we have been; it is also a keynote to the distinctive flavor and picturesque appeal that has been sensed by so many observers. . . . It is also a major reason why . . . everyone is in spontaneous agreement . . . that "we don't want another Williamsburg," a museum village perfectly "preserved" in all of its details.[2]

1. John Lawrence, Address to Friends of the Cabildo, 1964.
2. Bernard Lemann, *The Vieux Carre: A General Statement* (New Orleans, 1966), 33.

The problem is, How do we preserve a kaleidoscope? Obviously, to keep it, it is necessary to keep it in motion. Historic preservation can be a large part of planned development and growth management. The information it amasses can provide a basis for evaluating an environment and determining where changes, if needed, can best take place. In 1974, there was concern about the pell-mell demolition of structures in New Orleans' Central Business District, upriver from the Vieux Carre, and a recognition of the need to revitalize the stagnant economy of the area. A distinguished ecological planning firm that was hired as a consultant developed several data maps, one of which defined the matrix of action and another the probability of change.[3] In the designated area, which extended the limits of the official Central Business District, it evaluated every structure for its structural integrity, historic importance, and probability of future reuse in a growth management plan. It made suggestions as to ways investors might plan for growth and change in the long, middle, and short range.

The probability of change was in large part judged by reference to the strength and continuity the nineteenth and early-twentieth-century stock of architecture provided. More recent high-rise structures completed the data base. The patterns of economic and residential use in the older neighborhoods had had a stabilizing effect. Several older neighborhoods were included in the expanded Central Business District, thus maintaining human scale and continuity. Buildings of newer types and improvements in public infrastructure were proposed to round out the realistic urban plan. The Downtown Development District became a reality when the growth management plan was approved and an entity established with taxation power to fund the plan. Today the plan has been somewhat revised. A number of warehouses have been made into apartments or condominiums, old buildings have been converted into law offices, new hotels have been built and others fashioned out of old buildings, art galleries and other small businesses have been established. It is a lively, viable neighborhood and stands as an excellent prototype for urban change and growth.

Historic preservation provides the context for education and learning. The scholar J. René Jules Dubos wrote in 1969, "The environment men create through their wants becomes a mirror that reflects their civilization; more importantly it also constitutes a book in which is written the formula of life that they communicate to others and transmit to succeeding generations. The characteristics of the environment are therefore of importance not only because they affect the comfort and quality of present-day life, but even more because they condition the development of young people and thereby of society." Dubos quoted Winston Churchill's compressed statement "We

3. Donald A. Wallace, Ian L. McHarge, William H. Roberts, and Thomas A. Todd, *Central Area New Orleans Growth Management Program: Technical Report, Containing the Proposed CBD Community Improvement Plan and Program, 1974 to the Year 2000* (Philadelphia, 1975), esp. 16, 19.

shape our buildings and afterwards our buildings shape us," and then went on to say, "While the total environment certainly affected the way men feel and behave, more importantly it conditions the kind of persons their descendants will become, because all environmental factors have their most profound and lasting effects when they impinge on the young organism during the early stages of its development."[4]

When young people feel out of sync with the world in which they are growing up, that is in considerable measure because they lack a clear concept of what they have for a future. In both city and country they are all too often part of a throwaway society that values nothing except immediacy and hence misprizes the lines running from the past that could project a continuity into the future. For city children, whole neighborhoods—and thereby the children's very image of their situation in the world—alter through demolition or neglect. There is little sense of personal worth to be found in a society that seems to value nothing except momentary satisfactions. Historic preservation allows the young imaginatively to reenact the great failures and successes of history where they occurred. Experiencing a place firsthand lends momentous happenings a tangibility, at the same time that the realization dawns that each participant in the happenings was human and had personal desires and needs.

Every year since 1977, the program Education Through Historic Preservation, which a specialist in the St. Charles Parish public school system and I founded, has carried out a project that seeks to introduce students at an early age to experiencing historic environments directly and creatively, as both worthwhile in itself and a step to further learning. A number of programs for school children in other parts of Louisiana also employ historic settings as learning environments for the young. The premise is that if our environment is destroyed or its integrity compromised, the basic preservation of self and society becomes questionable. For the first year's program, Homeplace plantation was the setting. The eighty-year-old owner shared many stories of his childhood and life. Old family photographs and mementos gave the working field trips the concreteness of the familiar. Students learned to draw the individual details of the house and then assembled them to record the whole. Or they wrote their descriptions or composed poetry about how life once was on a Louisiana sugar plantation. They heard about the sorrows and joys of the many families who had built or maintained Homeplace and called it home for almost two hundred years. They learned about slavery and freedom. They met an eighty-year-old woman whose mother had been a slave at the plantation before the Civil War. She told the students about the hindrances to schooling that had stood in her way and about how she had dropped out at a very young age to work in the fields and

---

4. J. René Jules Dubos, *So Human an Animal* (New York, 1968), 170–71.

cut sugarcane. She told them the great value of education. And she was so in-spired by the enthusiasm of the school children that she went back to school herself, becoming the oldest person to obtain her general equivalency degree in Louisiana. In 1981, this program received the first Honor Award in Edu-cation given by the National Trust for Historic Preservation. The relation-ship between historic preservation and education has been recognized na-tionally.

The environmental renewal and neighborhood conservation figuring in historic preservation provide the foundation for sound economic develop-ment that can include cultural tourism. As Samuel Wilson, Jr., predicted in the 1940s, the Vieux Carre has proved its capacity to generate revenue for New Orleans and Louisiana. It has become integral to the perception out-siders have of the state. Visitors come to Louisiana from all parts of the United States and from foreign lands to see the French Quarter and to expe-rience the plantation houses and cultures of the region. The Cajun and other regional cultures also attract visitors. Every parish makes a contribution to cultural tourism, and in virtually every one, the interest for visitors begins with preserved historic buildings. In Lincoln Parish, there is the Absalom Autrey House, a log house. In Alexandria, the Arna Bontemps House was the home of a major author of the Harlem Renaissance. The Association for the Preservation of Historic Natchitoches owns and operates three proper-ties: the Melrose plantation, where, not least, the folk artist Clementine Hunter painted; the Kate Chopin/Bayou Folk Museum; and the Lemee House, dating from 1830. The number of visitors has grown steadily. In 1938, for example, 4,487 people visited Melrose plantation; in 1993, there were 14,746 visitors.

Cultural tourism is the second largest industry in Louisiana, after agri-culture. It results in thousands of jobs and adds millions of dollars to the state's economy. Several federal agencies and the National Trust for Historic Preservation have helped put Louisiana in contention for the tourist's spend-ing. The National Register for Historic Places has listed fifty-five historic dis-tricts outside New Orleans. The National Main Street Center, initiated by the National Trust in 1977, tenders planning and design assistance to historic downtowns. But local preservation societies and organizations, as well as nonprofit and for-profit housing and neighborhood rehabilitation corpora-tions, are also helping, by working to renovate and restore our built and nat-ural environment so as to provide dwellings and a sense of place.

HABS compiles archival-quality drawings of ink on polyester film in order to assemble a permanent record of historic buildings' plans and details. Notes are appended to the drawings, and photographic documentation shows each building in its context, with all the patina it has acquired. The initial focus of HABS in Louisiana, as elsewhere, was on recording the earli-est structures and those threatened with demolition. In recent years the focus has been on buildings that are especially characteristic of Louisiana, such as sugarhouses. There has been no comprehensive record made of late-nineteenth- and twentieth-century structures, and this book suggests many that remain to be documented. HABS complements the state's parish surveys of historic buildings.

The very first structure HABS documented was the handsome Beauregard-Keyes House, dating from 1826, in the French Quarter of New Orleans. At the time it was recorded, it was a macaroni factory threatened with demolition. The attention HABS brought the house led to its purchase and restoration by the author Frances Parkinson Keyes as her writing studio and a salon for meetings concerned with historic preservation and arts and literature. Today, it is one of several restored houses open as museums in New Orleans, each of which attracts a substantial number of visitors each year and each of which has an educational program for children.

Another landmark documented in the first phase of HABS was the principal house, completed in 1857, at Belle Grove plantation. It was a masterpiece of the mid-nineteenth-century architect Henry Howard, the largest plantation house in Louisiana, and one of the finest structures to be built in the United States. After the 1920s, it fell gradually into ruin, and on March 15, 1952, it was consumed by a fire. Today, we have the HABS documentation, a partial grove of large live oak trees, and a subdivision of modern houses. Had there been an effort to save the landmark at the time the HABS drawings were made, it could have become invaluable for cultural tourism and education.

HABS far surpasses other surveys in the wealth of information it provides. It has been a goad to the many people who have rescued important buildings and retained and rebuilt their neighborhoods and towns, with the aim not only of preserving this structure or that block but of nurturing a quality of life responsive to the way the past is a foundation for the present and the future. If we are aware and care for our environment, we are caring for future generations.

THE LOUISIANA HABS CATALOG
Julie H. McCollam

INTRODUCTION

The Historic American Buildings Survey, inaugurated in 1933, was one of the sweeping projects that President Franklin Delano Roosevelt's Works Progress Administration undertook in response to the severe economic crisis of the Great Depression. Like other WPA projects, the far-reaching social and political consequences of which are still being felt, the survey had both practical and idealistic purposes. Unemployed architects might be put to work evaluating and recording America's historic buildings, and the National Park Service, the American Institute of Architects, and the Library of Congress were logical partners in the envisioned assembling of architectural information. It was later recalled, "As we saw examples of our characteristic buildings, both great and humble, slip out of memory without record, we recognized a collective loss. From the Atlantic to the Pacific, we began to look at what our immigrant civilization had built in little more than three centuries, and what native American cultures had produced still earlier. The Historic American Buildings Survey was our first national attempt to preserve this heritage through graphic and written records of our built environment."[1] Perhaps HABS's most valuable technical achievement was the standard format it introduced for recording and making available the information the teams of architects gathered. The survey, which is the only WPA-founded program still functioning today, continues to employ that format.

Charles E. Peterson, the first director of HABS, was an architect who, after graduating from the University of Minnesota, had worked in the western office of the National

1. Russell E. Dickenson, Robert Broshar, and Daniel J. Boorstin, Foreword to *Historic America: Buildings, Structures, and Sites,* ed. C. Ford Peatross (Washington, D.C., 1983), ix.

Park Service in its early days and then for three years at the Colonial Williamsburg restoration project. As the director of HABS, he particularly sought to recruit architects whose success and recognition derived from the restoration of historic buildings. To head the Louisiana HABS team, he found what he sought in Richard Koch, a native of New Orleans and a partner in the firm of Armstrong and Koch. That firm had restored Shadows-on-the-Teche, in New Iberia, in 1922 and Oak Alley plantation, in Vacherie, in 1926. A graduate of Tulane, Koch had studied in Paris for two years and had worked for several years in New York before returning to New Orleans. His team for HABS in Louisiana included F. Monroe Labouisse, Samuel Wilson, Jr., and Douglass Freret, Jr., all recent architectural graduates of Tulane. Koch, a perfectionist, brought to the Louisiana project a meticulous attention to detail, closely monitoring the quality of the drawings by his staff. Also included on the staff was A. Boyd Cruise, a gifted artist whose finished watercolors in the Library of Congress record the character and color of selected buildings in the survey. His drawings of hardware, cast iron, plasterwork, and other architectural details make an invaluable contribution to many of the HABS measured-drawing sheets. Other distinguished delineators among the many talented draftsmen on Koch's staff were R. G. Crump, Jr., H. H. Dowling, O. C. Kottermann, and Chester Wicker.

Koch himself chose the buildings to be measured, on the basis of age, uniqueness, vulnerability to demolition, and stage of decay. In 1934, he compiled a list of buildings and complexes of buildings that he considered worthy of being measured. Of the 150 projects on his list, about half had been measured or photographed and accepted by HABS in Washington by 1941, when World War II caused the program to be suspended.[2]

Researchers turned to parish conveyance offices to trace titles and to uncover historical information. Koch was also interested in the photography of architecture and was influenced by Frances Benjamin Johnston and Robert W. Tebbs, well-known pre–World War II photographers whose work is in the Library of Congress. Koch traveled and photographed extensively with Tebbs in Louisiana. But other team members produced photographs as well. Between 1934 and 1941, the Louisiana HABS team measured, photographed, and recorded numerous structures. The originals of their drawings went to the Library of Congress, which has made copies available for general use.

In abeyance during World War II, the HABS program resumed after the war in modified form. It continued to accept sets of drawings that adhered to the same standards and procedures as before but with-

out hiring professional architects. In the summer of 1978, Sibyl McCormac Groff led a group of students to the state and established a precedent for further projects whereby teams of architectural students working under supervision would do the research and drawing.

In 1981, the Louisiana State Historic Preservation Office established a continuing HABS program. The division, under Ann Jones as director, with Barbara SoRelle Bacot as grants manager, funded Eugene Darwin Cizek, of the Tulane School of Architecture, to make measured drawings according to HABS standards. The collaboration between the State Historic Preservation Office and Tulane continued successfully under Cizek's direction, and in 1985 Jonathan Fricker, who had succeeded Jones, expanded the program to involve other universities. Michael Pitts, William R. Brockway, and Barrett C. Kennedy, of the School of Architecture at Louisiana State University, became participants, as did Jay D. Edwards of the Department of Geography and Anthropology there, with Sid Gray as a consultant; Lestar Martin, of the School of Architecture at Louisiana Tech University; and Dan Branch, of the School of Architecture at the University of Southwestern Louisiana.

As from the beginning, the HABS office in Washington receives the original sheets of measured drawings, sometimes accompanied by photographs and historical and descriptive data. The policy of the

2. HABS Buildings list 5, in HABS Office Materials, Richard Koch and Samuel Wilson, Jr., Addenda, Box 6, Southeastern Architectural Archive, Tulane University.

survey from its inception has been to accept auxiliary documentation only if it does not duplicate what is in the official measured drawings. Many repositories in the state hold copies of the material in Washington. The illustrated listing of HABS buildings by parish that begins on page 358 tells what kind of information is available in the various repositories.

There exists from the prewar phase of HABS a body of preliminary work leading to, but vastly different from, the final measured drawings. This forms a sort of exuberant subtext to the standardized end product. It is a disorderly and whimsical miscellany harboring all the idiosyncrasy expunged from the finished work. Three repositories in New Orleans—the Louisiana State Museum, the Southeastern Architectural Archive at the Howard-Tilton Memorial Library of Tulane University, and the Historic New Orleans Collection—are rich in such material.

Koch sent field notebooks, preparatory watercolor studies, and odds and ends left in the New Orleans HABS office when it closed in 1941, as well as his personal collection, to the Louisiana State Museum. Separating what part of this collection is material never submitted to Washington or returned by Washington to HABS in Louisiana and what part is from Koch's private collection is complicated, but the documents can offer insights, sometimes amusing, into the way the Louisiana team operated under Koch.

The watercolor sketches by Cruise at the Louisiana State Museum do not conform to a standard size, and were not accepted by HABS in 1941. Samuel Wilson, Jr., reported in an address in 1940 that adding Cruise to the HABS staff was not approved, was in fact roundly disapproved, by Washington. Nonetheless, the Library of Congress accepted forty-seven of Cruise's finished and highly detailed watercolors. The Louisiana State Museum retained his unofficial preliminary work. The rapid freehand sketches, line drawings, and spontaneous watercolors, often unsigned and unidentified, stand to HABS's architectural drawings as an artist's experimental preparatory studies stand to the final form of a painting. The drawings that HABS accepted do not have the spontaneity of the studies. The technical complexity and sheer mechanical virtuosity of the measured drawings are indicative of tools with a serious purpose, whereas the fresh and expressive character of the preliminary renderings connects them with the lively realm of the imagination.

The Louisiana State Museum catalogs this hodgepodge in its entirety as HABS, though some of it duplicates completed, official HABS archives and some is only loosely related to them, conforming not at all to the documentation requirements HABS set forth in "Transmitting Documentation to HABS/HAER:WASO," its official guidelines. Most buildings recorded in this part of the collection have no

identification whatever, much less a HABS number label. Koch himself included under the HABS heading many buildings that had been researched, photographed, or sketched by Boyd Cruise, or for which floor plans and elevations had been drawn, but that were never formally measured nor accepted by Washington. Buildings in this category do not appear in the periodically issued official HABS Checklist. Other items, such as a group of drawings by Ellsworth Woodward and a wonderful collection of 1930s photographs, are labeled HABS as well, although their only connection to the survey seems to lie in their sharing with it, as subjects, certain historic buildings.

The Southeastern Architectural Archive benefited also from Koch's generosity. Among its mélange is a large collection of correspondence between Koch, in New Orleans, and Peterson, in Washington. One poignant exchange evinces the mounting frustration of the two men as they desperately cast about for ways to save Uncle Sam plantation. Other letters concern the exhibition in 1936 of Cruise's watercolors at the Arts and Crafts Club and the club's show of photography, *Ante-Bellum Houses of the Mississippi Valley*, in November, 1941. In another exchange, the two men address the idea of relocating the Louisiana HABS office to the Pontalba Building, in New Orleans, in the hope of establishing a permanent exhibit there. The correspondence displays Koch's judgments about people, programs, houses, and the history of styles, as well as his taste and opinions. Preferring the Louisiana Colonial style over the Greek Revival, he wrote Peterson, "I am not too fond of huge Greek columns on a dwelling." Other letters bring to light disagreements between the two men regarding stylistic derivation, show the kinds of scholarly information they shared, and give indications of their criteria for choosing buildings for measurement. The letters allow an unexpected glimpse into the working relationship between the two colleagues in their ambitious enterprise.

The records at the Southeastern Architectural Archive include documentation of the extensive historical and title research the Louisiana HABS team conducted before the war. In the records are trackings of successive ownership, photographs of legal instruments, information about remodeling, and demonstrations of the difficulty or impossibility of establishing dates of buildings in the French Quarter because of frequent rebuilding and remodeling during the last one hundred years. There, also, are the progress reports, the field sketches of floor plans, the notes, and the photographs that led to the final measured drawings. Thirty-five photographs of the houses measured by HABS up to 1941 are in the collection, as well as seventeen copies of measured drawings. Cabildo files, legal annals and plan books, city archives, newspaper

files, cemeteries, and the colonial archives in Paris were just some of the sources consulted in determining ownership transfers. There are such oddities as a manuscript copy of a 1728 archival plan of New Orleans taken from a French source and a copy of an insulting patois quatrain directed at the buckskin-clad "Kaintucks" whose rough-and-ready presence offended residents of the Creole city. The material gathered is so varied that it almost defies cataloging. At present the Southeastern Architectural Archive keeps it in boxes labeled HABS, to differentiate it from other holdings that Koch donated.

The ancillary material at the Historic New Orleans Collection is less preliminary and random than at the other two repositories. The Historic New Orleans Collection has eighty photographs of HABS-measured buildings, accompanied by historical data on microfiche. Although there is a disclaimer by the Library of Congress attached to the historical information, much of interest is included, such as the identification of houses belonging to free people of color in nineteenth-century New Orleans. Sixteen photographs are of buildings measured in the late fifties and early sixties. Particularly evocative are the photographs of now-razed buildings, like the Louisiana Sugar Exchange, in New Orleans. There is a photograph from 1899 of the barn and *pigeonnier* at Homeplace plantation, in St. Charles Parish, as well as descriptive data and early pho-

tographs, plans, and drawings of Square No. 62, in New Orleans, known in the survey as the Vieux Carre Squares (Chapter 2, Figures 35, 36). Also in the collection are copies of original drawings by James Gallier of the Forstall House, a rare Italianate-style building at 920 St. Louis Street, which Koch's team measured (Chapter 5, Figure 77), and a drawing from the architectural firm of Dakin and Dakin of St. Patrick's Catholic Church, at 724 Camp Street. (Chapter 5, Figure 49).

The collection possesses a helpful digest of HABS operations in loose-leaf-binder form. Produced by an intern from the art department of Newcomb College, this includes a brief history of the HABS program nationally and in Louisiana, biographical sketches of the major figures of the HABS team before World War II, a list of HABS photographers along with photocopied samples of their work, and an index of microfiche photographs arranged alphabetically by parish and accompanied by photocopies of the photographs.

The Louisiana State Archives, in Baton Rouge, is the repository for duplicate full-size measured drawings made beginning in 1993 under the aegis of the State Historic Preservation Office, that is, the Division of Historic Preservation. It also holds the photographs for HABS by Jim Zietz.

In the illustrated listing by parish beginning on page 358 there is a brief presentation of information for every building in Louisiana that HABS recorded from its inception through 1988. A photograph or drawing in each case accompanies the information. Material for buildings measured and photographed between 1989 and 1993 is still being processed.

HABS BUILDINGS
ALPHABETICAL LISTING

Academy, near Union, St. James Parish

Afton Villa (restored gardens, ruins of house), U.S. Highway 61, St. Francisville, West Feliciana Parish

Alma sugarcane plantation, Lakeland, Pointe Coupee Parish

Angelina plantation (dovecote, dollhouse), Highway 1, Mount Airy, St. John the Baptist Parish

Archbishopric, 1114 Chartres Street, New Orleans, Orleans Parish

Arsenal, 615 St. Peter Street, New Orleans, Orleans Parish

Ashland (Belle Helene) plantation, near Geismar, Ascension Parish

Austerlitz plantation, Highway 1, near Oscar, Pointe Coupee Parish

Autrey House, Highway 151, Dubach, Lincoln Parish

Avery Island Salt Mine Village, Avery Island, Iberia Parish
    Baptist church
    Bradford Club
    Company store
    Salt workers' houses Nos. 1–6

Avery Island Sugar House, Avery Island, Iberia Parish

Bagatelle plantation, near Sunshine, Iberville Parish (moved from St. James Parish)
    North kitchen support building
    South kitchen support building
    South slave cabin
    Stables

Baillio, Peter, House (Kent House), Bayou Rapides, near Alexandria, Rapides Parish

Balcony Building, 120 Washington Street, Natchitoches, Natchitoches Parish

Bank of Lafayette (Old City Hall), 217 West Main Street, Lafayette, Lafayette Parish

Bank of the United States, 339 Royal Street, New Orleans, Orleans Parish

Barbarra (Rose) plantation (*garçonnière*), near St. Rose, St. Charles Parish

Beauregard House, 1113 Chartres Street, New Orleans, Orleans Parish

Beauregard, René, House, Mississippi River, Chalmette Battleground Park, Chalmette, St. Bernard Parish

Belle Grove plantation house, near White Castle, Iberville Parish

Belle Helene (Ashland) plantation, near Geismar, Ascension Parish
    Pigeonnier

Bermuda (Oakland) plantation, Highway 494, Bermuda, Natchitoches Parish

Blum House, 630 Louisiana Avenue, Baton Rouge, East Baton Rouge Parish

Bosque House, 617–619 Chartres Street, New Orleans, Orleans Parish

Bosworth-Hammond House, 1126 Washington Avenue, New Orleans, Orleans Parish

Bourbon Street, 701 (commercial building), New Orleans, Orleans Parish

Bourbon Street, 941 (Lafitte's Blacksmith Shop), New Orleans, Orleans Parish

Brame (Brame-Bennett) House, Highway 36, Clinton, East Feliciana Parish

Brevard, Alfred Hamilton, House, 1239 First Street, New Orleans, Orleans Parish

Burnside (Houmas House), Highway 1, Ascension Parish

Cabildo, Jackson Square, New Orleans, Orleans Parish

Castillon House (Tremoulet's Hotel), Decatur and St. Peter Streets, New Orleans, Orleans Parish

Central Congregational Church, South Liberty and Cleveland Streets, New Orleans, Orleans Parish

Chartres Street Building, Chartres Street, New Orleans, Orleans Parish

Chesneau Mansion, 533 St. Louis Street, New Orleans, Orleans Parish

Chrétien Point plantation, near Sunset, St. Landry Parish

Church of the Immaculate Conception, 132 Baronne Street, New Orleans, Orleans Parish

City (Gallier) Hall, 545 St. Charles Avenue, New Orleans, Orleans Parish

Clinton (East Feliciana Parish) Courthouse, St. Helena Street, Clinton, East Feliciana Parish

Columbia plantation, Edgard, St. John the Baptist Parish

Columbia (Paramount) Theatre, Riverside Mall, Baton Rouge, East Baton Rouge Parish

Convent of Notre Dame, 835 Josephine Street, New Orleans, Orleans Parish

Convent of the Holy Family, 717 Orleans Street, New Orleans, Orleans Parish

Convent of the Sacred Heart, Grand Coteau, St. Landry Parish

Cooley, G. B., House, 1011 South Grand Street, Monroe, Ouachita Parish

Crescent Farm plantation (Robicheaux House, Hymel House), SW of River Road, St. James Parish

Crowell Lumber Mill, U.S. Highway 165, Longleaf, Rapides Parish

Dabney, Lavinia C., House, 2265 St. Charles Avenue, New Orleans, Orleans Parish

Daneel Street, 3417–3419, New Orleans, Orleans Parish

Daneel Street, 3421–3423, New Orleans, Orleans Parish

Labatut plantation, River Road, N of
New Roads, Pointe Coupee Parish
Main House
La Cour, Nicholas, House, Rougon,
Pointe Coupee Parish
Lafitte's Blacksmith Shop, 941 Bourbon
Street, New Orleans, Orleans Parish
Lakeside plantation (*pigeonniers*),
Batchelor, Pointe Coupee Parish
Lanoix, Louis, House, 514–518
Toulouse Street, New Orleans,
Orleans Parish
La Rionda Cottage, 1218-1220 Burgundy
Street, New Orleans, Orleans Parish
Lastrapes House, N of Opelousas, St.
Landry Parish
Latour and Laclotte's Atelier, 625–627
Dauphine Street, New Orleans,
Orleans Parish
Laura plantation, River Road, Vacherie,
St. James Parish
Laurel Street Station, 1801 Laurel Street,
Baton Rouge, East Baton Rouge
Parish
Lawyer's Row, St. Helena Street and
Liberty Road, Clinton, East Feliciana
Parish
Layton Castle, 1133 South Grand Street,
Monroe, Ouachita Parish
Lear, Alston, House, 2016–2018
Louisiana Avenue, New Orleans,
Orleans Parish
Le Beau (Nicholas La Cour) House,
Rougon, Pointe Coupee Parish
Lehmann House, Hahnville, St. Charles
Parish
Lemee House, 308–309 Jefferson Street,
Natchitoches, Natchitoches Parish
Le Prêtre Mansion, 716 Dauphine Street,
New Orleans, Orleans Parish
Live Oak plantation house (Old Powers
Place), Highland Road, south of
Baton Rouge, East Baton Rouge
Parish (moved from St. Landry Parish)
Live Oak plantation house, between
Weyanoke and Bains, West Feliciana
Parish

Lombard Manor House, 3931 Chartres
Street, New Orleans, Orleans Parish
Louisiana Avenue, 2000-2001, New
Orleans, Orleans Parish
Louisiana Avenue, 2010-2010 1/2, New
Orleans, Orleans Parish
Louisiana State Bank, 403 Royal Street,
New Orleans, Orleans Parish
Louisiana State (Old State) Capitol,
North Boulevard, St. Philip, America,
Front Streets, Baton Rouge, East
Baton Rouge Parish
Louisiana State Museum Buildings, New
Orleans, Orleans Parish
Calaboose Building, 616 Orleans
Alley
Jackson House, St. Peter Street
and Cabildo Avenue (Pirate's
Alley)
Louisiana State Prison (prison store,
warden's house), 703 Laurel Street,
Baton Rouge, East Baton Rouge Parish
Louisiana State University Livestock
Judging Pavilion, Louisiana State
University, Baton Rouge, East Baton
Rouge Parish
Louisiana Sugar Exchange, North Front
and Bienville Streets, New Orleans,
Orleans Parish
Lyons Warehouse, Water and Main
Streets, Washington, St. Landry Parish

Madame John's Legacy, 632 Dumaine
Street, New Orleans, Orleans Parish
Magnolia Mound plantation house, 2161
Nicholson Drive, Baton Rouge, East
Baton Rouge Parish
Magnolia plantation, Highway 119,
Natchitoches, Natchitoches Parish
Blacksmith shop
Corncrib
Cotton gin press
Hospital
Magnolia store
Pigeonnier, fattening pen
Privy
Slave quarters

Magnolia Ridge plantation house, De
Jean Street, Washington, St. Landry
Parish
Marine Hospital, New Orleans, Orleans
Parish
Martin House, St. Martinville, St.
Martin Parish
Meeker Sugar Cooperative, U.S. Highway
71, near Lecompte, Rapides Parish
Administrative office
Chemist's office
Sugar mill
Syrup canning building
Warehouse, privy
Melrose (Yucca) plantation, Highway
119, Natchitoches, Natchitoches Parish
Africa House
Slave hospital
Yucca House
Michel-Pitot House, 1440 Moss Street
(moved from 1370 Moss Street), New
Orleans, Orleans Parish
Montegut (Logue) plantation, La Place,
St. John the Baptist Parish

Nicholson House, Corso Street,
Washington, St. Landry Parish
Nicolas, Valery, House (Casa Flinard,
Casa Hinard), 723 Toulouse Street,
New Orleans, Orleans Parish
Northwestern State University Women's
Gymnasium, U.S. Highway 6,
Natchitoches, Natchitoches Parish

Oakland (Bermuda) plantation,
Highway 494, Bermuda, Natchitoches
Parish
Barn
Carpenter's shop
Carriage house
Chicken coop
Cook's house
Corral shed
Doctor's house
Fattening pen
North *pigeonnier*
Overseer's house

HABS BUILDINGS NOT YET CATALOGED BY THE LIBRARY OF CONGRESS

St. Gabriel Catholic Church, St. Gabriel, Iberville Parish, 1993

Starhill plantation billiard hall, West Feliciana Parish, 1996

Wells-Buard House, Natchitoches, Natchitoches Parish, 1996

Woodlawn plantation, Plaquemines Parish, 1996

HABS BUILDINGS
ILLUSTRATED LISTING BY PARISH
ABBREVIATIONS
Holdings

MD   Measured drawings

P   Photographs

O   Other material, such as sketches, watercolors, compilations of data

Repositories

C   Centenary College Library

HNOC   Historic New Orleans Collection

HT   Louisiana Collection, Howard-Tilton Memorial Library, Tulane University

LC   Prints and Documents Division, Library of Congress

LSA   Louisiana State Archives

LSL   Louisiana State Library

LSMM   Louisiana State Museum (Mint)

LSU   Louisiana and Lower Mississippi Valley Collections, Hill Memorial Library, Louisiana State University

---

Further information about the Historic American Buildings Survey is available through the Library of Congress, Prints and Photographs Section, Washington, D.C. Reproductions of HABS material are available through the Library of Congress, Photoduplication Services. HABS submissions to the Library of Congress after 1989, however, are not yet cataloged. Reproductions of HABS material from 1981 and later are available from the Louisiana State Archives, Baton Rouge. The number to the right of each name here—*e.g.,* LA-80—is useful in requesting information or reproductions.

LT   Louisiana Tech University Library

NOR   New Orleans Reproduction

SEAA   Southeastern Architectural Archive, Howard-Tilton Memorial Library, Tulane University

SHPO   Division of Historic Preservation, Department of Culture, Recreation and Tourism, State Historic Preservation Office

TU   School of Architecture, Tulane University

USL   University of Southwestern Louisiana Library

ASCENSION PARISH

HABS, Richard Koch

Ashland (Belle Helene) plantation /LA-80
Geismar

1841
Attributed to James Gallier or James Dakin, architect

HNOC: MD, P, O. LC: MD, P, O. LSA: MD. LSMM: P. SEAA: P, O. SHPO: MD, P. USL: MD, P, O.

HABS, Richard Koch, 1936

Houmas House /LA-26
Burnside

Early nineteenth century, rebuilt 1840

HNOC: MD, P, O. HT: MD. LC: MD, P, O. LSMM: MD, P. LSU: MD. SEAA: MD, P. TU: MD. USL: MD, P, O.

ASSUMPTION PARISH

HABS, Richard Koch, 1937

Woodlawn plantation house /LA-20
Napoleonville

Main house, 1840; wings, 1850; demolished
Henry Howard, architect

C: MD. HNOC: MD, P, O. LC: MD, P, O. LSA: MD. LSL: MD. LSMM: MD, P, O. NOR: MD. SEAA: MD, P. TU: MD. USL: MD, P.

CADDO PARISH

HABS, T. C. Smith, 1978

United States Post Office and Courthouse /LA-1125
Texas and Marshall Streets, Shreveport

1910–1912
James K. Taylor, architect for Treasury Department

HNOC: MD, P. LC: MD, P, O. USL: MD, P, O.

EAST BATON ROUGE PARISH

Blum House /LA-1126
630 Louisiana Avenue, Baton Rouge
Mid– to late nineteenth century
LC: MD, P, O. LSL: P.

Columbia (Paramount) Theatre /LA-1133
Riverside Mall, Baton Rouge
1920; demolished
Walter E. Stephens, of Prather and Stephens, architect
LC: P, O. LSL: MD, P.

Grand Theatre /LA-1128
133 South Twelfth Street, Baton Rouge
1915; demolished
LC: P, O. LSL: P.

Knox Cottage /LA-1129
1029 America Street, Baton Rouge
1890s; demolished
LC: P, O. LSL: P.

Laurel Street Station /LA-1127
1801 Laurel Street, Baton Rouge
1924–1925
W. T. (or T. T.) Nolan, architect
LC: MD, P, O. LSL: P.

Live Oak plantation house (Old Powers Place) /LA-1188
Highland Road, south of Baton Rouge (moved from St. Landry Parish)
1825
LC: MD, P, O. SHPO: MD.

Louisiana State (Old State) Capitol /LA-1132
North Boulevard, St. Philip, America, Front Streets, Baton Rouge

1847–1849, damaged by fire 1862, rebuilt and enlarged 1880–1882
James H. Dakin, architect 1847–1849; William A. Freret, architect 1880–1882
LC: P, O. LSL: P.

Louisiana State Prison: Prison store, warden's house /LA-1140
703 Laurel Street, Baton Rouge
1838–1839, remodeled 1945
A. Hays Town, architect for remodeling
LC: P, O. LSL: P.

Louisiana State University Livestock Judging Pavilion (Building No. 23) /LA-1207A
Tower Drive, Baton Rouge
1923
Theodore C. Link, architect
LC: MD, O. LSU: MD. LSA: MD, O. SHPO: MD.

Magnolia Mound plantation house /LA-1130
2161 Nicholson Drive, Baton Rouge
Ca. 1790, enlarged *ca.* 1815
LC: MD, P, O. LSA: MD, O. SHPO: MD, P.

Planter's cabin /LA-1135
7815 Highland Road, Baton Rouge
Late 1700s, early 1800s; demolished
LC: P, O. LSL: P.

Post Office (City Club) /LA-1131
355 North Boulevard, Baton Rouge
1894–1897
LC: P, O. LSL: P.

St. James Episcopal Church /LA-1136
208 North Fourth Street, Baton Rouge
1895
Colonel W. L. Stephens, architect
LC: P, O. LSL: P.

Santa Maria plantation /LA-1137
Perkins Road, Baton Rouge

1870s
LC: P, O. LSL: P.

**Suburb Gracie (The Lakes): Five
houses** /LA-1138, 1138A–D
1660 Gracie Street, Baton Rouge (one
example)
First quarter of twentieth century
LC: P, O. LSL: P.

Tessier Building /LA-1139
342–348 Lafayette Street, Baton Rouge
1820–1850
LC: P, O. LSL: P.

**United States Arsenal Powder
Magazine** /LA-1215
East Garden, State Capitol Grounds,
Baton Rouge
1838
LC: MD, O. LSA: MD. SHPO: MD, P.

United States (Pentagon) Barracks /LA-
1134
Riverside Mall, Capitol Avenue, Front
Street, Baton Rouge
1819–1824
Captain James Gadsden, U.S. Army
engineer, architect
LC: P, O. LSL: P.

Willow Grove plantation /LA-1238
18367 Perkins Road, Baton Rouge
Early nineteenth century
LC: MD, O. LSA: MD. LSU: MD. SHPO:
MD, O.

EAST FELICIANA PARISH

Brame (Brame-Bennett) House /LA-40
Highway 36, Clinton
1832–1842
HNOC: MD, P, O. HT: MD. LC: P, O.
LSL: MD, P. LSMM: MD, P, O. LSU:
MD. NOR: MD. SEAA: MD, P. TU:
MD. USL: MD, P, O.

HABS, Richard Koch, 1936

East Feliciana Parish Courthouse LA-30

St. Helena Street, Clinton

Finished 1839–1840

S. J. Savage, architect; Lafayette Sanders, builder

HNOC: MD, P, O. HT: MD. LC: MD, P, O. LSA: MD. LSL: MD, P. LSMM: MD, P, O. LSU: MD. NOR: MD. SEAA: MD, P. TU: MD. USL: MD, P, O.

HABS, Richard Koch

Lawyers' Row /LA-31

St. Helena Street and Liberty Road, Clinton

Ca. 1841

HNOC: MD, P, O. LC: MD, P, O. LSA: MD. LSL: MD, P. LSMM: MD, O. LSU: MD. NOR: MD. SEAA: MD, P. TU: MD. USL: MD, P.

IBERIA PARISH

HABS

HABS

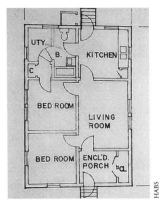

HABS

Avery Island Salt Mine Village: Baptist church, Bradford Club, company store, salt workers' houses Nos. 1–6

/LA-1120, 1120A–H

Avery Island

1899

LC: MD, O. SHPO: MD, P.

La Cour, Nicholas, House. *See* **Le Beau House, under Pointe Coupee Parish**

HABS, Frances Benjamin Johnston, 1936

Shadows-on-the-Teche (David Weeks House) /LA-75

Main and Weeks Streets, New Iberia

1832

Jeremiah Clark, brickmason; James Bedell, carpenter

HNOC: MD, P, O. LC: P, O. LSL: MD, O. LSMM: P, O. LSU: MD. SEAA: MD, P. USL: MD, P, O.

HABS

Tango Village: Tabasco Deli company store, Tabasco workers' houses Nos. 1–3 /LA-1219

Avery Island

1910

LC: MD, O. LSA: MD. SHPO: MD. USL: MD.

IBERVILLE PARISH

SHPO

Bagatelle plantation: North kitchen support building, south kitchen support building, south slave cabin, stables /LA-1142, 1142A–D

Near Sunshine (moved from St. James Parish)

1841–1842

LC: P (LA-1142, 1142A–D), O (LA-1142).

HABS, Thomas Waterman

Belle Grove plantation house /LA-36

Near White Castle

1857; demolished

Henry Howard, architect

C: MD. HNOC: MD, P, O. HT: MD. LC: P, O. LSL: P. LSMM: P, O. LSU: MD. NOR: MD. SEAA: MD, P, O. TU: MD. USL: MD, P, O.

Iberville Parish Courthouse /LA-1208
209 Main Street, Plaquemine

1848

Henry Howard, architect

LC: MD, O. LSA: MD, O. SHPO: MD, P.

Kroll House: Plantation /LA-1179
Near Iberville (moved from St. John the Baptist Parish)

Ca. 1825

LC: MD, O. LSA: MD. SHPO: MD. SEAA: MD.

Variety plantation /LA-1141
Highway 3066, Bayou Plaquemine

Ca. 1855

LC: MD, O. SHPO: P.

LAFAYETTE PARISH

Bank of Lafayette (Old City Hall) /LA-1154
217 West Main Street, Lafayette

Ca. 1898

George Knapp, architect

LC: P, O.

Sears Department Store (Lafayette City Hall) /LA-1157
705 West University Avenue, Lafayette

1956–1957

George H. Dahl and Associates, architects; G. E. Bass, builder

LC: P, O.

LINCOLN PARISH

Autrey House /LA-1217A
Highway 151, Dubach

1849

LC: MD, O. LSA: MD. LT: MD. SHPO: MD.

Nolan House /LA-1217B
Highway 151, Dubach

1840; demolished

LC: MD, O. LSA: MD, O. LT: MD. SHPO: MD.

NATCHITOCHES PARISH

Balcony Building /LA-2-3
120 Washington Street, Natchitoches

1830

Triscini and Soldini, architects

HNOC: P, O. LC: P, O LSMM P.

Bermuda (Prudhomme family) plantation. *See* Oakland (Bermuda) plantation

Church of the Immaculate Conception /LA-2-4
Second and Church Streets, Natchitoches

1856

HNOC: P, O. LC: P, O.

Duplex columns /LA-2-5

312 Jefferson Street, Natchitoches

Ca. 1850

HNOC: P, O. LC: P, O. LSMM: P.

Lemee House /LA-2-193

308–309 Jefferson Street, Natchitoches

Ca. 1830

Triscini and Soldini, architects

HNOC: MD, P, O. HT: MD. LC: P, O.
LSL: MD, P. LSMM: MD. LSU: MD.
NOR: MD. SEAA: MD. TU: MD. USL:
MD.

**Magnolia plantation: Blacksmith
shop, corncrib, cotton gin press,
hospital, Magnolia store,** *pigeonnier*
**and fattening pen, privy, slave
quarters (house in slave quarters
illustrated)** /LA-1193, 1193A–H

Highway 119, Natchitoches

1830–1880

Ambrose Lecompte II, builder

LC: MD, P, O. LSA: MD. SHPO: MD.

**Melrose (Yucca) plantation: Africa
House, slave hospital** /LA-2-69, 2-
69A, B

Highway 119, Natchitoches

Ca. 1820; main house, 1830s

Marie Therese "Coin-Coin," Henry
family, builders

Melrose: HNOC: MD, P, O. LC: P, O.
LSL: P.

Africa House: C: MD. HNOC: MD. HT:
MD. LSL: MD, P. LSU: MD. NOR: MD.
SEAA: MD. TU: MD.

Slave hospital: HNOC: P, O. LC: P, O.

Yucca House: SHPO: MD. LSA: MD.
LSU: MD.

**Northwestern State University
Women's Gymnasium** /LA-1209A

U.S. Highway 6, Natchitoches

1923

Favrot and Livaudais, architects

LC: MD, O. LSA: MD, O. SHPO: MD, P.

**Oakland (Bermuda) plantation: Barn
(1), carpenter's shop (2), carriage
house, chicken coop, cook's house,
corral shed, doctor's house (3),
fattening pen, north** *pigeonnier* **(4),
overseer's house (5), plantation store
and post office (6), settling pen,**

slave quarters, south *pigeonnier*, stables, storage shed, washhouse /LA-1192, 1192A–Q
Highway 494, Bermuda
Ca. 1820
HNOC: MD, P, O. LC: MD, P, O. LSA: MD. SHPO: MD.

Prudhomme-Hughes Building / LA-2-7
Natchitoches
Ca. 1845
HNOC: P, O. LC: P, O. LSA: P. LSMM: P.

Tauzin-Wells House /LA-2-8
Natchitoches
Late eighteenth century
HNOC: P, O. LC: P, O. LSMM: P.

Trinity Episcopal Church /LA-2-6
Natchitoches
1857
HNOC: P, O. LC: P, O.

ORLEANS PARISH

Archbishopric (Ursuline Convent) /LA-18-2
1114 Chartres Street, New Orleans
1745
Ignace François Broutin, architect; C. Dubreuil, builder
HNOC: MD, P, O. HT: MD. LC: MD, P, O. LSA: MD. LSMM: MD, P, O. LSU: MD. NOR: MD. SEAA: MD, P. TU: MD. USL: MD, P, O.

Arsenal /LA-18-6
615 St. Peter Street, New Orleans
1839
James Harrison Dakin, of Dakin and Dakin, architect
HNOC: MD, P. HT: MD. LC: MD, P, O. LSA: MD. LSL: MD, P. LSMM: MD, O. LSU: MD. NOR: MD. SEAA: MD, P, O. TU: MD. USL: MD, P, O.

Bank of the United States /LA-1159
Location: 339 Royal Street, New Orleans
1800
Attributed to Barthelemy Lafon, architect
LC: O.

Beauregard House /LA-18-1
Location: 1113 Chartres Street, New Orleans
1826
François Edouard Correjolles, architect; James Lambert, builder
HNOC: MD, P, O. HT: MD. LC: MD, P, O. LSA: MD. LSMM: MD, P, O. LSU: MD. NOR: MD. SEAA: MD, P. TU: MD, O. USL: MD, P, O.

Bosque House /LA-81
617–619 Chartres Street, New Orleans
1795, rebuilt prior to 1816

HNOC: MD. HT: MD. LC: MD, P, O. LSMM: MD, P, O. LSU: MD. NOR: MD. SEAA: MD. TU: MD, O. USL: MD.

Bosworth-Hammond House /LA-1143
1126 Washington Avenue, New Orleans

1859

Thomas K. Wharton, architect

LC: P, O.

Bourbon Street: Commercial buildings /LA-1144
701 Bourbon St.

Ca. 1811

LC: P, O.

Bourbon Street Cottage (Lafitte's Blacksmith Shop) /LA-24
941 Bourbon Street, New Orleans

Ca. 1795

HNOC: MD, P, O. HT: MD. LC: MD, P, O. LSA: MD. LSMM: MD, O. LSU: MD. NOR: MD. SEAA: MD, P. TU: MD. USL: MD.

Brevard, Alfred Hamilton, House /LA-1118
1239 First Street, New Orleans

1857

James B. Calrow, architect; Charles Pride, builder

HNOC: MD, P. HT: MD. LC: MD, P, O. LSU: MD. SEAA: MD. TU: MD. USL: MD.

Cabildo /LA-18-4
Jackson Square, New Orleans

1795, mansard roof added 1850s
Gilberto Guillemard, architect

HNOC: MD, P, O. HT: MD. LC: MD, P, O. LSA: MD. LSL: MD, P. LSMM: MD. NOR: MD. SEAA: MD, P, O. TU: MD. USL: MD, P, O.

Castillon House (Tremoulet's Hotel) /LA-191
Decatur and St. Peter Streets, New Orleans

1811; demolished
Latour and Laclotte, architects; Joseph Guillot, Claude Gurley, builders

HNOC: O. LC: MD. LSMM: P.

Central Congregational Church /LA-22
South Liberty and Cleveland Streets, New Orleans

1846; demolished
Samuel Jamison, James McIntosh, architects

HNOC: MD, P, O. HT: MD. LC: MD, P, O. LSA: MD. LSMM: MD. LSU: MD. NOR: MO. SEAA: MD, P. TU: MD. USL: MD, P, O.

Chartres Street Building /LA-1144
Chartres Street, New Orleans

1850s; demolished

LC: P, O.

Chesneau Mansion /LA-1190
533 St. Louis Street, New Orleans

1801–1803

LC: MD, O. LSA: MD, O. SHPO: MD.

HABS

Church of the Immaculate Conception
/LA-1147
132 Baronne Street, New Orleans

1857, rebuilt 1927–1928

T. E. Giraud, Hogan and Bernard, architects; James Freret, architect for high altar

LC: P, O. SEAA: P, O.

HABS

City (Gallier) Hall /LA-193
545 St. Charles Avenue, New Orleans

1850

James Gallier, architect

HNOC: P. LC: P, O.

HABS, Richard Koch

Convent of Notre Dame /LA-1102
835 Josephine Street, New Orleans

1854

HNOC: P. LC: P, O. SEAA: P.

Convent of the Holy Family. *See* **Orleans Ballroom**

HABS

Dabney, Lavinia C., House /LA-1113
2265 St. Charles Avenue, New Orleans

1857

James Gallier, Jr., John Turpin, architects

HNOC: P. LC: P, O.

Julie H. McCollam, 1994

Dauphine Street House /LA-1173
631–633 Dauphine Street, New Orleans

Probably *ca.* 1810

Probably Latour and Laclotte, architects

LC: O. LSMM: P.

Julie H. McCollam, 1994

Dauphine Street House /LA-1172
1113–1115 Dauphine Street, New Orleans

1825

LC: O. LSMM: P, O.

Julie H. McCollam, 1996

Dujarreau-Rouquette House /LA-1170
413 Royal Street, New Orleans

1804–1807

LC: O. LSMM: P, O.

R. Christopher Goodwin and Associates, Kathryn M. Kuranda

Duncan, Albert, House /LA-1223
2010–2010 1/2 Louisiana Avenue, New Orleans

Early twentieth century; demolished

LC: P, O.

Duplantier family tomb /LA-1107

St. Louis Cemetery No. 2, North Claiborne Avenue, New Orleans

1842

J. N. B. de Pouilly, architect; P. H. Monsseaux, builder

HNOC: MD. LC: MD, P, O. LSU: MD.

Faubourg Marigny: Filling station /LA-27G

Burgundy and St. Roch Streets, New Orleans

1840s; demolished

LC: P, O.

Faubourg Marigny: General view /LA-27B

Kelerec and Pauger Streets, New Orleans

1815–1890

LC: P, O.

Faubourg Marigny: House /LA-27D

2519 Dauphine Street, New Orleans

1870s

LC: P, O.

Faubourg Marigny: Laundry (Cardau Drugs) /LA-27C

Spain and Burgundy Streets, New Orleans

Second half of nineteenth century; demolished

LC: P, O.

Faubourg Marigny: House /LA-27A

2447–2449 Royal Street, New Orleans

1880s

LC: P, O.

Faubourg Marigny: General view /LA-27B

Spain and Burgundy Streets, New Orleans

1850–1870

LC: P, O.

Faubourg Marigny: House /LA-27F

1451 Pauger Street, New Orleans

1870s

LC: P, O.

Faubourg Marigny: House /LA-27E

1463 Pauger Street, New Orleans

1870s

LC: P, O.

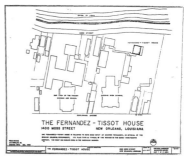

Fernandez-Tissot House /LA-1117

1400 Moss Street, New Orleans

Prior to 1819, remodeled 1850–1860; demolished
André Fernandez, architect

HNOC: MD. LC: P. LSMM: P. LSU: MD.

Ferrera Tenement House I /LA-1226

3417–3419 Daneel Street, New Orleans

Early twentieth century; demolished

LC: P, O.

R. Christopher Goodwin and Associates, Kathryn M. Kurandia

Ferrera Tenement House II /LA-1227

3421–3423 Daneel Street, New Orleans

Early twentieth century; demolished

LC: P, O.

HABS, Richard Koch, 1938

First Presbyterian Church /LA-1103

South Street, New Orleans

1857; demolished
Henry Howard, architect

LC: P, O. SEAA: P.

Julie H. McCollam, 1994

First skyscraper (Lemonnier House)
/LA-21

638 Royal Street, New Orleans

Ca. 1795

Probably Bartolome Lafon, first
architect; Latour and Laclotte,
architects for completion in 1811

HNOC: MD, P, O. HT: MD. LC: MD, P,
O. LSA: MD. LSL: MD, P. LSMM: O.
LSU: MD. NOR: MD. SEAA: MD, P.
TU: MD. USL: MD, P, O.

Julie H. McCollam, 1994

Forstall, Edmund J., House /LA-1114

920 St. Louis Street, New Orleans

Ca. 1845
James Gallier, Jr., John Turpin, architects

HNOC: P, O. LC: P, O.

Julie H. McCollam, 1995

Fouche House /LA-1148

619 Bourbon Street, New Orleans

1810–1812
Latour and Laclotte, architects

HT: MD. LC: MD, P, O. LSMM: P. SEAA:
MD. TU: MD, O. USL: MD.

Julie H. McCollam, 1994

Gaillard House /LA-69

915–917 St. Ann Street, New Orleans

1824

LC: P, O. LSMM: P.

Gallier Hall. *See* **City (Gallier) Hall**

Gallier House /LA-1211

1132 Royal Street, New Orleans

1857
James Gallier, Jr., architect

LC: MD, O. LSA: MD. SEAA: O. SHPO:
MD.

HABS, Richard Koch

Gally House /LA-29

536 Chartres Street, New Orleans

1830
Gurlie and Guillot, architect-builders

HNOC: MD, P, O. HT: MD. LC: MD, P,
O. LSA: MD. LSMM: MD, O. NOR:
MD. SEAA: MD, P. TU: MD. USL: MD.

Gaudet House /LA-1149
Chestnut and Josephine Streets, New
Orleans

Late 1850s

LC: P, O.

Girod (Napoleon) House /LA-18-9
500–506 Chartres Street, New Orleans

1814

Probably Hyacinthe Laclotte, architect

HNOC: MD, P, O. HT: MD. LC: MD, P,
O. LSA: MD. LSL: MD, P. LSMM: MD,
P, O. LSU: MD, NOR: MD. SEAA: MD,
P, TU: MD. USL: MD, P, O.

Governor Nicholls Street House /LA-
1150
524 Governor Nicholls Street, New
Orleans

1836–1838
Attributed to Claude Gurlie, architect-
builder

LC: P, O. LSMM: P, O. SEAA: P.

Grailhe family tomb /LA-1108
St. Louis Cemetery No. 2, North
Claiborne Avenue, New Orleans

1850
J. N. B. de Pouilly, architect; P. H.
Monsseaux, builder

HNOC: MD, P. LC: MD, P, O. LSU:
MD.

**Grinnan, Robert A. (Grinnan-
Henderson-Reily), House** /
LA-1120
2221 Prytania Street, New Orleans

1850
Henry Howard, architect

HNOC: MD. HT: MD. LC: MD, P, O.
LSL: P. SEAA: MD, P. TU: MD. USL:
MD.

**Grinnan, Robert A. (Grinnan-
Henderson-Reily), House:**
Garçonnière /LA-1121
2221 Prytania Street, New Orleans

1920s

LC: P, O.

Hermann-Grima House /LA-1122
820 St. Louis Street, New Orleans

Ca. 1831
William Brand, architect

HNOC: P. LC: P, O. LSMM: P. SEAA:
P, O.

Hermann-Grima House: *Garçonnière*
and kitchen /LA-1123
820 St. Louis Street, New Orleans

Ca. 1831

William Brand, architect

HNOC: P. LC: P, O.

Irish Channel Historic District:
General view /LA-28A

Fourth Street, New Orleans

1870s

LC: P, O.

Irish Channel Historic District:
General view /LA-28B

Rousseau Street, New Orleans

Late 1830s

LC: P, O.

Lanoix, Louis, House /LA-1115

514–518 Toulouse Street, New Orleans

1818–1820

HNOC: MD, P. HT: MD. LC: MD, P, O.
LSU: MD. SEAA: MD, O. TU: MD.
USL: MD.

La Rionda Cottage /LA-192

1218–1220 Burgundy Street, New Orleans

1810; demolished

HNOC: MD. HT: MD. LC: MD, P, O.
LSMM: MD, O. LSU: MD. NOR: MD.
SEAA: MD, P. TU: MD.

Latour and Laclotte's Atelier /LA-1151

625–627 Dauphine Street, New Orleans

1811

Latour and Laclotte, architects; Gurlie
and Guillot, builders

HT: MD. LC: MD, P, O. NOR: MD.
SEAA: MD. TU: MD. USL: MD.

Lear, Alston, House /LA-1224

2016–2018 Louisiana Avenue, New Orleans

Early twentieth century; demolished

LC: P, O.

Le Prêtre Mansion /LA-53

716 Dauphine Street, New Orleans

1836

Frederick Roy, architect

HNOC: MD, P, O. HT: MD. LC: MD, P,
O. LSA: O. LSMM: MD, P, O. LSU:
MD. NOR: MD. SEAA: MD, P. TU:
MD. USL: MD.

Lombard Manor House /LA-1197

3931 Chartres Street, New Orleans

1826

LC: MD, O. LSA: MD. SEAA: MD.
SHPO: MD.

Louisiana State Bank /LA-18-8

403 Royal Street, New Orleans

Ca. 1820

Benjamin Henry Latrobe, architect;
Benjamin Fox, builder; Diboll, Owen
and Goldstein, architects for
restoration in 1910–1911

HNOC: MD, P. HT: MD. LC: MD, P, O.
LSA: MD, O. LSMM: MD, P, O. LSU:
MD. NOR: MD. SEAA: MD, P. TU:
MD. USL: MD, P, O.

Julie H. McCollam, 1996

**Louisiana State Museum: Calaboose
Building** /LA-18-10A
616 Orleans Alley, New Orleans

Ca. 1850

HNOC: P. LC: P, O. LSL: P. SEAA: P.

Julie H. McCollam, 1996

**Louisiana State Museum: Jackson
House** /LA-18-10B
St. Peter Street and Cabildo Avenue
(Pirate's Alley), New Orleans

Ca. 1933
Weiss, Dreyfous and Seiferth, architects

HNOC: P. LC: P, O. SEAA: P. USL: P.

HABS, Dan Leyrer, 1963

Louisiana Sugar Exchange /LA-1110
North Front and Bienville Streets, New
Orleans

1883–1884; demolished
James Freret, architect; Joseph R. Turck,
builder

HNOC: P. LC: P, O.

HABS, Lester Jones

Madame John's Legacy /LA-39
632 Dumaine Street, New Orleans

Prior to 1776; restored 1972–1973

HNOC: MD, P, O. HT: MD. LC: MD, P,
O. LSA: O. LSL: P. LSMM: MD. SEAA:
MD, P, O. SHPO: MD. TU: MD, O.

HABS

Marine Hospital /LA-1153
New Orleans

1838–1849; demolished

LC: P, O.

HABS, Frances Benjamin Johnston

Michel-Pitot House /LA-116
1440 Moss Street (moved from 1370 Moss
Street), New Orleans

1800–1805
Hilaire Boutte, builder

HNOC: MD, O. LC: MD, P, O. LSMM: P.
LSU: MD. USL: MD.

HABS

**Nicolas, Valery, House (Casa Flinard,
Casa Hinard)** /LA-33
723 Toulouse Street, New Orleans

1808

HNOC: MD, P. O. LC: MD, P, O. LSA:
MD. LSMM: MD, P, O. LSU: MD.
NOR: MD. SEAA: P, O. TU: MD.

HABS, Richard Koch, 1934

**Olivier, David, House (Olivier
plantation)** /LA-70
4111 Chartres Street, New Orleans

Ca. 1820, outbuildings later;
demolished

HNOC: MD, P, O. HT: MD. LC: MD, P, O. LSMM: P, O. LSU: MD. SEAA: MD. TU: MD. USL: MD.

Orleans Ballroom (Convent of the Holy Family) /LA-1155

717 Orleans Street, New Orleans

Original building, prior to 1816; second building, 1817; demolished

Henry S. Latrobe, architect for original building; William and John Brand, architects for second building

HT: MD. LC: MD, P, O. SEAA: MD. TU: MD, O. USL: MD.

Our Lady of Guadalupe Catholic Church (Mortuary Chapel of St. Anthony of Padua) /LA-1104

411 North Rampart Street, New Orleans

1827

Joseph Pilie, architect; Gurlie and Guillot, builders

HNOC: P. LC: MD, P, O. LSMM: P. SEAA: P, O.

Pauger Street Cottage /LA-23

1436 Pauger Street, New Orleans

1820

Jean Louis Dolliole, builder

HNOC: MD, P, O. HT: MD. LC: MD, P, O. LSL: MD, P. LSMM: MD, O. NOR: MD. SEAA: MD.

Presbytère /LA-18-5

Jackson Square, New Orleans

1789

Gilberto Guillemard, architect

HNOC: MD, P. HT: MD. LC: MD, P, O. LSA: MD. LSL: MD, P. LSMM: MD, O. LSU: MD. NOR: MD. SEAA: P. TU: MD. USL: MD, P, O.

Pumping Station No. 6, New Orleans Sewerage and Water Board /LA-1235

Orpheum Avenue and Hyacinth Street, New Orleans

Ca. 1900

LC: MD. LSA: MD. LSU: MD. SHPO: MD.

Robinson-Jordan House /LA-1156

1415 Third Street, New Orleans

1850s

Attributed to James Gallier, architect

LC: P, O. LSMM: O. SEAA: P, O.

Rouselle House /LA-1225

2012–2014 Louisiana Avenue, New Orleans

Early twentieth century; demolished

LC: P, O.

Royal Street Commercial Buildings /LA-176

New Orleans

1830s

LC: P, O.

Royal Street House /LA-1175

600 Royal Street, New Orleans

1805–1815, remodeled 1825, third floor
   added to service wing 1841
Box, Bickle and Hamblet, architects-
   builders for third floor on service
   wing
LC: O.

**St. John the Baptist Catholic
   Church** /LA-1105
1101 Dryades Street, New Orleans
1869
Albert Diettel, architect; Thomas
   Mulligan, builder
HNOC: P. LC: P. SEAA: P, O.

St. Patrick's Catholic Church /LA-1111
724 Camp Street, New Orleans
1838
Dakin and Dakin, James Gallier,
   architects
HNOC: P, O. LC: P, O.

St. Philip Street House /LA-1174
514–516 St. Philip Street, New Orleans
1830–1831
LC: O.

Seven Oaks (Petit Desert) plantation
   /LA-1158
New Orleans
Ca. 1840; demolished
LC: P, O.

Short, Colonel Robert Henry, House
   /LA-1112
1448 Fourth Street, New Orleans
1859–1866
Henry Howard, Albert Diettel,
   architects; Robert Huyghe, builder
HNOC: P. LC: P, O.

**St. Mary's Assumption Catholic
   Church** /LA-1106
2030 Constance Street, New Orleans
1858
HNOC: P. LC: P, O.

St. Philip Street House /LA-160
931 St. Philip Street, New Orleans
1805
LC: P, O. LSMM: P.

South Street House /LA-1171
618 South Street, New Orleans
1856
William Freret, architect
LC: O. SEAA: P.

HABS, Richard Koch

Spanish Custom House /LA-18-3
1300 Moss Street, New Orleans

1780

C: MD. HNOC: MD, P. HT: MD. LC:
MD, P, O. LSMM: MD, P, O. LSU: MD.
NOR: MD. SEAA: P. TU: MD. USL:
MD, P, O.

HABS

**Spanish Fort Ruins (Fort St. John
Ruins, Bayou St. John Hotel Ruins)**
/LA-18-25
Bayou St. John at Lake Pontchartrain,
New Orleans

1808
U.S. War Department, builder of Fort
St. John

HNOC: MD, P. HT: MD. LC: MD, P.
LSA: MD. LSL: MD, P. LSMM: MD, P,
O. NOR: MD. SEAA: P. TU: MD.

Julie H. McCollam, 1992

Taney, C. H., House /LA-1160
908 St. Louis Street, New Orleans

1835
Edward W. Sewell, builder

LC: P, O.

HABS, 1992

Teche Street House /LA-25
1617–1619 Teche Street, New Orleans

1899

LC: P, O. LSA: P. LSL: P.

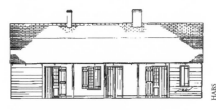

HABS

Troxler-Psayla Cottage /LA-196
919 St. Philip Street, New Orleans

Prior to 1782; demolished

HNOC: MD. HT: MD. LC: MD, O.
LSMM: MD. LSU: MD. NOR: MD.
SEAA: MD. TU: MD. USL: MD.

Julie H. McCollam, 1995

**United States Branch Mint (Federal
Jail)** /LA-1119
400 Esplanade Avenue, New Orleans

1835–1844
William Strickland, architect; John
Mitchell, Benjamin Fox, builders

HNOC: P, O. LC: P, O. LSMM: P.
SEAA: P, O.

Julie H. McCollam, 1996

United States Custom House /LA-1109
423 Canal Street, New Orleans

1849–1861
Alexander Thompson Wood, T. R.
Wharton, Dakin and Gallier,
architects; P. G. T. Beauregard for U.S.
government, builder

HNOC: P, O. LC: P, O. SEAA: P, O.
SHPO: P.

Julie H. McCollam, 1992

**Ursuline Row Houses: Commercial
buildings** /LA-1101-41
1107–1133 Decatur Street, New Orleans

1830–1831
Gurlie and Guillot, builders

LC: P, O. SEAA: P.

**Vieux Carre Squares: 2nd District,
Square No. 62** /LA-1100
Square block bounded by Royal,
Bourbon, St. Louis, Toulouse Streets,
New Orleans

HNOC

**Vieux Carre Squares: Site of Felix de
Armas House** /LA-1100C
513 Royal Street, New Orleans

First House, 1821–1828; present building, 1840s
HNOC: P, O. LC: MD. SEAA: O.

Vieux Carre Squares: Service wing of Peychaud House /LA-41
727 Toulouse Street, New Orleans

Ca. 1830
Gurlie and Guillot, builders

HNOC: MD. HT: MD. LC: MD, O. LSA: MD. LSL: MD. LSMM: MD, O. LSU: MD. TU: MD. USL: MD.

Vieux Carre Squares: Poeyfarre House /LA-1100T
532 Bourbon Street, New Orleans
1848; present building, 1948
HNOC: P, O. LC: MD. SEAA: O.

Vieux Carre Squares: Merieult House /LA-1100O
527–533 Royal Street, New Orleans
1792
HNOC: P, O. LC: MD. LSMM: O.

Vieux Carre Squares: Jean Lacoste Cottage /LA-1100N
526 Bourbon Street, New Orleans
Prior to 1827
HNOC: P, O. LC: MD. SEAA: O.

Vieux Carre Squares: Meilleur House /LA-1100X
511–515 Bourbon Street, New Orleans
1831
HNOC: O. HT: MD. LC: MD, P. LSMM: O. LSU: MD. SEAA: MD.

Vieux Carre Squares: Coffini Cottage /LA-1100G
726–728 Toulouse Street, New Orleans
Prior to 1830
HNOC: O. LC: MD. SEAA: O.

Vieux Carre Squares: Countinghouse of William Nott and Co.—Antoine's restaurant service building—Spanish *commandancia* /LA-1100H
519 Royal Street, New Orleans

Main building and warehouse, *ca.* 1890; two warehouses, 1827
HNOC: P, O. LC: MD. LSMM: O. SEAA: O.

Vieux Carre Squares: Site of Jayme Jorda House /LA-1100J
521–523 Royal Street, New Orleans
1798
HNOC: P, O. LC: MD.

Vieux Carre Squares: Site of Jourdan property /LA-1100K
500 Bourbon Street, New Orleans
Nineteenth century, remodeled twentieth century
HNOC: O. LC: MD. SEAA: O.

Vieux Carre Squares: Vincent Nolte House—Court of the Lions /LA-1100Q
535–541 Royal Street, 708 Toulouse Street, New Orleans
1819
HNOC: P, O. LC: MD, O. LSMM: P, O. SEAA: O.

Vieux Carre Squares: Kohn-Anglade House—Lafcadio Hearn domicile /LA-1100L

516 Bourbon Street, New Orleans

1830s

HNOC: P, O. LC: MD. LSMM: O. SEAA: O.

Vieux Carre Squares: Kohn-Anglade dependencies /LA-1100M

508 Bourbon Street, New Orleans

1827–1836

HNOC: P, O. LC: MD. LSMM: O.

Vieux Carre Squares: Site of Baker d'Acquin House /LA-1100D

720–724 Toulouse Street, New Orleans

1805

HNOC: O. LC: MD. LSMM: O. SEAA: O.

Vieux Carre Squares: Site of Pension de Boulanger /LA-1100R

727–733 St. Louis Street, New Orleans

Prior to 1832

HNOC: P, O. LC: MD. LSMM: O. SEAA: P, O.

Vieux Carre Squares: Site of Planter's Association office /LA-1100S

714 Toulouse Street, New Orleans

Late nineteenth century

HNOC: O. LC: MD.

Vieux Carre Squares: Antoine's restaurant—James Ramsey commercial buildings /LA-1100B

713–717 St. Louis Street, New Orleans

Prior to 1823

HNOC: P, O. LC: MD. LSMM: O. SEAA: O.

Vieux Carre Squares: Rouzan residence /LA-1100W

522 Bourbon Street, New Orleans

Ca. 1840

HNOC: P, O. LC: MD. LSMM: O. SEAA: P, O.

Vieux Carre Squares: Antoine's Restaurant annex /LA-1100A

719–725 St. Louis Street, New Orleans

Ca. 1827, altered *ca.* 1870
William Brand, architect

HNOC: P, O. LC: MD. SEAA: O.

Vieux Carre Squares: Boimare-Schloeman Building /LA-1100E

509–511 Royal Street, New Orleans

1835

HNOC: P, O. LC: MD. LSMM: O. SEAA: O.

Julie H. McCollam, 1995

Vieux Carre Squares: Merieult Stables—Royal House Hotel /LA-1100P

718 Toulouse Street, New Orleans

Original building, *ca.* 1821–1829

HNOC: o. LC: md. SEAA: o.

HNOC

Vieux Carre Squares: Grandchamp's Pharmacie /LA-1100I

501 Royal Street, New Orleans

1800–1820

Antonio Peytavin, Jean Reanaud, architects

HNOC: p, o. LC: md. LSMM: o. SEAA: p, o.

HNOC

Vieux Carre Squares: Widow Roche House /LA-1100V

505 Royal Street, New Orleans

1820, remodeled 1850

HNOC: p, o. LC: md. SEAA: o.

HNOC

Vieux Carre Squares: Poeyfarre Houses /LA-1100U

734–740 Toulouse Street, 540 Bourbon Street, New Orleans

Prior to 1824

HNOC: p, o. LC: md. LSMM: o.

HABS

Vieux Carre Squares: Café Toulousin /LA-1100F

732 Toulouse Street, New Orleans

Prior to 1806

HNOC: p, o. LC: md. LSMM: o. SEAA: p, o.

HABS

Villa Meilleur /LA-1216

1418 Governor Nicholls Street, New Orleans

1828

LC: md, o. LSA: md. SEAA: o. SHPO: md. TU: md.

OUACHITA PARISH

SHPO

Cooley, G. B., House /LA-1230

1011 South Grand Street, Monroe

Designed 1908, built 1926
Walter Burley Griffin, architect

LC: md, o. LSA: md. LT: md.

HABS

Layton Castle /LA-1231

1133 South Grand Street, Monroe

Original house, 1814; present renovation, 1912

LC: md, o. LSA: md. LT: md.

PLAQUEMINES PARISH

HABS, Samuel Wilson, Jr.

Frank's Island Lighthouse /LA-19

Northeast Pass, Mississippi River

1820–1823
Benjamin Henry Latrobe, architect; Winslow Lewis, builder

HNOC: md, p. HT: md. LC: md, p. LSA: md. LSL: md, p. LSMM: md. LSU: md. NOR: md. SEAA: md, p, o. TU:md. USL: md.

POINTE COUPEE PARISH

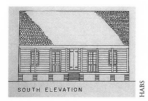

SOUTH ELEVATION

HABS

Alma sugarcane plantation /LA-1239
Lakeland

Early twentieth century

LC: MD, O. LSA: MD. USL: MD.

SHPO

Austerlitz plantation /LA-1228
Highway 1, near Oscar

Ca. 1830

LC: MD, O. LSA: MD. LSU: MD. SHPO:
MD.

HABS, Richard Koch, 1936

Fannie Riche plantation /LA-35
Highway 30, New Roads

1825–1835

C: MD. HNOC: MD, P. LC: MD, P, O.
LSA: MD. LSL: MD, P. LSMM: MD, P.
LSU: MD. NOR: MD. SEAA: MD, P, O.
TU: MD.

HABS

Fannie Riche Cabin /LA-35A
Highway 30, New Roads

1825–1835

LC: P, O. SEAA: P.

HABS

Labatut plantation house /LA-1205A
River Road, N of New Roads

Late eighteenth century

LC: MD, O. LSA: MD, P, O. SEAA: MD.
SHPO: MD.

HABS

Lakeside plantation: *Pigeonniers* /LA-1180A
Batchelor

Ca. 1850

LC: MD, O. LSA: MD. SHPO: MD.

HABS

Le Beau (Nicholas La Cour) House
/LA-95
Rougon

1840

LC: P, O. LSA: MD. LSMM: P. SEAA:
P, O.

HABS, Richard Koch, 1936

Parlange plantation /LA-34
Highway 93, New Roads

Late eighteenth century to 1810

C: MD. HNOC: MD, P. LC: MD, P, O.
LSA: MD. LSL: MD, P. LSMM: MD, P.
LSU: MD. NOR: MD. SEAA: MD, O.
TU: MD. USL: MD.

HABS

Pleasant View Farms /LA-152
New Roads

1820

LC: P, O.

SHPO

Riverlake plantation /LA-1187
North Bend, near Oscar

1823

LC: MD, O. LSA: MD, O. SHPO: MD, P.

HABS

Riverlake plantation: Sugar mill /LA-146
North Bend, near Oscar

1823; demolished

LC: P, O.

Riverlake plantation: *Pigeonniers* **No. 1 and No. 2** /LA-1187A, B
North Bend, near Oscar

1823

LC: MD, O. LSA: MD, O. SHPO: MD.

RAPIDES PARISH

HABS, Lester Jones, 1940

Baillio, Peter, House (Kent House)
/LA-2-1
Bayou Rapides, near Alexandria

Ca. 1795

HNOC: P. LC: P, O. LSMM: P.

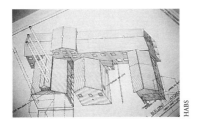

HABS

Crowell Lumber Mill /LA-1233
U.S. Highway 165, Longleaf

1892, renovated 1910, 1920, 1950s

LC: MD, O. LSA: MD. SHPO: MD. USL: MD.

Meeker Sugar Cooperative /LA-1191
U.S. Highway 71, near Lecompte

1912

L. A. Toussaint, brickmason

LC: MD, O. LSA: MD. SHPO: MD.

Meeker Sugar Cooperative: Administrative office /LA-1191E
U.S. Highway 71, near Lecompte

1912

L. A. Toussaint, brickmason

LC: MD, O. LSA: MD. SHPO: MD.

Meeker Sugar Cooperative: Chemist's office /LA-1191D
U.S. Highway 71, near Lecompte

1912

L. A. Toussaint, brickmason

LC: MD, O. LSA: MD. SHPO: MD.

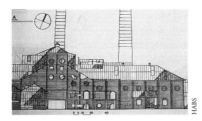

HABS

Meeker Sugar Cooperative: Sugar mill
/LA-1191A
U.S. Highway 71, near Lecompte

1912

L. A. Toussaint, brickmason

LC: MD, O. LSA: MD. SHPO: MD.

Meeker Sugar Cooperative: Syrup canning building /LA-1191B
U.S. Highway 71, near Lecompte

1912

L. A. Toussaint, brickmason

LC: MD, O. LSA: MD. SHPO: MD.

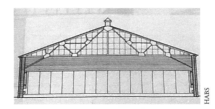

HABS

HABS

NORTHEAST

Meeker Sugar Cooperative: Warehouse and privy /LA-1191F
U.S. Highway 71, near Lecompte

1912

L. A. Toussaint, brickmason

LC: MD, O. LSA: MD. SHPO: MD.

HABS

O'Shee House /LA-1177
Bayou Rapides (moved from Alexandria)

Ca. 1915

LC: P, O.

SHPO

Rosalie plantation: Sugarhouse /LA-1232A
Near Chambers

Early nineteenth century

LC: MD, O. LSA: MD. USL: MD.

ST. BERNARD PARISH

HABS, Richard Koch, 1936

Beauregard, René, House /LA-18-7
Mississippi River, Chalmette Battleground Park, Chalmette

1833

C: MD. HNOC: MD, P. LC: MD, P, O.
LSA: MD. LSMM: MD. LSU: MD.
NOR: MD. SEAA: MD. TU: MD. USL: MD.

St. Charles Parish

HABS

Barbarra (Rose) plantation:
Garçonnière /LA-18-12
St. Rose

1820

C: MD. HNOC: MD, P. LC: MD, P, O.
LSL: MD, P. LSMM: MD, P. SEAA:
MD, P.

HABS

Destrehan plantation /LA-1212
River Road, Destrehan

1787–1790, remodeled late 1830s
Charles (free man of color), builder

LC: MD, O. LSA: MD. SEAA: P. SHPO:
MD.

Julie H. McCollam, 1995

Destrehan plantation: *Garçonnières*
/LA-1212
River Road, Destrehan

Late 1830s
Charles (free man of color), builder

LC: MD, O. SEAA: P.

HABS, Lester Jones, copy of photo taken before 1899

Homeplace plantation /LA-155
River Road, Hahnville

Ca. 1800

Possibly Charles (the free man of color
who built Destrehan), builder

C: MD. HNOC: MD, P. HT: MD. LC:
MD, P, O. LSL: MD, P. LSMM: MD, P.
NOR: MD. SEAA: P. TU: MD. USL:
MD.

HABS, Lester Jones, 1940

Lehmann House /LA-194
Hahnville
Early nineteenth century; demolished
HNOC: P. LC: P, O. LSMM: P.

Julie H. McCollam, 1996

Ormond plantation /LA-18-13
Highway 1, near St. Rose

1803; wings, 1811–1819
probably Henry S. Latrobe, architect for
wings

C: MD. HNOC: MD, P. HT: MD. LC:
MD, P, O. LSA: MD. LSL: MD, P.
LSMM: MD, P, O. LSU: MD. NOR:
MD. TU: MD.

HABS

Zeringue House /LA-1181
Hahnville
1810–1820
LC: MD, O. LSA: MD, P. SHPO: MD.

St. James Parish

HABS, Thomas Waterman, 1937

Academy /LA-1161
Near Union

1840s

HNOC: P. LC: P, O. SHPO: P.

Bagatelle plantation. *See under*
Iberville Parish

Crescent Farm plantation. *See*
Robicheaux House, Hymel House

SHPO

Graugnard Farms plantation /LA-1202
St. James

1790–1820

LC: MD, O. LSA: MD. SEAA: MD. SHPO:
MD.

SHPO

**Hymel House, Crescent Farm
plantation** /LA-1200
SW of River Road on Crescent Farm
plantation

1810; demolished

LC: MD, O. LSA: MD. SEAA: MD. SHPO:
MD.

Julie H. McCollam, 1996

Laura plantation /LA-1213

River Road, Vacherie

1810

LC: MD, O. LSA: MD. SHPO: MD.

HABS

Robicheaux House, Crescent Farm plantation /LA-1199

SW of River Road on Crescent Farm plantation

1810–1820; demolished

LC: MD, O. LSA: MD. SEAA: MD. SHPO: MD.

HABS, Richard Koch

Uncle Sam plantation /LA-74

Near Convent

1837, rebuilt 1849; demolished

C: MD. HNOC: MD, P. LC: MD, P, O. LSL: MD, P. LSMM: MD, P. LSU: MD. NOR: MD. SEAA: MD, P. USL: MD.

St. John the Baptist Parish

HABS, Richard Koch, 1935

Angelina plantation: Dovecote, dollhouse /LA-18-14

Highway 1, Mount Airy

1830–1850; demolished

Probably George Roussel family, builders of dovecote and dollhouse, *ca.* 1850s

C: MD. HNOC: MD, P. HT: MD. LC: MD, P, O. LSA: MD. LSL: P. LSMM: MD, P. TU: MD.

HABS

Columbia plantation: Cabins /LA-1204

Edgard

1815; demolished

LC: MD, O. LSA: MD. SEAA: MD. SHPO: MD.

Julie H. McCollam, 1996

Evergreen plantation /LA-1236

Near Reserve

1832

John Carver, builder

LC: MD, O. LSA: MD. SHPO: MD. TU: MD.

HABS, Robert Tebbs

Glendale plantation /LA-150

Lucy

1801

HNOC: P. LC: MD, P, O. LSA: MD. SEAA: MD. SHPO: MD.

Kroll House. *See under* **Iberville Parish**

SHPO

Montegut (Lougue) plantation /LA-1189

La Place

1810

LC: MD, O. LSA: MD. SEAA: MD, P, O. SHPO: MD, P.

HABS, Robert Tebbs

Whitney plantation: Main house /LA-1194

Highway 18, Wallace

Ca. 1804

LC: MD, O. LSA: MD. LSMM: P. SEAA: MD, O. SHPO: MD, P.

Julie H. McCollam, 1996

Whitney plantation: Outbuildings /LA-1194A

Highway 18, Wallace

Ca. 1804

LC: MD, O. LSA: MD. SEAA: MD, P, O. SHPO: MD.

St. Landry Parish

HABS, Lester Jones, 1940

Chrétien Point plantation /LA-64

Near Sunset

1831–1832

Samuel Young, Jonathan Harris, architects

C: MD. HNOC: MD, P. HT: MD. LC: MD, P, O. LSL: MD, P. LSMM: MD, P, O. LSU: MD. NOR: MD. SEAA: MD. TU: MD. USL: MD.

HABS, Lester Jones, 1940

Convent of the Sacred Heart /LA-54

Grand Coteau

1830

HNOC: P. LC: P, O. LSMM: P.

SHPO

SHPO

Dupré, Governor Jacques, gravesite tomb figures /LA-1196

Opelousas Cemetery, Opelousas

Ca. 1846

LC: MD, O. LSA: MD. SEAA: MD. SHPO: MD.

SHPO

Dupré, Governor Jacques, House /LA-1201

Highway 10 and U.S. Highway 167, Opelousas

Ca. 1810

LC: MD, O. LSA: MD. SEAA: MD. SHPO: MD.

HABS, Lester Jones, 1940

Hebrard House /LA-83

304 Bellevue Street, Opelousas

1830–1840

HNOC: P. LC: P, O. LSMM: P.

Julie H. McCollam, 1992

Hinckley House /LA-1162

De Jean Street, Washington

Ca. 1850

LC: MD, O. LSA: MD. USL: MD, O.

Julie H. McCollam, 1991

Immaculate Conception Catholic Church /LA-1163

Moundville Street, Washington

Ca. 1890, begun 1851, tower begun 1856

LC: MD, O. LSA: MD. USL: MD, O.

HABS, Lester Jones, 1940

Lastrapes House /LA-89

N of Opelousas

Brick wall, 1801; rest of building later

C: MD. HNOC: MD, P. HT: MD. LC: MD, P, O. LSMM: MD, P. LSU: MD. NOR: MD. SEAA: MD, O. TU: MD. USL: MD.

Live Oak plantation house (Old Powers Place). *See under* **East Baton Rouge Parish**

Julie H. McCollam, 1991

Lyons Warehouse /LA-1164

Water and Main Streets, Washington

First part, 1810; addition, *ca.* 1830

LC: MD, O. LSA: MD. USL: MD, P.

Julie H. McCollam, 1991

Magnolia Ridge House /LA-1165

De Jean Street, Washington

1830

LC: MD, O. LSA: MD. USL: MD, O.

Julie H. McCollam, 1991

Nicholson House /LA-1166

Corso Street, Washington

Prior to 1839

LC: MD, O. LSA: MD, O. USL: MD, O.

HABS

Petetin's Store /LA-86

Grand Coteau

1834

HNOC: P. LC: P, O.

Julie H. McCollam, 1991

Pierrel, A. S., House /LA-1167

De Jean Street, Washington

1851

LC: MD, O. LSA: MD. USL: MD, O.

HABS, Lester Jones, 1940

Schmit Hotel /LA-195

Washington

1866

HNOC: P. LC: P, O. LSMM: P.

Julie H. McCollam, 1991

Schulze House /LA-1168

Water Street, Washington

First part, 1826; second part, 1852

LC: MD, O. LSA: MD. USL: MD, O.

Julie H. McCollam, 1991

Wartelle plantation /LA-1203

Washington

1827

LC: MD, O. LSA: MD, O. SEAA: MD, O. SHPO: MD.

Julie H. McCollam, 1991

Wolff, J., House /LA-1169

Main Street, Washington

1870

LC: MD, O. LSA: MD. USL: MD, O.

St. Martin Parish

SHPO

Fontenette House /LA-1182

Main and Hamilton Streets, St. Martinville

1817–1819

LC: MD, O. LSA: MD, O. SHPO: MD, P. USL: MD, O.

SHPO

Foti Townhouse /LA-1184

132 South Main Street, St. Martinville

1875

LC: MD, O. LSA: MD, O. SHPO: MD. USL: MD, O.

Julie H. McCollam, 1993

Gary Building /LA-1183

214–216 South Main Street, St. Martinville

1857–1860

Alphonse Tertrou, architect

LC: MD, O. LSA: MD. SHPO: MD, P. USL: MD.

HABS

Martin House /LA-1185

St. Martinville

1800–1820

Louis Gary, architect

LC: MD, O. LSA: MD. SHPO: MD, P.

Julie H. McCollam, 1993

St. John plantation /LA-1186
Highway 347, near St. Martinville
1850
LC: MD, O. LSA: MD. SHPO: P.

Julie H. McCollam, 1993

**St. John plantation: Creole cottage
No. 1** /LA-1186A
Highway 347, near St. Martinville
1866
LC: MD, O. LSA: MD. SHPO: MD.

SHPO

**St. John plantation: Creole cottage
No. 2** /LA-1186B
Highway 347, near St. Martinville
Ca. 1860
LC: MD, O. LSA: MD. SHPO: MD.

St. Mary Parish

SHPO

Sterling Sugar Mill /LA-1210
Sterling Road, Franklin
Mid–nineteenth century
LC: MD, O. LSA: MD. SHPO: MD, P.

West Feliciana Parish

HABS

Afton Villa /LA-63
U.S. Highway 61, St. Francisville
Ca. 1850; demolished
Possibly James Dakin, architect
HNOC: P. LC: P, O. LSL: P.

HABS

Greenwood (Ventress) plantation /LA-
16
Bains
Kitchen building and box garden, 1820;
main house, 1850
C: MD. HNOC: MD. HT: MD. LC: MD,
O. LSA: MD. LSMM: MD, P. LSU: MD.
NOR: MD. SEAA: MD. TU: MD.

SHPO

Live Oak plantation house /LA-17
Between Weyanoke and Bains

1800–1810
Peter Murray, maker of interior
woodwork
C: MD. HNOC: MD, P. HT: MD. LC:
MD, P, O. LSA: MD, O. LSMM: P, O.
LSU: MD. NOR: MD. SEAA: MD.

HABS

Rosedown plantation: Gazebo /
LA-1101
St. Francisville
Main house, 1835; wings, 1844–1845
Wendell Wright, architect for main
house; T. S. Williams, architect for
wings
HNOC: P. LC: P, O. LSMM: P, O.

HABS

St. Mary's Episcopal Church /
LA-1218
Highway 66, Weyanoke
1857
Sometimes attributed to Frank K. Wills,
architect
LC: MD, O. LSA: MD. SHPO: MD.

Glossary

ACANTHUS. A stylized Classical design based on the leaves of a common Mediterranean plant, as on a CAPITAL of the CORINTHIAN ORDER.

ADAMESQUE. Of a delicate neoclassical design based on Roman Pompeii as interpreted in the eighteenth century by the English architects Robert Adam and James Adam.

ALLÉE. A tree-lined walk or drive.

ANTHEMION. A Classical decorative ornament of radiating clusters represented flat or in RELIEF and always from the side, and based on floral and foliate forms, especially of the palmetto.

ARCHITRAVE. 1. A beam resting directly on top of columns, and the lowermost division of an ENTABLATURE. 2. A MOLDING around a doorway or window, often projecting on both sides at the top.

ASHLAR. 1. A squared stone used for facing. 2. Stucco with SCORING to resemble stone, or wooden blocks made to resemble stone.

BALLOON FRAME. The structural members of a building when nailed together rather than joined by MORTISE AND TENON. Balloon frames continue in use by architects and builders today.

BALUSTER. An upright support for the handrail on a flight of stairs, a balcony, or a GALLERY.

BALUSTRADE. A row of BALUSTERS supporting a rail.

BANQUETTE. A sidewalk (from the French term for a footway of a road).

BAS-RELIEF. Low RELIEF.

BATTEN DOOR, BATTEN SHUTTER. A door or shutter constructed of vertical boards nailed to two or more horizontal boards.

BATTURE. The land between water and LEVEE.

BAY. Any of a series of major divisions or units in a structure, as window, door, or archway openings, or the spaces between columns or PIERS. A reference to the number of bays usually concerns the number of openings across an elevation.

BAY WINDOW. A window or set of windows projecting from an outer wall and creating a polygonal, rounded, or rectangular alcove for the room inside.

BLIND. A window shutter with LOUVERS.

BOARD AND BATTEN. Vertical FLUSH board siding with narrow strips of wood, that is, battens, covering the joints.

BOUSILLAGE. A mixture of mud, Spanish moss, and animal hair laid in loaf shapes on a series of horizontal laths as NOGGING between the posts of a timber-FRAME structure.

BOX COLUMN. A rectangular column with one of the two wider sides facing forward.

BRACKET. A supporting member for EAVES, shelves, or other overhangs, often more decorative than functional.

Briquette entre poteaux. A form of construction with low-fired bricks as NOGGING between the posts of a timber-FRAME structure.

BUTTRESS. A projecting support that strengthens or stabilizes a wall.

CAPITAL. The uppermost part of a column, PILASTER, or the like, usually molded or otherwise decorated, as with VOLUTES (IONIC ORDER) or ACANTHUS designs (CORINTHIAN ORDER) or both (COMPOSITE ORDER).

CARTOUCHE. An ornamental shield, scroll, or oval, often with an inscription.

CASEMENT. A window that swings open on hinges, as opposed to one with sashes that can be raised and lowered.

CAST IRON. Iron that, when molten, is poured into sand molds. Elaborate GALLERY railings, window hoods, and FACADES are possible in cast iron.

CHAIR RAIL. A broad MOLDING along the walls of a room or front GALLERY at approximately the height of a chair back.

CHAMFER. The beveled corner of a post or other structural member.

CHINKING. The material, usually a clay mixture, that fills the gaps between the logs of a log house.

CLAPBOARD. A board with one edge thicker than the other, so as to permit horizontal overlapping.

Colombage. A heavy timber FRAME.

COLONNETTE. A wooden column or turned post of the TUSCAN ORDER having the shape of an elongated vase and used as a GALLERY support on the principal level of some CREOLE houses.

COMPOSITE ORDER. An ORDER of Classical Roman architecture that combines the ACANTHUS of the CORINTHIAN ORDER and the VOLUTE of the IONIC ORDER.

CONCESSION. A French land grant in Louisiana.

CORINTHIAN ORDER. The most ornate of the three Classical Greek ORDERS, having a bell-shaped CAPITAL embellished with ACANTHUS designs.

CORNICE. 1. The topmost horizontal division, usually molded and projecting, of an

ENTABLATURE. 2. The horizontal projecting member at the top of a wall.

CREOLE. 1. A person born in the New World of parents from France or Spain, or with ancestors from those countries and from Africa. 2. Resulting from the blend of European with African, and sometimes also Native American, cultures. 3. Of the architecture in Louisiana derived from this heritage. 4. Of a sort specifically Louisianian.

CREVASSE. A break in a LEVEE.

CRIB. A wooden enclosure for storing grain.

CUPOLA. A small structure on top of a roof for observation or ventilation or simply to complete a design.

DADO. The lower part of an interior wall with special decoration—paneling, paper, or color—and the baseboard and CHAIR RAIL.

DENTIL. A small rectangular block in a series projecting like teeth, usually under a CORNICE.

DOGTROT. An open breezeway between the two main rooms of a log—or sometimes a frame—house, the floor being at the same level as the floor of the rooms.

DORIC ORDER. The oldest and simplest of the three Classical Greek ORDERS, with a rounded CAPITAL, a FRIEZE of TRIGLYPHS and METOPES, and a SHAFT with FLUTES.

DORMER. A window set vertically in a small GABLE that projects from the slope of a roof.

EAVES. The edge of a roof, usually overhanging a wall.

ELL. An addition or extension to a building at right angles to the principal block of the building.

EMBRASURE. A flared opening in a thick wall for a window or door, so that the opening is larger on one side of the wall.

En suite. Having rooms opening into one another rather than into a hall.

Enfilade. En suite, with rooms and doors in a line.

ENGAGED. Partly embedded in or bonded to, as a column on a wall.

ENTABLATURE. The ornamented horizontal upper section of a Classical building, usually supported on columns or PILASTERS,

and comprising, from bottom to top, the ARCHITRAVE, the FRIEZE, and the CORNICE.

FACADE. The face of a building, usually the front elevation.

FANLIGHT. A semicircular or semielliptical window, with radiating MUNTINS or tracery, placed over a door, a window, or FRENCH DOORS.

FASCES. A Classical Roman design incorporating a representation of tied reeds or rods with a projecting ax blade. It was a symbol of Roman authority.

FASCIA. A flat horizontal facing or MOLDING, usually under a CORNICE or EAVES.

Faux bois. Painted with a grain to resemble a decorative wood.

FENESTRATION. The arrangement, proportions, and ornamentation of windows in a building.

FLUSH. With boards applied to make a smooth wall rather than to overlap.

FLUTE. A curved channel or groove, usually one in a parallel vertical series on the SHAFT of a column or PILASTER.

FRAME. 1. The wooden or steel structural members of a building fitted together to form a skeleton. 2. A basic structural unit that when fitted with other parts forms a whole.

FRENCH DOOR. A door the upper section of which is multipaned and the lower section paneled, often in pairs within a single doorframe, both doors opening from a central vertical axis.

FRIEZE. The division of an ENTABLATURE between the ARCHITRAVE and the CORNICE. It is usually plain in Greek Revival architecture but often ornamented in low RELIEF in ancient Greek temples.

GABLE ROOF. A roof having two pitched slopes that meet at their uppermost edge.

GABLE. The usually triangular section of wall at the end of a pitched roof.

GALLERY. A covered porch, veranda, or piazza, usually functioning as an outdoor living space.

Garçonnière. A building near a main house for the young men of a household.

GAZEBO. A garden house or summerhouse, usually open at the sides and often polygonal.

GRAINING. A decorative painting technique that simulates the grain of a wood, either real or imaginary.

GUILLOCHE. An ornament or design composed of loosely intersecting curvilinear bands.

GUTTA. One of a series of small cylindrical or truncated conical ornaments on a frieze of the DORIC ORDER.

HIP ROOF. A roof with four uniformly pitched sides.

HOOD MOLD. The projecting MOLDING over a window or door.

IMBRICATION. The overlapping of tiles or, usually, pointed, rounded, or shaped wooden shingles to form a pattern.

IONIC ORDER. The ORDER in Classical Greek and Roman architecture that is distinguished by four downward VOLUTES on its CAPITAL.

JIB WINDOW. A sash window with hinged panels that can open as a doorway when the lower sash is raised.

JIGSAW WORK. Decorative flat woodwork, usually in intricate patterns, made with a jigsaw.

LAMB'S TONGUE. A carved or cut tapering tongue, usually between the CHAMFERS and square sections of a post.

LEVEE. A man-made embankment along waterways to prevent flooding.

LIGHT. A glass pane of a window or door.

LINTEL. The supporting horizontal member spanning an opening.

LOGGIA. A roofed open GALLERY recessed into the main block of a structure, usually at the rear.

LOTUS CAPITAL. A CAPITAL with the shape of a stylized Egyptian lotus bud.

LOUVER. One of the horizontal slats in a FRAME, as of a shutter, spaced for ventilation and shade and tilted to admit air but to shed rain.

LOZENGE. A decorative element in the shape of a diamond.

MANSARD ROOF. A roof with two slopes on each of four sides, with steeper lower slopes. It is named for the seventeenth-century French architect François Mansard.

MARBLEIZING. A decorative painting technique that simulates marble on wood or stucco, usually on a mantel or baseboard or on the facade of a gallery.

METOPE. The area between two TRIGLYPHS on a Doric FRIEZE, usually plain in Greek Revival architecture, often with low-RELIEF carving in ancient Greece.

MOLDING. A decorative contoured surface or strip, usually of wood, plaster, or stucco, and frequently combined with others, often to function as a CORNICE.

MORTISE AND TENON. A technique of joinery in which the pieces are put together by projecting parts, that is, tenons, which fit into holes, that is, mortises. In timber-FRAME construction, a wooden peg is driven through two members to secure a joint.

MUNTIN. A vertical or horizontal bar separating the glass panes of a window.

NECKING. A small raised MOLDING at the top of a column SHAFT and below the CAPITAL.

NEWEL. The main post at the foot of the railing on a flight of stairs, or the main post on a landing.

NOGGING. The fill in the open spaces of a wooden FRAME.

NORMAN TRUSS. A form of timber roof construction employing MORTISE AND TENON and associated with Normandy.

NOTCHING. The cutting and shaping of logs where two join together.

OGEE. 1. A MOLDING the profile of which is a double curve, the curvature at the top of the molding being concave, and at the bottom convex. 2. Having the outline of such a MOLDING.

ORDER. A COLUMN and ENTABLATURE taken together as a unit in a Classical style. The Romans added the TUSCAN ORDER and COMPOSITE ORDER to the DORIC ORDER, IONIC ORDER, and CORINTHIAN ORDER of the Greeks.

OVERLIGHT. A short, wide window above a door or doorway with SIDELIGHTS.

OVERMANTEL. An ornamental structure of decorative cabinetwork above a mantel.

PARAPET. A low wall rising at the edge of a roof, porch, or terrace. A parapet is sometimes the extension of a wall above the level of a flat or nearly flat roof, often as a decorative crown on masonry buildings.

PARTY WALL. A wall shared by adjoining buildings.

PATERA. A round or oval medallion with an ornamental design, usually a sunburst.

PAVILION. 1. An ornamental building in a park or garden. 2. A high HIP ROOF. 3. A central or end section of a large building.

PEDIMENT. 1. A wide, low-pitched GABLE above the FACADE of a Classical building. 2. Such a triangular form over a door, window, niche, or the like.

PEN. A four-sided log enclosure, forming a room.

PERGOLA. An arbor or passageway, usually a double row of columns with an openwork FRAME above.

PERIPTERAL. On all sides.

PIANO NOBILE. The main or principal floor of a house.

PIER. A vertical support or pillar for an arch or LINTEL, either a freestanding wall or of a section of wall between two openings.

PIEUX. A fencing of cypress planks with pointed tops, and bottoms set in a trench.

PIGEONNIER. A pigeon house or dovecote. In Louisiana, this is a substantial square or polygonal building with the pigeons roosting in the upper level.

PILASTER. A shallow section of column—not excluding a COLONNETTE or BOX COLUMN—attached to a wall and treated like a column with base, SHAFT, and CAPITAL.

PLATE. A horizontal timber supporting the trusses or rafters of a roof.

POINTING. The mortar in a wall of brick or stone.

PORTE COCHERE. 1. A gateway by which vehicles enter a courtyard. 2. A covered porch attached to a building at ground level where passengers alight.

PORTICO. A porch or walkway with a roof supported by columns, often at the entrance to a building.

POTEAUX EN TERRE. A method of early CREOLE building construction in which sharpened logs are set in the ground and held in place by the framing of the roof.

POTEAUX SUR SOL. A method of early CREOLE building construction in which the sill is laid directly on the ground.

REEDING. A set of long, parallel half-round MOLDINGS, for an effect the opposite of FLUTES.

RELIEF. The projection of sculptural figures from a background. In low relief the projection is slight; in high relief it is half or more of the full form.

RISER. The upright, vertical member between the TREADS of a stairway.

ROUNDEL. A circular window or panel.

RUSTICATION. The cutting of stone or SCORING of stucco to produce strongly emphasized beveled or recessed joints, often roughly textured. Rustication was frequent for the ground floor of buildings during the Renaissance.

SCORING. Marking with lines or notches to resemble stone blocks, usually on exterior stucco.

SEGMENTAL ARCH. A rounded arch in the form of a segment of a circle less than a semicircle.

SHAFT. The long, slender part of a column, between the BASE and the CAPITAL.

SHOTGUN. A house one room wide and three or more rooms deep with a GABLE facing the street. A double shotgun is a pair of shotguns with a PARTY WALL. A camelback is usually a double with a second story over the rear rooms only.

SIDEHALL. A hall with a room or rooms on only one side. In Louisiana, this is principally a stair hall.

SIDELIGHT. One of the narrow windows that sometimes flank a door, often with a TRANSOM or OVERLIGHT above.

SILL. 1. A heavy horizontal timber or masonry wall supporting the walls of a structure. 2. The horizontal timber at the bottom of the frame of a wooden structure, resting on brick, stone, or cypress piers, or directly on the ground in some early CREOLE houses.

SOFFIT. The exposed underside of a structural part, such as an overhanging roof, cornice, or balcony.

TRANSOM. A horizontal, usually rectangular, window over a door or full window.

TREAD. The flat, horizontal surface of a step or stair.

TRIGLYPH. A slightly projecting block incised and beveled to make a tripartite ornament that alternates with the METOPES on a FRIEZE of the DORIC ORDER.

TROMPE L'OEIL. Decorative painting that suggests three dimensions, usually architectural elements, and often includes graining and marbling (from the French for "fool the eye").

TUSCAN ORDER. A Classical Roman ORDER with a SHAFT lacking FLUTES and with a plain molded CAPITAL.

VOLUTE. A spiral, scroll-like ornament, as on a CAPITAL of the IONIC ORDER.

WAINSCOTING. Wood paneling on the walls of a room, usually on only the lower section.

WROUGHT IRON. Iron soft enough to be pounded into shapes, usually for railings, gates, and fences.

Glossary of Styles

ART DECO. A style, employed in Louisiana primarily in the 1930s and for commercial and, especially, public buildings, that is typified by zigzag, chevron, and lozenge decorations, along with bas-reliefs, metal windows, grilles, and panels, and monumental size, often with the center of the facade set back. See Chapter 8, Figure 23.

ART MODERNE. A style that in Louisiana won its greatest acceptance in Shreveport in the 1930s and 1940s and that is characterized by flat roofs, smooth walls, horizontal bands of windows, and a suppression of ornamentation, giving a building a streamlined effect, sometimes emphasized by curved windows or walls. See Chapter 8, Figure 32.

BEAUX ARTS. A style adopted in the state for commercial and public buildings during roughly the first two decades of the twentieth century and based on designs developed at the Ecole des Beaux Arts, in Paris. Buildings in the style manifest a grandiose Classicism and are often faced in stone and embellished with monumental, frequently paired columns, heavy balustrades, enriched details (such as cartouches) and moldings, and pronounced cornices and pediments. See Chapter 8, Figure 39.

BUNGALOW. A residential style, in favor from about 1900 into the 1930s in Louisiana for one- and two-story houses, that is distinguished by a broad gable facing the street and usually over a front porch, tapered porch posts typically resting on high piers, open brackets, broad, multiple-window openings, shed dormers, and exposed rafter ends. See Chapter 8, Figure 7.

COLONIAL REVIVAL. A style reinterpreting some of the architectural features common along the upper eastern seaboard in the mid– and late eighteenth century that was influential in Louisiana from approximately 1895 to 1920. Structures in the style, commonly residences, are larger than the colonial originals and combine elements from several sections of the Northeast. The buildings may have wide single-light windows, often with multipaned upper sashes, clapboard siding, oversized dormers, doors with one light in the upper panel, and a generous provision of columns and porches. See Chapter 7, Figure 33.

EASTLAKE. A style of ornamentation based on the furniture designs of Charles Eastlake that in the 1880s and 1890s was appropriated for the adornment of houses essentially in the Queen Anne style and that is recognizable by its heavy turned posts, post brackets, spindle work, and incised patterns.

EGYPTIAN REVIVAL. A style occasionally favored in the state in the 1840s and 1850s and based on ancient Egyptian temples that is typified by pylon gates, lotus capitals, and such decorative adjuncts as the winged solar disk. See Plate J.

FEDERAL. A style developed in the new republic of the United States and reaching Louisiana during the first three decades of the 1800s that was based on an Adamesque interpretation of imperial Rome, with light, airy Classical features. The impact of the style in the state was primarily on the decoration of Creole buildings and on the design of public buildings of American character. See Chapter 5, Figure 2.

GOTHIC REVIVAL. A style based on medieval castles and churches that in its castellated form shaped monumental buildings in the 1840s and 1850s and in its ecclesiastical form continued as an option for Eclecticism in church architecture well into the twentieth century. Buildings in the style may have lancet windows, steeply pitched roofs, crenellations, quatrefoils, tracery windows, and crockets. See Chapter 5, Figures 60, 32.

GREEK REVIVAL. A style widely embraced in Louisiana from the 1830s through the 1860s based on temples exhibiting the Doric, Ionic, and Corinthian orders, with columns, friezes, pediments, and low roofs. See Chapter 5, Figure 13.

INTERNATIONAL. A style that evolved in Europe between the World Wars and gained a following in Louisiana from the 1930s into the 1950s for its flat roofs without eaves and its uniform wall surfaces, glass walls, metal casement windows, asymmetry, and rejection of ornamentation. See Chapter 8, Figure 28.

ITALIANATE. A style based on the Italian villas of the Renaissance and a source of designs for houses and commercial buildings from the 1850s through the 1880s that usually resulted in asymmetrical structures but that in Louisiana lent itself to peculiarly local and often symmetrical adaptations. Buildings in the style may possess segmental arches between columns that create high basements, as well as parapets, rounded windows and doors, and brackets under the eaves, often in pairs. See Chapter 5, Figure 89.

PRAIRIE. A style based on the residential designs of the American architect Frank Lloyd Wright that, though not generating great enthusiasm in the state, has several examples there from the years between about 1900 and 1920. The one- and two-story houses in the style are of brick or stucco with low, horizontal lines, projecting eaves, higher central sections, low roofs, and casement windows often grouped in horizontal bands. See Chapter 7, Figure 59.

QUEEN ANNE. A popular style in the state between about 1880 and 1915 that was named in England to classify vernacular buildings, usually brick or masonry, built before and during Queen Anne's reign but that in the United States usually involved wood-frame construction. Buildings in the style, generally residences, have irregular plans, front- and side-facing gables, steep roofs, towers, turrets, and a multitude of wraparound galleries, porches, and projecting dormers. See Chapter 7, Figure 8.

RENAISSANCE REVIVAL. A style, based on Italian Renaissance palaces, of only a few houses in Louisiana, from during and shortly after the 1850s, and some public buildings, from the early twentieth century, the marks of which are symmetry, ashlar finishes, pediments over windows and doors, and balustrades, often above the cornice. See Chapter 7, Figure 42.

ROMANESQUE REVIVAL. A style based on early medieval European churches and accepted by architects in the state from the 1880s into the twentieth century. The Richardsonian Romanesque, which produced highly styled buildings reflecting the designs of H. H. Richardson, who was born in Louisiana and developed a unique personal interpretation, is considered a separate style emphasizing mass, volume, scale, and broad planes, always in brick or stone, with rounded windows and arches and short round towers. See Chapter 7, Figure 50.

SECOND EMPIRE. A style based on the town houses of Renaissance France and employed in Louisiana, though rarely, around the 1880s that is identified chiefly by its mansard roofs.

References

Ackerman, James S. *Distance Points: Studies in Theory and Renaissance Art and Architecture.* Cambridge, Mass., 1991.

Ashe, Thomas. *Travels in America, Performed in 1806.* Vol. III of 3 vols. London, 1808.

Bacot, Barbara SoRelle, "Marie Adrien Persac, Architect, Artist, and Engineer." *Magazine Antiques,* November, 1991, pp. 806–15.

Bacot, H. Parrott. "Magnolia Mound Plantation House in Baton Rouge, Louisiana." *Magazine Antiques,* May, 1983, pp. 1054–61.

Baillardel, A., and A. Prioult, eds. *Le Chevalier de Pradel: Vie d'un colon français en Louisiane au XVIIIe siècle.* Paris, 1928.

Bernhard, duke of Saxe-Weimar-Eisenach. *Travels Through North America During the Years 1825–1826.* Vol. II of 2 vols. Philadelphia, 1828.

Brand, Stewart. *How Buildings Learn: What Happens After They're Built.* New York, 1994.

Brasseaux, Carl A., Glenn R. Conrad, and R. Warren Robison, *The Courthouses of Louisiana.* Lafayette, La., 1977.

Brooklyn Museum. *The American Renaissance, 1876–1914.* New York, 1979.

Butler, W. E. *Down Among the Sugar Cane: The Story of Louisiana Sugar Plantations and Their Railroads.* Baton Rouge, 1980.

Cable, George Washington. *Old Creole Days.* New York, 1879.

Cable, Mary. *Lost New Orleans.* New York, 1980.

Caldwell, Joan. "Italianate Domestic Architecture in New Orleans, 1850–1880." Ph.D. dissertation, Tulane University, 1975.

Campbell, D. C., Jr. *Before Freedom Comes: African-American Life in the Antebellum South.* Charlottesville, Va., 1991.

Carter, Edward C., II, ed. *The Journals of Benjamin Henry Latrobe, 1799–1820: From Philadelphia to New Orleans.* New Haven, 1980.

Christovich, Mary L., *et al. The American Sector.* Gretna, La., 1972. Vol. II of *New Orleans Architecture.* 7 vols.

———. *The Esplanade Ridge.* Gretna, La., 1977. Vol. V of *New Orleans Architecture.* 7 vols.

Collot, Victor. *A Journey in North America.* Vol. II of 2 vols. Paris, 1826.

Cowdrey, Albert E. *Land's End: A History of the New Orleans District, U.S. Army Corps of Engineers, and Its Lifelong Battle with the Lower Mississippi and Other Rivers Wending Their Way to the Sea.* New Orleans, 1977.

Craig, Lois, ed. *The Federal Presence: Architecture, Politics, and Symbols in U.S. Government Buildings.* Cambridge, Mass., 1978.

Cullison, William R., III. "Design and Construction of Orange Grove." M.A. thesis, Tulane University, 1975.

———, ed. *Architecture in Louisiana: A Documentary History.* New Orleans, 1983.

Darby, William. *The Emigrants' Guide to the Western and Southwestern States and Territories.* New York, 1818.

Davis, Edwin A. *Louisiana: A Narrative History.* Baton Rouge, 1971.

Downing, Andrew Jackson. *The Architecture of Country Houses.* 1850; rpr. New York, 1964.

Dubos, René. *So Human an Animal.* New York, 1968.

Duncan, Patricia. "New Orleans: Port of Distinction." *Preservation in Print,* February, 1989.

Durrell, Edward [H. Didimus]. *New Orleans As I Found It.* New York, 1845.

Edwards, Jay D. "Cultural Identifications in Architecture: The Case of the New Orleans Townhouse." *Traditional Dwellings and Settlements Review,* forthcoming.

———. *Louisiana's Remarkable French Vernacular Architecture, 1700–1900.* Baton Rouge, 1988.

———. "The Origins of Creole Architecture." *Winterthur Portfolio,* XXIX (1994), 155–99.

Eyrau, Jean M. *A History of St. John the Baptist Parish, with Biographical Sketches.* Marrero, La., 1939.

Farnsworth, Jean M., and Ann M. Masson, eds. *The Architecture of Colonial Louisiana: Collected Essays of Samuel Wilson, Jr., F.A.I.A.* Lafayette, La., 1987.

Ferguson, John. "Captain Milton Doullut and His Fantastic House: 400 Egania Street." *Preservation in Print,* September, 1990.

———. "The Colonial Revival Style in New Orleans: A Study of Six Houses." M.A. thesis, Tulane University, 1979.

———. "History for Sale: Buckner-Soule Mansion." *Preservation in Print,* May, 1988.

———. "The Howard Memorial Library: Decline and Resurrection." *Preservation in Print,* December, 1989.

———. "The Howard Memorial Library: Renaissance of a Masterpiece." *Preservation in Print,* October, 1989.

Flint, Timothy. *Journal . . . : From the Red River to the Ouachita . . . in Louisiana, in 1835.* Philadelphia, 1836.

Forman, L. Ronald, and Joseph Logsdan. *Audubon Park: An Urban Eden.* New Orleans, 1985.

Franklin, John Hope, ed. *Reminiscences of an Active Life: The Autobiography of John Ray Lynch.* Chicago, 1970.

Fricker, Donna. "The Greek Revival Architecture of Keachi." *Preservation in Print,* November, 1988.

Fricker, Jonathan. "Temples in the Country." *Preservation in Print,* April, 1991.

Friends of the Cabildo. *Jefferson City.* Gretna, La., 1989. Vol. VII of *New Orleans Architecture.* 7 vols.

Garrison, Ervan G., *et al. Archaeological Investigations at Two Nineteenth-Century Well Sites, Lucy, Louisiana.* College Station, Tex., 1980.

Gibson, John. *Gibson's Guide and Directory of the State of Louisiana and the Cities of New Orleans and Lafayette.* New Orleans, 1838.

Glassie, Henry. *Pattern in the Material Folk Culture of the Eastern United States.* Philadelphia, 1969.

Gowans, Alan. *The Comfortable House.* Cambridge, Mass., 1986.

———. *Styles and Types of North American Architecture.* New York, 1992.

Grootkerk, Paul. "Artistic Images of Mythological Reality: The Antebellum Plantation." *Southern Quarterly,* XXXII. (Summer, 1994), 33–44.

Hall, Captain James Basil. *Travels in North America in the Years 1827 and 1828.* Vol. III of 3 vols. Edinburgh, 1829.

Hall, Mrs. Basil. *The Aristocratic Journey.* Edited by Una Pope-Hennessy. New York, 1931.

Halsted, Byron D., ed. *Barns, Sheds, and Outbuildings.* 1881; rpr. Brattleboro, Vt., 1977.

Hamlin, Talbot. *Greek Revival Architecture in America.* New York, 1964.

Heck, Robert W., and Otis B. Wheeler. *Religious Architecture in Louisiana.* Baton Rouge, 1995.

Historic Shreveport: A Guide. Shreveport, La., 1980.

Huber, Leonard. *Landmarks of New Orleans.* New Orleans, 1991.

———. *Louisiana: A Pictorial Guide.* New York, 1975.

Huber, Leonard, *et al. The Cemeteries.* Gretna, La., 1974. Vol. III of *New Orleans Architecture.* 7 vols.

Hussey, Christopher. *The Picturesque.* London, 1927.

Ingraham, Joseph Holt. *Travels in the Southwest by a Yankee.* 2 vols. 1835; rpr. Ann Arbor, Mich., 1966.

Jacobs, Jane. *The Death and Life of Great American Cities.* New York, 1961.

Jones, Katharine M. *The Plantation South.* New York, 1957.

Jordan, Terry G. *American Log Buildings: An Old World Heritage.* Chapel Hill, N.C., 1985.

———. "Cultural Preadaptations and the American Frontier: The Role of New Sweden." In *Rereading Cultural Geography,* edited by Kenneth E. Foote *et al.* Austin, Tex., 1994.

Kemp, John R., and Linda Orr King, eds. *Louisiana Images, 1880–1920: A Photographic Essay by George François Mugnier.* Baton Rouge, 1975.

Kingsley, Karen. *Modernism in Louisiana: A Decade of Progress, 1930–1940.* New Orleans, 1984.

Kirk, Susan Lauxman, and Helen Michel Smith. *The Architecture of St. Charles Avenue.* Gretna, La., 1977.

Kniffen, Fred B. *Cultural Diffusion and Landscapes.* Edited by H. Jesse Walker and Randall A. Detro. Baton Rouge, 1990.

———. *The Indians of Louisiana.* Baton Rouge, 1945.

Kniffen, Fred B., and Henry Glassie. "Building in Wood in the Eastern United States." *Geographical Review,* LVI (1966), 58–59.

Kruty, Paul. "The Gilbert Cooley House: A Prairie Style Masterpiece in Monroe." *Preservation in Print,* June, 1994.

Lafayette: Its Past, People, and Progress. Baton Rouge, 1988.

Lane, Mills. *Architecture of the Old South: Louisiana.* New York, 1990.

Latrobe, Benjamin Henry. *Impressions Respecting New Orleans.* Edited by Samuel Wilson, Jr. New York, 1951.

Latrobe, John H. B. *Southern Travels: Journal . . . 1834.* Edited by Samuel Wilson, Jr. New Orleans, 1986.

Le Gardeur, René J., Jr., *et al. Green Fields: Two Hundred Years of Louisiana Sugar.* Lafayette, La., 1980.

Lemann, Bernard. *The Lemann Family.* Donaldsonville, La., 1965.

———. *The Vieux Carre: A General Statement.* New Orleans, 1966.

Lemann, Bernard, Malcolm Heard, Jr., and John P. Klingman, eds. *Talk About Architecture: A Century of Architectural Education at Tulane.* New Orleans, 1993.

Le Page Du Pratz. *The History of Louisiana.* 1774; rpr. Baton Rouge, 1975.

Lester, Julius, ed. *To Be a Slave.* New York, 1968.

Leyburn, James G. *The Scotch-Irish: A Social History.* Chapel Hill, N.C., 1962.

Loudon, John C. *An Encyclopedia of Cottage, Farm, and Villa Architecture and Furniture.* London, 1883.

Louisiana Writers' Program of the WPA. *Louisiana: A Guide to the State.* New York, 1971.

Lynch, Kevin. *The Image of the City.* Cambridge, Mass., 1960.

McAlester, Virginia, and Lee McAlester. *A Field Guide to American Houses.* New York, 1984.

McDonald, Roderick A. *The Economy and Material Culture of Slaves: Goods and Chattels on the Sugar Plantations of Jamaica and Louisiana.* Baton Rouge, 1993.

Martin, F. Lestar. *Folk and Styled Architecture in Northern Louisiana.* Ruston, La., 1988.

Moody, V. Alton. *Slavery on Louisiana Sugar Plantations.* New Orleans, 1924.

Morrison, Hugh. *Early American Architecture: From the First Colonial Settlements to the National Period.* New York, 1952.

Mosser, Monique, and Georges Teyssot, eds. *The Architecture of Western Gardens.* Cambridge, Mass., 1991.

Newton, Milton. *Atlas of Louisiana: A Guide for Students.* Baton Rouge, 1972.

———. "Cultural Readaptation and the Upland South." *Geoscience and Man,* V (1974), 143–57.

Norman, Benjamin Moore. *Norman's New Orleans and Environs.* New Orleans, 1845.

Northup, Solomon. *Twelve Years a Slave.* New York, 1857.

O'Gorman, James F. *H. H. Richardson: Architectural Forms for an American Society.* Chicago, 1987.

Olmsted, Frederick Law. *The Cotton Kingdom: A Traveller's Observations on Cotton and Slavery.* 2 vols. New York, 1861.

———. *A Journey in the Back Country.* 1860; rpr. New York, 1970.

Overdyke, William D. *Louisiana Plantation Homes: Colonial and Ante Bellum.* New York, 1965.

Owsley, Frank L. *Plain Folk of the Old South.* Baton Rouge, 1949.

Palladio, Andrea. *The Four Books of Architecture.* 1738; rpr. New York, 1964.

Parker, A. A. *Trip to the West and Texas.* Boston, 1836.

Parker, H. Hanley. "New Orleans Architecture As Others See It." *Architectural Art and Its Allies,* II (January, 1908), 1–3.

Peatross, C. Ford, ed. *Historic America: Buildings, Structures, and Sites.* Washington, D.C., 1983.

Pevsner, Nikolaus. *From Mannerism to Romanticism.* London, 1968. Vol. I of Pevsner, *Studies in Art, Architecture, and Design.* 2 vols.

Pierson, William H. *The Colonial and Neoclassical Styles.* New York, 1970. Vol. I of Pierson, *American Buildings and Their Architects.* 2 vols.

Pintard, John. "New Orleans, 1801." Edited by David Lee Sterling. *Louisiana Historical Quarterly,* XXXIV (1951), 217–33.

Pittman, Philip. *The Present State of the European Settlements on the Mississippi: A Facsimile Reproduction of the 1770 Edition.* Gainesville, Fla., 1973.

Poesch, Jessie. *The Art of the Old South: Painting, Sculpture, Architecture, and the Products of Craftsmen, 1560–1860.* New York, 1983.

Posey, Zoe. *Plantations and Planters of Louisiana.* Baton Rouge, 1900.

Postell, William Dosite. *The Health of Slaves on Southern Plantations.* Baton Rouge, 1951.

Prichard, Walter, ed. "Inventory of the Paris Duvernay Concession in Louisiana, 1726." *Louisiana Historical Quarterly,* XXI (1938), 979–94.

———. "Lease of a Louisiana Plantation and Slaves, 1727." *Louisiana Historical Quarterly,* XXI (1938), 995–97.

———. "Minutes of the Police Jury of St. Helena Parish, August 16–19, 1813." *Louisiana Historical Quarterly,* XXIII (1940), 405–27.

Reeves, Sally Kittredge. *Legacy of a Century: Academy of the Sacred Heart in New Orleans.* New Orleans, 1987.

Reeves, Sally Kittredge, and William Reeves. *Historic City Park, New Orleans.* New Orleans, 1982.

Rehder, John Burkhardt. "Sugar Plantation Settlements of Southern Louisiana: A Cultural Geography." Ph.D. dissertation, Louisiana State University, 1971.

Ripley, Eliza. *Social Life in Old New Orleans.* New York, 1912.

Roach-Langford, Susan. "The Regional Folklife of North Louisiana." In *Louisiana Folklife: A Guide to the State,* edited by Nicholas R. Spitzer. Baton Rouge, 1985.

Robin, C. C. *Voyage to Louisiana.* Edited and translated by Stuart O. Landry, Jr. New Orleans, 1966.

Robison, R. Warren. *Louisiana Church Architecture.* Lafayette, La., 1984.

Russell, F. Whitehead. "The Old and the New South." *Architectural Record,* XXX (July, 1911), 1–56.

Schuler, Stanley. *American Barns: In a Class by Themselves.* Exton, Pa., 1984.

Schultz, Christian. *Travels on an Inland Voyage. . . . Through the . . . Territories of Indiana, Louisiana, Mississippi, and New Orleans.* Vol. II of 2 vols. New York, 1810.

Scully, Arthur. *James Dakin: His Career in New York and the South.* Baton Rouge, 1973.

Serlio, Sebastiano. *On Domestic Architecture: Different Dwellings from the Meanest Level to the Most Ornate Palace . . .—the Sixteenth-Century Manuscript of Book VI in the Avery Library of Columbia University.* Edited by Myra Nan Rosenfeld; introduced by James S. Ackerman. New York, 1978.

Sibley, J. Ashley, Jr. *Louisiana's Ancients of Man.* Baton Rouge, 1967.

Sitterson, J. Carlyle. "Magnolia Plantation, 1852–1862." *Mississippi Valley Historical Review,* XXV (1938), 197–210.

———. *Sugar Country: The Cane Sugar Industry in the South.* Frankfort, Ky., 1953.

Stahls, Paul F. *A Bicentennial Guide to Louisiana.* Baton Rouge, 1976.

Starr, S. Frederick. *Southern Comfort.* Cambridge, Mass., 1989.

Stokes, George H. "Lumbering in Louisiana: A Study of the Industry as a Culturo-Geographic Factor." Ph.D. dissertation, Louisiana State University, 1954.

Swanson, Betsy. *Historic Jefferson Parish from Shore to Shore.* Gretna, La., 1975.

Taylor, Joe Gray. *Negro Slavery in Louisiana.* New York, 1963.

Thorpe, T. B. "Sugar and the Sugar Region of Louisiana." *Harper's New Monthly Magazine,* VII (1853), 746–67.

Toledano, Roulhac, *et al. The Creole Faubourgs.* Gretna, La., 1974. Vol. IV of *New Orleans Architecture.* 7 vols.

———. *Faubourg Treme and the Bayou Road.* Gretna, La., 1980. Vol. VI of *New Orleans Architecture.* 7 vols.

Vlach, John Michael. *The Afro-American Tradition.* Cleveland, 1978.

———. *Back of the Big House.* Chapel Hill, N.C., 1993.

———. "The Shotgun House: An African Architectural Legacy." In *Common Places: Readings in American Vernacular Architecture,* edited by Dell Upton and John Michael Vlach. Athens, Ga., 1986.

Warden, D. B. *A Statistical, Political, and Historical Account of the United States of North America.* Edinburgh, 1819.

Wharton, Thomas Kelah. "Diary, 1856–1868." Microfilm in Howard-Tilton Library Tulane University.

Whiffen, Marcus, and Frederick Koeper. *American Architecture.* 2 vols. Cambridge, Mass., 1983.

Wilson, Samuel, Jr. "The Building Contract for Evergreen Plantation, 1832." *Louisiana History,* XXI (1990), 399–406.

———. "Gulf Coast Architecture." In *Spain and Her Rivals on the Gulf Coast,* edited by Ernest F. Dribble. Pensacola, Fla., 1971.

———. *The Lower Garden District.* Gretna, La., 1991. Vol. I of *New Orleans Architecture.* 7 vols.

———. *The Vieux Carre, New Orleans: Its Plan, Its Growth, Its Architecture—Historic District Demonstration Study.* New Orleans, 1968.

———, ed. *Autobiography of James Gallier, Architect.* New York, 1968.

Wilson, Samuel, Jr., and Leonard Huber. *Landmarks of New Orleans.* New Orleans, 1991.

Wooldridge, Laura A. "The East Feliciana Parish Court House and Lawyers' Row in Clinton, Louisiana: A Study in the Greek Revival." M.A. thesis, Tulane University, 1973.

Zacherie, James S. *New Orleans Guide.* New Orleans, 1902.

Ziegler, Arthur P., Jr. *Historic Preservation in Inner City Areas: A Manual of Practice.* Pittsburgh, 1971.

CONTRIBUTORS

BARBARA SORELLE BACOT, an architectural historian, manages the areas of technical preservation and tax incentives for historic buildings in the Louisiana Division of Historic Preservation. She has published on the architect and artist Marie Adrien Persac and has written a number of articles for *Preservation in Print*.

JOAN G. CALDWELL, an art historian, is in charge of the Louisiana Collection at the Howard-Tilton Memorial Library, of Tulane University, and is the curator of the university art collection. She has written on Italianate architecture in New Orleans and on Renaissance iconography. One of the authors of *A Guide to New Orleans Architecture,* published by the New Orleans chapter of the American Institute of Architects, she is currently involved in preparing an updated edition.

EUGENE DARWIN CIZEK, an architect, is a professor at the School of Architecture of Tulane University. He is also on the faculty of the Roger Thayer Stone Center for Latin American Studies and is codirector of the Education Through Historic Places program. He has led teams of students in the Historic American Buildings Survey, many of whom have won awards in the Charles E. Peterson competition. He is the author of over thirty publications regarding Louisiana's architectural heritage.

JONATHAN FRICKER, an architectural historian, serves as director of the Louisiana Division of Historic Preservation and deputy state historic preservation officer. Formerly the state's coordinator of the program for the National Register of Historic Places, he has inspected and researched more than six hundred historic buildings and districts. He has published numerous articles in *Preservation in Print*.

KAREN KINGSLEY, an architectural historian, is a professor at the School of Architecture of Tulane University. She prepared *Modernism in Louisiana:*

A Decade of Progress, 1930–1940 for an exhibition she organized. She is currently readying a volume on Louisiana for the series Buildings of the United States, sponsored by the National Society of Architectural Historians.

JULIE H. McCOLLAM, an art historian, is chairman of the editorial committee of *Preservation in Print.* In earlier service as managing editor of that periodical, she received a Louisiana Preservation Alliance Honor Award in heritage education. She currently holds an appointment to the New Orleans Historic District Landmarks Commission.

JESSIE POESCH, an art historian, is a professor emerita of the Newcomb Department of Art, of Tulane University, where she held the Maxine and Ford Graham chair in art. Her publications include *The Art of the Old South: Painting, Sculpture, Architecture, and the Products of Craftsmen, 1560–1860.* She is currently publications chairman for the Louisiana Landmarks Society.

ELLEN WEISS, an architectural historian, is an associate professor at the School of Architecture of Tulane University. She is the author of *City in the Woods: The Life and Design of an American Camp Meeting on Martha's Vineyard.* She is currently at work on a biography of the black architect Robert R. Taylor, the designer of the buildings of Tuskegee University.

INDEX

Heterick Memorial Library
Ohio Northern University

DUE	RETURNED		DUE	RETURNED
FEB 1 ~ FEB 0 5 2001 1.			13.	
AUG 3 1 200 2.	MAY 9 200 14.			
3.			15.	
4.			16.	
5.			17.	
6.			18.	
7.			19.	
8.			20.	
9.			21.	
10.			22.	
11.			23.	
12.			24.	

WITHDRAWN FROM
OHIO NORTHERN
UNIVERSITY LIBRARY

Heterick Memorial Library

3 5111 00438 6888

DATE DUE ON LAST PAGE

HETERICK MEMORIAL LIBRARY
OHIO NORTHERN UNIVERSITY
ADA, OHIO 45810

LE PETIT THEATRE DU VIEUX CARRE - 99

LE PETIT SALON-19 O'HARA'S SNUFF FACTORY-163

JEAN LACOSTE HOUSE-162

OLD FREN

CARPENTIER — BEAUREGARD HOUSE - 1

FLECHIER - BURGESS HOUSE - 114

HURST - STAUFFER HOUSE 107

TRICOU-WOGAN HOUSE COURTYARD-156

ELKIN - SARAH HENDERSON HOUSE 159

DELORD SARPY HOUSE - 45

VIEUX CARRÉ
NEW ORLEANS
AND ITS
ENVIRONS

MISSISSIPPI

RIVER

GARDEN DISTRICT

GENERAL JACKSON'S
UPPER LINE
TAKEN FROM THE GENE
JACKSON MAP OF F.B.ODOY

BASIN STREET

RAMPART

BURGUNDY

DAUPHIN

BOURBON

ROYAL

CHARTRES

LEVEE

CANAL STREET

LIBERTY STREET

ST. PAUL STREET

ST. PETER STREET

ST. JOHN STREET

CAMP STREET

MAGAZINE STREET

TCHOPITULAS ST

COMMERCE ST

MISSISSIPPI

SCALE